Echoes of Chivalry

# International Studies on Military Ethics

THE SERIES IS EDITED UNDER THE AUSPICES OF THE INTERNATIONAL SOCIETY FOR MILITARY ETHICS IN EUROPE (EUROISME)




VOLUME 15



The titles published in this series are listed at *brill.com/isme*

# Echoes of Chivalry

*Military Honour and Human Dignity in the Age of Professional Armies*

*By*

Francisco Lobo

BRILL | NIJHOFF

LEIDEN | BOSTON

Cover illustration: Johannes Vermeer (Dutch, 1632–1675), Officer and Laughing Girl, ca. 1657. Oil on canvas, 19 7/8 × 18 1/8 in. (50.5 × 46 cm). The Frick Collection, New York. Image © The Frick Collection.

The Library of Congress Cataloging-in-Publication Data is available online at https://catalog.loc.gov

Typeface for the Latin, Greek, and Cyrillic scripts: "Brill". See and download: brill.com/brill-typeface.

ISSN 2214-7926
ISBN 978-90-04-75408-9 (hardback)
ISBN 978-90-04-75409-6 (e-book)
DOI 10.1163/9789004754096



This book is printed on acid-free paper and produced in a sustainable manner.

Chivalry cannot stop the wheels of war, that is clear. But as its waters wash away blood, they enable us to see the chariot wheels, the circles of sacrifice and grief, more clearly. Chivalry reminds us why there is war: not because God wills it, as Honoré Bouvet claimed, not simply because the world is enmeshed in cycles of violence, as René Girard claims, but because ideas and traditions can be worth dying for – and worth killing for.

ALLEN J. FRANTZEN

## Contents

# Acknowledgements

Herman Melville, the author of *Moby Dick*, once famously described the enterprise of whaling as a "four-year voyage". Spanning over the same period, writing a doctoral thesis feels like a similar undertaking, whatever the white whale one happens to be after. Yet, it is not a lonely voyage, as there are plenty of hands to thank. In the style of Marcus Aurelius, I count each of their contributions as precious gifts I have been granted along the way:

From the Chilean National Agency for Research and Development (ANID), generous financial support for this endeavour.

From the School of Security Studies at King's College London, both the War Studies Department and the Defence Studies Department, a wonderful community to conduct engaging and impactful research.

From my supervisor Professor David Whetham, guidance and support in the perilous journey of multi-disciplinary studies as I ventured from law into military ethics.

From Doctor Cian O'Driscoll, incredibly generous feedback and encouragement to dig deeper into the history of chivalry.

From my dear friend Javier Gallego Saade, long-lasting intellectual community and the key that unlocked my passion for the study of human dignity.

From the late Professor José "Pepe" Zalaquett, everything I know about human rights and the laws of war, as well as living proof that chivalry is not dead, it just traded the sword for the pen.

From my family back in Chile, my values, education, love and support despite the distance.

From my son Alexander, Sashko, love innocent and pure, and patience beyond his years.

Finally, from my beautiful wife Kimberly, love of my life, the most unconditional support and faith in me beyond measure or reason, as well as a home, a safe haven to share all my thoughts and replenish my heart with every wonderful conversation.

# Prologue

## 1 Highway to Hell

The legacy of the first Gulf War is a mixed one. To use Dickens' famously ambivalent formula: "It was the best of times, it was the worst of times".

That conflict was an example of the use of force in full compliance with the international security system envisaged in the UN Charter – almost five decades after its original inception. Indeed, this war "is widely remembered as one of the cleanest, most precise, and most legal wars".[1] The Cold War was over, and the world agreed that an unjust act of aggression should be met with the legitimate use of force to assist a sovereign nation in the exercise of its inherent right to self-defence, all done with the approval of the United Nations Security Council. It was the best of times, at least for the rules-based international order.

But it was also a time of war, and that means not only that all the mechanisms for the pacific settlement of disputes listed in the UN Charter[2] have failed; on a human level, armed conflict always brings about death, destruction, and suffering for all those involved, whether they take part in the hostilities or not. It was the worst of times, as war always is a "function of loss".[3]

There is one murky episode from this "clean" war that has been of particular interest to scholars of the ethics of war over the years. It is known as "The Highway of Death". During the early hours of 26 February 1991, a convoy of Iraqi forces fled Kuwait City. The convoy was intercepted en route by American aircraft on its way to Basra, back in Iraqi territory. What ensued that day has been described as a veritable "feeding frenzy" or "turkey shoot" whereby combined aircraft from the U.S. Air Force, Marines, and Navy deployed their fire

---

1 Craig Jones, *The War Lawyers. The United States, Israel, and Juridical Warfare* (Oxford: Oxford University Press, 2020), p. 117.

2 Art. 33: "1. The parties to any dispute, the continuance of which is likely to endanger the maintenance of international peace and security, shall, first of all, seek a solution by negotiation, enquiry, mediation, conciliation, arbitration, judicial settlement, resort to regional agencies or arrangements, or other peaceful means of their own choice.

2. The Security Council shall, when it deems necessary, call upon the parties to settle their dispute by such means".

3 Cian O'Driscoll, *Victory. The Triumph and Tragedy of Just War* (New York: Oxford University Press, 2020), p. 151.

 | DOI:10.1163/9789004754096_002

power over the "target-rich environment" made up by the stranded vehicles on the ground.[4]

The targets of the attack were reportedly combatants for the most part, and they were not technically *hors de combat* or out of combat such that legal protection had to be afforded to them under international law, but merely retreating or withdrawing from Kuwait City. The convoy, moreover, comprised military vehicles that needed to be destroyed to prevent further hostilities, including the threat of impending chemical weapons attacks.[5] As the attack was arguably proportionate given the military advantage anticipated, targeting the convoy, even if the troops on the ground were unable to flee or fight back, was perfectly legal.

A similar scenario is presented to us in the BBC show *SAS Rogue Heroes* (2022), where we can see a fictionalized account of events in the North Africa front during the Second World War.[6] After a night raid where the fabled special forces destroy an entire airfield, including all the grounded planes as well as several German and Italian airmen caught off guard, some of the characters feel uneasy about what they have done since they were met with no resistance. One of them finds solace in the notion that, armed or unarmed, they are the enemy. This view on the targetability of combatants even if they are off duty and as long as they are not injured or surrendering, arguably based in customary international law at the time[7] – and certainly no worse than Hitler's *Kommandobefehl* ordering to execute all special forces upon capture without a trial – renders these actions, again, perfectly legal.

Yet, legal does not equal "clean". Indeed, and even though the age of the machine gun supposedly put an end to the idea of fairness in war,[8] some pilots who took part in the Highway of Death operation reportedly felt revulsion at what they were doing and requested permission not to go back on new sorties.[9] Some military officers were "sickened by what they saw".[10] This

---

4 Martin L. Cook and Phillip A. Hamann, 'The Road to Basra: A Case Study in Military Ethics', *The Annual of the Society of Christian Ethics*, 14 (1994), p. 216.

5 Ibid., pp. 218–221.

6 'SAS Rogue Heroes', https://www.bbc.co.uk/iplayer/episodes/p0d5z0xy/sas-rogue-heroes, 22 September 2023.

7 As reflected, for example, in the Hague Convention (IV) Respecting the Laws and Customs of War on Land (1907): "*Art. 24. Ruses of war and the employment of measures necessary for obtaining information about the enemy and the country are considered permissible*".

8 Sebastian Junger, *War* (New York: Twelve, 2011), p. 139.

9 Cook and Hamann, 'Basra', p. 223.

10 Gabriella Blum, 'The Dispensable Lives of Soldiers', *Journal of Legal Analysis*, 2:1 (2010), p. 70.

included General Colin Powell, who even advised the U.S. President against "killing for the sake of killing".[11] As a professional soldier, Powell believed that he had to honour the "warrior's code", and this excluded such an unchivalrous or ungallant way of killing the enemy.[12] This echoes the British government's view about the possibility to assassinate Hitler in 1938 as a course of action to prevent war, which was eventually ruled out as such an act was considered to be "unsportsmanlike".[13] Sometimes, playing by the book is not good enough for the players themselves.

Thus, the main question this investigation attempts to answer is: Is the instruction in the laws of war, otherwise known as International Humanitarian Law or the Law of Armed Conflict, enough to ensure the appropriate behaviour of combatants on the battlefield, or are additional normative standards of an ethical nature needed to protect both civilians from unjustified harm and combatants themselves from moral injury?[14] Where could such standards be found? Is there something in the language used by contemporary professionals that is reminiscent of the ancient code of chivalry and what is the importance of this for the main research question of this book?

---

11 Rain Liivoja, 'Law and Honor: Normative Pluralism in the Regulation of Military Conduct', in Jan Klabbers and Touko Piiparinen (eds.), *Normative Pluralism and International Law: Exploring Global Governance* (Cambridge: Cambridge University Press, 2013), p. 144.

12 Ibid. See also Neil C. Renic, *Asymmetric Killing. Risk Avoidance, Just War, and the Warrior Ethos* (Oxford: Oxford University Press, 2020), pp. 147–151.

13 Ward Thomas, 'Norms and Security: The Case of International Assassination', *International Security*, 25 (2000), p. 113.

14 Moral injury is defined as "debilitating psychological or spiritual damage resulting from transgression of deeply held moral beliefs and expectations" that harms both warriors and their communities. See Brad Allenby and Tom Frame, 'Moral Injury', in Center on the Future of War, Arizona State University, *Moral Injury: Towards an International Perspective* (Tempe: Arizona State University, 2017), p. 6. See also Shannon E. French, *The Code of the Warrior. Exploring Warrior Values Past and Present*. 2nd ed. (Lanham: Rowman and Littlefield Publishers, 2017), p. 257. A comprehensive monograph can be found in Tine Molendijk, *Moral Injury and Soldiers in Conflict* (Oxon: Routledge, 2021). For a more critical analysis of moral injury vis-à-vis the Just War tradition see Robert Emmet Meagher, *Killing from the Inside Out. Moral Injury and Just War* (Eugene: Cascade Books, 2014). For a recently proposed typology including lost trust, guilt, and harm to one's capacity for right and virtue, see Edward Barrett, 'Moral Injury: A Typology', *Journal of Military Ethics*, 22:3–4 (2023), pp. 158–167. For a psychological study applying the so-called "Moral Injury Questionnaire-Military Version" as a psychometric instrument see Joseph M. Currier, Jason M. Holland, Kent Drescher, and David Foy, 'Initial Psychometric Evaluation of the Moral Injury Questionnaire – Military Version', *Clinical Psychology and Psychotherapy*, 22 (2015), pp. 54–63.

The main working hypothesis is that the question should be answered in the negative and that there is indeed a need for additional normative standards to ensure appropriate behaviour in the sense that they not only secure allegiance to the law, but further promote the practice of virtues that are beneficial for society at large and for the military in particular.[15] It will be argued here that these additional standards may be found in the concepts of military honour and human dignity, both containing echoes of the erstwhile code of chivalry. Once they have been defined and connected, that is, once the content of the normative message is ascertained, the next logical step is to find the most effective way to convey it to the military, for which training and education by using manuals and codes of ethics codifying the foremost military virtues, including references to honour and dignity therein, becomes crucial.

## 2 This Is Not Who We Are

As we found ourselves in the middle of the 2020s, the world is witnessing several armed conflicts both among states and between states and non-state actors. One of the rallying cries that has been heard most often in recent years is that of respect for the 'rules-based international order', a concept for which entire nations are willing to fight and die.[16] Even in the face of renewed violence in the Middle East after the surprise Hamas offensive against Israel in 2023, President Joe Biden made a point of saying: "We uphold the laws of war – the law of war. It matters".[17] And more recently, in the middle of Ukraine's 2024 offensive in Kursk, President Volodymyr Zelensky made a point of saying: "It is important that Ukraine fights by the rules".[18]

But respecting the rules and the will to sacrifice life and limb for them is apparently not enough for the military professional. This phenomenon has even been acknowledged by the International Committee of the Red Cross,

15 Peter Olsthoorn, *Military Ethics and Virtues* (New York: Routledge, 2011), pp. 14–15.

16 Francisco Lobo, 'Defending the Rules-Based Order: The US at a Crossroads', https://rusi.org/explore-our-research/publications/commentary/defending-rules-based-order-us-crossroads, 26 September 2023.

17 'Remarks by President Biden on the Terrorist Attacks in Israel', https://www.whitehouse.gov/briefing-room/speeches-remarks/2023/10/10/remarks-by-president-biden-on-the-terrorist-attacks-in-israel-2/, 11 October 2023.

18 Mick Ryan, 'Kursk and the Battle of Wills', https://mickryan.substack.com/p/kursk-and-the-battle-of-wills, 21 August 2024.

which has admitted in a report that "ethical values appear to play a strong complementary role to the law, a hybrid of formal and informal norms that aims to discourage unwanted behaviour not only because it is 'against the rules' but also because it is 'not who we are'".[19] This approach was reaffirmed by some ethicists a year into the armed conflict in Gaza and Lebanon.[20] Admittedly, ethical arguments can also be instrumentalized and abused by states,[21] not unlike any other kind of standard. But *corruptio optimi pessima est* is not enough of an argument to drop our standards altogether, especially when they are held in high esteem by key actors such as professional soldiers.

Indeed, the military seem to feel the need to find solace and guidance in additional normative concepts such as 'honour', 'warrior's code', 'sportsmanship', and the like. Furthermore, some military manuals include statements such as to serve "with honour, dignity, courage and integrity"[22] (South Africa); "to behave with dignity and honour"[23] (Ukraine); "to protect the weak and defenceless" as a matter of "military chivalry"[24] (India); "to preserve human dignity" with "purity of arms"[25] (Israel); to recognize "the intrinsic dignity and worth of all people, treating them with respect"[26] (United States); that "every soldier is to treat with dignity all enemies who have surrendered"[27] (Chile); to

19 ICRC, *The Roots of Restraint in War* (Geneva: ICRC, 2018), p. 32; Andrew Bell, 'Can IHL training influence military conduct in war?', https://blogs.icrc.org/law-and-policy/2024/05/07/can-ihl-training-influence-military-conduct-in-war/, 13 May 2024.

20 Elke Schwarz and Neil Renic, 'Beyond Law: Reaffirming the Centrality of Ethics in War', https://www.justsecurity.org/103464/beyond-law-reaffirming-the-centrality-of-ethics-in-war/, 8 October 2024.

21 Jessica Wolfendale, 'Beyond Law: When States Use Ethics to Excuse War Crimes', https://www.justsecurity.org/104969/states-ethics-excuse-war-crimes/, 21 November 2024.

22 South African National Defence Forces, 'Code of Conduct', https://www.resdal.org/Archivo/d0000124.htm#:~:text=I%20accept%20personal%20responsibility%20for,risk%20of%20my%20own%20life., 10 July 2023.

23 'On the Disciplinary Statute of the Armed Forces of Ukraine', https://zakon.rada.gov.ua/laws/show/551-14#Text, 14 November 2024.

24 Headquarters Army Training Command, *Indian Army Doctrine* (Shimla: Headquarters Army Training Command, 2004).

25 Israel Defense Forces, 'The Spirit of the IDF', https://www.idf.il/en/mini-sites/spirit-of-the-idf/, 6 July 2023.

26 U.S. Army, 'ADRP-1: The Army Profession', https://irp.fas.org/doddir/army/adrp1.pdf, 25 May 2023, pp. 2-6–2-7.

27 Chilean Army, *Manual: Ethos del Ejército de Chile. MOLD – 02005* (Santiago: Ejército de Chile, Comando de Educación y Doctrina, 2018), pp. 3-5–3-6.

always act “with honour, courage and dignity”[28] (France); and to respect dignity as the “best defence against ethical failure in war or peace”[29] (Australia).

What do all these concepts mean? What are the definitions of the echoes of chivalry we call military honour and human dignity, and how do these concepts connect and interact in times of war? Answering this question is the main task of this book. Acknowledging the empirical reality of the usage of these concepts and categories, thus, becomes a first descriptive step in this inquiry, while at the same time representing the embers of a chivalric tradition waiting to be reignited through earnest intellectual discussion.

If targeting combatants who are at a disadvantage or who cannot fight back makes soldiers uneasy sometimes, attacking off-duty military personnel as they are engaged in leisurely activities can be even more off-putting. An illustration comes from the case-law of the International Criminal Tribunal for the former Yugoslavia (‘ICTY’). On 1 June 1993, several residents of Dobrinja, in Sarajevo, gathered to hold a football tournament in an improvised pitch in a parking lot of a residential area controlled by Bosnian forces (the ‘ABiH’). The crowd included approximately 200 people, among whom there were women and children. Some members of the ABiH were reportedly among the players, but they were not donning any uniforms or carrying any weapons as they were on leave. As the game unfolded, suddenly two shells coming from Bosnian-Serbian SRK controlled territory impacted the field, killing at least 10 people and injuring over 100.

The Trial Chamber of the ICTY found that this attack was unlawful, but with an important qualifier: “Although the number of soldiers present at the game was significant, an attack on a crowd of approximately 200 people, including numerous children, would clearly be expected to cause incidental loss of life and injuries to civilians excessive in relation to the direct and concrete military advantage anticipated”.[30] In other words, what made the shelling illegal was not the fact that it was directed at unarmed soldiers on leave; it was the collateral damage to civilians, infringing upon the principles of proportionality and distinction that are central in International Humanitarian Law, that made the

---

28 État-major de l’armée de Terre, ‘Honneur, courage et dignité. Le comportement du soldat de l’armée de Terre’, https://www.info-reglement.terre.defense.gouv.fr/images/multimedia/photo/illustrations/livre_orange-Comportement_du_soldat-web-VD.pdf, 7 July 2023, p. 13.

29 Australian Defence Forces, ‘Military Ethics’, https://theforge.defence.gov.au/sites/default/files/2021-12/ADF-P-0%20Military%20Ethics%20Ed%201_0.pdf, 10 December 2022, p. 39.

30 International Criminal Tribunal for the Former Yugoslavia, Trial Chamber, *Prosecutor v. Galić*, Judgment, 5 December 2003, Case No. IT-98-29-T, para. 387.

attack unlawful in the court's view.[31] The unarmed combatants presenting no immediate threat were, therefore, fair game.

There is no way of knowing what was on the mind of the artillery troops that targeted the football game that day. A similar scenario is, however, recounted in the memoirs of a former officer of the United States Marine Corps in his capacity as an advisor to the Iraqi counter-terrorism forces in 2016:

> We had a drone over this part of the city now [Fallujah], and everyone on the JOC floor was watching the live footage displayed on the big screen. It was a volleyball game. A group of ISIS fighters were battling it out on a makeshift court, their weapons stacked neatly to one side, cheered on by a small crowd of their comrades. We watched transfixed, and, with no sense of irony, became lost in the game, cheering points and groaning at near misses. As the ball bounded out of play the strike cell leader turned to me:
>
> 'Sir, do you want to take them out.' The drone was carrying Hellfire missiles. Jeff and I looked at one another and shook our heads simultaneously. 'No, let them finish the game.'[32]

Even if the targets were completely legitimate under the Law of Armed Conflict, and despite the fact that collateral damage was not an issue and therefore the principle of proportionality would be complied with, there was something about attacking a group of men gathered together in sportsmanlike delectation that did not sit well with the soldiers in that surveillance room.

A similar aversion may be observed in the popular Just War theory trope known as the 'naked soldier'.[33] Contrary to Vladimir Putin's infamous vow to kill Chechen fighters even if they are found in the toilet,[34] there appears to be a widespread discomfort with the idea of shooting a naked soldier. "The same tale", Michael Walzer writes in *Just and Unjust Wars*, "appears again and again in letters from the front. It has this general form: a soldier on patrol or on sniper duty catches an enemy soldier unaware, holds him in his gunsight, easy to kill, and then must decide whether to shoot or let the opportunity pass. (...) No doubt, a deep psychological uneasiness about killing plays a part in

31 Blum, 'Dispensable', p. 113.

32 Andrew Milburn, *When the Tempest Gathers* (Bransley: Pen & Sword, 2020), pp. 457–458.

33 Larry May, *War Crimes and Just War* (Cambridge: Cambridge University Press, 2007), pp. 108–117.

34 Nathan Hodge, 'https://edition.cnn.com/2022/02/08/europe/putin-coarse-remarks-ukraine-intl/index.html', 22 September 2023.

these cases".[35] Walzer goes on to recount the way some insightful personalities recall their own experience when encountering the naked soldier, including Robert Graves and George Orwell.[36] He concludes that, despite this reluctance to kill someone clearly engaged in activities that have "the savor of peace"[37] – for example, playing football or volleyball – the rules of war do not prohibit targeting said individuals as they belong to a class, i.e. fighters, that is liable to attack by definition, for each soldier "has allowed himself to be made into a dangerous man".[38]

The uneasiness of the soldier who has his or her finger on the trigger is mirrored by the discomfort some authors express about the permissiveness of the laws of war as portrayed by Walzer. Thus, some proposals to revise the war convention in order to alter the status-based targetability of combatants have been advanced in recent years, including a threat-based approach,[39] and the inclusion of a liability/non-liability criterion alongside the justice/injustice criterion that may result in the characterization of a combatant as unjust (because the war his or her superiors started is unjust) yet non-liable (i.e. not culpable due to forced conscription, for instance), and therefore not necessarily targetable in a moral sense.[40]

But putting chivalry and philosophy on hold for a moment, we may ask what is the cause of this seemingly widespread discomfort about killing naked, non-threatening soldiers? What is a combatant's connection to them that makes them hesitate until the very last second of that momentous decision?

## 3 A Plea from Another World

War is usually thought of as a descent into chaos and madness, a return to the dreaded Hobbesian 'state of nature' amounting to a "*bellum omnium contra omnes*" ("war [...] of every man, against every man").[41] In other words, it is *Lord of the Flies* time, as famously immortalized by William Golding in his 1954 novel. Never mind that real life cases of boys stranded on a desert island

35 Michael Walzer. *Just and Unjust Wars. A Moral Argument with Historical Illustrations.* 4th ed. (New York: Basic Books, 2006), pp. 138–139.

36 Ibid., pp. 139–140.

37 Ibid., p. 142.

38 Ibid., p. 145.

39 Blum, 'Dispensable', pp. 108–114.

40 Marcela Prieto Rudolphy, *The Morality of the Laws of War: War, Law, and Murder* (Oxford: Oxford University Press, 2023), pp. 214–215.

41 Thomas Hobbes, *Leviathan* (Oxford: Oxford University Press, 1998), p. 84.

have not ineluctably ended in bloodshed and horror but have even resulted in cooperation and survival;[42] our fascination with the mythical state of nature and *Lord of the Flies* trope often makes us search for our identity as human beings by looking into some of the darkest mirrors of our own making, like Golding's desert island.

But there is a time even in *Lord of the Flies* when the rules are still binding on the island, still in place to guide the small community of what Thomas Hobbes would have called "strong and sturdy children".[43] These standards of behaviour and civilisation are symbolized by the conch the children use to assemble. As they began their slow descent into chaos, however, the rightful leader, Ralph, calls out the head of the hunters' camp, Jack, for not abiding by the terms of their social contract:

> 'The rules!' shouted Ralph, 'you're breaking the rules!'
> 'Who cares?'
> Ralph summoned his wits.
> 'Because the rules are the only thing we've got!'
> But Jack was shouting against him.
> 'Bollocks to the rules! We're strong – we hunt! If there's a beast, we'll hunt it down! We'll close in and beat and beat and beat –!'.[44]

The denouement of this bleak tale of the jungle is well known, and it is supposed to confirm the worst realist assumptions about our flawed human nature. There is a time, however, at the beginning of the story where the shipwrecked children still believe in rules, conventions, and principles – the same standards Ralph hopelessly clings to in the exchange above. Aside from the artificial authority of the conch, they carry with them some boundaries that they have learned from society during their short time on this earth, as illustrated by two additional characters playfully throwing rocks at one another:

> Roger gathered a handful of stones and began to throw them. Yet there was a space round Henry, perhaps six yards in diameter, into which he dare not throw. Here, invisible yet strong, was the taboo of the old life. Round the squatting child was the protection of parents and school and

---

42 Rutger Bregman, *Humankind. A Hopeful History* (London: Bloomsbury Publishing, 2021), pp. 21–38.

43 Thomas Hobbes, *Man and Citizen* (Indianapolis: Hackett, 1991), p. 100.

44 William Golding, *Lord of the Flies* (Pomodoro Books, 2023), p. 100.

> policemen and the law. Roger's arm was conditioned by a civilization that knew nothing of him and was in ruins.[45]

This invisible blanket provided by what Tim O'Brien calls "civilized trappings",[46] indeed, gradually starts to fade in an exceptional enclave where rules make little or no sense – say, a desert island, or perhaps even a modern battlefield. In such settings, these boundaries must certainly seem and feel outlandish to those immersed in them. In his famous memoir from the Great War, *Storm of Steel*, Ernst Jünger narrates an encounter with a frightened British officer in the trenches: "he reached into his pocket, not to pull out a weapon, but a photograph (…). I saw him on it, surrounded by numerous family (…). It was a plea from another world. Later, I thought it was blind chance that I let him go and plunged onward".[47] Something as trivial as showing family pictures to another person becomes, in times of war, a device for parlay, a chance to buy time or even negotiate our way out of mortal danger. It is also an opportunity to remove the veil of enmity and embrace our common humanity even among enemies, much like King Priam once did when he shared his sorrow with Achilles, the slayer of his own son.[48]

In a place where the main currency is death, an appeal for life must, no doubt, seem like a plea from another world. Similar views are expressed in other accounts of modern war[49] where the introduction of images and memories of loved ones back home are perceived as otherworldly in what Siegfried Sassoon once called 'death's grey land'.

## 4 The Better Angels of Our Nature

Even amidst the hell that is war we want rules. That is the meaning behind the often invoked 'rules-based international order'[50] even (or especially) in the face of such a blatant act of aggression as the Russian full-scale invasion of Ukraine in 2022. "The rules are what make us better" is what an FBI agent tells Jack Bauer in one episode of the famous TV show *24* – which epitomized the

45 Ibid., p. 67.
46 Tim O'Brien, *The Things They Carried* (London: 4th Estate, 2015), p. 212.
47 Ernst Jünger. *Storm of Steel* (London: Penguin, 2004), pp. 233–234.
48 Simone Weil, 'The Iliad, or the Poem of Force', *Chicago Review*, 18:2 (1965), pp. 8–9.
49 O'Brien, *Things*, p. 15; Milburn, *Tempest*, pp. 458–459.
50 Francisco Lobo, 'Defending the Rules-Based Order: The US at a Crossroads', https://rusi.org/explore-our-research/publications/commentary/defending-rules-based-order-us-crossroads, 26 September 2023.

spirit of the hapless 'War on Terror', with all its excesses and missteps. "Not today" is what the zealot anti-terrorist hero replies. But if not today, then when?

The Just War Tradition ('JWT') will be the main normative framework this investigation will rely on, as it stands as the most honed articulation of the intuitive idea of the rules of war. These rules take the form of what is known in the JWT as the 'war convention', as we shall see throughout this investigation. As Michael Walzer puts it: "We want to have it both ways: moral decency in battle and victory in war; constitutionalism in hell and ourselves outside".[51] We do not need to fall prey to an inflexible approach to the rules, an "asinine ethics" of sorts, in order to appreciate their importance for practical matters.[52] And it is through such vehicles, these civilized trappings that we carry with us into battle, or the conventions that we make up and honour as we go along, that the better angels of our nature guide us in our journey across hell.

Now, it is not only in reels and scrolls that we find appeals to normative standards in combat. Practice also informs our views about what is right and what is wrong in war, what is admissible and what is unacceptable, why we fight and how we are supposed to go about it. A recent study shows how more often than not war memoirs support the ideals underpinning the Just War Tradition, admittedly not without a sense of irony and the absurd at their lack of efficacy in practice.[53]

One particular episode from the Iraq War reveals how even some shocking actions are sometimes attempted to be justified by relying on normative concepts. This was the case of U.S. Army Captain Roger Maynulet, who in 2005 testified in his own court-martial that he shot a wounded Iraqi citizen as a case of 'mercy killing'. The driver allegedly transported a high-value target inside the vehicle; after a car chase, he crashed and was severely injured. Maynulet justified shooting him after that: "He was in a state I didn't think was *dignified*. I had to put him out of his misery. (...) It was the right thing to do. It was the *honorable* thing to do"[54] (added emphasis).

Whether Maynulet is simply a hypocrite, or if he was truly assisted by the better angels of our nature on that day in Iraq is hard to tell. It is worth noting that he was convicted of assault with intent to commit voluntary manslaughter,

51 Walzer, *Just*, p. 47.

52 Ibid., p. 225.

53 Liane Hartnett and Cian O'Driscoll, 'Sad and laughable and Strange: At War with Just War', *Global Society*, 35:1 (2021), pp. 27–44.

54 'Maynulet testifies in own defense, says killing wounded Iraqi "right thing to do"', https://www.stripes.com/news/maynulet-testifies-in-own-defense-says-killing-wounded-iraqi-right-thing-to-do-1.31154, 26 September 2023.

and that he was sentenced to dismissal from the service, a decision affirmed by two appellate bodies.[55]

What is of more interest here is that this short statement from the court's record contains references to two of the most salient normative concepts in today's Just War thinking and practice, and precious relics preserved from the days of chivalry: honour and dignity. It will be the main purpose of this inquiry to critically ascertain the meaning of these concepts, as well as the importance of the connection between military honour and human dignity, in order to provide a satisfactory answer to the main question regarding the need for education in additional normative categories beyond the laws of war in order to prevent unjustified harm to civilians and moral injury to soldiers.

The concepts of military honour and human dignity that are the main focus of this investigation have not been selected arbitrarily, as they are both well-established in military doctrinal publications (see section II above), as well as in moral public discourse (as will be shown in Chapters 2–4 of this study). As we shall see, even though it is pervasive in military doctrine, the interpretive concept of honour is also not always easy to define and, thus, the expectations it encloses are not always clear and this can have an impact in the way such an important profession as the military is performed and assessed in practice. At the same time, even though human dignity is a household expression in moral discourse and legal language, there are several competing conceptions of the concept and it is therefore not entirely certain which one people mean when they invoke it, as it happens with any such essentially contested concept, a philosophical category which will be further developed in this book. In addition, sometimes human dignity is said to be present as a form of "shadow"[56] normative category that is not mentioned by name, but that is still honoured insofar as similar notions such as 'humanity' or 'intrinsic value' are protected.

Finally, for all their development in the literature as discrete categories, a connection is yet to be established between military honour and human dignity. It will be the main purpose of this inquiry to bridge this gap in the literature with a proposal that may spark further discussion in the fields of Professional Military Ethics ('PMEt') and Professional Military Education ('PME').[57]

55 United States Court of Appeals for the Armed Forces, *United States v. Rogelio M. Maynulet, Captain, U.S. Army*, Crim. App. No. 20050412, Decided 3 March 2010.

56 Ginevra Le Moli, *Human Dignity in International Law* (Cambridge: Cambridge University Press, 2021), p. 137.

57 The acronym 'PME' is used in the literature to signify 'Professional Military Education' (for instance, by Roger Wertheimer). For an alternative use see Sally Rohan's meaning of the acronym as 'Professional Military Ethics'. See Roger Wertheimer, 'Preface', in Roger

## 5 Paint It Black

*Officer and Laughing Girl* is one of Johannes Vermeer's lesser-known paintings – certainly not as famous as, for instance, his *Girl with a Pearl Earring*. Painted sometime between 1657 and 1658, *Officer and Laughing Girl* depicts a simple scene from Dutch social life in the 17th century: A man in military uniform sits with his back to the viewer, as he faces a woman sitting opposite him. They seem to be engaged in friendly banter, perhaps leading to courtship suggested by her joyful expression, rosy cheeks and open palm, as the daylight illuminates the small room through an open window located to the left of the frame, as is the artist's style. Indeed, master of shadow and light, Vermeer manages to highlight the main features of the scene, namely the lively young lady dressed in ivory, black and gold, as well as the map of the Low Countries hanging in the back, another one of his signature tropes. Conversely, shadows engulf the military officer sitting in the dark corner, and the only glimpses of his humanity we are allowed to access are his darkened profile and partially covered hands.

Many contrasts and reversals are portrayed in this scene, mirroring the changes that Dutch society was undergoing at the time "from military to civil society, from monarchy to republicanism, from Catholicism to Calvinism, merchant house to corporation, empire to nation, war to trade".[58]

Indeed, the contrast between military and civil society can be immediately grasped by the viewer of *Officer and Laughing Girl*. Despite the lack of definition and opacity of his features, we can see that the man is dressed in military uniform, donning a scarlet coat the dim tone of which is a reminder that the blood-shedding business of this gentleman, war, is only temporarily paused as he fraternizes with a civilian. Is the officer on leave from the battlefield? Is he about to depart to the front, or to be shipped off *ad noctum* to a faraway land newly conquered by the emerging Dutch empire? Is he just a clerk in the increasingly complex bureaucracy of modern national armies of the time? We cannot know. He appears collected and pensive. Whatever he is telling the laughing girl, it seems to be working. She looks charmed. But perhaps it is also what he is *not* telling her that allows this friendly exchange to continue smoothly.

---

Wertheimer (ed.), *Empowering our Military Conscience. Transforming Just War Theory and Military Moral Education* (New York: Routledge, 2010); Sally Rohan, 'An organic professional military ethic and the educational challenge', in Don Carrick, James Connelly and David Whetham (eds.), *Making the Military Moral. Contemporary Challenges and Responses in Military Ethics Education* (New York: Routledge, 2018), p. 71.

58 Timothy Brooks, *Vermeer's Hat. The Seventeenth Century and the Dawn of the Global World* (London: Profile Books, 2009), pp. 28–29.

There is another famous depiction of an exchange between a man returning from the outposts of civilization and a woman who stays behind in the tranquillity of urban peace. In his acclaimed novel, *Heart of Darkness*, Joseph Conrad tells the story of a man looking for a rogue agent of the Belgian empire in Congo in the late nineteenth century. After finding Kurtz only to witness his last days and to register his last words – the famous formula "The horror! The horror!" – the main character, Marlow, travels back to Brussels to return some letters addressed to Kurtz's fiancée, or his 'Intended'. A parallel may be drawn between *Officer and Laughing Girl* and Marlow's exchange with Kurtz's Intended, in the sense that both the military officer and the imperial agent have been probably exposed to more violence and brutality than the European women staying in the rear-guard of civilisation. Even Conrad's description of the fiancée, her forehead remaining smooth, white and illuminated as the room grows darker, could perfectly fit Vermeer's image of the laughing girl.[59]

More importantly, both men seem to be keeping the harsh truth from their innocent interlocutors. Just as Marlow decides to lie to the fiancée by telling her that it was her name that Kurtz chose to utter as his last words – the actual words "The horror! The horror!" deemed simply too dark to convey to a grieving soul – Vermeer's officer appears to be lost in thought, possibly shellshocked or experiencing PTSD over what he has seen or done in the battlefield. It is, again, simply too dark a truth to throw into a conversation with a lady.

In their insightful literary analysis of Conrad's novel, Birgit and Daniel Maier-Katkin criticize Marlow's decision to sugar-coat the realities of European imperialism, however noble his intentions, as an instance of what Hannah Arendt calls the 'banality of evil' that allows tyranny and totalitarianism to endure whenever decent, common folk don't have the courage to speak up against it.[60] Similarly, Primo Levi also regrets how the German people were reduced in the time of Nazism to "a cowardice which became an integral part of mores, and so profound as to prevent husbands from telling their wives, parents their children".[61]

59 Joseph Conrad, *Heart of Darkness and Other Tales* (New York: Oxford University Press, 2008), p. 184.

60 Birgit Maier-Katkin and Daniel Maier-Katkin, 'At the Heart of Darkness: Crimes against Humanity and the Banality of Evil', *Human Rights Quarterly*, 26:3 (2004), pp. 597–602. On the original conceptualization of the banality of evil, see Hannah Arendt, *Eichmann in Jerusalem. A Report on the Banality of Evil* (London: Penguin, 2006).

61 Primo Levi, *The Drowned and the Saved* (London: Abacus, 2013), p. 6.

Soldiers returning from war may experience the same reluctance to openly talk about what happened, as documented in works such as *Achilles in Vietnam* by Jonathan Shay[62] and *On Combat* by Dave Grossman and Loren Christensen.[63] Similarly, in his war memoir, *The Things They Carried*, Tim O'Brien recounts how when his (fictional) daughter was nine, she asked him if he had ever killed anyone when he was in Vietnam. In an attempt to shield his little girl from the horror, he reportedly replies "Of course not", hoping that someday she would ask again.[64] It would appear that this lie is not so different from the ones we, as a society, like to tell ourselves.

The deceptive shield, however, can become a heavy burden on the back of the soldier returning from combat. By not talking about what happened, even if it is with the noble intention to protect the innocence of those untouched by war, they further harm themselves, thus deepening moral injury. It also keeps their principal, civil society, in the dark as to what its agents are up to. The shield, then, like that of Perseus, must become a mirror into which society can look to find its own image, that the medusa of wilful blindness may be defeated. As General Sir John Hackett puts it: "What a society gets in its armed services is exactly what it asks for, no more and no less. What it asks for tends to be a reflection of what it is. When a country looks at its fighting forces it is looking in a mirror; the mirror is a true one and the face that it sees will be its own".[65]

As will be explained in this book, it is of the utmost importance to develop a culture within the military that promotes routine, healthy ethical discussions across all ranks and throughout the entire time spent in the service. Such discussions should take place, ideally, not only among the military themselves, but also by engaging with the societies that task them to fight on their behalf. By reflecting on several ethical questions bearing on the concepts of military honour and human dignity, this work is intended as a contribution for developing such a dialectic critical spirit in the armed forces and civil society, that the military honour embodied by our *Officer* may meet the human dignity personified by our *Laughing Girl* through genuine, transformative conversation.

---

62 Jonathan Shay, *Achilles in Vietnam. Combat Trauma and the undoing of Character* (New York: Scribner, 2003).

63 Dave Grossman and Loren W. Christensen, *On Combat. The Psychology and Physiology of Deadly Conflict in War and Peace*. 4th ed. (New York: Open Road Media, 2022).

64 O'Brien, *Things*, p. 139.

65 John Hackett, *The Profession of Arms* (London: Sidgwick & Jackson, 1983), p. 158.

## 6 Back to the Future

Uniforms are an integral part of any military unit's identity. They are a parchment upon which the deeds of many are recounted and remembered. They can also be a clean canvas where new feats may be imprinted in days to come. In 2021, the sixth branch of the U.S. armed forces, the recently created United States Space Force, released a prototype of its new uniform. The dark blue jacket is sleek looking and retro-futuristic. As the garment of a newly created unit, naturally, it has no history. Only the future may reveal its importance in the wars to come.

Conversely, around the same time the Space Force prototype was in the making, another branch of the service decided it needed a change of image. In 2019 the U.S. Army also announced a change in its uniform, although they decided to go in the opposite direction: instead of adopting a more modern-looking apparel, they recommissioned the old 'Army Greens', the fabled uniform donned by American soldiers during the Second World War, admittedly the country's greatest military achievement shouldered by the 'Greatest Generation'.[66] It was thus decided that the best way to face the national and global security challenges of the future would be by honouring one of the proudest moments in that country's past.

Revivals are quite common to look for guidance and comfort in an ever-changing world like ours. In his most recent book, *Limited Force and the Fight for the Just War Tradition*, Christian Nikolaus Braun remarks that three main revivals have taken place since the second half of the 20th century: the reappearance of the Just War Tradition thanks to the work of Michael Walzer; the reappreciation of casuistry as a time-honoured method of moral reasoning; and a new-found popularity of the school of virtue ethics as promoted by neo-Aristotelian and Thomistic scholarship.[67] In an attempt to bring the past back into the future, in this inquiry I shall rely on two of those revivals, namely the Just War Tradition as a theoretical framework, as well as virtue ethics as the school of moral philosophy admittedly most favoured in the fields of PMEt and PME.

Furthermore, the concepts of military honour and human dignity have been selected as the main focus of this research due not only to their prevalence in

66 Dave Philipps, 'To Stand Out, the Army Picks a New Uniform With a World War II Look', https://www.nytimes.com/2019/05/05/us/new-army-greens-uniform.html, 28 September 2023.

67 Christian Nikolaus Braun, *Limited Force and the Fight for the Just War Tradition* (Washington, DC: Georgetown University Press, 2023), pp. 7; 34; 61.

practice, but also because they carry the potential to operate as vehicles or portals through which we may metaphorically travel back in time and return to the future again by ascertaining the many overlapping contents between these two morally rich normative ideas. This way, traditional military honour and modern human dignity act as wormholes of sorts, each located at one end of the space-time continuum across which history traverses, whereby military honour offers us a window into medieval chivalry whereas human dignity opens for us a gate into our contemporary world.

Accordingly, I shall also dig into the past to look for answers that may be waiting to be unearthed in order to better understand war and the professionals that wage it in the present. In Hackett's words:

> It is therefore of high importance to form a clear idea of what society looks for in its professional man-at-arms. To recognize what we need demands an understanding of what we have. To understand what we have we must ask how the man-at-arms came to be what he is and this in turn requires a journey into the past, into the very roots of Western culture. To see where we are going we must know where we are and to know where we are we must discover how we got here.[68]

The contrast between past and future, aptly epitomized by the Army and Space Force uniforms, can be also found in the two main concepts this inquiry aims to define and clarify, namely military honour – firmly grounded in the past and in tradition – and human dignity – a modern value shaping our views of the world we want to build for ourselves and for future generations. But perhaps these are, after all, new-old categories that keep haunting us in our search for meaning. Interestingly, the old Roman concept of *dignitas* was used also by a 17th century cartographer who drew up the first ever map of the Moon, including among its many regions a name that, although it did not stick in astronomy, will sound familiar enough to us: *Terra Dignitatis* – "Land of Dignity".[69]

As we venture, *ad noctum*, into the heart of darkness to face the depths of our human condition during the worst of times, we must not forget to look up at the stars, *ad astra*, where the Land of Dignity that we mapped out for ourselves may yet become a reality to which we can aspire even as the fog of war obscures everything around us.

---

68 Hackett, *Profession*, p. 7.

69 Philip Parker, *The Atlas of Atlases* (London: Ivy Press, 2022), p. 159.

## 7 Research Questions, Methodology, and Structure

As stated above, the main puzzles this inquiry attempts to solve are: Is the instruction in the laws of war, otherwise known as International Humanitarian Law or the Law of Armed Conflict, enough to ensure the appropriate behaviour of combatants on the battlefield, or are additional normative standards of an ethical nature needed to protect both civilians from unjustified harm and combatants themselves from moral injury? Where could such standards be found? Is there something in the language used by contemporary professionals that is reminiscent of the ancient code of chivalry and what is the importance of this for the main research question of this book?

The importance of these questions cannot be overstated considering the great impact modern warfare has on the bodies and minds of those who fight, but also – and perhaps more critically – of those at the receiving end of the violence, especially considering that, however culturally universal the principle of protection of civilians might be, "the struggle for civilian immunity is far from won".[70]

As also stated, the chief working hypothesis is that the question should be answered in the negative and that there is indeed a need for additional normative standards to ensure appropriate behaviour. It will be argued here that these additional standards can be found in the concepts of military honour and human dignity that are prevalent in theory and practice in both the military and the civilian worlds, both concepts containing echoes of the erstwhile code of chivalry and keeping that tradition alive.

In this sense, the thesis makes "*a moral argument with doctrinal illustrations*", to paraphrase Michael Walzer. It does so by drawing on established normative categories still in use such as honour and dignity, as they are both applied to the specific context of war and to the professionals who wage it.

Furthermore, the moral argument presented here will establish the conceptual connection between military honour as heir to the humanitarian tradition of the code of chivalry, and human dignity as a contemporary humanitarian value that calls for respect for every human being simply because of their status in both times of peace and war.

Accordingly, it will be argued that training and education in the legal categories stemming from IHL must be complemented by ethical standards that may ensure restraint even in the heat of battle, where the fog of war clouds

70 Alex Bellamy, *Massacres and Morality: Mass Atrocities in the Age of Civilian Immunity* (Oxford: Oxford University Press, 2012), pp. 12; 17–18.

everything and where there is no police or judge available to tell the soldier what the right course of action is.

In order to solve the puzzles presented by the research question an appropriate methodology must be employed. The appropriateness of said methodology will depend fundamentally on the type of contribution this qualitative research intends to deliver. To the extent that this inquiry aims at clarifying the different understandings of two key concepts, military honour and human dignity, as well as the possible connections and interplay among them, it is a *conceptual* contribution. Additionally, insofar as said concepts function as vessels enclosing a rich payload of longstanding ethical conceptions and universal legal standards, their study is at the same time a *normative* contribution. Accordingly, this investigation is intended to result in a significant "conceptual-normative contribution"[71] to the literature on JWT, PMEt, PME, international law, legal theory, and human rights.

Two good examples of this type of conceptual-normative contribution are Michael Walzer's *Just and Unjust Wars*[72] and Nancy Sherman's *Stoic Warriors.*[73] After the Vietnam War, Walzer famously reactivated the dormant debate on the Just War by providing what he calls "A Moral Argument with Historical Illustrations", drawing on examples bearing on both *jus ad bellum* and *jus in bello* dilemmas from ancient China and Greece, the American Civil War, and the Second World War, to name just a few. Sherman, on the other hand, refurbishes the classic teachings of Stoicism by connecting the transcending thoughts of Epictetus, Cicero, Seneca, and Marcus Aurelius to practical ethical dilemmas faced by contemporary military personnel. In her own words: "The book is hybrid in content, taking seriously both military matters and Stoic theory. But it is also hybrid in methodology. It adopts the standard method of philosophers – namely, analysis of text and argument – but also the method of ethnographers who collect stories and anecdotes".[74]

In this inquiry I would like to follow Walzer's and Sherman's methodology and writing style to produce a volume containing sound philosophical analysis of text and argument, complete with interpretation of legal, doctrinal and other normative standards, all under the light of broader narratives[75]

71 Henry E. Brady and David Collier, *Rethinking Social Inquiry: Diverse Tools, Shared Standards* (Lanham, MD: Rowman & Littlefield, 2004), p. 127.

72 Walzer, *Just.*

73 Nancy Sherman, *Stoic Warriors. The Ancient Philosophy Behind the Military Mind* (New York: Oxford University Press, 2005).

74 Ibid., pp. x–xi.

75 Aside from Walzer's masterpiece, some excellent accounts of battle conditions experiences of common soldiers throughout history can be found in Keegan, *Face*; Ernst Jünger.

that might help to ascertain the connection between the revered concepts of military honour and human dignity in both theory and practice. Although it looks into the past to better make sense of the present, this investigation does not amount to a history of ideas or a simple documentation of an admittedly contested historical record,[76] but rather a philosophical study that draws on time-honoured categories used in normative discourse. In other words, this book does not amount to a history of ideas that traces the way certain notions and concepts evolve over time. On the contrary, this book attempts to show how some of these concepts actually have *not* changed despite the passing of time, at least not in their essence or core meaning; "points of continuity, not disjunction, are my focus" to borrow a phrase from Allen Frantzen's study on chivalry during the Great War, a conflict he asserts did not kill chivalry, "for these [medieval] ideas, old though they are, help to explain violence in the modern world".[77] Thus, it becomes a theoretical attempt at better understanding some notions that have been bequeathed to us by centuries of evolution in the way we think about war and political violence in general. In that sense, it is a quest to salvage our best traditions, preserved in those doctrinal embers waiting to be rekindled, that we may harness them for the present and the future.

The foregoing also means that the select examples of military doctrine included in this investigation will be used illustratively, and they will remain subordinated to the conceptual-normative nature of the contribution, their argumentative value being measured against their explanatory potential to illustrate the arguments and theories under the 'overarching narrative'[78] of the interplay between military honour and human dignity. Accordingly, as stated above, this will not be an empirical study, but "*a moral argument with doctrinal illustrations*", to paraphrase Walzer.

Finally, the book will be structured as follows. The Introduction briefly describes the historical development and core tenets of the medieval code of chivalry, tracing its trajectory from the Middle Ages into Modernity and the age of professional armies, mainly through customary international law. Chapter 1, titled "War Is Our Business: Taking What Military Professionals Do Seriously",

---

*Storm*; Ernest Hemingway (ed.), *Men at War* (New York: Berkeley Publishing, 1958); Eugene B. Sledge, *With the Old Breed. At Peleliu and Okinawa* (New York: Presidio Press, 2007); Tim O'Brien, *Things*; Sebastian Junger, *War* (New York: Twelve, 2011); and Milburn, *Tempest.*

76 Helen M. Kinsella, *The Image before the Weapon. A Critical History of the Distinction between Combatant and Civilian* (Ithaca: Cornell University Press, 2011), p. 26.

77 Allen J. Frantzen, *Bloody Good. Chivalry, Sacrifice, and the Great War* (Chicago: University of Chicago Press, 2004), pp. 2; 8–9.

78 Pat Bazeley, *Qualitative Data Analysis* (London: SAGE, 2013), p. 115.

attempts to explore the factual background conditions making the normative question of the investigation possible and necessary. Thus, this first chapter presents a theoretical proposal to conceptualize the factors potentially leading to war, as well as an explanation of the particular kind of professional that is needed to manage this outcome, in order to contextualize later discussions on PMEt and PME. This way, war and its circumstances are taken seriously and so are its main practitioners.

The following three chapters then proceed analytically to ascertain the meaning of each of the core concepts listed above, as well as their potential connections. Thus, in Chapter 2, "Military Honour", I analyse this defining professional trait of the modern soldier, first inquiring into the theoretical framework surrounding this normative category and later proposing a working definition of the concept.

In Chapter 3, titled "Human Dignity", I study the concept that has become a household expression in moral discourse and a foundational value underpinning both International Human Rights Law and International Humanitarian Law. The analysis includes a study of the four main conceptions of human dignity, including the welfare, the autonomy, the *imago Dei*, and the rank conceptions, the last one being particularly developed for the purposes of this inquiry.

Chapter 4, "Military Honour and Human Dignity", attempts to bridge the gap between the two main concepts of this inquiry, which will become the main contribution of the book. Thus, after contextualizing the need for such a contribution to better understand military honour and human dignity in the context of armed conflict, I explain how their respective normative propositions may be merged under the banner of a new *Jus Armorum* or Law of Arms that rejuvenates our traditional views of chivalry refurbished with a modern humanitarian content.

But it is not enough for philosophers alone to grasp the right message. It needs to be communicated to those who actually go to war in ways that resonate with their shared practices and codes of behaviour. Equipped with the appropriate normative contents unveiled by these analytical chapters, the next step must then focus on the most effective ways to convey their message and instil their meaning in the professionals of arms. Thus, in Chapter 5, titled "Professional Military Ethics Education", I focus on the pedagogical aspects pertaining to the ways in which we inculcate understanding and respect for such concepts in the military, including the importance of new methods and technologies to get the message across, as well as the power of tried and trusted pedagogical devices such as military manuals and codes of ethics.

Chapter 6, called "Military Virtues Revisited", then applies all these theoretical contents to empirical examples of normative standards of behaviour as found in different military manuals and codes of ethics around the world by way of illustration, including Australia, Canada, Chile, France, Germany, India, Israel, Japan, New Zealand, South Africa, Spain, Ukraine, the United Kingdom, and the United States. These varied cases show that fighting for values is not the preserve of the so-called "Western way of war".[79] Since virtue ethics is the most popular school of thought among military professionals today, it becomes appropriate to scrutinize and assess the argumentative quality of these official documents through the prism of that moral tradition that seems to thrive within the military milieu. Due to space constraints, I focus on the four cardinal virtues as applied to PMEt, namely: justice, prudence or practical wisdom, courage, and temperance.

Lastly, I offer some final thoughts in the Conclusions. After problematizing the distinction between 'warrior' and 'soldier' in light of the contents developed throughout the investigation, I propose to think of professionalism, not as another military virtue, but as the epitome of all military virtues, its reward being honour as redefined in this final section. Thus, the Conclusions summarize the way in which this investigation will contribute to filling the gap that exists in theory and practice as to the understanding of the often-invoked concepts of military honour and human dignity, as well as the way they interact under a new *Jus Armorum* for the 21st century.

---

79 Peter Roberts, *The Western Way of War* (Havant: Howgate, 2024), p. 10.

INTRODUCTION

# Reliquaries of Honour

> Chivalry marked off knights from mere ruffians and bandits and also from peasant soldiers who bore arms as a necessity. I suppose that it survives today: some sense of military honor is still the creed of the professional soldier, the sociological if not the lineal descendent of the feudal knight.
>
> MICHAEL WALZER, *Just and Unjust Wars*

∵

## 1 In the Halls of the Knights of Old

*Crusade in Europe* is one of the most famous war memoirs ever written. Its pages depict gallant feats of arms and epic deeds aimed at defeating a formidable foe during one of the darkest periods in history. It narrates a true fight of good versus evil in which no compromise was possible, and which could only end with the unconditional surrender of the forces of darkness. Yet, it does not recount the events of some medieval war or the military efforts to recapture sacred sites. *Crusade in Europe* was actually written by General Dwight D. Eisenhower and published in 1948 as "*A Personal Account of World War II*".

Although it does not directly refer to the original crusades or to the deeds of the knights of old, Eisenhower's war memoir does include an interesting passage that calls to mind one of the most fabled military orders emerging from the crusades in the 12th century AD, the Order of Knights of the Hospital of Saint John of Jerusalem, or Knights Hospitaller, today continued as the Sovereign Military Order of Malta. Before the 1943 Cairo Conference between Winston Churchill and Franklin Delano Roosevelt, the British Prime Minister made a stop at a small island in the middle of the Mediterranean to confer with one of the top men of the American President, General Eisenhower. The author of *Crusade in Europe* recalls the events as follows:

> In the old palace of the Knights of Malta the Prime Minister presented [General] Alexander and me each a specially designed medal sent to us by the King; no others identical to them were ever to be produced. The

 | DOI:10.1163/9789004754096_003

> occasion was informal; one of the guests commented that such an event in the same palace, four hundred years earlier, would have called for days of jousting, pageantry, and roistering in the garrison.[1]

With or without jousting, pageantry, and roistering, Eisenhower certainly saw America's involvement in the Second World War as a true crusade to liberate Europe, both in the experience of his troops interrupting their own lives and crossing the Atlantic to risk life and limb for a greater cause,[2] as well as for himself. His own personal feelings on the matter are compellingly captured in a passage referring to his refusal to allow a defeated Nazi general to partake in the time-honoured martial tradition of paying his respects to the victorious commander:

> When Von Arnim was brought through Algiers on his way to captivity, some members of my staff felt that I should observe the custom of bygone days and allow him to call on me. The custom had its origin in the fact that mercenary soldiers of old had no real enmity toward their opponents. Both sides fought for the love of a fight, out of a sense of duty or, more probably, for money. A captured commander of the eighteenth century was likely to be, for weeks or months, the honored guest of his captor. The tradition that all professional soldiers are really comrades in arms has, in tattered form, persisted to this day. For me World War II was far too personal a thing to entertain such feelings. Daily as it progressed there grew within me the conviction that as never before in a war between many nations the forces that stood for human good and men's rights were this time confronted by a completely evil conspiracy with which no compromise could be tolerated. Because only by the utter destruction of the Axis was a decent world possible, the war became for me a crusade in the traditional sense of that often misused word.[3]

Eisenhower's total commitment to individual liberty and its foundation, human dignity,[4] could not but move him to reimagine what was expected of his role as a military commander in a total war of the 20th century, the brutality of which would have been probably unconscionable for any eighteenth

1 Dwight D. Eisenhower, *Crusade in Europe. A Personal Account of World War II* (New York: Vintage, 2021), p. 234.

2 Ibid., p. 68.

3 Ibid., p. 188.

4 Ibid., p. 569.

century soldier (or civilian) for whom such niceties were originally envisaged. Against such existential odds, then, he was only too happy to lead an Allied Expeditionary Force what he would characterize as "a mighty engine of righteous destruction".[5]

And yet, for all his self-righteousness and personal conviction, Eisenhower did not choose to call his memoir *Dirty War in Europe, Guerrilla Warfare in Europe, Vendetta in Europe*, or *Manhunt for Hitler*. He deliberately chose a concept originated in the Middle Ages to designate the kind of existential armed conflict that is believed to represent a true battle between good and evil: a crusade. However misguided in both their conceptualization and their execution throughout history,[6] the fact is that the crusades loomed large in the imaginary of a 20th century battle commander, and that is how he even characterized the war effort when addressing his troops on the eve of the largest military operation in history, D-Day.[7] Is this an anomaly, or are there more examples?

## 2 Echoes of Chivalry in the Age of Total War

During the Second World War there was no love lost between Allied military commanders and their Axis counterparts. Eisenhower's reported disdain as described above is one instance of this. Another famous illustration comes from the Pacific Theatre of Operations. After Japan's defeat, General Yamashita was put on trial for the crimes committed against civilians by his troops during the occupation of The Philippines, including large scale murder and rape. The American military commission passing judgment on this occasion decided that Yamashita was guilty, even if he did not commit or order the commission of any crimes, because of what he, as a commander, must have known or should have known. This case would go down in history as the main precedent for command responsibility for war crimes under International Criminal Law, as codified in the 1998 Rome Statute (Art. 28.1).[8]

---

5 Ibid., p. 510.

6 For an account from the standpoint of the recipients of such fanatical violence see Amin Maalouf, *The Crusades through Arab Eyes* (London: Saqi Books, 2012).

7 'General Dwight D. Eisenhower's Order of the Day (1944)', https://www.archives.gov/milestone-documents/general-eisenhowers-order-of-the-day, 14 October 2024.

8 Article 28 Responsibility of commanders and other superiors
In addition to other grounds of criminal responsibility under this Statute for crimes within the jurisdiction of the Court:
1. A military commander or person effectively acting as a military commander shall be criminally responsible for crimes within the jurisdiction of the Court committed by forces

Yamashita was sentenced to death by hanging on December 7, 1945, on the anniversary of the attack on Pearl Harbor. After the defence filed an appeal, General Douglas MacArthur himself confirmed the sentence, choosing to do so in the following terms:

> Rarely has so cruel and wanton a record been spread to public gaze. Revolting as this may be in itself, it pales before the sinister and far-reaching implication thereby attached to the profession of arms. The soldier, be he friend or foe, is charged with the protection of the weak and unarmed. It is the very essence and reason for his being …
>
> This officer, of proven field merit and entrusted with a high command involving authority adequate to his responsibility, has failed this irrevocable standard; has failed his duty to his troops, to his country, to his enemy, and to mankind; he has failed utterly his soldier faith. The transgressions resulting therefrom as revealed by the trial are a blot upon the military profession, a stain upon civilization, and constitute a memory of shame and dishonor that can never be forgotten.[9]

This professional commitment that the modern soldier shows to protecting those who cannot protect themselves[10] is what lies at the heart of the code of chivalry, as we shall see in the next section. Therefore, every time one military professional reminds another about the standards of behaviour they are supposed to observe, and more importantly, whenever they call out those who fail at this, chivalry is reenacted and its essence rejuvenated, even if shrouded in different trappings.

---

under his or her effective command and control, or effective authority and control as the case may be, as a result of his or her failure to exercise control properly over such forces, where:

(a) That military commander or person either knew or, owing to the circumstances at the time, should have known that the forces were committing or about to commit such crimes; and

(b) That military commander or person failed to take all necessary and reasonable measures within his or her power to prevent or repress their commission or to submit the matter to the competent authorities for investigation and prosecution.

9 Kelly Ashkin, 'Treatment of Sexual Violence in Armed Conflicts: A Historical Perspective and the Way Forward', in Anne-Marie Brouwer et al (eds), *Sexual Violence as an International Crime: Interdisciplinary Approaches* (Cambridge: Intersentia, 2013), pp. 48–49; Michael Walzer. *Just and Unjust Wars. A Moral Argument with Historical Illustrations*. 5th ed. (New York: Basic Books, 2015), p. 317.

10 Dave Grossman and Loren W. Christensen, *On Combat. The Psychology and Physiology of Deadly Conflict in War and Peace*. 4th ed. (New York: Open Road Media, 2022), pp. xx–xi; 176.

Now, the Second World War is typically regarded as the archetype of a "good" or a "just" war – so much so that not even the main proponent of the revisionist school of thought within the Just War tradition, Jeff McMahan, dares to undermine the foundations of such a universal instance of a just cause (at least when it comes to the war the Allies fought against the Nazis, not vice versa).[11] The deadliest armed conflict in history and the paradigm of total war, the Second World War stands in the middle of the 20th century as the fulcrum upon which other armed conflicts can be balanced, situated, and understood in their significance and impact. That applies, for instance, to the immediate cause of the Second World War, the conflict known as the Great War at the beginning of the century. It also applies at the other end, as we witness the decline of the international relations paradigm resulting from the Second World War in what could be very easily the swan song of the rules-based international order, the 2022 war in Ukraine. Interestingly, we can also find echoes of chivalry on both of these extremes in the relatively short arc of history tracing the path of total war.

Beyond the historical back alleys and political inroads that led to the assassination of Franz Ferdinand in Sarajevo in 1914 and Great Britain's involvement in the Great War, the words written in 1919 by the former commander in chief of the British Expeditionary Force, Douglas Haig, are illustrative of the attitude towards this conflict at the time: "We were doing battle for a higher form of civilisation, in which man's duty to his neighbour finds a place more important than his duty to himself, against an Empire built up and made great by the sword, efficient indeed, but with an efficiency unredeemed by any sense of chivalry or of moral responsibility towards the weak".[12]

Accordingly, Leo Braudy points out, "[t]o buttress these ideals, World War I was suffused with the imagery of the chivalric – in posters, in poetry, and in propaganda",[13] all of which are masterfully compiled by Allen J. Frantzen in his book *Bloody Good. Chivalry, Sacrifice, and the Great War*.[14] Perhaps the most conspicuous embodiment of this chivalric revival was the figure of Lawrence of Arabia, who was, according to Braudy, "a romantic medievalist whose head was filled with stories of knights and conquests, a kind of modern Don Quixote. But unlike Quixote, he actually led or helped lead a guerrilla army

11 Jeff McMahan, *Killing in War* (New York: Oxford University Press, 2009), p. 5. For more critical approaches of the justness of the Second World War see Ted Grimsrud, *The Good War That Wasn't – and Why It Matters* (Eugene: Cascade Books, 2014); Uwe Steinhoff, *The Ethics of War and the Force of Law. A Modern Just War Theory* (New York: Routledge, 2021).

12 Leo Braudy, *From Chivalry to Terrorism* (New York: Vintage Books, 2005), p. 460.

13 Ibid., p. 461.

14 Allen J. Frantzen, *Bloody Good. Chivalry, Sacrifice, and the Great War* (Chicago: University of Chicago Press, 2004).

of sword-wielding horsemen, warriors who seemed to Lawrence to be brothers across the centuries to medieval knights".[15] It would be also the war in the desert that would inspire the American reporter Lowell Thomas to dub the war against the Ottomans as "the last crusade".[16]

Back from the sands of Arabia, this chivalric revival would be also famously acted out in the skies of Europe with the dawn of aerial warfare. As Neil Renic observes:

> The emergence of the aircraft, and specifically, the practice of 'dogfighting' – close range aerial battle between opposing pilots – stood as one of the most powerful military counters to this trend [of industrialised killing in the trenches]. Among both observers and participants, aerial fighting was seen to possess an element of knightly chivalry that had been all but extinguished in the trenches of Europe.[17]

However, as the new "cavalry of the clouds"[18] regaled in epic pageantry up in the air, the bleak reality for the common soldier during the Great War was the brutality of trench warfare. As Braudy remarks: "The warrior honor of the nineteenth century, which in the images of the Arthurian quest for the Holy Grail promised a purification that transcended the body, had to face the din, dirt, death, and annihilation of the trenches".[19]

Today, there is another conflict where trench warfare has become a popular military tactic. It is not a war between empires, although it is a confrontation taking place in the throes of lost power whereby one agonizing empire attempts to recover some of its past lustre. It is the war of aggression Russia started in 2014 when it annexed part of the territory of Ukraine, intensified in 2022 when the former began a full-scale invasion of its western neighbour. Indeed, while the war in Ukraine has become known as the first "drone war",[20] at the same time it has rehabilitated an old method of warfare that the world thought belonged in the sepia-toned recollections of century-old horrors from the Great War.

15 Braudy, *From*, p. 499.

16 Ibid., p. 501.

17 Neil C. Renic, *Asymmetric Killing. Risk Avoidance, Just War, and the Warrior Ethos* (Oxford: Oxford University Press, 2020), p. 139.

18 Ibid.

19 Braudy, *From*, p. 467.

20 Isabelle Khurshudyan, Mary Ilyushina and Kostiantyn Khudov, 'Russia and Ukraine are fighting the first full-scale drone war', https://www.washingtonpost.com/world/2022/12/02/drones-russia-ukraine-air-war/, 15 October 2024.

Nevertheless, as the portentous wonders of the age of industrialized killing bring armies to a literal standstill, the echoes of chivalry can be heard even amidst this latest iteration of modern warfare against the backdrop of what is perceived as an epic battle between the forces of good and the evil "orc" occupier.[21] A case in point are the names of the weaponry used by Ukraine to fend off Russia's aggression, including the self-propelled howitzer cannon named "Paladin",[22] the 155mm "Excalibur" projectile,[23] and the ubiquitous "Javelin" anti-tank missiles – so powerful in the popular imagination that the weapon was even informally canonized as the "Saint Javelin".[24] These modern weapons evoking chivalric motives currently being used to defend Ukraine belong in the same panoply as the "Crusader" tank in service during the Second World War,[25] or the contemporary submarine hunter "Merlin" helicopter.[26]

Furthermore, several units in the Ukrainian Armed Forces have emblazoned their green fatigues with medieval and chivalric themes embroidered in their respective insignias, including knights in full armour, iron helmets, gauntlets wielding swords and mazes, and gallant battle steeds.[27] Perhaps even more tellingly, chivalry has even made its way into Ukrainian official military doctrine, as codified alongside other military traditions (arguably received from the Cossack citizen-knight of centuries past[28]) in the following terms in the 1999 *Code of Honour of an Officer of the Armed Forces of Ukraine*:

---

21 Francisco Lobo, 'The quest for the Ukrainian "Araucana". The case for the humanization of the Orc', *Revista Electrónica Iberoamericana*, 18:2 (2024), pp. 241–263.

22 'Servicemen of Ukraine trained with Paladin self-propelled howitzers', https://mil.in.ua/en/news/servicemen-of-ukraine-trained-with-paladin-self-propelled-howitzers/, 16 October 2024.

23 'Ukrainian soldiers showcased operations with M982 Excalibur shells', https://mil.in.ua/en/news/ukrainian-soldiers-showcased-operations-with-m982-excalibur-shells/, 16 October 2024.

24 Christian Borys, 'The story of Saint Javelin', https://www.nato.int/docu/review/articles/2024/02/22/the-story-of-saint-javelin/index.html, 16 October 2024.

25 'Crusader II Cruiser Tank', https://www.iwm.org.uk/collections/item/object/70000137, 16 October 2024.

26 'Merlin', https://www.royalnavy.mod.uk/equipment/aircraft/merlin, 16 October 2024.

27 Including the 46h Separate Air Assault Brigade; the 23rd Separate Tank battalion of Assault Troops; the 14th Separate Motorized Infantry Brigade; the 65h Separate Motorized Infantry Brigade; the 117th Separate Mechanized Brigade; the 12th Separate Tank Battalion; the 3rd Separate Tank Brigade; the 1st Separate Tank Brigade; the 4th Separate Tank Brigade; the Logistics Forces Command; the Support Forces Command; and the Ukraine Ground Forces Command. See 'Ukraine and Soviet Military', http://www.military.biz.ua/, 16 October 2024.

28 Zbigniew Rau, '"Free with the free, equal with the equal". Knightly freedom-lovingness against Moscow despotism is a common heritage of the First Polish-Lithuanian

> 3.9 Knightly spirit.
> Under no circumstances can an officer be forced to change his or her beliefs, faith, or to betray the military oath. An officer considers it beneath his dignity to disregard the spiritual values of others. An officer is a model of chivalrous attitude towards the sick, wounded, and civilians.[29]

If chivalry is indeed dead, and if the rules-based international order seems to be headed for the same fateful end, then why do we keep encountering such a rich normative language enclosed in these reliquaries of honour? Why do we keep hearing these echoes of chivalry even in the age of total war? A reconstruction of the essential contents and the historic trajectory of the code of chivalry may assist us in answering this most perplexing puzzle.

## 3 The Code of Chivalry Decoded

As already stated in the Prologue, this book does not amount to a history of ideas. Rather, it is a theoretical attempt at better understanding some notions that have been bequeathed to us by centuries of evolution in the way we think about war and political violence in general. In that sense, it is a quest to salvage our best traditions, preserved in those doctrinal embers waiting to be rekindled, that we may harness them for the present and the future.

Accordingly, the purpose of this book is not to undertake a specialized study of the code of chivalry, but merely to understand its core elements and its trajectory across history that has resulted in modern combatants still talking about it and drawing inspiration from it. For a dedicated analysis of this medieval phenomenon there are several scholars whose work can be of assistance, including Johan Huizinga,[30] Richard W. Kaeuper,[31] Theodor Meron,[32]

---

Commonwealth in the political culture of Poland and Ukraine', in in Dmytro Kuleba (ed.), *Війна і нові горизонти* (Kyiv: Knygolove, 2024), pp. 193–230.

29 'Code of honor of an officer of the Armed Forces of Ukraine', https://sprotyvg7.com.ua/lesson/kodeks-chesti-oficera-zbrojnix-sil-ukraini, 16 October 2024.

30 Johan Huizinga, *The Autumn of the Middle Ages* (Chicago: The University of Chicago Press, 1996).

31 Richard W. Kaeuper, *Chivalry and Violence in Medieval Europe* (New York: Oxford University Press, 1999).

32 Theodor Meron, *Bloody Constraint: War and Chivalry in Shakespeare* (New York: Oxford University Press, 1998).

Allen J. Frantzen,[33] Leo Braudy,[34] David Whetham,[35] Hellen M. Kinsella,[36] and Neil Renic,[37] just to name a few. In this section I shall merely outline the core elements of the code of chivalry as a historic phenomenon, such that we may attempt to distil its essence to guide us in our journey to rediscover this trove of ethical principles for the modern soldier.

First, it is important to understand that, although it crystalized during the Middle Ages around the twelfth century,[38] chivalry is not an exclusively medieval phenomenon. As understood by its own practitioners, chivalry has its roots in Antiquity. As Chrétien de Troyes writes in the prologue to his 12th century romantic tale of a knight named Cligès: "our books teach us … that Greece first had renown in chivalry and knowledge. Then came chivalry to Rome, and the whole of knowledge, which has now come into France. God grant that she may stay there".[39] Accordingly, Huizinga points out that "Knightly life is a life without historical dimensions. It makes little difference whether its heroes are those of the Round Table or those of classical antiquity. (…) Knighthood itself was considered to be Roman".[40] Thus, there is no reason to necessarily confine this social practice and its ethos to one single period in history. On the contrary, just at it made its way from Antiquity to the Middle Ages, chivalry seems to be an ideal that can be rediscovered, rejuvenated, and reforged in every period in history, including ours.

Now, as to its core elements, Kaeuper summarizes what he calls the "fusion of chivalric elements" in the following terms:

> Chivalry came into being as a powerful, mutually reinforcing fusion of several major functions, roles, and rights. Above all, the chivalrous defended honour through the violence of personal prowess; to this fusion they added a formal and rather independent piety, asserting God's blessing on their demanding and violent lives; they claimed an elite, usually

33 Frantzen, *Bloody*.

34 Braudy, *From*.

35 David Whetham, *Just Wars and Moral Victories. Surprise, Deception, and the Normative Framework of European War in the Later Middle Ages* (Leiden: Brill, 2009).

36 Helen M. Kinsella, *The Image before the Weapon. A Critical History of the Distinction between Combatant and Civilian* (Ithaca: Cornell University Press, 2011).

37 Neil C. Renic, *Asymmetric Killing. Risk Avoidance, Just War, and the Warrior Ethos* (Oxford: Oxford University Press, 2020).

38 Kaeuper, *Chivalry*, p. 47.

39 Josephine Quinn, *How the World Made the West. A 4,000 Year History* (New York: Random House, 2024), p. 394.

40 Huizinga, *Autumn*, p. 75.

> noble, status and established their nobility by the practice of a chivalric way of life; they sought to regulate relationships between males and females on their own terms, exclusively linking love, too, with prowess and honour.[41]

Similarly, Braudy refers to the main contents this code is supposed to espouse: "Briefly stated, the chivalric values (…) are loyalty (to the knight's political superior); prowess (which includes both praise of the rash willingness to throw oneself into danger – *hardiesse* – and the skill to deal with that danger); *franchise*, or an openhanded largesse to one's fellows and followers; and courtesy to women, children, and the elderly".[42] Among these core elements, Frantzen also highlights self-sacrifice as the knight's way to emulate the archetype of everything that is good and noble, Jesus Christ, turning a violent trade into a purposeful activity of the highest order: "The soldier of Christ, who was himself the epitome of nonviolence, does God's work by engaging in holy warfare. During the Crusades, war was defined as a form of worship and an act of penitence. Christ's antisacrifice became sacrifice: the renunciation of violence became the justification of violence in Christ's name".[43]

Furthermore, according to Huizinga chivalry served a double purpose in medieval society: it supported the order of divine and human laws, while at the same time protecting people, to the extent possible, from the pervasive violence of war characteristic of the times.[44] Accordingly, chivalry amounted not only to an aesthetic ideal of warrior prowess and bravado, but at the same time it aspired to become an ethical ideal for those partaking in it.[45] As such, it runs parallel to that other medieval normative edifice that is the Just War tradition (sometimes also contributing as a source or sub-tradition thereof[46]), with the latter mainly focusing on the victims of war, whereas the code of chivalry was aimed chiefly at the warrior in the form of an ethos.[47]

Admittedly, as Meron points out, chivalry was in actuality "a mix of reality, poetry, and legend. While humanizing warfare, chivalry also contributed to the legitimizing of war".[48] To be sure, the above rosy and romanticized view of chivalry does not address its foremost shortcomings, not least its

41 Kaeuper, *Chivalry*, p. 302.
42 Braudy, *From*, p. 118.
43 Frantzen, *Bloody*, p. 19.
44 Huizinga, *Autumn*, p. 70.
45 Ibid., p. 73.
46 Alex Bellamy, Just Wars. From Cicero to Iraq (Malden: Polity Press, 2012), pp. 40–44.
47 Renic, *Asymmetric*, p. 69.
48 Meron, *Bloody*, p. 5.

anti-egalitarianism manifested in the two vices of benign misogyny and radical xenophobia. Indeed, as Kinsella argues:

> The prowess of the knight was most frequently demonstrated in the protection of his lady from the advances of other knights. Indeed, one scholar of the period writes that 'even when idealized or adored, women seem to have been considered property in much chivalric literature, prizes to be won by knightly prowess or to be defended against the prowess of another'. (…) Thus, the identification of women as weak and defenseless required effort, concerted effort made visible in the gilded codes of martial and courtly chivalry.[49]

Further, chivalry came to be fully defined in contrast to the warrior class of the main religious enemy at the time, Islam, the crusades representing its historical climax.[50] Thus, it was a code of conduct reserved only for the interactions between Christians, and not even every Christian the knight errant would encounter, but only other warriors deemed of equal standing and status in medieval society. Even among equals the restraint and shows of respect that are characteristic of chivalry were not necessarily inspired by ethical considerations, but often much more pragmatic ones. As Whetham soberingly remarks:

> While medieval chroniclers may have tried to cast a 'golden spell of chivalry', the reality of Medieval warfare remained an extremely unpleasant business – 'Chivalry was in fact compatible with stark, ruthless slaughter'. Certain aspects of the violence were simply restrained for a time as those who considered themselves as belonging to Christendom's knighthood generally respected the code relating to the laws of ransom. This was thanks to a professional class of fighters who successfully employed agreements that limited their potential losses in what was, for the most part, a financial exercise. Knights were not unchivalrous for not attempting to limit the effects of war on anyone else for 'as a code, chivalry had next to nothing to do with ordinary people'. This, then, was what chivalry was about. There was no idealism or romantic sentiments here, just hard-nosed business sense. Within this context, honour can be seen as simply the way of holding together this business relationship.[51]

49 Kinsella, *Image*, pp. 43–44.
50 Huizinga, *Autumn*, pp. 92; 105.
51 Whetham, *Just*, pp. 15–16.

And yet, this pragmatic corporate spirit might hold the key to unlock chivalry's full potential in the age of professional armies, as we shall see throughout this investigation, in which I will attempt to show that it is indeed possible to distil chivalry's essence to get rid of the detritus of misogyny, hypermasculinity, and racism against "infidels". Mindful of the dangers of nostalgia and presentism when approaching the subject, as we shall see, a rejuvenation of the concept of chivalry through military honour understood as respect for human dignity in the age of professional armies is possible. Such a rejuvenation of chivalry reforged with modern humanitarian contents will be the main task of the following chapters.

## 4 Chivalry Lost and Found

With the end of the Middle Ages came the demise of the code of chivalry, or so the story goes. But did chivalry actually die the same death as the Middle Ages? Or did its embers stay stubbornly burning across the centuries, waiting to be reignited? Was the code of chivalry lost and perhaps found again within a different container? Could that new reliquary of the chivalric tradition be something more familiar to us like international law?

Mindful of the excesses of too rosy a view of medieval violence and war, Huizinga once remarked:

> Even if it were no more than a fiction, these fancies of war as a game of honour and virtue have still played an important part in developing civilization, for it is from them that the idea of chivalry sprang and hence, ultimately, of international law. Of these two factors, chivalry was one of the great stimulants of mediaeval civilization, and however constantly the ideal was belied in reality it served as a basis for international law, which is one of the indispensable safeguards for the community of mankind.[52]

In a recent article titled *War's Rustic Code of Honor* Jens David Ohlin contends that, amidst a serious crisis in confidence experienced by international law (and international lawyers) in the face of the massacres being perpetrated in places like Gaza or Ukraine, we should draw inspiration from the "rustic" or simple and reliable chivalry underlying the sophisticated laws of war. He concludes that "It is no surprise that the law of war is built on ancient traditions

52 Johan Huizinga, *Homo Ludens* (London: Routledge and Kegan Paul, 1980), p. 96.

of chivalry and honor, a tradition that goes back to the use of knights to fight battles, and the rules and customs of knighthood that emerged from that process".[53] He adds that the rustic character of the laws of war is to be celebrated, as it infuses this normative body with three positive attributes: (i) it relies on intuitive and widely shared commitments to the standards of chivalry (e.g. sparing non-combatants from harm); (ii) it is made up of clear norms; and (iii) it is embodied and reinforced through military professionalism and unit discipline.[54] It is important to point out here that to some chivalry also fulfils an important gap-filling function with regard to the laws of war.[55]

How did chivalry come to inform such an important and universally respected legal regime as the laws of war of the 21st century, as its modern-day reliquary? According to Meron, the normative contents of chivalry survived the passing of time in the form of a particular source of international law, namely customary law, and eventually codified under another source, that is treaty law. Thus, he states that "Such chivalric principles, now regarded as the customary law of nations, clearly appear in the 1899 and the 1907 Hague Convention (No. IV) on Laws and Customs of War".[56]

As a result of this historical cross-fertilization between the laws of war and the code of chivalry, the former have acquired a distinct set of contents. As Ohlin also remarks:

> The chivalric code is embodied in the specific legal rules that are codified in treaties and customary international law. The intentional killing of civilians is a war crime. Killings that are performed perfidiously are also illegal. A soldier cannot feign being injured to gain a military advantage and kill the enemy through deception. Nor can a soldier impersonate a civilian organization such as the red cross. Poison and other forms of perfidious killings are illegal. It's all illegal because it violates the chivalric code.[57]

Meron further asserts that chivalry informs the famous Martens Clause found in the 1907 Hague Regulations, which originally stated: "in cases not included in the Regulations adopted by them, the inhabitants and the belligerents remain

53 Jens David Ohlin, 'War's Rustic Code of Honor', https://ssrn.com/abstract=4931591, 12 September 2024, p. 18.

54 Ibid., p. 42.

55 Evan Wallach, 'Pray Fire First Gentlemen of France: Has 21st Century Chivalry Been Subsumed by Humanitarian Law?', *Harvard National Security Journal*, 3 (2012), pp. 431–469.

56 Meron, *Bloody*, p. 14.

57 Ohlin, 'Rustic', p. 47.

under the protection and the rule of the principles of the law of nations, as they result from the usages established among civilized peoples, from the laws of humanity, and the dictates of the public conscience".[58] The Martens Clause is the minimum legal yardstick codifying the principle of humanity under International Humanitarian Law.[59] Most importantly, the 2004 British *Joint Service Manual of the Law of Armed Conflict* indicates that the Martens Clause "incorporates the earlier rules of chivalry that opposing combatants were entitled to respect and honour. From this flowed the duty to provide humane treatment to the wounded and those who had become prisoners of war".[60]

Finally, there are two additional considerations with regard to the vehicle that transported the code of chivalry from the Middle Ages to the wars of the 21st century, customary international law. The first one refers to the absence of what is known as the "persistent objector" phenomenon with relation to the chivalric contents kept alive through customary law and codified under subsequent treaty law. According to general international law, a state may opt-out of a customary rule if it can prove that it has consistently and from the inception of a new rule objected to its contents. Although it is debatable whether this doctrine can be applied to International Humanitarian Law or the laws of war because of the importance of the values safeguarded by that regime (such as human dignity),[61] the fact is that no state has ever objected to such basic norms of behaviour as the protection of civilians in wartime or the appropriate treatment of prisoners of war. The most infamous time a state official, namely legal counsel to George W. Bush Alberto Gonzales, haplessly remarked that the Geneva Conventions were "quaint" and "obsolete", and thus not suited for the so-called war on terror,[62] this did not prevent the U.S. Supreme Court from

58 Hague Convention (IV) on War on Land and its Annexed Regulations, 1907.

59 Ginevra Le Moli, *Human Dignity in International Law* (Cambridge: Cambridge University Press, 2021), p. 177.

60 Ministry of Defence of the United Kingdom of Great Britain and Northern Ireland, 'The Joint Service Manual of the Law of Armed Conflict', https://assets.publishing.service.gov.uk/government/uploads/system/uploads/attachment_data/file/27874/JSP3832004Edition.pdf, 20 June 2022, pp. 23–24. See also Ohlin, 'Duty', p. 1270; Oeter, '(Non)Importance', pp. 54–55; Kinsella, *Image*, p. 105; Francisco Lobo, 'The "capture or kill" debate revisited: Putting the "human" back in "human enhancement of soldiers"', *The Military Law and the Law of War Review*, 58:1 (2020), p.109.

61 Jean-Marie Henckaerts and Louise Doswald-Beck, *Customary International Humanitarian Law. Vol. I: Rules* (New York: Cambridge University Press-ICRC, 2009), p. xlv.

62 'Memorandum for the President', https://nsarchive2.gwu.edu/NSAEBB/NSAEBB127/02.01.25.pdf, 6 November 2024.

eventually ruling that the United States is legally bound by such legal instruments and other legal standards even as it wages war on terrorism.[63]

The second consideration bears on the nature of customary law in terms of how it comes to exist and is identified. According to the UN International Law Commission, a rule of customary international law exists when there is a general practice that is accepted as law, or with regard to which there is an *opinio juris*. One important form of evidence of such *opinio juris* are official publications.[64] In the specific case of International Humanitarian Law, military manuals are a critical instance of such official publications.[65] Accordingly, some historic military manuals have been undoubtedly influential in shaping the laws of war and preserving its contents (including the tenets of chivalry) alive across the centuries. A case in point is the fabled "Lieber Code" issued in 1863 for the U.S. Army, an ambitious piece of military doctrine that intended "not only to establish rules to govern the conduct of the Union Army but to set down in a short, usable form the accumulated customary rules binding all the armies of the extended European world".[66] Indeed, the Lieber Code would be well received across the Atlantic and some of its provisions would make their way into the Hague regulations and the subsequent Geneva Conventions.[67]

Chivalry, however, is not explicitly mentioned in the Lieber Code, although some of its contents may be identified therein in vestigial form, including: the prohibition of cruelty and bad faith concerning engagements concluded with the enemy during war (Art. 11); the prohibition of torture or inflicting unnecessary suffering as falling outside the concept of military necessity (Art. 16); the prohibition of rape, pillage, and wanton violence (Art. 44); the protection of prisoners of war (Art. 56); the banning of poison (Art. 70); the prohibition of treacherous attacks incompatible with honourable warfare (Art. 101); and the possibility to release prisoners of war honour-bound by parole (Art. 120).

Today, echoes of chivalry can be further found in contemporary military manuals, for example, in the aforementioned 1999 *Code of Honour of an Officer of the Armed Forces of Ukraine*, which prescribes a chivalrous attitude towards the sick, wounded, and civilians. Such echoes can also be clearly heard in the

63 Wayne McCormack, *Understanding the Law of Terrorism* (Danvers: Lexis Nexis, 2007), pp. 330–333.

64 UN International Law Commission, 'Draft conclusions on identification of customary international law', https://legal.un.org/ilc/texts/instruments/english/draft_articles/1_13_2018.pdf, 11 January 2023.

65 Henckaerts and Doswald-Beck, *Customary*, p. xxxviii.

66 John Fabian Witt, *Lincoln's Code* (New York: Free Press, 2012), p. 15.

67 Ibid., pp. 16–17.

U.S. Department of Defense 2015 Law of War Manual, updated in 2023 – a true heir to the Lieber Code. The Manual defines the legal principle of "Honor" thus:

> *Honor* demands a certain amount of fairness in offense and defense and a certain mutual respect between opposing military forces. (...) *Honor* has also been called *chivalry*. (...) *Chivalry* is often associated with a specific historical context – a code of behavior for knights in Europe during the Middle Ages. Rather than refer to this specific context, the term *honor* is used in this manual to indicate more clearly that the law of war principle of *honor* draws from warriors' codes from a variety of cultures and time periods.[68]

Three further examples of military manuals carrying the voices of chivalry are the Canadian *Law of Armed Conflict Manual* (2001), the Indian *Army Doctrine* (2004), and the Spanish *Values of the Land Army* (2018). According to the first:

> The concept of chivalry is difficult to define. It refers to the conduct of armed conflict in accordance with certain recognized formalities and courtesies. An armed conflict is rarely a polite contest. Nevertheless, the concept of chivalry is reflected in specific prohibitions such as those against dishonourable or treacherous conduct and against misuse of enemy flags or flags of truce. The concept of chivalry makes armed conflict slightly less savage and more civilized for the individual combatant.[69]

The Indian *Army Doctrine* codifies the "Code of the Warrior" taken from the *Bhagavad Gita*, including pledge to always protect the weak, be humane, cultured and compassionate.[70] Moreover, the section specifically devoted to

68 US Department of Defense, *Law of War Manual* (Washington D.C.: DoD, 2023), pp. 66–67. Against the inclusion of the idea of chivalry see Sean Watts, 'The DOD Law of War Manual's Return to Principles', https://www.justsecurity.org/24270/dod-law-war-manuals-return-principles/, 26 August 2024; Rachel Van Landingham, 'The Law of War is Not About "Chivalry"', https://www.justsecurity.org/24773/laws-war-chivalry/, 26 August 2024; Richard Salomon, '2023 DoD Manual Revision – What's Chivalry Got to Do with It?', https://lieber.westpoint.edu/whats-chivalry-got-to-do-with-it/, 26 August 2024.

69 Canadian Armed Forces, 'Joint Doctrine Manual: Law of Armed Conflict at the Operational and Tactical Levels', https://www.fichl.org/fileadmin/_migrated/content_uploads/Canadian_LOAC_Manual_2001_English.pdf, 10 June 2022, par. 202.7. See also G. Corn, V. Hansen, R. Jackson, C. Jenks, E. Talbot Jensen and J. Schoettler, *The Law of Armed Conflict: An Operational Approach* (New York: Wolters Klumer, 2012), p. 202.

70 Headquarters Army Training Command, *Indian Army Doctrine* (Shimla: Headquarters Army Training Command, 2004).

professionalism and the military *ethos* incorporates contents bearing on "The conduct of military operations within prescribed norms such as the laws of armed conflict and the concept of military chivalry"; and "The requirement for members of the profession to uphold a high standard of discipline to protect the weak and defenceless and to always act for the common good".[71] Finally, the Spanish *Values of the Land Army* state: "Honour is based and grounded in a well-formed conscience, in which several other values are thoroughly cultivated such as integrity, chivalry, justice, integrity and respect for the dignity of others as well as our own".[72]

## 5 Decoding Lions

"We use words like honor, code, loyalty. We use these words as the backbone of a life spent defending something. You use them as a punchline!" This is a quote from Jack Nicholson's famous "You can't handle the truth!" speech, playing USMC Colonel Jessup in the 1992 film *A few good men*. Although it is a work of fiction, Colonel Jessup's indictment of civilian inability to grasp the core concepts of the military mindset resonate in a 2024 article written by Jeffrey Goldberg exposing Donald Trump's proverbial contempt for the service. Goldberg concludes this piece by saying: "In Trump's mind, traditional values – values including those embraced by the armed forces of the United States having to do with honor, self-sacrifice, and integrity – have no merit, no relevance, and no meaning".[73] What if Trump is not alone in this?

Ludwig Wittgenstein once famously said: "If a lion could talk, we wouldn't be able to understand it".[74] He was referring to the lack of a shared experience between us and lions that could enable mutual understanding, for language is in the end about more than just uttering the right words or sounds; it is about a common form of life.[75] A form of life in this context should be understood as "the underlying consensus of linguistic and nonlinguistic behaviour,

71 Ibid., para. 7.16.

72 Free translation from Spanish. See Spanish Army, 'Los Valores en el Ejército de Tierra', https://ame1.org.es/wp-content/uploads/2018/03/EME-Valores-del-Ejercito-de-Tierra-2018.pdf, 31 July 2023, p. 23.

73 Jeffrey Goldberg, 'Trump: "I Need the Kind of Generals that Hitler Had"', https://www.theatlantic.com/politics/archive/2024/10/trump-military-generals-hitler/680327/, accessed 24 October 2024.

74 Ludwig Wittgenstein, *Philosophical Investigations* (Croydon: Blackwell Publishing, 2009), p. 235.

75 Ibid., p. 15.

assumptions, practices, traditions, and natural propensities which humans, as social beings, share with one another, and which is therefore presupposed in the language they use".[76]

There is a strange mismatch in the modern military profession of our age, one that brings to mind Wittgenstein's observation as societies take their cubs and lionize them to go to war, when institutions take in thousands of civilians to undergo military training and turn them into soldiers. Societies send their 'warriors' into battle equipped with state-of-the-art technology, the latest weaponry, and the most advanced tools and gadgets any science fiction writer could only dream of. And they are using them to maximum effect, as the unpredictable, multipolar world of today becomes ever more securitised by entrusting the military with increasingly more functions, not least warfighting under its most professionalized guise in history.

And yet, though they are supposed to act on behalf of the societies that fund them, field them, and send them into battle, these military professionals are discharging their duties by speaking in almost incomprehensible terms for the rest of us, just as the language of lions would. This has nothing to do with military acronyms, although there is plenty of obscurity surrounding those as well, not unlike countless other contemporary bureaucracies. As evidenced by the doctrinal documents cited above carrying the echoes of chivalry, modern soldiers are waging contemporary wars using the language of the knights of old, and that kind of rhetoric defines who they are, who they believe they represent and stand for, in a critical and often unexamined way. It also bears on the way they are expected to deal with transgressions of said standards, such as war crimes, as we shall see in this investigation. Societies that don't pay attention to the words their soldiers use and to the oaths they take risk not understanding them at all.

Indeed, the preceding doctrinal illustrations confirm that respecting the rules and the will to sacrifice life and limb for their communities is apparently not enough for the military professional. In other words, the soldier needs more than just the "Laws of War" and "Rules of Engagement" abridged version of the moral reality of war that is succinct enough to fit in one Power Point slide during basic training. The modern soldier needs more, as acknowledged by the International Committee of the Red Cross, which admitted in a 2018 report, after initially favouring an exclusively legalistic approach, that "ethical values appear to play a strong complementary role to the law, a hybrid of

76 A.C. Grayling, *Wittgenstein. A Very Short Introduction* (New York: Oxford University Press, 2001), p. 97.

formal and informal norms that aims to discourage unwanted behaviour not only because it is 'against the rules' but also because it is 'not who we are'".[77]

How can the military know who they really are and what the right thing to do is in today's modern, messy warfare, beyond the legal baseline they are taught during training? The answer lies in their own institutionalized beliefs about what works in war, that is, military doctrine,[78] which carries within a most precious normative payload, the echoes of chivalry. As we shall see towards the end of this book, perhaps the easiest way to access doctrine is by consulting military manuals and official publications. These are pithy documents rich with prescriptive content and are considered an integral part of what it means to be a military professional today. Yet, concepts contained in those manuals are rarely defined or discussed in society, as civilians take comfort in the fact that their armed forces are getting the proper Law of Armed Conflict training that in turn is supposed to inform the Rules of Engagement.

Beyond a baseline training in the Law of Armed Conflict, the military seem to feel the need to find solace and guidance in additional normative concepts such as 'honour', 'warrior's code', 'sportsmanship', and the like, all shibboleths that, to quote Wittgenstein, seem to "strike a note on the keyboard of the imagination"[79] of contemporary military professionals. Such concepts have been codified in the manuals and doctrinal publications listed above and in many others, therefore constituting empirical evidence that modern militaries are still thinking in these quaint terms and applying them in practice. Acknowledging the empirical reality of the usage of these concepts and categories, in other words being aware of the language of lions, thus, becomes a first descriptive step in this inquiry, while at the same time representing the embers of a tradition waiting to be reignited through earnest intellectual discussion. That is what this book offers the reader.

However, as mentioned in the Prologue, this book is not a descriptive study. It is a conceptual-normative investigation, or a prescriptive work probing the meanings and implications of these normative categories taken from military doctrine and moral philosophy. What do all these concepts mean? What is the importance of chivalry for today's military professionals? What are the definitions of military honour and human dignity, and how do these concepts connect and interact in times of war? Answering these questions is the main task of this book.

---

77 ICRC, *The Roots of Restraint in War* (Geneva: ICRC, 2018), p. 32.

78 Harald Høiback, *Understanding Military Doctrine* (New York: Routledge, 2017), p. 1.

79 Wittgenstein, *Investigations*, p. 7.

Now, it would be naïve to think that these quaint words preserved in such reliquaries of honour will strike the same note in the keyboard of every person's imagination. As a matter of fact, what they may evoke in some people is not something at all serious or solemn, but rather something laughable, such as when we encounter certain parodies of chivalry and military honour like Don Quixote or the Black Knight from *Monty Python and the Holy Grail*.[80] As we shall see at the end of Chapter 4, these parodies are there to remind us about the serious realities upon which they are built, so we should not be always so ready to just take these comical devices at their face value, unexamined, as they may tell us more about us than we would care to admit.

The orthodoxy of parody, thus, can be a prison from which the mind may not easily escape, and which may prevent it from understanding reality, especially when we are confronted, not only with the comical, but with the ludicrously farcical. The latter may happen as we encounter the language of chivalry in some rather unexpected sources, for example, terrorist actors. Masters of social media engagement and propaganda warfare, ISIS at one point characterized its online recruits as veritable "Knights of the Uploading".[81] Or take the case of the "Knights Templar of Michoacán" ("*Caballeros Templarios de Michoacán*"), a Mexican drug cartel founded a decade ago, which enacted its own "Code of Chivalry", featuring such contents as an oath to always fight to protect the oppressed, widows and orphans, as well as to conduct themselves with honour, dignity, total discipline, loyalty and honesty, and even love and selflessly serve all of humankind while respecting natural justice and fundamental rights.[82]

When it comes to state-sponsored terrorism, the Russian military machine is yet another example of this farcical instantiation of chivalry, as that aggressive regime drapes its illegal war on Ukraine in the blazonry of the Order of Saint George – a military order founded in 1769 by Catherine II and inspired by the fabled dragonslayer[83] – and pins its cross upon the chest of hundreds of fighters for the 'brave' feat of terrorizing the Ukrainian civilian population

80 Francisco Lobo, 'Parody or deadly-serious commitment? Non-state armed groups upholding humanitarian standards in war', (https://www.kcl.ac.uk/parody-or-deadly-serious-commitment-non-state-armed-groups-upholding-humanitarian-standards-in-war), 08 June 2022.

81 David Patrikarakos, *War in 140 Characters. How Social Media Is Reshaping Conflict in the Twenty-First Century* (New York: Basic Books, 2017), p. 238.

82 Lobo, 'Parody'.

83 'The Military Order of the Saint Grand Martyr and the Triumphant George has been established', https://www.prlib.ru/en/history/619789, 21 October 2024; Frantzen, *Bloody*, p. 18.

day in and day out, with no military justification whatsoever and no reprieve since the full-scale invasion started in 2022. All these cases of terrorist actors embracing the language and the imagery of chivalry are a sobering reminder that, far from being a joke, the motivations driving people to commit the most atrocious acts are never to be taken lightly, but we should rather think of them as deadly serious, just as serious as the death and destruction they can bring about.

Chivalry, then, is not dead. As Frantzen concludes after his study of chivalry in the beginning of the 20th century: "Chivalry did not die with World War 1".[84] It appears to be in good health a century later, at least in the minds of soldiers and fighters, most notably in the echoes that can be heard in military doctrine, as well as in the weaponry and the understated military regalia deployed in the battlefields of the 21st century. It appears today as a faint radio signal echoing through time, or as embers of sorts preserving the all but extinct fire of heroic societies. What remains of it, under which language and with what degree of intensity is the object of the present reappraisal of military honour as respect for human dignity. However, before venturing into the lofty domains of honour and dignity, we must first have a real conversation about what soldiers do and why they do it.

---

84 Frantzen, *Bloody*, p. 8.

CHAPTER 1

# War Is Our Business: Taking What Military Professionals Do Seriously

## 1 Introduction

The main questions this book aims to answer have been stated as follows: Is the instruction in the laws of war, otherwise known as International Humanitarian Law or the Law of Armed Conflict, enough to ensure the appropriate behaviour of combatants on the battlefield, or are additional normative standards of an ethical nature needed to protect both civilians from unjustified harm and combatants themselves from moral injury? Where could such standards be found? Is there something in the language used by contemporary professionals that is reminiscent of the ancient code of chivalry and what is the importance of this for the main research question of this book? As they pertain to legal and ethical standards of behaviour, these are normative questions. However, they are predicated on factual background conditions making them possible and necessary. In this first chapter I shall explore said factual conditions before venturing into the normative implications arising from the main issue, whose contents and pedagogical possibilities shall make up the rest of the investigation.

During late 2021 and early 2022 numerous Russian forces were amassed at the Ukrainian border unimpeded, threatening an invasion. Tensions continued to rise among world powers in the face of an impending armed conflict. Pundits and intellectuals articulated at the time what international organizations were too paralysed to vocalize. One of them, Yuval Noah Harari, the renowned author of *Sapiens*, wrote in The Economist just a few weeks before war eventually broke out: "At the heart of the Ukraine crisis lies a fundamental question about the nature of history and the nature of humanity: is change possible? Can humans change the way they behave, or does history repeat itself endlessly, with humans forever condemned to re-enact past tragedies without changing anything except the décor?"[1]

1 Yuval Noah Harari, https://www.economist.com/by-invitation/2022/02/09/yuval-noah-harari-argues-that-whats-at-stake-in-ukraine-is-the-direction-of-human-history?itm_source=parsely-api, 14 February 2022.

 | DOI:10.1163/9789004754096_004

Arguing against the pessimistic view envisaging human beings forever governed by the 'law of the jungle', Harari advocated the thesis that change is possible, and that war is indeed in decline: "Unlike gravity, war isn't a fundamental force of nature. (...) The decline of war didn't result from a divine miracle or from a change in the laws of nature. It resulted from humans making better choices".[2]

He was wrong, as it turns out. Before the month was out war would return to European soil, against all hopes and calculations. Prompted by the same kind of optimism underlying Harari's reflections, UN Secretary General Antonio Guterres reacted declaring war to be "an absurdity in the 21st century".[3] Similarly, several months into the conflict Indian Prime Minister Narendra Modi admonished his ally Vladimir Putin by stating outright that ours is "not an era of war".[4]

If change is possible, if war is an absurdity in our century and if this is no longer an era for such a form of human interaction, an opinion undergirded by the tireless efforts of countless men and women fighting to outlaw war over the centuries,[5] how did it come to this? How can we make sense of a phenomenon that defies all our wishes and modern assessments of the human condition?

The truth is that contemporary optimism about peace and its resulting inability to comprehend the abject failure of such a lofty promise, namely war, is not something new. Erasmus already argued against war as a stupid, irrational human endeavour in the 16th century.[6] The root causes of such stupidity were of no concern to him, however. As Michael Howard posits, Erasmus "was the first in that long line of humanitarian thinkers for whom it was enough to chronicle the horrors of war in order to condemn it; men who may command one's instinctive agreement, but provide little constructive advice as to how to deal with the phenomenon which they find so abhorrent to nature and reason".[7] Howard then concludes:

---

2 Ibid.

3 'UN Secretary General describes war in Ukraine as "absurdity" in 21st century', https://www.theguardian.com/world/2022/apr/28/un-secretary-general-describes-war-in-ukraine-as-absurdity-in-21st-century, 28 April 2022.

4 'Narendra Modi chides Vladimir Putin over Ukraine war', https://www.ft.com/content/d0ac0361-c101-4605-ba22-ee20f9f92233, 21 September 2022.

5 Oona Hathaway and Scott Shapiro, *The Internationalists. How a Radical Plan to Outlaw War Remade the World* (New York: Simon & Schuster, 2017).

6 Michael Howard, *War and the Liberal Conscience* (London: Hurst, 2008), p. 6.

7 Ibid., p. 8.

> At the root of this dilemma of liberal thinkers lies the habit, far older even than Erasmus, of seeing war as a distinct and abstract entity about which one can generalise at large. It was this habit of thought that made possible the ludicrous confusion of the interwar years when liberals declared themselves passionately opposed to 'war' but in favour of 'military sanctions' to enforce collective security or, even more strongly, in favour of 'resistance to Fascism'. It has made it possible for enthusiasts in our own day to declare their opposition to war but their support for struggles of national liberation. But 'war' is simply the generic term for the use of armed force by states or aspirants to statehood for the attainment of their political objectives.[8]

We may find a more constructive view of the kind Howard wishes for in the work of historian Graham Allison, author of *Destined for War. Can America and China Escape Thucydides's Trap?* No matter how ominous its title and however premonitory its contents might prove in the future, Allison's volume ends on a more positive note by pointing out that history is made up of the choices that people make freely. Ever since Antiquity "Destiny dealt the hands, but men played the cards."[9]

That might be the case, but what is the deck actually made of? Instead of merely denouncing war as an absurdity, Allison takes up the realist challenge of examining the causes of war and the forces or 'traps' that push us, albeit not inevitably, towards such an undesirable outcome. The proverbial trap Allison refers to goes back to the days when Thucydides identified three main causes of war: honour, fear, and interest,[10] all of them later revisited by Thomas Hobbes and his realist successors.[11]

Although these three causes are somewhat generic and may explain human behaviour in any number of situations outside of war (e.g. business, politics, social relations, etc.), they represent at least an honest intellectual attempt to make sense of the reality of war instead of just wishing it away from the pulpit. Before venturing into the conceptual analysis of military honour and human dignity as the linchpins of this investigation, in this first chapter I will attempt

8 Ibid., p. 118.

9 Graham Allison, *Destined for War. Can America and China Escape Thucydides's Trap?* (New York: Houghton Mifflin Harcourt, 2017), p. 232.

10 Donald Kagan, *On the Origins of War and the Preservation of Peace* (New York: Doubleday, 1995), p. 8.

11 Thomas Hobbes, *Leviathan* (Oxford: Oxford University Press, 1998), p. 83; Samuel Zilincik, 'Why the "Fear, Honour and Interest" Trinity Harms Our Understanding of War', *The RUSI Journal*, (2021), pp. 2–9.

a similar feat by laying the groundwork for understanding the circumstances that make of war a permanent possibility in human affairs, albeit not an unregulated activity but, on the contrary, a highly normative one. This has crucial implications for the professionals charged by society with the task of managing such an ominous outcome. Indeed, only a specific kind of professional can be tasked with managing the outcome of such a portentous set of conditions. By taking the circumstances making of war a permanent possibility seriously, we come closer to a better understanding of the professionals in charge of administering their impactful effects, such that we may take the military and what they do also seriously. If war is indeed back in our "post-heroic societies"[12] of today, then we owe this kind of earnest consideration to our troops, as well as to ourselves.

## 2 The 'Circumstances of War' (CoW): a Proposal

### 2.1 *Formulation*

In his seminal *A Theory of Justice*, John Rawls coined the phrase 'circumstances of justice' to refer to "the normal conditions under which human cooperation is both possible and necessary".[13] These are the background conditions bearing on the cooperative and competitive nature of human beings from which arises the need for institutional arrangements of distributive justice. In other words, they are the hard facts on which social institutions are built and that warrant their existence. Every human society is characterized by these circumstances.[14] Thus, Rawls concludes: "Unless these circumstances existed there would be no occasion for the virtue of justice, just as in the absence of threats of injury to life and limb there would be no occasion for physical courage".[15]

Rawls further divides these conditions in objective and subjective circumstances.[16] *Objective* circumstances pertain to the existence of a human group over the same territory and at the same time, their similar physical and mental capabilities as well as vulnerabilities, and finally the condition of moderate scarcity of resources. *Subjective* circumstances, on the other hand, refer to the personal interests, conceptions, purposes and plans of mutually

12 Tine Molendijk, 'War Is Back in Post-Heroic Europe: Change and Continuity in the Relationship Between the Armed Forces and Society', *Armed Forces and Society*, 00 (2024), pp. 1–25.

13 John Rawls, *A Theory of Justice* (Cambridge: Harvard University Press, 2005), p. 126.

14 Ibid., p. 130.

15 Ibid., p. 128.

16 Ibid., pp. 126–127.

disinterested individuals belonging to a social group, such that each requires a fair share to further their own goals.

In order to build his theory of the circumstances of justice, Rawls expressly relied on the works of other thinkers, such as H.L.A. Hart and, especially, David Hume.[17] Hart notably constructed his notion of the 'minimum content of Natural Law' that every legal system presupposes to achieve the modest purpose of survival, based on a few 'truisms' about human nature that amount to what Rawls would later call the (objective/subjective) circumstances of justice: (i) human vulnerability; (ii) approximate equality of capacities; (iii) limited altruism; (iv) limited resources; and (v) limited understanding and strength of will.[18]

Hume's account of the circumstances of justice is, according to Rawls, the most perspicuous.[19] Reflecting on the origins of property and justice in *A Treatise of Human Nature*, Hume highlights some obstacles to the common enterprise of social union. Among them we find our 'natural temper,' and in particular our selfishness, which amount to the subjective circumstances in Rawls's own account. As to the objective factors, Hume calls them 'outward circumstances,' bearing on three different types of goods that we can possess: the internal satisfaction of our mind, the external advantages of our body, and the enjoyment of possessions acquired through our industry and good fortune. The latter are liable to being transferred and that makes then unstable; if we add to this the fact that they are also scarce, then a formidable obstacle for social cooperation arises, hence the need for social conventions in the form of property and distributive justice.[20] Thus Hume advances the following proposition: "*that 'tis only from the selfishness and confin'd generosity of man, along with the scanty provision nature has made for his wants, that justice derives its origin*" (original italics).[21]

Building on this theoretical framework, I would like to propose the notion of the 'Circumstances of War' ('CoW'),[22] namely the group of those background

17 Ibid., p. 126.

18 H.L.A. Hart, *The Concept of Law*, 3rd ed. (Oxford: Oxford University Press, 2012), pp. 185–200.

19 Rawls, *Theory*, p. 127.

20 David Hume, *A Treatise of Human Nature*, Vol. 1 (New York: Oxford University Press, 2007), pp. 313–315. See also David Hume, *An Enquiry Concerning the Principles of Morals* (Indianapolis: Hackett, 1983), pp. 21–24.

21 Hume, *Treatise*, p. 318.

22 I do not use the term in the same sense as Walzer in the postscript to the 5th edition of *Just and Unjust Wars*, namely as the characteristics of war as it unfolds. I refer to the factors *leading to* war. See Michael Walzer. *Just and Unjust Wars. A Moral Argument with*

conditions that, considered together in a logical (not a chronological) sense,[23] give rise to war as a "perennial feature"[24] or permanent *possibility*,[25] however much we may want more optimistic accounts of human nature to be right,[26] and thus lending credence to George Santayana's *dictum* – erroneously attributed to Plato: "only the dead have seen the end of war".[27]

I contend that the CoW amount to the interplay between the following three theses:

> (i) *The interest thesis* (T1): Self-interested or strategic, goal-seeking[28] entities, such as human beings, groups of people and states, may find themselves in one of the following situations: a) their vital interests – otherwise known in the literature as "drivers" or "motivations"[29] – might not conflict or overlap at all with those of other self-interested entities;

---

*Historical Illustrations*. 5th ed. (New York: Basic Books, 2015), p. 339. The CoW also differ from the 'Correlates of War' ('COW') project, in that my CoW are an analytical framework whereas the COW are a quantitative database.

23 This logical-chronological distinction is used by Steven Pinker to probe the origins of violence. See Steven Pinker, *The Better Angels of Our Nature. Why Violence Has Declined* (New York: Penguin, 2012), p. 31. On different theories explaining the causes of war from the perspective of the major human sciences (biology, psychology, anthropology, and ecology), history, social and political sciences see Richard Overy, *Why War?* (New York: w.w. Norton & Co., 2024).

24 William O'Brien, *The Conduct of Just and Limited War* (New York: Praeger Publishers, 1981), p. 2.

25 Yitzhak Benbaji and Daniel Statman, *War by Agreement. A Contractarian Ethics of War* (New York: Oxford University Press, 2019), pp. 139; 193; 199–200; N. Fotion and Gerard Elfstrom, *Military Ethics. Guidelines for Peace and War* (New York: Routledge, 2021), p. 1; Juan Moliner, *La ética militar como como marco de reflexión sobre la guerra y la profesión militar* (Madrid: Ministerio de Defensa, 2022), p. 34. As a conceptualization of a permanent possibility, this theoretical proposal needs not take sides on the decades old debate in the social sciences between nature and nurture regarding war throughout human history. For a summary of said debate see Wilbur J. Scott, Karin Modesto De Angelis, and David R. Segal, *Military Sociology. A Guided Introduction* (New York: Routledge, 2023), pp. 38–54.

26 Rutger Bregman, *Humankind. A Hopeful History* (London: Bloomsbury Publishing, 2021); Darcia Narvaez, 'Evolution, child raising, and compassionate morality', in Paul Gilbert (ed.), *Compassion. Concepts, Research and Applications* (New York: Routledge, 2017), pp. 173–186.

27 'George Santayana 1863–1952. Spanish-born philosopher and critic', https://www.oxfordreference.com/view/10.1093/acref/9780191843730.001.0001/q-oro-ed5-00009114, 5 April 2021.

28 Pinker, *Angels*, p. 31.

29 Beatrice Heuser, *War. A Genealogy of Western Ideas and Practices* (New York: Oxford University Press, 2022), p. 127.

b) their vital interests might coincide with those of other self-interested entities, enabling cooperation; or c) their vital interests might collide with those of other self-interested entities. In the latter case, the conflict might be resolved by resorting to one of the following mechanisms: c.1) adjudication by a superior authority; c.2) negotiation between the parties, including the possibility of designating a mediator; c.3) voluntary submission of one party to the other; or, should all of the above fail – perhaps as the result of an insufficient bargaining process over time[30] – c.4) recourse to force.[31] Indeed, according to Clausewitz "War is a clash between major interests, which is resolved by bloodshed – that is the only way in which it differs from other conflicts."[32] People's "visceral emotions and their *will to fight*"[33] will be ever fuelled by their perceived interest (dis)satisfaction over major/minor differences or antitheses strong enough to reach the threshold of enmity[34] – however much violence may have admittedly declined (but not disappeared) in recent human history.[35]

(ii) *The mortality thesis* (T2): Human beings are mortal creatures afflicted in roughly equal measure by physical and mental vulnerability leading to the ultimate outcome of death, which has a definite impact on the way we live and organize our societies.

Some prominent thinkers have made of this feature a cornerstone of their philosophical anthropology, most notably Philipp Mainländer[36] and Martin Heidegger.[37]

(iii) *The technology thesis* (T3): Human beings are technological creatures, otherwise known as *homo faber*,[38] who in that capacity have

30 Jack McDonald, *What is War For?* (Bristol: Bristol University Press, 2023), p. 27.

31 José Zạlaquett, 'Prólogo', in Francisco Lobo, *Teoría y Práctica de la Intervención Humanitaria en la Tradición de la Guerra Justa* (Mexico D.F.: Tirant lo Blanch, 2016), p. 17; José Ortega y Gasset, *Obras Completas*. Vol. IV. 6th ed. (Madrid: Revista de Occidente, 1966), p. 289.

32 Carl von Clausewitz, *On War* (New York: Oxford University Press, 2008), p. 100.

33 Arnel P. David, Sean Acosta and Nicholas Krohley (eds.), *Warrior Diplomats. Civil Affairs Forces on the Front Lines* (Amherst: Cambria, 2023), p. 9.

34 Carl Schmitt, *The Concept of the Political* (Chicago: The University of Chicago Press, 2007), p. 37.

35 Pinker, *Angels*.

36 Philipp Mainländer, *Filosofía de la redención* (Santiago: FCE, 2011).

37 Martin Heidegger, *Being and Time* (Cornwall: Blackwell, 2005).

38 Hannah Arendt, *The Human Condition*, 2nd ed. (Chicago: University of Chicago Press, 1998), p. 207; Martin Heidegger, *Filosofía, ciencia y técnica* (Santiago: Editorial Universitaria, 2004); Christopher Coker, *Barbarous Philosophers. Reflections on the Nature of War from Heraclitus to Heisenberg* (London: Hurst & Company, 2010), pp. 213–219.

> invented and perfected the means of their own destruction, up to and including weapons of mass destruction, without the possibility of those means of destruction to ever be "disinvented",[39] and with said means also becoming increasingly cheaper and more accessible[40] – as borne out, for example, by drone technology.[41] Indeed, "the history of combat can be seen as the evolution of a series of ever more efficient devices to enable humans to kill and dominate their fellow human beings".[42]

As a result, I contend that **the interaction between T1, T2, and T3 results in the permanent possibility of war.** Why is this relevant for professional military ethics and the practice of war by the military in general? The military are the professionals tasked with managing the outcome of the interplay between the three theses, namely war. By trying to ascertain the conditions that lead to such an outcome, we gain a better understanding of the need and the importance of the profession of arms. Put negatively, if we pay heed to the calls to abolish armies and we remove the military profession from the equation,[43] the Circumstances of War would still exist and their outcome, war, would still have to be dealt with by unprepared, unprofessional agents. This risks not only more harm to civilians, but also to said agents in the form of moral injury or psychological damage due to the potential transgression of deeply held moral beliefs, as a result of such lack of preparedness and awareness of this phenomenon, all in the name of a society that did not offer them the chance to prepare for the many rigours of war.

Further, as we shall see in this investigation, taking the military profession seriously entails not only acknowledging the need and importance of this sector for the Circumstances of War and all its trying possibilities, but also, and as importantly, it requires us to provide military professionals with adequate training and education that will ensure they will have a fighting chance and

39 Francisco Lobo, 'Abolishing atomic warfare? Nuclear power and natural-international law in the twenty-first century', *Transnational Legal Theory* (2019), pp. 1–27; John Finnis, Joseph Boyle and Germain Grisez, *Nuclear Deterrence, Morality and Realism* (Oxford: Clarendon Press, 1987), p. 73.

40 Niall Ferguson, *Colossus. The rise and fall of the American empire* (New York: Penguin Books, 2004), p. 300.

41 Michael Boyle, 'The Cost and Consequences of Drone Warfare', *International Affairs*, 89:1 (2013), p. 22.

42 Dave Grossman and Loren W. Christensen, *On Combat. The Psychology and Physiology of Deadly Conflict in War and Peace*. 4th ed. (New York: Open Road Media, 2022), p. 196.

43 Adam Henschke, 'Rethinking the Nature of States and Political Violence', *Ethics and International Affairs*, 35:1 (2021), pp. 145–158.

not lose their humanity or risk moral injury in the process. Societies owe it to the professionals tasked with managing the most atrocious of scenarios to endow them with the physical, psychological and moral armour[44] they require to fight and win well and to protect them from moral injury.

Two things are worth noting at this point about the three theses. First, lest they become generic truisms applicable to any number of human activities – not unlike the Thucydidesian triad of honour-fear-interest – all three theses need to be qualified to truly become the CoW: Regarding T1, We talk about *vital* interests, not just trivial ones, and we have to think in a *plurality* of interests belonging to many individuals, inasmuch as the potential for their clash is predicated on the premise of the *zoon politikon's* "unsociable sociability";[45] as for T2, we deal with mortality in its *existential* dimension, in the sense that it is a fact of social life of which human beings (unlike animals) are aware and that profoundly affects our individual and collective decisions; and, concerning T3, we refer to *deadly* technology that can bring about our own destruction, a feat no other species on the planet has ever accomplished.

Secondly, it is important to note that it is the *interplay* between the three theses that gives rise to the phenomenon of war. In other words, if we remove but one of these theses the CoW would not fully operate and therefore the result of war would not obtain.

For example, and in a most obvious sense, if we remove T2, the *mortality thesis*, from the equation, then war as we understand it cannot arise – the image of Borges's 'Immortals' from *El Aleph*, who suffer from a deprivation of all that is "preciously precarious" in life comes to mind. Perhaps among such immortals a 'deathless warfare' in the form of a sports-like competition may take place if they still have interests and are technological, such as the Olympic Games – literally, the contests of the gods inhabiting Mount Olympus in Greek mythology. Games have that ability to suspend normal social life, including acts of retaliation and vendettas, while preserving competition.[46]

Alternatively, if we imagine beings that, while not immortal, are nonetheless impervious to external attacks, the same result of a bloodless competition obtains. We may think, for instance, of the fictional creatures Hart envisions to illustrate, negatively, his point about the minimum content of natural law:

---

44 Shannon E. French, *The Code of the Warrior. Exploring Warrior Values Past and Present.* 2nd ed. (Lanham: Rowman and Littlefield Publishers, 2017), pp. 12; 257.

45 David Luban, 'A Theory of Crimes Against Humanity', *Yale Journal of International Law*, 29 (2004), p. 112; Moliner, *Ética*, p. 35.

46 Johan Huizinga, *Homo Ludens* (London: Routledge and Kegan Paul, 1980), p. 12.

> [s]uppose that men were to become invulnerable to attack by each other, were clad perhaps like giant land crabs with an impenetrable carapace, and could extract the food they needed from the air by some internal chemical process. In such circumstances (the details of which can be left to science fiction) rules forbidding the free use of violence and rules constituting the minimum form of property – with its rights and duties sufficient to enable food to grow and be retained until eaten – would not have the necessary nonarbitrary status which they have for us, constituted as we are in a world like ours.[47]

We might add that in a world inhabited by such *testudos* war would look very different to what it is for us, to the point that we probably would not be able to call it war at all. Perhaps the rapid development of autonomous weapons systems will lead someday to such a scenario whereby invulnerable creatures engage one another in perpetual competition.[48]

Furthermore, the interplay between the mortality thesis and the other theses makes even more acute the existential dread we experience when confronting death. If death can endow human existence with meaning, albeit elliptically as it provides a sense of completion at the end of the road, it is also true that this 'possibility of our impossibility' as Heidegger calls it can be a dauting prospect for human beings, which is a direct result of the premium we put on its opposite, life.

Indeed, reflecting on the so-called 'sanctity' or 'intrinsic value' of life argument often invoked in abortion and euthanasia debates, Ronald Dworkin wonders what it is about preserving human life that is so compelling as to bring together different people on issues surrounding the deliberate termination of life. The value we assign to human life, he concludes, is informed by a sense of shame or lamentation when witnessing the untimely cessation of two interconnected processes: biological evolution (the same despondency we experience when learning that an animal species has gone extinct, whether it is accompanied or not by religious beliefs about a creator of such life forms); and cultural development (as when we experience sadness at the destruction of a great work of art that is a testimony to human creativity and capacity for admiring beauty). These are, according to Dworkin, the two creative traditions of the sacred.[49]

---

47 H.L.A. Hart, 'Positivism and the Separation of Law and Morals', *Harvard Law Review*, 71:613 (1958), p. 623.

48 I thank Christian Nikolaus Braun for pointing this out to me.

49 Ronald Dworkin, *Life's Dominion* (New York: Alfred A. Knopf, 1993), p. 82.

Thus, the loss of a human life that is the culmination of an evolutionary process and cultural history going back thousands of years prompts in us a sense of "cosmic shame"[50] because we realize what a waste it is for something with such a rich history to come to an end and not have the opportunity to flourish and thrive building on such a legacy, as the traditions of the sacred look both backwards (from whence we came) and forward (everything we could become and do). It is, ultimately, the feeling we experience at the frustration of "an adventure already under way", like a poem without a last stanza or a play without a final scene.[51] This extends even to unborn generations to which we owe some sort of fair treatment.[52] In Dworkin's own poignant words: "The horror we feel in the wilful destruction of a human life reflects our shared inarticulate sense of the intrinsic importance of each of these dimensions of investment".[53]

Such wilful destruction of life becomes an unequivocal reality when we think about warfare, even if – or perhaps because – life expectancy has improved in the past centuries and dying in war has become less frequent compared to most of human history.[54] It is then that the tragedy of the mortality thesis, in combination with the technology and the interest theses as the means of destruction are put to use in the pursuit of vital interests, is felt more intensely. Then, this sense of 'cosmic shame' becomes particularly acute at the sight of the wastage of human life and potential on a massive scale. For example, in his memoirs as a Marine fighting in the Pacific Theatre during the Second World War, Eugene B. Sledge recalls what it felt like to see one of his fallen comrades on the sands of Peleliu island, a young man whose dream was to become a doctor after the war: "A bright young mind that aspired to delve into the mysteries of the human brain to alleviate human suffering had itself been destroyed by a tiny chunk of metal. What a waste, I thought. War is such self-defeating, organized madness the way it destroys a nation's best".[55]

Incidentally, this sensitivity to the waste of human life and potential in the midst of war is arguably also one of the main drivers behind the principle of military necessity in International Humanitarian Law, which has been articulated following a logic of frugality that allows for the preservation of what is deemed valuable even in times of war:

50 Ibid., p. 75.
51 Ibid., pp. 88; 199.
52 Ibid., p. 77.
53 Ibid., p. 84.
54 McDonald, *What*, p. 56.
55 Eugene B. Sledge, *With the Old Breed. At Peleliu and Okinawa* (New York: Presidio Press, 2007), p. 114.

> Military necessity permits a state engaged in an armed conflict to use only that degree and kind of force, not otherwise prohibited by the law of armed conflict, that is required in order to achieve the legitimate purpose of the conflict, namely the complete or partial submission of the enemy at the earliest possible moment *with the minimum expenditure of life and resources* (emphasis added).[56]

On the other hand, if we dispense with T3, the *technology thesis*, then it is conceivable that mortal, self-interested human beings will still resort to deadly violence should alternative mechanisms of conflict resolution fail, but we could not call such deadly violence 'war' unless we were also ready to characterize violent behaviour among animals of the same species as war. But war is actually a uniquely human activity, as it is organized violence dating back to the invention of agriculture and the territorial disputes entailed therein.[57] As noted by José Ortega y Gasset: "war is not an instinct but an invention. It is unknown to animals and it is a purely human institution, like science or administration".[58] Accordingly, Pierre Clastres discards the theories characterizing war as natural fact, like hunting among animals, as he prefers to explain the phenomenon of war in primitive societies as the unique human expression of a social unit that reasserts itself through the fight with external enemies.[59] Similarly, for John Searle hunting can be considered a social (collective) fact performed by animals, but never an institutional fact,[60] of which war is an example as we shall see in the next section.

Thus, war can be characterized as an expression of culture, following John Keegan,[61] besides the familiar Clausewitzian conception of it as a "continuation of political intercourse, with the addition of other means".[62] But whether stemming from culture, from politics, or both, what is certain is that in this fight

56 Ministry of Defence of the United Kingdom of Great Britain and Northern Ireland, 'The Joint Service Manual of the Law of Armed Conflict', https://assets.publishing.service.gov.uk/government/uploads/system/uploads/attachment_data/file/27874/JSP3832004Edition.pdf, 20 June 2022, pp. 21–22.

57 John Keegan, *A History of Warfare* (New York: Vintage Books, 1993), p. 122.

58 "La guerra no es un institnto, sino un invento. Los animals la desconocen y es pura institución humana, como la ciencia o la administración". See Ortega y Gasset, *Obras*, p. 287. See also Christopher Coker, *Barbarous Philosophers. Reflections on the Nature of War from Heraclitus to Heisenberg* (London: Hurst & Company, 2010), p. 28.

59 Pierre Clastres, *Archeology of Violence* (Los Angeles: Semiotext(e), 2010); Chantal Mouffe, *The Return of the Political* (Brooklyn: Verso, 2005).

60 John Searle, *The construction of social reality* (New York: The Free Press, 1995), p. 38.

61 Keegan, *History*, p. 12.

62 Clausewitz, *War*, p. 252.

technology plays a crucial role, as pointed out also by Clausewitz: "Force, to counter opposing force, equips itself with the inventions of art and science".[63]

Finally, if we remove T1, the *interest thesis*, war is deprived of one of its fundamental causes, what Clausewitz calls the universal "hostile intentions" between human beings.[64] Indeed, if human beings were not self-interested entities, then no conflict resolution mechanisms to arbitrate between those vital interests would need to be in place, including the ultimate possibility of the use of force.[65] It would still be possible for such mortal creatures to apply their technology in their mutual destruction, but now the main motives for such destruction, i.e. the opposition of vital interests, would be absent. Some other causes for such a result might be imagined, such as a collective belief in the evil nature of human beings warranting suicide *en masse*. Yet, we would be hard-pressed to call such a bleak hypothesis 'war'.[66]

### 2.2 *The CoW and War as Institutional Fact*

By seriously analysing the CoW, we may gain a better understanding of war as its outcome and, by implication, of the military profession that is charged with managing it. Thus, by taking the CoW seriously, we take the military seriously. We owe it to the people we task with going to war on our behalf to think about what we ask them to do in the most rigorous way possible, that we may understand their sacrifice and avoid asking for it with too much profligacy and too little regard for their physical and psychological integrity. Accordingly, in this section I reflect on the outcome of the CoW and its institutional nature.

It is of the utmost importance, first, to clearly distinguish between the CoW and war itself. The CoW are all those facts whose interplay leads, it is submitted here, to the permanent *possibility* of war. But war as a phenomenon is not the same as its conditions of possibility, namely the CoW, not any more than rain could be said to be the same as the weather factors causing it such as clouds, air temperature, or ocean tides. War is, moreover, not just a natural result or

63 Ibid., p. 13.

64 Ibid., p. 14.

65 The idea of a utopian, pacific world where there are no collisions of interests will be dealt with in the last part of this section, with regard to the debate within the Just War Tradition between 'traditionalists' and 'revisionists.'

66 Interestingly, the Albigensian Crusade conducted against the Cathars in southern France during the 13th century was proclaimed to fight a sectarian belief in the absolute corruption and evil of the material world that called for general sexual abstention, among other political causes. Far from embracing their own material destruction and therefore the liberation of their entrapped souls, which would have been consistent with their own beliefs, the Cathars resisted by waging war against their enemies.

outcome inevitably stemming from the CoW, such as death. War, like justice or property, is an *institution*, a human artifice particularly devised to address the problems arising from the CoW. As Hume would put it: "The remedy, then, is not deriv'd from nature, but from *artifice*" (original italics).[67]

If war is human artifice to address the CoW, there is no need to adhere to the postulate of war as a deterministic reality from which human beings cannot escape. What is ineluctable, the 'hand' dealt by destiny, are the CoW, war being a device of human making to deal with such background conditions. Accordingly, following Harari's and Allison's optimism, there is always the possibility that a skilful management of all three CoW may lead to an outcome other than war – for instance, the interest thesis can be managed such that different vital interests are ranked and organized so as to know when it is necessary to risk everything to secure them, and, just as importantly, when to let go and compromise. Similarly, the technology thesis can be managed such that every new invention must abide by certain standards as to development, manufacture and use, including the rules of war.[68] Even the mortality thesis can be managed to a limited extent if science and technology allow for a delayed and less frequent recurrence in death. What is important to bear in mind is that the outcome, war, is always "a function of loss"[69] to be avoided to the extent possible.

To be sure, Hume himself was sceptical of the idea of human conventions being able to remain in place amidst the intensity of war.[70] Yet, there is support in the literature for the conceptualization of war itself as a 'social institution',[71] or more precisely, an 'institutional fact',[72] however often the rules may be

67 Hume, *Treatise*, p. 314.

68 Additional Protocol I to the Geneva Conventions, Article 36: "New Weapons. In the study, development, acquisition or adoption of a new weapon, means or method of warfare, a High Contracting Party is under an obligation to determine whether its employment would, in some or all circumstances, be prohibited by this Protocol or by any other rule of international law applicable to the High Contracting Party".

69 Cian O'Driscoll, *Victory. The Triumph and Tragedy of Just War* (New York: Oxford University Press, 2020), p. 151.

70 Hume, *Enquiry*, p. 23.

71 McDonald, *What*, p. 13.

72 François Bugnion, 'Just wars, wars of aggression and international humanitarian law', *International Review of the Red Cross*, 847:84 (2002), pp. 523–546; Hanneke van Schooten, 'War as an Institutional Fact: Semiotics and Institutional Legal Theory', *International Journal for the Semiotics of Law*, 22:3 (2009), pp. 307–320; Harald Hoiback, *Understanding Military Doctrine* (New York: Routledge, 2017), p. 94.

breached,[73] such that "the practice of war is still therefore often shaped by the institution of war".[74] But what is an institutional fact?

According to John Searle, a 'brute fact', for instance, a piece of paper, can reach the quality of an 'institutional fact' if there is a convention establishing a constitutive rule that assigns to the original fact a new status from which stems a new function, for instance, paper money. Crucially, Searle indicates war as an example of an institutional fact on several occasions.[75] Admittedly, what Searle had in mind was a classic concept of war between sovereign units declaring their hostile intentions upfront, what Yoram Dinstein calls "war in the technical sense" as opposed to the material sense or the actual use of force, declared or not,[76] the latter usually referred to today as 'armed conflict'.[77]

However, whether classic or modern, labelled as 'war' or designated as 'armed conflict,' the essence of war was distilled into one simple definition offered by Clausewitz almost two centuries ago: "*War is thus an act of force to compel our enemy to do our will*" (original italics).[78] And it is the CoW that cause such an act to arise.

However, as an institutional fact, war cannot simply be the display of sheer force, just as the sports of fencing or boxing are not just about applying oneself to hit another human being willy-nilly with a pointy stick or a clenched fist. There are rules that are both constitutive and regulative of said activities,[79]

---

73 Heuser, *War*, p. 307.

74 McDonald, *What*, p. 82.

75 Searle, *Construction*, pp. 32; 34; 36; 79; 84; 89; 96; 115; 116; 119.

76 Yoram Dinstein, *War, Aggression and Self-Defence*. 5th ed. (Cambridge: Cambridge University Press, 2012), par. 37.

77 Heuser, *War*, pp. 107–108; Ian Brownlie, *International Law and the Use of Force by States* (Oxford: Clarendon Press, 1963), p. 27.

78 Clausewitz, *War*, p. 13.

79 John Rawls, 'Two Concepts of Rules', *The Philosophical Review*, 64:1 (1955), pp. 3–32. Admittedly, the law mostly *regulates* previous brute or physical actions or objects, assigning a new institutional (legal) meaning to them, whilst creating (*constituting*) the possibility of new forms of behaviour, for instance, sheer violence turned into the terms of art 'common crimes' and 'war crimes'. See Fernando Atria, *On Law and Legal Reasoning* (London: Bloomsbury Publishing, 2002), p. 29. See a further explanation in Frederick Schauer, *Playing by the Rules: A Philosophical Examination of Rule-Based Decision -Making in Law and Life* (Oxford: Oxford University Press, 1993), p. 7: "Although sets of constitutive rules establish institutions such as games, universities, corporations, and language, these constitutive rules lose their constitutive character within those institutions, serving instead to regulate antecedently defined behavior. The rule has a double aspect – first defining the behavior and then regulating it. Take the rule prohibiting clipping in American football. Although it is possible to hit a person from behind without reference to the rules of football, clipping is different, being constituted by certain of those rules. Yet the same rules also prohibit clipping, and the prohibitory side of the rules about clipping

as "[t]he point of the institution of boxing is not to regulate fights (as, e.g., criminal law does), *but to create a new, institutional, form of fighting*".[80] In other words, there are conventions that make of war a *normative* activity.[81] And it is precisely on the 'war convention' that Michael Walzer, the patriarch of modern Just War thinking,[82] builds his theory.

Walzer submits that war is endowed with a normative or moral reality that is reflected in the way we talk about it and discuss its many complexities. Thus, terms such as 'aggression,' 'self-defence,' 'appeasement,' 'cruelty,' 'ruthlessness,' 'atrocity,' or 'massacre' are all normative judgments indicating an underlying moral reality of war understood as such by its own practitioners, that is, by people who find themselves involved in war.[83] Such normative judgments hinge on the existence of a set of standards known as the 'war convention'. Walzer defines the war convention, otherwise known as the 'common law of combat,' as follows: "I propose to call the set of articulated norms, customs, professional codes, legal precepts, religious and philosophical principles, and reciprocal arrangements that shape our judgments of military conduct *the war convention*" (original italics).[84]

War is, thus, a social construct or creation. As Walzer remarks: "What is war and what is not-war is in fact something that people decide".[85] Or in Searle's own words: "part of being a war is being thought to be a war".[86] It is worth noting here that the law is an integral part of the war convention as a framework for a veritable 'construction' of the institution of war. As Marcela Prieto Rudolphy put it recently, war is "a legally regulated tragedy".[87] Or as similarly proposed by Nathaniel Berman: "rather than standing in opposition to war, law has long been directly involved in *the construction of war* – the construction of war as a separate sphere of human activity in which the 'normal' rules of social

operates in the same way within the institution of football as a rule prohibiting driving in excess of 55 miles per hour operates outside that institution".

80 Atria, *Law*, p. 44. See also on the legal paradigm of combatant targetability, Jens David Ohlin, 'War's Rustic Code of Honor', https://ssrn.com/abstract=4931591, 12 September 2024, p. 24.

81 Coker, *Barbarous*, p. 149. On the importance of law and rules in war see Andrew Clapham, *War* (Oxford: Oxford University Press, 2021), p. xii.

82 O'Driscoll, *Victory*, p. 135.

83 Michael Walzer. *Just and Unjust Wars. A Moral Argument with Historical Illustrations*. 4th ed. (New York: Basic Books, 2006), pp. 3; 15.

84 Ibid., p. 44.

85 Ibid., p. 24. See also Heuser, *War*, p. 17.

86 Searle, *Construction*, p. 34.

87 Marcela Prieto Rudolphy, *The Morality of the Laws of War: War, Law, and Murder* (Oxford: Oxford University Press, 2023), p. 1.

life, codified, for example, in the domestic criminal law regulating violence, do not operate."[88]

Now, it was the great merit of Walzer to revive the Just War Tradition ('JWT') right at a time when a normative and conceptual apparatus for the critique of largely resisted military adventures, such as the Vietnam War, was needed to articulate society's attitudes toward both *some* wars and *war* itself. The JWT provided such a framework. It can further explain how and why moral injury among soldiers takes place when said standards are breached.[89] But Walzer's work is only one of the latest sprouts of the many branches growing out of the tree of the JWT, whose roots dive deep into the soil of history. Indeed, the possibility of passing moral and legal judgment on war, including both the recourse to war in the first place (*jus ad bellum*) and the conduct of hostilities (*jus in bello*), has been entertained by thinkers such as Augustine, Aquinas, Christine de Pizan, Francisco de Vitoria, Hugo Grotius, Emmerich de Vattel, Immanuel Kant, James Turner Johnson, and Paul Ramsey. Alongside Walzer, all of them are part of the JWT, which may be thought of as a timeless dialogue[90] about war not only among towering scholars, but as a collective enterprise in which society at large is permanently engaged,[91] including contemporary military and political elites.[92]

### 2.3 *'First to go, last to know': the Unsung Heroes of the Just War Tradition*

At this point it is worth asking: what role do the actual practitioners of war, namely military professionals, play in this inveterate normative tradition? Does the JWT amount to a mere exercise in 'metaethics'? Andrew Fisher uses football as an analogy to explain the differences between applied ethics, normative ethics, and metaethics. While it is the players on the field that follow and apply the rules of the game (i.e. applied ethics), it is for the referee to interpret and enforce those standards (normative ethics), whereas pundits

88 Nathaniel Berman, 'Privileging Combat? Contemporary Conflict and the Legal Construction of War', *Columbia Journal of Transnational Law*, 43:1 (2004), pp. 1–72.

89 Tine Molendijk, 'Just War Theory for Morale and Moral Injury: Beyond Individual Resilience', https://www.tandfonline.com/doi/full/10.1080/15027570.2024.2442802?src=, 17 January 2025.

90 Alex Bellamy, *Just Wars. From Cicero to Iraq* (Malden: Polity Press, 2012), p. 2; Daniel Brunstetter, *Just and Unjust Uses of Limited Force. A Moral Argument with Contemporary Illustrations* (New York: Oxford University Press, 2021), p. 14.

91 Michael Walzer, *Arguing about War* (New Haven: Yale University Press, 2004), p. x; John Kelsay, 'Just War Thinking as a Social Practice', *Ethics and International Affairs*, 27:1 (2013), pp. 67–86.

92 O'Driscoll, *Victory*, p. 3.

and commentators attempt to analyse and understand the nature of the game without taking part in it, from the benches as it were (metaethics).[93]

Is the JWT mere analysis from the benches, or do the players also have something to say? Building on Walzer's definition of the war convention and the normative language mirroring it, the moral reality of war, it becomes evident that people who wage war are also governed by those standards and thus become active users of its normative vocabulary. In other words, soldiers are also part of the JWT,[94] and they have a lot to contribute to the conversation from their perspective as professionals of war, as borne out by the echoes of chivalry presented in the Prologue and the Introduction, as well as by the military doctrine documents to be analysed in Chapter 6. Forgetting about these professionals and the language they use only increases the chances that they will behave unprofessionally on the battlefield, as well as the risk of suffering moral injury as a result of such neglect. But what makes a professional?

In the literature on professional ethics, the following traits are frequently listed to identify a profession: (1) professionals are licensed by society and/or the state to perform a certain act; (2) they belong to a group of similarly enfranchised individuals who live by common rules of behaviour; (3) they possess specialized or 'esoteric' knowledge that is not widespread in the rest of the community; (4) they exercise autonomy in their work; and (5) they publicly pledge to render assistance to those in need of their services.[95]

More specifically, in his renowned work *The Soldier and the State* Samuel Huntington characterizes the military (mainly the officer corps) as professionals to the extent that they fulfil the following criteria informing the concept of a profession: (i) Expertise, namely specialized knowledge and skill in a significant field; (ii) Responsibility to society for the services rendered; and (iii) Corporateness, or the sense of organic unity among the members of the same profession.[96]

Thus, as applied to the military profession the features listed by Huntington acquire a colour of their own. Firstly, the expertise the military possess boils down to the "management of violence".[97] Huntington clarifies that it is the

---

93 Andrew Fisher, *Metaethics. An Introduction* (New York: Routledge, 2014), pp. 1–2.

94 For an excellent study of soldiers' narrative accounts of the JWT in war memoirs see Liane Hartnett and Cian O'Driscoll, 'Sad and laughable and Strange: At War with Just War', *Global Society*, 35:1 (2021), pp. 27–44.

95 Daryl Koehn, *The Ground of Professional Ethics* (New York: Routledge, 1994), p. 56.

96 Samuel Huntington, *The Soldier and the State* (Cambridge: Harvard University Press, 2000), pp. 8–10.

97 Ibid., p. 11. See also Morris Janowitz, *The Professional Soldier* (New York: Free Press, 2017), p. xvii.

management of violence, not necessarily its practice, that is within the purview of the military officer.[98] But given the *factum* of the CoW, we are well advised to remember the words of General Sir John Hackett: "There will be violence and those whose business is its management now assume a more important place in our societies than ever before".[99] Accordingly, the military's specific professional identity is shaped by the unique function they perform.[100]

Two points are worth mentioning in this sense. First, a professional soldier is sometimes deemed as something more than just a warrior, held to a higher ethical and legal standard as evinced by the Australian *Brereton Report's* rebuke of the 'warrior culture' that was allowed to fester within Special Forces units in Afghanistan.[101] Conversely, institutions like the U.S. Army and the New Zealand Army still view the concept of warrior under a positive light.[102] I shall revisit the 'soldier vs. warrior' debate in the Conclusions, in particular as it pertains to professionalism. Second, the military professional is tasked with the management of violence that is a direct *result of* the CoW, not with managing the CoW themselves. That task falls to people engaged in statecraft, who are expected to manage the CoW such that they find peaceful solutions to the interest thesis and that the mortality and technology theses do not have to come into play should they fail. This is the essence of Victor Hugo's firm belief in the possibility of eradicating, if not the suffering that comes naturally with existence, at least man-made misery,[103] which in his view includes wars among nations.[104]

---

98 Huntington, *Soldier*, p. 13.

99 John Hackett, *The Profession of Arms* (London: Sidgwick & Jackson, 1983), p. 7.

100 Canadian Armed Forces, 'Duty with Honour: The Profession of Arms in Canada', https://www.canada.ca/en/department-national-defence/corporate/reports-publications/duty-with-honour-2009.html, 21 March 2023, p. 20.

101 Inspector-General of the Australian Defence Force, *Afghanistan Inquiry Report* (Canberra: Commonwealth of Australia, 2020), pp. 33; 115; 325; 330; 334; 471–472; 499–502. See also David Whetham, 'Special Operations Command: Leadership and Ethics Review', in Inspector-General of the Australian Defence Force, *Afghanistan Inquiry Report* (Canberra: Commonwealth of Australia, 2020), p. 515. For an alternative account promoting a healthy version of warrior culture see Andrew Hastie, 'SAS must put honour before glory', https://www.adso.org.au/andrew-hastie-sas-must-put-honour-before-glory/, 14 December 2022.

102 U.S. Army, 'ADRP-1: The Army Profession', https://irp.fas.org/doddir/army/adrp1.pdf, 25 May 2023, p. B-3; New Zealand Army, 'The Way of the New Zealand Warrior', https://www.nzdf.mil.nz/assets/Uploads/DocumentLibrary/Way-of-the-New-Zealand-Warrior-2020.pdf, 23 May 2023, p. 13.

103 Victor Hugo, 'Détruire la misère', https://www2.assemblee-nationale.fr/decouvrir-l-assemblee/histoire/grands-discours-parlementaires/victor-hugo-9-juillet-1849, 27 June 2023.

104 Victor Hugo, 'Speech to the Peace Congress at Paris', https://trove.nla.gov.au/newspaper/article/12914658, 27 June 2023.

This desideratum of successfully managing the CoW to prevent the dreaded outcome arguably connects with what is known as "Phase Zero" operations whereby "Joint and multinational operations – inclusive of normal and routine military activities – and various interagency activities are performed to dissuade or deter potential adversaries and to assure or solidify relationships with friends and allies".[105] It also arguably bears on a special hybrid professional located at the intersection between statecraft and warfare, namely the Civil Affairs community within some militaries, such as the U.S. Army, also dubbed "warrior diplomats".[106]

Should people in charge of statecraft fail and misery endure, military professionals stand at the ready to manage the consequence of such a failure, namely war (both its permanent nature and evolving characteristics).[107]

The concept of management further suggests an attempt at approaching the essence of war, i.e. violence or force, in a rational and legitimate way, such that a return to a situation of no-violence that defuses the lethal potential enclosed within the CoW is possible.[108] It is of the utmost importance to highlight that only a professional management of such variables can make a return to peace more likely, thus confirming the relevance of Professional Military Ethics ('PMEt'[109]) for the adequate administration of the outcome of the CoW and the possibility of a lasting peace.[110] Anyone can wage violence unfettered like there is no tomorrow; it takes a professional to do it in a restrained, ethical way that reflects a deeper understanding of the true meaning and purpose of the services rendered, namely the restoration of peace or the (admittedly elusive) idea of victory.[111]

105 Scott W. Orr, 'Just War Theory Reloaded: The Ethics of SOF in Modern Conflict', https://apps.dtic.mil/sti/pdfs/AD1060027.pdf, 6 June 2023, p. xiii.

106 Arnel P. David, Sean Acosta and Nicholas Krohley (eds.), *Warrior.*

107 On the canonical, Clausewitzian distinction between the nature and the characteristics of war, see Rosa Brooks, 'Fighting words. Has the nature of "war" changed since the days of Clausewitz?', https://foreignpolicy.com/2014/02/04/fighting-words/, 04 February 2014.

108 Juan Moliner, 'La educación y formación en ética militar', in Centro Conjunto de Desarollo de Conceptos, *Cuestiones sobre ética militar* (Madrid: Ministerio de Defensa, 2022), p. 24; Moliner, *Ética*, p. 29. See also Immanuel Kant, *Toward Perpetual Peace and Other Writings on Politics, Peace, and History* (New Haven: Yale University Press, 2006), p. 70.

109 See Sally Rohan, 'An organic professional military ethic and the educational challenge', in Don Carrick, James Connelly and David Whetham (eds.), *Making the Military Moral. Contemporary Challenges and Responses in Military Ethics Education* (New York: Routledge, 2018), p. 71.

110 Moliner, 'Educación', p. 29; Moliner, *Ética*, p. 34.

111 O'Driscoll, *Victory.*

The foregoing considerations set the military profession apart from what Karma Nabulsi has dubbed 'martialism' in her book *Traditions of War*. Martialism corresponds to the glorification of war and military conquest for their own sake, taking war and the violence it entails as "the ultimate realization of all human endeavour".[112] The professional account of the military, on the contrary, conceives of their craft as essentially instrumental and subordinate to the goals set by society and the state which have commissioned said professionals to manage violence, as war is seen as "a tool in international politics"[113] and not an end in itself. This is also a distinctive feature of this particular group as the only one endowed with "the capacity to make war".[114]

This leads to another salient feature of the military profession, that of service and the responsibility arising from it. In her book *The Ground of Professional Ethics*, Daryl Koehn locates trust at the heart of every client-professional relationship.[115] Such trust stems from the commitment shown ('professed') by the expert to use their skill and knowledge to *serve* another person's interests, regardless of the material reward.[116] In the case of war, the phenomenon of service becomes particularly intense as almost all the freedoms an individual enjoys as a civilian in peacetime are heavily curtailed to the point of evanescence. A doctor treating Vietnam veterans with PTSD puts it in the following terms:

> The social institution of modern war makes the soldier a captive, but unlike other forms of captivity, the role of his captor is continuously shared by the enemy and the soldier's own army. (…) If he flees toward the enemy he may be shot out of hand when his surrender is not accepted, or he may be imprisoned as a POW. If he flees toward his own rear, he may be summarily shot or imprisoned as a deserter. The front line is thus a narrow zone of fear and death lying between two prisons. In this narrow zone two massive social organizations compete to enslave the soldier. The social institution of war creates total captivity with opposing

112 Karma Nabulsi, *Traditions of War* (New York: Oxford University Press, 2007), p. 81. On the celebration of war as an ethical enterprise, see G.W.F. Hegel, *Elements of the Philosophy of Right* (Cambridge: Cambridge University Press, 2003), p. 361; Alexis de Tocqueville, *Democracy in America* (Indianapolis: Liberty Fund, 2010), Vol. 4, Part III, Ch. 22, p. 1159.

113 McDonald, *What*, p. 140.

114 Fotion and Elfstrom, *Military*, p. 2.

115 Koehn, *Ground*, p. 15.

116 Ibid., p. 19. See also Paul Camenisch, 'Business Ethics: On Getting to the Heart of the Matter', *Business and Professional Ethics Journal*, 1:1 (1981), pp. 59–69.

> armies working in perfect harmony to keep the soldiers in place and at each other.[117]

Now, is not necessary to take at face value Shay's point about military *service* amounting to effective *servitude*; we just need be mindful that such an extreme situation remains a possibility prompted by the excruciating conditions of modern warfare. But whether service or servitude, to whom does the soldier pledge his or her allegiance? Is it mainly an inter-personal professional relationship with an individual client, like the one doctors and lawyers have?

The ethics governing the military profession is, in fact, an "ethics of institutions", not of personal relations, as remarked by Fotion and Elfstrom.[118] According to Koehn, all professionals have been entrusted by their respective communities to fulfil a specific function no one else has the expertise or skill to provide.[119] The main form of political organisation said communities have adopted for the past centuries has been the modern state, to which the military provide an essential service as the keepers and managers of the legitimate monopoly of physical violence claimed by this modern-day *Leviathan*.[120] As Michel Foucault puts it:

> The State acquired a monopoly on war. The immediate effect of this State monopoly was that what might be called day-to-day warfare, and what was actually called 'private warfare,' was eradicated from the social body, and from relations among men and relations among groups. (…)
>
> So, thanks to the establishment of this State monopoly and to the fact that war was now, so to speak, a practice that functioned only at the outer limits of the State, it tended to become the technical and professional prerogative of a carefully defined and controlled military apparatus. This led, broadly speaking, to the emergence of something that did not exist as such in the Middle Ages: the army as institution.[121]

As James Scott explains in *Seeing Like a State*, by serving the state professional armies aided this modern construct to make the amorphous, organic mass that was the medieval society more "legible" and "regimented" for all sorts of

117 Jonathan Shay, *Achilles in Vietnam. Combat Trauma and the undoing of Character* (New York: Scribner, 2003), p. 93.

118 Fotion and Elfstrom, *Military*, p. 4.

119 Koehn, *Ground*, p. 48.

120 Max Weber, *The Vocation Lectures* (Indianapolis: Hacket, 2004), p. 33.

121 Michel Foucault, *Society Must Be Defended* (London: Penguin Books, 2003), pp. 48–49.

administrative and political purposes.[122] We must bear in mind, nevertheless, as Hackett remarks, that the main function of the military professional remains "the ordered application of force in the resolution of a social problem".[123]

Now, what is the service provided by military professional to the state and to the community it represents? It is fairly evident that the main service supplied by state forces is that of security, a social goal so cherished it has even been elevated to the status of a fundamental right in the Universal Declaration of Human Rights of 1948.[124]

In one of his latest contributions to the JWT, Michael Skerker postulates that professional norms are teleological standards for institutional actors to achieve the goals of core human rights or moral goods their professions are tasked with securing. In the particular case of the military profession, the rules governing this activity are devised to achieve one specific purpose or service to the community, which Skerker calls the "security standard". This standard comprises two first-order rules that define the contours of the professional duty of state agents charged with providing security to the population, in the sense that what matters is not only that they provide security, but also that the *way* in which it is provided can be considered acceptable to the beneficiaries insofar as the service is respectful of people's rights as it draws on "the most reliable, efficacious, proportional, and efficient norms and tactics".[125]

National or collective security, thus, is a public good that is provided by the military profession, one that is offered to society for its own sake, or *pro bono publico*,[126] given its high importance for the survival of the community. Thus, professional soldiers are public agents that represent their respective states, holding a special commission issued by them,[127] in order to attain this important goal. And if, as Koehn postulates the client's vulnerability is one of the key features underlying any professional relationship,[128] then this precondition reaches maximum intensity when the good sought after is the very physical integrity and survival of the client, in this case, society as a whole. It is the CoW that make society particularly vulnerable to its dreaded consequence, war, leaving it in need of the services only a specialized professional force can

122 James C. Scott, *Seeing Like a State* (New Haven: Yale University Press, 2020), pp. 2; 15; 55.
123 Hackett, *Profession*, p. 9.
124 Art. 3: "Everyone has the right to life, liberty and the security of person".
125 Michael Skerker, *The Moral Status of Combatants. A New Theory of Just War* (New York: Routledge, 2020), p. 129.
126 Koehn, *Ground*, p. 51; Moliner, *Ética*, p. 121.
127 John Fabian Witt, *Lincoln's Code* (New York: Free Press, 2012), p. 206.
128 Koehn, *Ground*, p. 65.

supply in a way that is both effective and legitimate according to the security standard.

Finally, the third feature listed by Huntington, corporateness, becomes key in the military's self-image as members of a community governed by its own professional standards, including not only technical knowledge and expertise but also ethical codes of behaviour.[129] Chapter 5 will focus on 'Professional Military Education' ('PME'), bearing on the ways we try to instil respect for said standards during military training and education.

## 2.4 *The Military and 'Role-Morality': of Men in Black and Men against Fire*

Towards the end of Honoré de Balzac's novel *Colonel Chabert* one of the characters, Derville, declares after seeing the poor war veteran in abject destitution:

> [t]here are in modern society three men who can never think well of the world – the priest, the doctor, and the man of law (…) And they wear black robes, perhaps because they are in mourning for every virtue and every illusion. The most hapless of the three is the lawyer. When a man comes in search of the priest, he is prompted by repentance, by remorse, by beliefs which make him interesting, which elevate him and comfort the soul of the intercessor whose task will bring him a sort of gladness; he purifies, repairs and reconciles. But we lawyers, we see the same evil feelings repeated again and again, nothing can correct them; our offices are sewers which can never be cleansed.[130]

Tragically, despite his best efforts, the man in black of this tale could not help a veteran of the Napoleonic wars, Colonel Chabert, regain his lost honour and reputation.

Another man in black, a priest, reportedly once told General Roméo Dallaire, commanding officer of the UN forces deployed in Rwanda at the time of the 1994 genocide, and whose memoir of the atrocities is the archetypal articulation of moral injury as spiritual harm due to the breach of deeply held moral beliefs: "'Ahh, soldiers (…) You know, soldiers are very unusual people. On the outside, they are the hardest, most demanding, severe people, but underneath

129 Janowitz, *Professional*, p. 6.

130 Honoré de Balzac, 'Colonel Chabert', https://www.gutenberg.org/files/1954/1954-h/1954-h.htm, 3 October 2022.

that, they are the most human, the most feeling, the most emotionally attached people who exist'".[131]

These two passages of men in black engaging with soldiers raise the question about the possibility of including military professionals among said experts who 'can never think well of the world' as they too work in an environment of 'sewers which can never be cleansed'. Should soldiers be afforded the dubious honour of joining the brotherhood of men and women in black? After all, the dedication showed by military professionals has of old been compared to that of prelates.[132] And if soldiers are to join the brotherhood of black cloaks, what does it matter in terms of what society expects from them ethically?

These expectations have been pondered by lawyers for some time in debates surrounding professional ethics and so-called 'role-morality'. Already in the early 20th century, Émile Durkheim postulated the existence of a differentiated set of ethical rules for each profession, as "there are as many forms of morals as there are different callings",[133] resulting in a very mild form of social censure at misbehaviour, while at the same time becoming a more developed ethics the more stable and connected the profession is, such as the military.[134]

This thesis is predicated on what has been dubbed a veritable 'moral division of labour'[135] whereby different, albeit interconnected, professions are expected to carry out discrete actions within their respective remits, for instance, a judge and an executioner among whom there is ostensible 'role relativity'.[136] This division would eventually become known as 'role-morality' in legal professional ethics, in the sense that "a lawyer may not legitimately be held morally accountable for the actions she takes on behalf of her clients so long as there are within the bounds of the law and professional responsibility".[137]

Further, Michael Boulette formulates the distinction between a 'hard' and a 'soft' role-morality.[138] Hard role-morality is defended by authors such as

131 Roméo Dallaire, *Shake Hands With the Devil. The Failure of Humanity in Rwanda* (New York: Carroll & Graf, 2005), p. 16. On the connections between soldiering and the ministry see Janowitz, *Professional*, p. 115.

132 Hackett, *Profession*, p. 9.

133 Émile Durkheim, *Professional Ethics and Civic Morals* (New York: Routledge, 2019), p. 5.

134 Ibid., pp. 6; 9.

135 Yitzhak Benbaji, 'The War Convention and the Moral Division of Labour', *The Philosophical Quarterly*, 59:237 (2009), p. 611.

136 Arthur Applbaum, *Ethics for Adversaries: The Morality of Roles in Public and Professional Life* (Princeton: Princeton University Press, 1999), pp. 6; 15–42.

137 Michael Boulette, 'Two Concepts of Role-Morality', https://papers.ssrn.com/sol3/papers.cfm?abstract_id=1527253, 3 October 2022, p. 6.

138 Ibid., pp. 6 *et seq.*

Stephen Pepper[139] and Durkheim himself. According to this account, the professional is to be considered an "amoral technician", merely a tool of the client to serve the latter's interests,[140] thus truly honouring the client's autonomy or moral agency and responsibility for their choices.[141]

Alternatively, authors like Bradley Wendel,[142] Daryl Koehn,[143] and Paul Camenisch[144] favour a soft role-morality approach, such that the ethical rules applying to a certain profession do not replace wholesale the standards of general morality as they can be found and practiced in society, especially taking into account the fact of moral pluralism and the instrumental nature of services like legal justice to further and nurture such pluralism.

In other words, soft-role morality consists of the proposition that, while each profession is in principle governed by its own ethical standards, it cannot be entirely isolated from the society it has been tasked to serve and therefore it remains porous to general moral rules permeating its activities.[145] In the words of Nancy Sherman: "The roles we assume when we express individual temperaments and fulfill professional duties must ultimately be constrained by the fundamental role that stems from our shared humanity".[146]

I shall return to soft role-morality in the chapter devoted to Professional Military Education (Chapter 5) as the right approach for instilling respect for ethical and legal rules of behaviour among soldiers, on account of the importance of the public service supplied by the military profession, as "war is too serious a matter to entrust to military men".[147] It should be noted here, however, that it is soft role-morality that makes possible the phenomenon of moral injury, understood as psychological or spiritual damage experienced due to the transgression of deeply held moral beliefs by a soldier, beliefs he or she shares with the same society he or she feels betrayed by.[148]

---

139 Stephen Pepper, 'The Lawyer's Amoral Ethical Role: A Defense, A Problem, and Some Possibilities', *Law and Social Inquiry*, 11:4 (1986), pp. 613–634.

140 Boulette, 'Two', p. 19.

141 Pepper, 'Amoral', p. 617.

142 Bradley Wendel, 'Legal Ethics as Political Moralism or the Morality of Politics', *Cornell Law Review*, 93:6 (2008), pp. 1413–1436.

143 Koehn, *Ground*, pp. 153–154.

144 Paul Camenisch, 'On the Matter of Good Moral Character', *The Linacre Quarterly*, 45:3 (1978), pp. 273–283.

145 Fotion and Elfstrom, *Military*, p. 279.

146 Nancy Sherman, *Stoic Warriors. The Ancient Philosophy Behind the Military Mind* (New York: Oxford University Press, 2005), p. 57.

147 Hoiback, *Understanding*, p. 52.

148 Brad Allenby and Tom Frame, 'Moral Injury', in Center on the Future of War, Arizona State University, *Moral Injury: Towards an International Perspective* (Tempe: Arizona State University, 2017), p. 6.

It should also be noted here that there is also an alternative to (soft/hard) role-morality, which we may call 'universal morality'. This is the thesis advanced by David Luban, according to whom lawyers and other professionals are not merely accidentally, but permanently bound by general morality as they are endowed with a moral conscience and are not to be treated as mere tools or "hired guns" of the client or of the adversarial justice system. In his words, lawyers are expected to "cut corners" but never to "cut throats",[149] as there are some things evidently wrong from a moral point of view, like murder. He does concede, however, that there are exceptions to this moral ban on killing, precisely when it comes to war and the business of soldiering,[150] which makes soft role-morality more attractive than universal morality when thinking about what soldiers do.

Returning to our original analogy, although it is plausible to compare one type of men in black, lawyers, with another type of professional working in the sewers of war, soldiers, the truth is that all the men and women in black – lawyers, doctors, and priests – have in common that they are considered part of the "learned" or "liberal" professions,[151] namely those that provide intellectual services in an autonomous and personal manner.[152] In that sense, it seems somewhat inaccurate to compare the military with the liberal professions considering the former provide the public and tangible service of collective security on behalf of the state. It seems more fitting to compare the military with another profession whose stock in trade is the facing of physical danger for the delivery of security to the public. Indeed, much closer to what the military do is the service supplied by yet another group of men and women in black: firefighters.[153] These 'men and women against fire' provide the service of physical safety and security in the face of a longstanding threat to people's lives and property.

This service has been purveyed by both private and public initiative for over a century across the world, as one of the many ways the modern state has come to organize itself such that it can manage public threats not only coming from external aggression and civil unrest, but also from nature's destructive

149 David Luban, *Legal Ethics and Human Dignity* (Cambridge: Cambridge University Press, 2009), pp. 9; 63.

150 Ibid., pp. 23; 265–266.

151 Koehn, *Ground*, p. 12.

152 'Manifesto: Definitions of the concept of liberal profession at European level', https://www.eesc.europa.eu/en/documents/manifesto-definitions-concept-liberal-profession-european-level, 3 October 2022.

153 Moliner, *Ética*, p. 91.

forces.[154] Unsurprisingly for such a crucial and increasingly professional service, firefighters in countries such as the United States[155] and England[156] have adopted their own codes of ethics, both lending credence to soft-role morality as they enshrine values also held dear in common morality, including fairness, honesty, integrity, responsibility, loyalty, non-discrimination and respect for people's dignity. As we shall see in Chapter 6, many military codes of ethics across the world consecrate similar principles.

The analogy between military professionals and firefighters seems also more accurate considering the quintessentially dangerous nature of the service they both provide:[157] in the case of the military, they are tasked with managing or administering the result of the CoW, war, in a way that results satisfactory under the security standard. But they do not create, direct or control those CoW, just as firefighters are tasked with managing fire, but not with administering all the 'combustive' circumstances (chemical, economic, social, political) that cause fires in the first place.

## 3 The 'Ethics of Killing' Debate

It is time now to leave analogies behind and return to the issue of the original *Men Against Fire*, to use the words chosen by S.L.A. Marshall to name his famous study on the reluctance of soldiers to kill in war.

Taking the military seriously means taking what they do, war, and the circumstances leading to it, seriously. It also entails thinking in earnest about what war is essentially about, no matter how much its character may have changed over millennia. Simply stated, war is about *killing*. Therefore, taking war and the military seriously means also taking killing seriously. If we send them to kill in our name, we owe it to them to seriously ponder the significance of what we are asking them to do.

Thus far I have characterized the military as the particular type of professional tasked by society with a specific function: managing the result of the Circumstances of War, namely war itself, in order to provide the service of the security standard. But, alas, providing this service will require of the military

154 Shane Ewen, *Fighting Fires. Creating the British Fire Service, 1800–1978* (New York: Palgrave Macmillan, 2010).

155 'Firefighter Code of Ethics', https://www.usfa.fema.gov/downloads/pdf/code_of_ethics.pdf, 3 October 2022.

156 'Core Code of Ethics for Fire and Rescue Services – England', https://www.local.gov.uk/publications/core-code-ethics-fire-and-rescue-services-england, 3 October 2022.

157 Grossman Christensen, *Combat*, p. 304.

professional to eventually take the life of another human being, something for which they must be prepared both physically and mentally, including an understanding of the ethical aspects of killing. A cutting-edge debate within the millenary discourse of the JWT revolves around the ethics of killing in war, with so-called 'traditionalists' pitted against 'revisionists'. In this section I outline the debate in order to put to the test the CoW theory.

Just as the Vietnam War inspired the revival of Just War thinking in general, it took another perceived unjust war, the Iraq intervention of 2003, to move the discussion forward in the form of the debate between traditionalists and revisionists. It all began when Jeff McMahan published his provocative article titled *The Ethics of Killing in War* in 2004.[158] In that piece, McMahan challenged what he conceptualized as the three main tenets underlying traditional JWT: (1) the independence between *jus ad bellum* and *jus in bello*; (2) that unjust combatants can abide by the principles of *jus in bello* and not act wrongly if they do so; and (3) that only combatants are legitimate targets, whereas non-combatants enjoy immunity from attack.[159]

Eventually these traditional propositions were simplified by David Rodin into two main theses: (1) the 'symmetry thesis' according to which just and unjust combatants, based on what Walzer called the "moral equality of soldiers",[160] enjoy the same privileges and are bound by the same duties under *jus in bello*; and (2) the 'independence thesis' pursuant to which the *jus in bello* rights and obligations of a combatant are independent from the *jus ad bellum* causes of the war they are fighting. Conversely, and following McMahan's lead, scholars such as Rodin undertook the task of 'revising' such assumptions, in order to advance the following two theses instead: (1) the 'asymmetry thesis' stating that the content of *in bello* rights and obligations is essentially different between just and unjust combatants; and (2) the 'dependence thesis' posing that *in bello* rights are ultimately dependent on the *ad bellum* justice of the war being fought.[161] Interestingly, the contents of revisionism have made their way into legal discourse in the form of a General Comment, No 36, issued by the UN Human Rights Committee in 2018, where it is stated outright: "States parties engaged in acts of aggression as defined in international law, resulting

158 Jeff McMahan, 'The Ethics of Killing in War', *Ethics*, 114 (2004), pp. 693–733.

159 Ibid., p. 694.

160 Walzer, *Just*, p. 34.

161 David Rodin and Henry Shue (eds.), *Just and Unjust Warriors. The Moral and Legal Status of Soldiers* (New York: Oxford University Press, 2008), pp. 2–3. It is arguably based on the same calculus that the war guilt clause was inserted in the Treaty of Versailles (i.e. if the war is unjust then all 'loss and damage' are unjust and the sole responsibility of the aggressor). See Kagan, *Origins*, pp. 288–289.

in deprivation of life, violate ipso facto article 6 of the Covenant [the right to life]".[162]

For two decades now JWT thinkers have been actively engaged in this debate, with McMahan leading the revisionist charge alongside authors like Rodin, Helen Frowe,[163] and Victor Tadros;[164] while Walzer leads the effort to hold down the traditionalist fort, with the help of authors like Henry Shue,[165] Jeremy Waldron,[166] and Michael Skerker.[167] Some authors, most notably Uwe Steinhoff, remain 'free-lances' of sorts, charging often against revisionism, but not sparing traditionalism either.[168] Similarly, Christian Nikolaus Braun promotes a third way by calling for a revival of classical (Thomistic) thinking to help bring peace back into what he calls "the fight for the just war tradition".[169]

Now, this controversy provides an opportunity to test the CoW theory. Thereby, I will briefly outline some of the main problems affecting the revisionist position, followed by some arguments to reinforce the traditionalists defences.

Admittedly, the revisionist position does get right two fundamental facts. First, despite all the political rhetoric and occasional ambiguity of moral discourse, war is ultimately about killing, and no amount of speeches referring to 'saving lives', 'delivering justice', or 'achieving peace' will change that. War is about breaking things and hurting people, about violence[170] and the "power to hurt,"[171] and what military professionals train for at the end of the day is

162 Human Rights Committee, 'General Comment No 36 (2018) on article 6 of the International Covenant on Civil and Political Rights, on the right to life', https://tbinternet.ohchr.org/Treaties/CCPR/Shared%20Documents/1_Global/CCPR_C_GC_36_8785_E.pdf, 22 March 2022, par. 70.

163 Helen Frowe, *Defensive Killing* (Oxford: Oxford University Press, 2014).

164 Victor Tadros, *To Do, To Die, To Reason Why. Individual Ethics in War* (Oxford: Oxford University Press, 2020).

165 Rodin and Shue, *Just*.

166 Jeremy Waldron, 'Deep Morality and the Laws of War', in Seth Lazar and Helen Frowe (eds.), *The Oxford Handbook of Ethics of War* (Oxford: Oxford University Press, 2018), pp. 80–93.

167 Skerker, *Moral*.

168 Uwe Steinhoff, *The Ethics of War and the Force of Law. A Modern Just War Theory* (New York: Routledge, 2021).

169 Christian Nikolaus Braun, *Limited Force and the Fight for the Just War Tradition* (Washington, DC: Georgetown University Press, 2023).

170 Eric-Hans Kramer and Tine Molendijk, 'Introduction', in Eric-Hans Kramer and Tine Molendijk (eds.), *Violence in Extreme Conditions. Ethical Challenges in Military Practice* (Cham: Springer, 2023), pp. 1–2.

171 Thomas Schelling, *Arms and Influence* (New Haven: Yale University Press, 1966), p. 2.

killing.[172] Wertheimer insists on not putting too fine a point on this: "The warrior's tools and attendant skills are evaluated and evaluable by their proficiency, not in saving lives, but in causing death and destruction".[173] Making these harsh realities invisible, or sugar-coating their real impact through rhetoric, only make recourse to war more trivial and less reflective, something that Just War theorists should never forget if they want to take war, and its practitioners, seriously. For it is not only civilians who will suffer from excessive and irresponsible uses of force, but also the military in the form of moral injury whenever they are instrumentalized by society with little or no regard for their deeply held moral beliefs. As Cian O'Driscoll has so eloquently put it, war "is as much about Ares as it is about Athena".[174]

Secondly, revisionists are correct in assuming that wars, and warriors, can be ethically classified as just or unjust. The entire JWT enterprise is predicated on the possibility of such distinctions, and so any work on JWT should not shy away from utilizing such devices, but on the contrary, embrace them like revisionists have done of late. Undoubtedly, one of the great merits of the revisionist revival has been to remind us of the fact that, despite working assumptions such as the moral and legal equality of soldiers, there *are* causes that are justified and causes that are not, and consequently, just and unjust wars. Again, the revisionist's sobering voice inspires us to ponder the implications of going to war more seriously and to the utmost. As Heather M. Roff has put it, McMahan and the revisionists have "either intentionally or not (…) made us all better theorists, jurists or philosophers because we have had to craft coherent, robust and forceful responses to his work".[175] Furthermore, the critical thinking propelled by the revisionist challenge arguably also makes for better military leadership.[176]

That being said, there are three main critiques that can be levelled against the revisionist view:

172 Fotion and Elfstrom, *Military*, p. 3; Moliner, *Ética*, p. 25.

173 Roger Wertheimer, 'The Moral Singularity of Military Professionalism', in Roger Wertheimer (ed.), *Empowering our Military Conscience. Transforming Just War Theory and Military Moral Education* (New York: Routledge, 2010), p. 135; see also Christopher Coker, *The Warrior Ethos. Military Culture and the War on Terror* (New York: Routledge, 2007), p. 135.

174 O'Driscoll, *Victory*, p. 89.

175 Heather M. Roff, 'Jeff McMahan (1954–present)', in Daniel R. Brunstetter and Cian O'Driscoll (eds.), *Just War Thinkers* (New York: Routledge, 2018), p. 247.

176 Lonneke Peperkamp and Christian Nikolaus Braun, 'Contemporary Just War Thinking and Military Education', in in Eric-Hans Kramer and Tine Molendijk (eds.), *Violence in Extreme Conditions. Ethical Challenges in Military Practice* (Cham: Springer, 2023), p. 109.

### 3.1 *Unexplored Pacifism*

Similar to Luban's universal morality as applied to legal ethics, the revisionist view imports moral criteria from normal life in order to make them operative and available for judgment in times of war, namely the prohibition on killing. It does not adhere to the traditional thesis of the exceptional nature of war, as it views war and peace as a continuum where the same moral principles apply in every circumstance.

Now, normal social life is ideally a situation of peace and order, an 'ideal theory' of sorts as envisaged by a rich tradition of political philosophy reflecting on the ways humans can advance from a 'state of nature' to a state of 'social contract'.[177] In other words, human beings associate to live in a state of (perpetual) peace,[178] not of constant war. Such a situation of ideal peace is never completely achieved, as law enforcement institutions and government policing bear out in the domestic domain. But it is thanks to such institutional arrangements that people enjoy a situation as close as possible to peace within a society.

In the international realm, on the other hand, there are no such effective devices, and the ones in place (i.e. the UN collective security system and a few regional security arrangements such as NATO) are pale reflections of the full-fledged monopoly of force enjoyed by the modern state. Therefore, the state of (relative) peace that obtains in normal life within a society is not replicable *between* societies, and whenever that impossibility reaches its farthest extreme, we talk about war.[179]

Thus, by transposing peacetime categories to the international realm, revisionists assume that a situation of (relative) peace exists between states, just as between individuals in a community,[180] despite the obvious fact that there is no such thing as a world government and that we are now perhaps farther than ever from that possibility in our current multipolar world.

But why do revisionists assume this, nonetheless? I believe that their desire to export domestic categories into the international environment springs from an unexplored pacifism. I call it unexplored because it has not been sufficiently

---

177 Hobbes, *Leviathan*; John Locke, *Second Treatise of Government* (Indianapolis: Hackett, 1980); Jean-Jacques Rousseau, *The Social Contract* (Oxford: Oxford University Press, 1999).

178 Prieto Rudolphy, *Morality*, p. 75; Walzer. *Just* (2015), p. 341.

179 Michael Howard, *The causes of wars* (London: Counterpoint, 1983), pp. 11; 25. See also Benbaji and Statman, *Agreement*, p. 72.

180 David Rodin, *War and Self-Defense* (Oxford: Oxford University Press, 2002), p. 107; David Rodin, 'The Moral Inequality of Soldiers: Why *jus in bello* Asymmetry is Half Right', in Rodin and Shue, *Warriors*, pp. 45–46.

dealt with in either the revisionist or the traditionalist literature.[181] But the fact remains that peace is nowadays considered to be the 'natural' state of humanity, whilst war is taken as an aberration, resulting in "a failure in peacetime to consider the possibility of another war, which, in turn, has prevented the efforts needed to preserve the peace".[182]

Such unexplored pacifism may be of two types. First, it could be 'absolute' or utopian pacifism, advocating for the abolition of war altogether, including not only unjust wars, but also those that are deemed just. But such a utopian pacifism no longer belongs in the JWT, as pacifism is a discrete school of thought that represents an alternative to JWT.[183] Additionally, such absolute pacifism finds a formidable obstacle in the CoW, which transfer the *onus* of demonstrating that the abolition of war is at all possible to the pacifist,[184] who would now have to show either: (i) that at least one of the three theses of the CoW is false; or (ii) even if all true, that the interaction between the three theses does not result in the permanent possibility of war.

Since revisionists engage in earnest debate *within* the JWT,[185] believing at least some wars to be just – usually drawing conveniently on the paragon of Just War, the Second World War[186] – we may discard their adherence to said utopian pacifism. That leaves a 'relative' or contingent[187] form of pacifism, one that aims at projecting into the international stage the categories and institutions that enable peaceful or secure coexistence in the domestic realm. In other words, revisionists wish to see the 'just security' of home operating between states, a desideratum we may call 'securitism'.[188]

---

181 Some notable exceptions and good points of departure are: Yitzhak Benbaji, 'The Responsibility of Soldiers and the Ethics of Killing in War', *The Philosophical Quarterly*, 57:229 (2007), pp. 558–572; Benbaji and Statman, *Agreement*, p. 18. See also Steinhoff on 'contingent pacifism': Steinhoff, *Ethics*, p. 238; and Prieto Rudolphy, *Morality*, pp. 75–76.

182 Kagan, *Origins*, p. 567.

183 Anthony Coates, *The Ethics of War* (Manchester: Manchester University Press, 1997), p. 95.

184 Kagan, *Origins*, p. 4; Overy, *Why*, p. 226.

185 Braun, *Limited*, p. 49.

186 However, Steinhoff has challenged this widespread assumption, mostly due to *jus in bello* proportionality concerns regarding the Allies conduction of hostilities during that conflict. See Steinhoff, *Ethics*, pp. 102; 299. For a deeper probe into WW2's myth of redemptive violence, especially in the US, see Ted Grimsrud, *The Good War That Wasn't – and Why It Matters* (Eugene: Cascade Books, 2014).

187 Rawls, *Theory*, pp. 381–382; Larry May, *After War Ends. A Philosophical Perspective* (Cambridge: Cambridge University Press, 2012), Ch. 12.

188 On the perennial search for security (especially border security) as a main driver for war throughout history see Overy, *Why*, pp. 197 et seq.

But this brand of relative pacifism or securitism also has to face the ineluctable facts making up the CoW. In particular, T1 or the interest thesis poses an insurmountable challenge to revisionists when the only available option for conflict resolution is the use of force. This is so because there is not an adjudicator between states that can replicate the power and *imperium* of a domestic court aided by law enforcement institutions monopolizing force, thereby the adjudication option not being available.[189] This is a key difference with the domestic environment. As given facts, the CoW are always at play, whether in the domestic or the international realms. But the interest thesis is sufficiently neutralized in the domestic realm thanks to the existence of a legal system backed by the state's monopoly of force. Alternatively, if there is no effective negotiation or submission, then states will have to solve the conflict by the only remaining alternative, the use of force among (relatively) equal entities. And if war is a conflict resolution mechanism between states as horizontally aligned entities,[190] then the traditional 'moral equality of soldiers' should be construed as a device mirroring the 'political equality of states'.[191]

Additionally, regarding T2 or the mortality thesis, if the parties in conflict deem the interests at play to be vital enough, history shows that they will be willing to kill for them, and risk being killed. Given the formidable epistemic constraints surrounding just causes for war that afflict both governments and individuals,[192] those interests will probably also be deemed 'just' by both parties, thus arising a situation of 'ostensible simultaneous justice',[193] which lies at the heart of the symmetry thesis in the traditional view as it does not expect for soldiers to be so high-minded that they will be able to ascertain the justness of a war all by themselves.[194]

Further, and also as a consequence of its unexplored relative pacifism, the revisionist position seems to heavily rely on the belief in the absolute value of human life that operates in peacetime. This belief logically depends on the validity of the mortality thesis. In other words, were we immortal, then the protection of human life would lose all meaning. This belief in the absolute value of life is certainly commendable, and it is a good guiding principle in general. Yet, it becomes severely qualified in situations of armed conflict, as

189 Howard, *Liberal*, p. 117.

190 Rousseau, *Contract*, p. 51.

191 Dan Zupan, 'A Presumption of the Moral Equality of Combatants', in Rodin and Shue, *Warriors*, p. 216.

192 Rodin and Shue, *Warriors*, p. 7; Gregory Reichberg, Henrik Syse and Endre Begby (eds.), *The Ethics of War. Classic and Contemporary Readings* (Oxford: Blackwell, 2006), p. 318.

193 Bellamy, *Just*, p. 53.

194 Benbaji, 'Convention', p. 613.

acknowledged even by law.[195] But if the revisionist insists on the absolute value of life even in war, then there is no reason to restrict it only to benefit 'just warriors', as unjust warriors too have a right to have their life respected (especially if not liable for the injustice[196]), no matter how morally guilty or responsible they are for the threats they pose. This is what *absolute* means, after all.[197] And if every combatant has an equal right to self-defence, stemming from an equal right to the absolute value of human life, then the symmetry thesis holds up, and traditionalists carry the day after all.

### 3.2 *Reductive Individualism*

The second major flaw in revisionism is the thesis of 'reductive individualism,' yet another projection of domestic, peacetime rationale into the inter-state arena. In his recent contribution to the debate, Michael Skerker has attempted a systematic critique of revisionism for relying on what he characterizes as 'reductive individualism'.[198] This means that, motivated by the relative pacifism or securitism that underlies their position, revisionists project the individualist logic of peacetime morality into the battlefield. Put simply, they make war an affair between two individuals threatening and attacking each other, no different from a common brawl or mugging on the street, or "street crimes and marital disputes" in Walzer's own words.[199]

War is also sometimes redefined as a confrontation between an individual and a state military apparatus, in what is known as "individuated warfare."[200] And if war and normal life were no different from each other, then revisionists would be probably right. Or as Walzer eloquently put it when replying to McMahan's challenge: "What he actually provides, I think, is a careful and

---

195 European Convention on Human Rights, Art. 15: "Derogation in time of emergency:

1. In time of war or other public emergency threatening the life of the nation any High Contracting Party may take measures derogating from its obligations under this Convention to the extent strictly required by the exigencies of the situation, provided that such measures are not inconsistent with its other obligations under international law.
2. No derogation from Article 2 [right to life], *except in respect of deaths resulting from lawful acts of war*, or from Articles 3, 4 (paragraph 1) and 7 shall be made under this provision" (emphasis added).

196 Prieto, *Morality*, pp. 214–215.

197 Benbaji and Statman, *Agreement*, p. 14.

198 Skerker, *Moral*, p. 8.

199 Walzer, *Just* (2015), p. 338.

200 Jack McDonald, *Enemies Known and Unknown* (Oxford: Oxford university Press, 2017), pp. 137–164.

precise account of what individual responsibility in war would be like *if war were a peacetime activity*" (emphasis added).[201]

However, and irrespective of the usage of the duel between two individuals for analytical purposes – most famously by Clausewitz, as we shall see in a future chapter – Skerker correctly points out that war is special insofar as it is necessarily *collective*[202] violence where "military actions are irreducibly corporate actions, collective actions that are greater than the mere aggregate of their contributory actions".[203] Or as Neil Renic has suggested in a recent study on drone warfare, war is marked by a distinctive condition of 'structural reciprocal risk', or the notion that war is collective violence between structured groups composed of combatants, and it is thus irreducible to one-on-one violence among individuals. War thus becomes "a sustained and pervasive imposition of danger upon and between belligerent parties",[204] a true "dialectic of killing and dying".[205] The collective nature of the military profession[206] accordingly mirrors this key feature of war.

This fundamental lack of understanding of war as structural or collective violence by revisionists bears on a number of related issues in the field of war studies. To begin with the most obvious, war has of old been characterized as a state affair to further collective political objectives, as argued by towering personalities such as Sun Tzu,[207] Clausewitz,[208] Rousseau,[209] and Hegel.[210] Furthermore, a household concept in military science like the "centre of gravity" doctrine[211] would make no sense if war were not a collective enterprise amassing numbers of individuals together in mutual opposition. Nor would other aspects of war as a collective experience make sense, like the development of a *esprit de corps* of those "keeping together in time".[212]

---

201 Michael Walzer, 'Response to McMahan's paper', *Philosophia*, 34:43 (2006), p. 43.

202 Walzer. *Just* (2015), p. 340.

203 Skerker, *Moral*, p. 17.

204 Neil C. Renic, *Asymmetric Killing. Risk Avoidance, Just War, and the Warrior Ethos* (Oxford: Oxford University Press, 2020), p. 35.

205 Ibid., 53.

206 Canadian Armed Forces, 'Duty', p. 53; Canadian Armed Forces, 'The Canadian Armed Forces Ethos – Trusted to Serve', https://www.canada.ca/en/department-national-defence /corporate/reports-publications/canadian-armed-forces-ethos-trusted-to-serve.html, 21 March 2023, p. 41.

207 Sun Tzu, *The Art of War* (Pax Librorum, 2009), p. 3.

208 Clausewitz, *War*, p. 28.

209 Rousseau, *Contract*, p. 51.

210 Hegel, *Elements*, p. 361.

211 Clausewitz, *War*, p. 242.

212 William McNeill, *Keeping together in time* (Cambridge: Harvard University Press, 1995).

Further, only if war is conceived of as an exceptional situation, like traditionalists do,[213] some additional germane institutions and categories make sense. For instance, the institution of a war crime requires a special link or nexus to the exceptional circumstances surrounding armed conflict.[214] Without such a special requirement, there would be no technical difference between war crimes and common crimes. But being war the collective enterprise it is, the only way to bring forth the individual liability so dear to revisionists is to treat war crimes as acts exceptionally attributable to the combatant *qua* participant in an armed conflict between two or more groups.

In sum, our conceptions of war and the institutions and accounts built around it are premised on the fundamental fact of war as an exceptional, collective experience of armed violence, all of which makes revisionism a far less intuitive doctrine than its defenders make it out to be.

### 3.3 *Practical Consequences*

Finally, perhaps the greatest failure of revisionism as a practical moral doctrine is that its consequences in real life are simply unacceptable, since it justifies the targeting of non-combatants if they bear the required moral responsibility for posing an unjust threat to just warriors. This line of thinking borders on the absolutist mindset that is characteristic of both total war and terrorism,[215] and even McMahan himself has acknowledged its dangers.[216] More recently, thinking about the Russia–Ukraine war, McMahan revisits this problem by arriving at two equally problematic conclusions: first, targeting Russian civilians is acceptable and not tantamount to terrorism if they bear responsibility for the war and are, thus, liable to such harm (e.g. because they are adults who voted for the belligerent authorities and support the war). However, McMahan waters down his own argument here by introducing a plethora of qualifiers to such a lethal outcome ("it would be more just that a *smaller number* of civilians who bear *some tiny responsibility* for the fact that *some killings* are unavoidable should be killed",[217] emphasis added), an analytical manoeuvre that should not be necessary for a supposedly consistent doctrine as revisionism (that is

213 Military robotics experts also take this exceptional approach to war as they design systems to be applied only within the confines of "bounded morality". See Ronald Arkin, *Governing Lethal Behavior in Autonomous Robots* (Boca Raton: CRC Press, 2009), p. 69.

214 H. van der Wilt, 'War Crimes and the Requirement of a Nexus with an Armed Conflict', *Journal of International Criminal Justice*, 10:5 (2012), pp. 1113–1128.

215 Benbaji and Statman, *Agreement*, p. 27.

216 Jeff McMahan, *Killing in War* (New York: Oxford University Press, 2009), p. 209; 232.

217 Jeff McMahan, 'Just War Theory and the Russia-Ukraine War', *Studia Philosophica Estonica*, 17 (2024), p. 64.

what "asymmetry" entails, after all, so why entertain so many qualms about unjust civilians/warriors?) and which places McMahan closer to the civilian immunity tenet that lies at the heart of traditional Just War thinking. Second, the even more disturbing conclusion he arrives at, that some forms of terrorism are actually acceptable, even if civilians are not liable to harm, "but *terrorism that could be morally justified* as the lesser evil"[218] (added emphasis).

Moreover, the asymmetry thesis fostered by revisionists might cause the reluctance of combatants to depose arms, leading to the very extremes of total annihilation due to the fear of being captured, judged and convicted for the sole fact of having taken up arms to fight for their country, thus making it even more difficult to secure peace, as McMahan also concedes.[219]

It may, further, promote a mischaracterization of the profession of arms as their own members conceive it. Indeed, revisionists contend that only unjust warriors are ethically liable to be harmed or killed because they have picked the 'wrong side', as it were. However, every military professional, regardless of the validity of the cause they fight for, is supposed to accept what Hackett calls an "unlimited liability", or their legitimate exposure to harm (and to all the existential implications of T2, or the mortality thesis) in order to offset the awesome lethal power that has been conferred to them.[220] Such an integral element of the military professional identity can arguably solve the so-called "combatant's trilemma" between military advantage-force protection-civilian protection[221] in favour of the latter. But if, as revisionists contend, only some military professionals are liable to being attacked, then this key feature of the military profession would have to be redefined for this entire class, or at least extricated from the professional ethos of the 'just warriors', as it would be only

218 Ibid., p. 65.

219 McMahan, *Killing* p. 190; Jeff McMahan, 'The Morality of War and the Law of War', in Rodin and Shue, *Warriors*, p. 30.

220 Hackett, *Profession*, p. 202; Moliner, *Ética*, pp. 31; 113. See additionally some doctrinal documents incorporating the notion of unlimited liability, including: British Army, 'Values and Standards of the British Army', https://www.army.mod.uk/media/5219/20180910-values_standards_2018_final.pdf, 24 May 2023, p. 3; Canadian Armed Forces, 'The Canadian Armed Forces Ethos – Trusted to Serve', https://www.canada.ca/en/department-national-defence/corporate/reports-publications/canadian-armed-forces-ethos-trusted-to-serve.html, 21 March 2023, p. 34.

221 Andrew Bell, 'Combatant socialization and norms of restraint: Examining officer training at the US Military Academy and Army ROTC', *Journal of Peace Research*, 59:2 (2022), p. 183. In contrast, on favouring military lives and resources as a matter of the principle of stewardship, see Eric Patterson, 'Returning Military Necessity to the *Jus in Bello*', in Eric Patterson and Marc LiVecche (eds.), *Military Necessity and Just War Statecraft. The Principle of National Security Stewardship* (New York: Routledge, 2024), p. 6.

the unjust ones who are supposed to embrace such liability. It remains to be shown if just warriors would be satisfied with the removal of such an integral part of their chosen profession as they understand it, including General Hackett himself.

Moreover, the war convention, and in particular the laws of war, are the result of centuries of evolution in the practice of warfare for the interplay of several opposing interests that, although engaged in mortal competition, allow for a certain degree of accommodation. The result is the set of institutions and conventions that govern warfare to this day, the war convention. They are, as Jeremy Waldron has eloquently put it, "deadly serious rules" regulating a most deadly serious activity, war,[222] by acknowledging that its "inexorable necessities" cannot just be wished out of existence by law.[223] They are, in sum, workable standards honed by repetition and imbibed with the practical wisdom of centuries of experience in the breaking of things and the hurting of people. These rules are "passed down from theologians and jurists, soldiers and statesmen. They arise out of the hard experience of war itself. They are the product of real people dealing with the horrors of the wars of their day".[224]

This line of thinking arguably puts Waldron within the camp of so called 'contractarianism' within the JWT.[225] Contractarianism is predicated on the premise that states need to provide the public good of security to their communities, and that, on account of T1 or the interest thesis, they are the only ones who can supply such a service. Thus, what Skerker calls the security standard results in the corollary that "The same moral foundation by which military A is permitted to protect state A permits military B to protect state B".[226]

One of the main contractarian thinkers in contemporary literature is Yitzhak Benbaji. He has defended the traditionalist banner of the moral equality of soldiers and what he calls the "collectivized morality of the war convention", building his argument on the contractarian logic as applied to warfare: "Just combatants lose their right not to be attacked by unjust combatants because they subject themselves to a rule that disregards the distinction between just

222 Waldron, *Deep*, p. 87.

223 David Luban, 'What is Military Necessity? A Defense of the Marginal Interpretation', in Eric Patterson and Marc LiVecche (eds.), *Military Necessity and Just War Statecraft. The Principle of National Security Stewardship* (New York: Routledge, 2024), p. 42.

224 Joel H. Rosenthal, 'Foreword', in Daniel R. Brunstetter and Cian O'Driscoll (eds.), *Just War Thinkers* (New York: Routledge, 2018), p. xv.

225 Renic, *Asymmetric*, pp. 45–46.

226 Skerker, *Moral*, p. 132.

and unjust combatants. They do so because they know it is in their interest that this rule would be commonly followed".[227]

Why would this be in their interest? Because "soldiers and civilians live in states, which form an anarchical society. They would be vulnerable to large-scale unjust threats unless their right to life is protected by a powerful political entity. (…) efficient and well-ordered armies are necessary for protecting people's right to life".[228] As a result, soldiers from both sides waive the right not to be lethally attacked even by unjust combatants (i.e. they embrace unlimited liability), as it is still considered beneficial to adhere to the war convention.[229] In order to effectively satisfy the security standard, standing armies need to be obedient and follow the rules of war regardless of the causes of war, whose soundness may or may not be epistemically accessible, as "ignorance is built into the contractarian methodology".[230]

This contractarian approach might seem overly procedural as it divorces the conduct of war from its causes in order to safeguard respect for a minimum set of rules governing the ways most armies throughout history have agreed are the appropriate standard to conduct the business of war. A good way of making sense of this procedural outlook is to use a sports analogy, sadly not untainted by the vicissitudes of history: During the 1936 Olympic games hosted by Hitler's Nazi regime German athletes proudly wore the swastika on their uniforms and performed the Nazi salute before every game, including the football team. They were undoubtedly sporting the wrong colours and 'fighting' for the wrong cause from an *ad bellum* perspective. Yet, this does not mean that on the pitch the players of other teams were allowed to physically assault the German players or cheat them, as they still had to conform to the rules of the game of football – or the rules of boxing in Benbaji's analogy of choice to illustrate the rationale in-built in the war convention[231] – namely the *in bello* dimension of things, if what they were doing was in fact still play the game. Without said constitutive rules we may still call it a competition, probably not a very friendly one, but certainly we would not call such a pitched battle football.

227 Yitzhak Benbaji, 'A Defense of the Traditional War Convention', *Ethics*, 118 (2008), p. 487. See also Yitzhak Benbaji, 'The Responsibility of Soldiers and the Ethics of Killing in War', *The Philosophical Quarterly*, 57:229 (2007), pp. 558–572.

228 Benbaji, 'Defense', pp. 489–490.

229 Yitzhak Benbaji, 'The Moral Power of Soldiers to Undertake the Duty of Obedience, *Ethics*, 122 (2011), p. 5.

230 Ibid., p. 15.

231 Benbaji, 'Convention', pp. 599–601.

More recently, Benbaji and Daniel Statman have offered a more honed version of contractarianism[232] building on the premise that the conditions for the moral effectiveness of social rules are that: (i) they must be mutually beneficial and this must be known by the participants *ex ante* (not in a Rawlsian hypothetical 'veil of ignorance' way,[233] but simply in the way all commitments we actually enter are surrounded by the uncertainty of the future); (ii) they distribute burdens and benefits in a fair manner; and (iii) they are actually followed or adhered to by members of the community.[234] Applying these standard to war, the contractarian view concludes that rules agreed on beforehand (for instance, in an instrument such as the UN Charter) that allow for decent states to protect their own populations are beneficial, fair, and actual in such a way that it is worth maintaining the *jus ad bellum* regime set forth therein. This includes the possibility of resorting to armed force to uphold the very same regime, provided *jus in bello* standards are observed to that end.[235] It also entails the assumption of obedience armies owe even to unjust politicians, since this regime of self-help (and its potential for deterrence) in an anarchical environment cannot be effective unless it can count on soldiers obeying orders that are not manifestly illegal or immoral.[236]

It is arguably for these formidable considerations underwriting contractarianism and its parent doctrine, traditionalism, that the leader of the revisionist charge ultimately renounces the practical consequences of his own moral doctrine by arguing that his point is theoretical and bearing on a so-called 'deep morality' of war to work as "a guide to individual conscience",[237] whilst the institutional arrangements currently in place to regulate war should remain the same until such time as a proper adjudication system may come to the fore.[238] In other words, until such time as T1 or the interest thesis of the CoW can be struck down due to the advent of a functioning adjudication system among states, then the war convention and traditional Just War thinking prevail, including the symmetry thesis and the separation thesis.

A deep morality of war may indeed exist in the heads of philosophers with their imagined worlds filled with fanciful thought experiments involving

232 These arguments may be found in more embryonic form in Benbaji, 'Power', pp. 4; 8–9.

233 Rawls, *A Theory*, pp. 136–142. See also Tim M. Scanlon, *What We Owe to Each Other* (Cambridge: Harvard University Press, 2000).

234 Benbaji and Statman, *Agreement*, pp. 43–49.

235 Ibid., pp. 72–97.

236 Ibid., p. 118; Benbaji, 'Defense', p. 490.

237 McMahan, 'Ethics', p. 733.

238 McMahan, *Killing*, p. 190.

evil twins, ray guns and alien invasions,[239] which have been rightly called "far-fetched hypothetical cases that bear little or no resemblance with real-world scenarios".[240] But what combatants, as the professionals tasked with managing the results of the CoW and burdened with unlimited liability, truly need to guide them in making split-second life and death decisions on the battlefield is mostly the clarity and certainty that the war convention provides,[241] of which, as Ohlin notes, the code of chivalry is an integral part that facilitates compliance thanks to its simplicity, resilience and robustness.[242] It is then no wonder that revisionist works have so far not been very successful in making it into the curricula of military academies.[243] Their predilection for fanciful hypothetical examples that bear little or no resemblance with the realities of war brings to mind Hermann Hesse's novel *The Glass Bead Game* in which a group of scholars or *lusores* engage in cryptic, esoteric intellectual exercises with no practical application. At the same time, Just War scholarship is not supposed to be mere description or apology for realpolitik, lest it end up resembling Jorge Luis Borges' fictional cartographers who were so obsessed with precision that ultimately produced a 1:1 scale map the size of an entire empire and, as such, useless in its ludicrous redundancy.

## 4 Concluding Remarks

This investigation aims to answer the puzzles stated in the Introduction: Is the instruction in the laws of war, otherwise known as International Humanitarian Law or the Law of Armed Conflict, enough to ensure the appropriate behaviour of combatants on the battlefield, or are additional normative standards of an ethical nature needed to protect both civilians from unjustified harm and combatants themselves from moral injury? Where could such standards be found? Is there something in the language used by contemporary professionals that is reminiscent of the ancient code of chivalry and what is the importance of this for the main research question of this book? As they refer to legal and ethical standards of behaviour, these are questions of a normative nature. Yet, before answering them, in this chapter I have explored the factual background

239 Tadros, *To Do*, passim.

240 Peperkamp and Braun, 'Contemporary', p. 101. See also Braun, *Limited*, p. 37.

241 G. Corn, L. Blank, C. Jenks and E. Talbot Jensen, 'Belligerent Targeting and the Invalidity of a Least Harmful Means Rule', *International Law Studies*, 89 (2013), pp. 562; 613–14.

242 Jens David Ohlin, 'War's Rustic Code of Honor', https://ssrn.com/abstract=4931591, 12 September 2024, p. 23.

243 Peperkamp and Braun, 'Contemporary', p. 102.

conditions upon which the puzzle is predicated. Put differently, before venturing into what are the best ways to prepare military professionals so they fight in an appropriate way, it was necessary first to investigate the factual phenomenon that makes this question about fighting well possible and necessary to begin with.

It is suitable to conclude this first philosophical step with a quote by one of the most notable historians of war, Donald Kagan:

> The study of war and its causes is both sobering and challenging. No one can examine the grim history of the human race, repeatedly ravaged by the pain and horror of war, without feeling a great sadness at its ubiquity and perpetuity. Yet anyone who analyzes the origins of particular wars must also be struck by a sense that many of them were unnecessary. In spite of the weaknesses and conflicts inherent in human beings and the societies they create, a student of their wars must feel that it is necessary, but also possible, to do better. It is not toward the elimination of war that we must aim, for that is an implausible expectation. Nor would most people, even in the modern world, agree that war must always be avoided. In our time wars of national liberation or for religious or political freedom are thought widely to be justified and preferable to a peace under the old conditions. Few Americans, in retrospect, would condemn the American Revolution or the Civil War for breaking the peace to achieve national independence and the end of slavery. Yet it would also be wrong to despair of reducing the danger and frequency of wars. If war in general cannot be avoided, we may still hope to be able to reduce the danger of war for long stretches of time, to avoid particular wars, to pursue policies that make a satisfactory peace more likely and more lasting.[244]

In sum, the Circumstances of War make of war, and therefore the killing involved therein, a permanent possibility. In this sense, it would seem indeed that only the dead have seen the end of war. Such are the colours and suits the deck of the Circumstances of War is made of, that destiny deals and that we, as the free agents of history, decide to play. We need not make of war our only move. We just need to judiciously understand it as a possibility. The dead may be the only ones that have seen the end of war; but, until we join them, it is up to us to make of peace what we continue to see for the rest of our days.

244 Kagan, *Origins*, p. 566.

However, should we be unfortunate enough to experience the dreaded result of the CoW, we can rest assured that the killing involved therein is and must be treated always as exceptional, governed by its own special rules in the form of the war convention, as the traditionalists contend. This doesn't mean that the killing cannot and should not be restrained by certain moral and legal standards that apply even in the heat of battle. On the contrary, such standards are precisely what the war convention is made of, which we should strive to instil in the professionals we commission to represent us and protect us when the CoW result in this feared outcome. Only then can we say that we take war, and its practitioners, seriously. We shall now inquire about what those standards are and how we can best engrave them in the hearts of our fighting men and women such that they are shielded from moral injury and that they remain unsoiled even as they trudge through the sewers of modern warfare.

CHAPTER 2

# Military Honour

> There is no substitute for honor as a medium of enforcing decency on the battlefield, never has been and never will be.
>
> JOHN KEEGAN

∵

## 1 A Mere Scutcheon? Falstaff's Catechism

Once the factual background conditions upon which the main questions of this inquiry are predicated have been addressed, it is time to move on to the normative level of analysis that is reflected in the formulation of the puzzle. As stated before, the core research questions of this study can be formulated as follows: Is the instruction in the laws of war, otherwise known as International Humanitarian Law or the Law of Armed Conflict, enough to ensure the appropriate behaviour of combatants on the battlefield, or are additional normative standards of an ethical nature needed to protect both civilians from unjustified harm and combatants themselves from moral injury? Where could such standards be found? Is there something in the language used by contemporary professionals that is reminiscent of the ancient code of chivalry and what is the importance of this?

The main working hypothesis is that the first research question should be answered in the negative and that there is indeed a need for additional normative standards to ensure appropriate behaviour in times of war. In this chapter, I shall address one of these additional normative standards, namely military honour. As seen in the Introduction, this is a concept found at the forefront of the doctrine of the most powerful force in human history, the U.S. military, in the Department of Defense Law of War Manual published in 2015 and recently updated in 2023. Among its core LOAC principles, it includes "Honor", conceptualized as follows:

> *Honor* demands a certain amount of fairness in offense and defense and a certain mutual respect between opposing military forces. (…) *Honor* has also been called *chivalry*. (…) *Chivalry* is often associated with a specific

 | DOI:10.1163/9789004754096_005

> historical context – a code of behavior for knights in Europe during the Middle Ages. Rather than refer to this specific context, the term *honor* is used in this manual to indicate more clearly that the law of war principle of *honor* draws from warriors' codes from a variety of cultures and time periods.[1]

We shall deal with chivalry again in Chapter 4. First, it is necessary to understand the concept of honour, for which we may draw inspiration from the works of William Shakespeare. Sir John Falstaff is probably one of the most relatable characters to be found in the Bard's canon. However much we would like to think of ourselves as brave, noble, and heroic, the truth is that Falstaff epitomizes many a trait that all humans share, not least the instinct of self-preservation that has been the cornerstone of political philosophy for hundreds of years.[2] In *Henry IV. Part I*, after the Prince of Wales reminds him that he owes God a death as they prepare to go into battle, Falstaff allows himself a moment of complete candour once he is left alone:

> 'Tis not due yet, I would be loath to pay him before his day. What need I be so forward with him that calls not on me? Well, 'tis no matter, honour pricks me on. Yea, but how if honour prick me off when I come on? How then? Can honour set to a leg? No. Or an arm? No. Or take away the grief of a wound? No. Honour hath no skill in surgery then? No. What is honour? A word. What is in that word honour? What is that honour? Air. A trim reckoning! Who hath it? He that died a' Wednesday. Doth he feel it? No. Doth he hear it? No. 'Tis insensible then? Yea, to the dead. But will['t] not live with the living? No. Why? Detraction will not suffer it. Therefore I'll none of it, honour is a mere scutcheon. And so ends my catechism.[3]

---

1 US Department of Defense, *Law of War Manual* (Washington D.C.: DoD, 2023), pp. 66–67. Against the inclusion of the idea of chivalry see Sean Watts, 'The DOD Law of War Manual's Return to Principles', https://www.justsecurity.org/24270/dod-law-war-manuals-return-principles/, 26 August 2024; Rachel Van Landingham, 'The Law of War is Not About "Chivalry"', https://www.justsecurity.org/24773/laws-war-chivalry/, 26 August 2024; Richard Salomon, '2023 DoD Manual Revision – What's Chivalry Got to Do with It?', https://lieber.westpoint.edu/whats-chivalry-got-to-do-with-it/, 26 August 2024.

2 Thomas Hobbes, *Leviathan* (Oxford: Oxford University Press, 1998).

3 William Shakespeare, 'Henry IV. Part I. Act V, Scene I'. In: *The Complete Works* (Eirean Press, 2016).

Finally, after the battle he concludes: "Give me life, which if I can save, so; if not, honour comes unlook'd for, and there's an end".[4]

In an impressive monograph devoted to the influence of chivalry in the works of Shakespeare, Theodor Meron points out that Falstaff personifies harsh realism against romantic ideals. He further notes that Cervantes' *Don Quixote* similarly ridicules the excesses of the knight errantry. Yet, while Cervantes writes wistfully about a lost golden age, according to Meron Shakespeare seems more optimistic about the possibility to salvage the humanitarian values underlying chivalry: "Once stripped of its extreme and artificial rituals, Shakespeare's normative chivalry represents a noble and honourable code of behaviour that controls manifestations of violence through civilized behaviour. It is therefore as pertinent to our times as to the Middle Ages."[5]

It is worth highlighting that Meron is far from an ivory tower type of academic, as his eventful life led him to constantly stare at the darkness of the human heart ever since he fled Nazi occupied Poland as a child to escape the Holocaust, and later as a practitioner of international law and ultimately sitting as a judge at the International Criminal Tribunal for the former Yugoslavia.[6] The fact that, after such *sojourns* through different circles of hell, he remains a believer in upholding humanitarian values even amidst war and destruction, is both intellectually inspiring and morally encouraging.

Nevertheless, Meron could be an outlier, a quixotic scholar alone in his quest for nobility in the modern world. After all, how often do we invoke 'honour' in our daily lives? Is it not but a mere scutcheon, a punchline as we saw in the Introduction, or a simple word made up of air, like the Shakespearean character claims, '*una parola*' in the words of Verdi's own Falstaff?[7] Is it not as obsolete as the idea of chastity?[8] Admittedly, even in the most dire of situations, including war, honour does not seem to be talked about much, as one former NATO General is reminded in a recent interview on the conflict in Ukraine.[9]

4 Ibid., Scene III.

5 Theodor Meron, *Bloody Constraint: War and Chivalry in Shakespeare* (New York: Oxford University Press, 1998), p. 131.

6 Theodor Meron, *Standing Up for Justice* (New York: Oxford University Press, 2021).

7 Francisco Lobo, 'Military Honor in the Twenty-First Century: Some Contemporary Challenges', https://www.e-ir.info/2021/05/25/military-honor-in-the-twenty-first-century-some-contemporary-challenges/, 25 May 2021.

8 Peter Berger, 'On the Obsolescence of the Concept of Honor', *European Journal of Sociology*, 11:2 (1970), p. 339.

9 'Former NATO General: Western self-deterrence only prolongs Ukraine war', https://www.youtube.com/watch?v=QbwYBv_vARU&list=WL&index=6&t=157s, 26 September 2023, at 10:01.

Yet, as Kwame Anthony Appiah equally reminds us in the preface to his book *The Honor Code*, "We may think we have finished with honor, but honor isn't finished with us".[10] Appiah's words are arguably borne out by the joint statement released in early 2022 by Russia and China in which they pledge to firmly uphold the results and legacies of the Second World War: "In order to prevent the recurrence of the tragedy of the world war, the sides will strongly condemn actions aimed at denying the responsibility for atrocities of Nazi aggressors, militarist invaders, and their accomplices, besmirch and tarnish the *honour* of the victorious countries" (emphasis added).[11] It is interesting to see how these two rising powers usher in what they believe is a new era in international relations, while at the same time acknowledging the accomplishments of past struggles and the sense of honour they draw from them as two of the victors.

But how much has honour changed over the centuries? As pointed out by a historian of the military profession "if there is a term that describes military honour, it is adaptability".[12] This word's endurance in normative discourse can be better explained if we think of honour as what Ronald Dworkin once characterized as an 'interpretive concept', for instance, the rules of 'courtesy'. Such concepts are those around which an 'interpretive attitude' arises within a community. This attitude comprises two elements: (i) the assumption that the practice in question has value, that is, it serves some interest or purpose or enforces some principle, and therefore there is a point to it; and (ii) that the requirements of the practice are not immutable but are sensitive to its point, such that the rules have to be applied, interpreted, extended or modified according to said point or purpose.[13] Once such an interpretive attitude arises, Dworkin concludes, the practice ceases to be mechanical and acquires a *meaning*.

Applying the foregoing to the interpretive practice of courtesy, Dworkin points out how its practitioners take it to be the point of the practice that it is an opportunity to show respect to our social superiors. But our views about what respect demands are not static. Indeed, "People's views about the proper grounds of respect, for example, may change from rank to age or gender or

---

10 Kwame A. Appiah, *The Honor Code: How Moral Revolutions Happen* (New York: W.W. Norton & Company, 2010), p. xix.

11 'Joint Statement of the Russian Federation and the People's Republic of China on the International Relations Entering a New Era and the Global Sustainable Development', http://en.kremlin.ru/supplement/5770, 4 February 2022. Against, see Pinker, *Angels*, p. 261.

12 Alberto Cañas de Pablos, '"Worth More Than Life Itself": Military Honour and the Birth of Its Courts in Spain (1810–1870)', *Journal of Military Ethics*, 21:3–4 (2022), p. 315.

13 Ronald Dworkin, *Law's Empire* (Oxford: Hart Publishing, 1998), p. 47.

some other property".[14] Eventually, if the point of the practice, its core meaning, is lost, such that it becomes mere ceremony, then the interpretive attitude languishes and the practice will go back to its original mechanical form.[15] This is the case with titles formerly reserved to convey privilege and nobility, such as the *Don* that we inadvertently reserve for Cervantes' deluded knight errant – and for every Spanish speaker today, for that matter, not unlike the *Mister* and the *Monsieur* we mechanically put in front of any person's name in English or in French.[16]

Have we reached the demise of the interpretive practice of honour? Has it become mere ceremony, mechanical delivery, like Dworkin warns? Are we even equipped to understand such a transition so as to be able to adequately discern between the bona fide use of a genuine normative principle and the hypocritical invocation of a shibboleth?

The unearthing of moral truths in the works of Shakespeare, a feat attempted by Meron as we have seen, could be indication that we can. Furthermore, and perhaps contrary to what Meron himself suggests, there are treasures also to be found within Cervantes' work that we may carry with us back to our modern life, as Chesterton did with his novel *The Return of Don Quixote*. As Ortega y Gasset once remarked about *Don Quixote*: "There is no book as powerful in its symbolic references to the universal meaning of life, and yet, there is no book where we will find less revelations, less indications for its own interpretation. Therefore, confronted with Cervantes, Shakespeare seems like an ideologist".[17]

But even if both Shakespeare and Cervantes offered us their insights into the universal truths of life in a clear and workable way, would we still be able to grasp such transcendent concepts, like honour, bequeathed to us from times immemorial? Can we really understand the past from whence these time-honoured categories we use today came?

At the beginning of his philosophical inquiry titled *After Virtue*, Alasdair MacIntyre invites us to imagine a thought experiment whereby the natural sciences are blamed for a series of environmental disasters and then abolished – or, in our modern vernacular, 'cancelled'. Later on, however, there is a countermovement led by enlightened people who try to revive the natural sciences. They find relics and remnants of the old knowledge here and there, and they try to piece them together as best they can. They argue about

14 Ibid., p.48.
15 Ibid., p. 49.
16 Michael Walzer, *Spheres of Justice* (New York: Basic Books, 1983), p. 252.
17 José Ortega y Gasset, *Meditaciones del Quijote y otros ensayos* (Madrid: Alianza, 2014), p. 89 (free translation from the Spanish original).

the theory of relativity alongside the phlogiston thesis, and they parrot such concepts as 'neutrino', 'mass' and 'atomic weight' without really grasping their meaning. After painting this picture, MacIntyre explains:

> The hypothesis which I wish to advance is that in the actual world which we inhabit the language of morality is in the same state of grave disorder as the language of natural science in the imaginary world which I described. What we possess, if this view is true, are the fragments of a conceptual scheme, parts which now lack those contexts from which their significance derived. We possess indeed simulacra of morality, we continue to use many of the key expressions. But we have – very largely, if not entirely – lost our comprehension, both theoretical and practical, of morality.[18]

This unfortunate loss took place, according to MacIntyre, in the transition from the Middle Ages to Modernity. The author's solution to this epistemological quandary relies on virtue ethics and is yet to be fully explored in this book, especially given the premium that the military place on that particular school of thought, as we will see in Chapter 6. For now, we may count honour among such expressions that we may be parroting or using without fully understanding its complex moral meaning. This affects both people as well as countries, the example of the Russian–Chinese statement providing proof that these old categories or 'scutcheons' are still pretty much in fashion among the many competitors of our multi-polar world.

But if it affects people, then a subset of society such as the military is not exempt, and therefore an expression such as 'military honour' should invite the same scepticism and critical approach MacIntyre recommends for all moral inquiries in our modern age. In what follows, I will review the foremost literature on military honour to begin to tread the long path towards conceptual clarity that is the necessary first step in any normative investigation with practical applications.

## 2 Military Honour in the Literature

> What our fathers called honour above all was, truly speaking, only one of its forms. They gave a generic name to what was only a type. So honour

18 Alasdair MacIntyre, *After Virtue*, 3rd ed. (Notre Dame: University of Notre Dame Press, 2007), pp. 1–2.

> is found in democratic centuries as in times of aristocracy. But it will not be difficult to show that in the former it presents another physiognomy.
>
> ALEXIS DE TOCQUEVILLE

*Military honour* is a notion embedded within a normative subsystem of professional ethics, usually known in the literature as 'Professional Military Ethics' ('PMEt'), whereas the process whereby such ethical knowledge is instilled is known as 'Professional Military Education' ('PME'),[19] as we shall see in more detail in Chapter 5.

Before proceeding further in the study of military honour as found in specialized works on PMEt in this section, two caveats are in order. First, despite the general development of a literature specializing in professional ethics during the 20th century, PMEt scholarship is still relatively nascent after only a few decades of existence, especially when compared to the centuries-old tradition of moral philosophy. As I will explain in Chapter 5, the young discipline of PMEt makes use of this rich philosophical legacy, as it mainly revolves around the dialectics between the three foremost ethical schools of thought, that is virtue ethics, rules-based or deontological ethics, and utilitarian or consequentialist ethics, usually skewing in favour of the first two. Consequently, theoretical reflections around the concept of military honour may not be as abundant in this burgeoning field, as we will see in this chapter.

The second caveat concerns language, more specifically, the use of the words 'ethics' and 'morality'. Like any other kind of professional, the military person performs a social role[20] in order to supply the service represented by the security standard. As explained in Chapter 1, 'role-morality' can be either 'hard', whereby a person performing a role is immune from external criticism

---

19 The acronym 'PME' is used in the literature to signify 'Professional Military Education' (for instance, by Roger Wertheimer), as mentioned in the Introduction. For an alternative use of the acronym see Sally Rohan's meaning as 'Professional Military Ethics'. See Roger Wertheimer, 'Preface', in Roger Wertheimer (ed.), *Empowering our Military Conscience. Transforming Just War Theory and Military Moral Education* (New York: Routledge, 2010); Sally Rohan, 'An organic professional military ethic and the educational challenge', in Don Carrick, James Connelly and David Whetham (eds.), *Making the Military Moral. Contemporary Challenges and Responses in Military Ethics Education* (New York: Routledge, 2018), p. 71.

20 Paul Gilbert, 'Civilian Immunity in the "New Wars"', in Igor Primoratz (ed.), *Civilian Immunity in War* (Oxford, Oxford University Press, 2007), p. 206; Larry May, *War Crimes and Just War* (Cambridge: Cambridge University Press, 2007), pp. 63–64; Adam Roberts, 'The Principle of Equal Application of the Laws of War', in Rodin and Shue, *Warriors*, p. 238; Wertheimer, 'Singularity', p. 134; Benbaji and Statman, *Agreement*, pp. 37 et seq.

by the rest of society;[21] or it could be 'soft', such that anyone performing a social role has a duty to society at large.[22] I contend that the kind of role-morality bearing on the military professional must be soft role-morality, as their stock in trade, modern war, is a phenomenon affecting society as a whole.

Although throughout this study I shall use the terms 'ethics' and 'morality' interchangeably, I am fully aware of the importance of the proposed conceptual difference between 'morality' as a set of values and standards of behaviour bearing on society as a whole, and 'ethics' as a subset of standards applicable only to certain groups.[23] Still, as a defender of a soft role-morality approach, I shall strive here to bridge this gap between (society's general) morality and (specialized professional) ethics to make these concepts as seamless as possible, except when indicated otherwise – for instance, in the use of terms of art such as 'role *morality*', '*moral* courage', '*moral* injury', 'professional military *ethics*', or '*ethics* of killing'. Thus, unless stated otherwise, I shall use the terms 'ethics' and 'morality' as interchangeable, mirroring common discourse around these topics,[24] including as I conceptualize honour as an ethical/moral concept.

### 2.1 *Honour and Respect*

This chapter focuses on a particular kind of honour, namely *military* honour. Now, as to the concept of honour *simpliciter*, in its most generic meaning it refers to a sense of integrity stemming from acting according to one's own conscience ('internal honour'), or to social prestige or reputation ('external honour').[25]

---

21 Stephen Pepper, 'The Lawyer's Amoral Ethical Role: A Defense, A Problem, and Some Possibilities', *Law and Social Inquiry*, 11 :4 (1986), pp. 613–634.

22 Michael Boulette, 'Two concepts of role-morality – In search of a normative language of legal ethics', *AIO* 5:2 (2010), pp. 20–32. On the respect for dignity as a matter of social morality, see Oscar Schachter, 'Human Dignity as a Normative Concept', *American Journal of International Law*, 77 (1983), p. 853.

23 Paul Robinson, 'Introduction: Ethics Education in the Military', in Paul Robinson, Nigel De Lee and Don Carrick (eds.), *Ethics Education in the Military* (New York: Routledge, 2016), p. 1.

24 Juan Moliner, *La ética militar como como marco de reflexión sobre la guerra y la profesión militar* (Madrid: Ministerio de Defensa, 2022), p. 75.

25 Paul Robinson, *Military Honour and the Conduct of War. From Ancient Greece to Iraq* (New York: Routledge, 2006), p. 2. See also Peter Olsthoorn, *Military Ethics and Virtues* (New York: Routledge, 2011), p. 14; Peter Olsthoorn, 'Risks, Robots, and the Honorableness of the military Profession', in Bernhard Koch (ed.), *Chivalrous Combatants? The Meaning of Military Virtue Past and Present* (Baden-Baden: Nomos, 2019), p. 164; Federico Aznar, '¿Qué es el honor militar?', in Centro Conjunto de Desarollo de Conceptos, *Cuestiones sobre ética militar* (Madrid: Ministerio de Defensa, 2022), p. 61. For an attempt at rejuvenating the concept of honour in moral philosophy, see Appiah, *Honor*. For a description

This latter meaning is the one used by Montesquieu when he famously identified honour as the dominant passion or "principle" in monarchies, i.e. the passion driving people to act based on ambition and a desire for preference and distinction.[26] In international relations it has sometimes adopted the costume of 'credibility',[27] which is closer to this external dimension.

Ultimately, this external aspect of honour refers to what Appiah describes as "our deep and persistent concern with status and respect, our human need for what Georg Wilhelm Friedrich Hegel called *Anerkennung* – recognition".[28]

Honour, then, is about respect. Stephen Darwall famously distinguished between two kinds of respect: (i) 'recognition respect', which consists of a disposition to weigh appropriately some feature and act accordingly (up to and including restraining our own behaviour), for instance, granting respect to the law, social institutions, and people in general as human beings; and (ii) 'appraisal respect', which we reserve only for those who excel at something, for instance music, or ethical behaviour, and which does not require any actions from us other than the admiration we experience for them.[29] Similarly, Nancy Sherman points out that within the military what we find is "deference respect" or respect for rank and hierarchy (closer to appraisal respect), as opposed to the "dignitary respect" that is universal and is found outside that milieu[30] (more similar to recognition respect).

Honour has been traditionally associated with appraisal respect, for "honour is a privilege, the main essence of which is its rarity".[31] In other words, honour, like appraisal respect, is something that we must earn, not a given. However, building on Darwall's distinction, Appiah believes that honour in reality demands an enhanced kind of recognition respect ('positive recognition respect') that is halfway between simple recognition and appraisal respect, whereby a positive attitude develops evincing that we esteem people highly as our 'honour peers', without them having to earn that respect. Importantly for

---

of the connections between honour and dignity in hate speech laws, see James Whitman, 'Enforcing Civility and Respect: Three Societies', *The Yale Law Journal*, 109 (2000), pp. 1279–1378, especially pp. 1339–1341 on military notions of honour as the basis for the modern German law of human dignity.

26 Céline Spector, 'A Montesquieu Dictionary. Honor', http://dictionnaire-montesquieu.ens-lyon.fr/en/article/1376474900/en/, 16 March 2022.

27 Coker, *Barbarous*, pp. 166–167; Pinker, *Angels*, p. 34.

28 Appiah, *Honor*, p. xiii.

29 Stephen Darwall, 'Two Kinds of Respect', *Ethics*, 88:1 (1977), pp. 38–39.

30 Nancy Sherman, *Stoic Warriors. The Ancient Philosophy Behind the Military Mind* (New York: Oxford University Press, 2005), p. 51.

31 Michel de Montaigne, *The Complete Essays* (London: Penguin Books, 2003), p. 429.

this inquiry, Appiah eventually identifies this special type of universal respect with human dignity.[32]

Similarly, Walzer explains how moral recognition can be either simple, in the sense that we recognize every person we meet as a potential recipient of honour and admiration (hence the "Mr./Ms." automatically attached to their name); or it can be special recognition as someone excelling at something in particular,[33] for instance, an artist or a judge. There is also the possibility to experience 'self-respect', understood as "a proper regard for the dignity of one's person or one's position", to which the concept of honour is attached.[34] Walzer highlights that self-respect can exist even within a hierarchical society comprising many ranks, whereby each rank can harbour a sense of self-respect according to some abstract standard, e.g. the "proud aristocrat, the honest artisan, the loyal servant, and so on".[35] The notion of rank and its implications for a contemporary understanding of dignity shall be analysed in the next chapter.

### 2.2 *Honour and the Military*

In his sociological inquiry into the modern phenomenon of the professional soldier Morris Janowitz devotes a special chapter to the study of what he believes is the basis of the belief system of the armed forces: military honour. He thus opens by postulating: "Military honor is both a means and an end. The code of honor specifies how an officer ought to behave, but to be 'honorable' is an objective to be achieved for its own right".[36] Accordingly, the U.S. Department of Defense lists honour as a principle of the law of armed conflict alongside necessity, proportionality, distinction, and humanity.[37]

Indeed, honour is pervasive in the self-image that the military have of themselves as different from murderers.[38] This connects back to the norma-

32 Appiah, *Honor*, pp. 13–14; 128–130; 177.
33 Walzer, *Spheres*, p. 258.
34 Ibid., p. 274.
35 Ibid., p. 275.
36 Morris Janowitz, *The Professional Soldier* (New York: Free Press, 2017), p. 215.
37 U.S. Department of Defense, 'Directive 2311.01. DoD Law of War Program', https://www.esd.whs.mil/Portals/54/Documents/DD/issuances/dodd/231101p.pdf?ver=2020-07-02-143157-007, 11 December 2023, p. 3.
38 French, *Code,* p. 2; G. Corn, V. Hansen, R. Jackson, C. Jenks, E. Talbot Jensen and J. Schoettler, *The Law of Armed Conflict: An Operational Approach* (New York: Wolters Klumer, 2012), p. xxv; Jessica Wolfendale, 'What is the Point of Teaching Ethics in the Military?', in Paul Robinson, Nigel De Lee and Don Carrick (eds.), *Ethics Education in the Military* (New York: Routledge, 2016), p. 167; Larry May, *After War Ends. A Philosophical Perspective* (Cambridge: Cambridge University Press, 2012), Ch. 4; Tine Molendijk, *Moral Injury and Soldiers in Conflict* (Oxon: Routledge, 2021), p. 47.

tive causes of moral injury understood as the kind of spiritual harm that is indicative of a profound gap between deeply held moral beliefs and their betrayal in practice. Put more simply, the higher the sense of honour a soldier has, the harder he or she will experience the downfall that is moral injury. As Appiah remarks: "your honor is intimately associated in many ways with those aspects of your identity that derive from membership in social groups".[39] And thinking about modern challenges to honour, Appiah concludes: "Those who train our armies claim that military honor is essential in both motivating and civilizing the conduct of warfare. (...) I am inclined to believe them. (...) And if armies are a necessary evil, the life of professional soldiers is one of the places where we still need something close to the enduring culture of martial honor".[40]

Accordingly, Peter Olsthoorn believes that the military might be one of honour's few remaining strongholds in our time.[41] Indeed, the concept of honour can be readily connected to the phenomenon of armed violence. Thus, the pursuit of honour or 'glory' is, according to Hobbes, one of the main causes of conflict and war – following Thucydides, who narrowed down the causes of war to interest, fear, and honour[42] (respectively 'competition', 'diffidence', and 'glory' in Hobbes).[43] Thus, if there is in fact a connection between war and honour, then the professionals making of war their business should experience a special manifestation of this value. Accordingly, we can talk of *military honour*.[44]

In this qualified sense, military honour amounts to honour as applied to those engaged in the military profession. Here it is worth noting that the

39 Appiah, *Honor*, p. 61.

40 Ibid., p. 190.

41 Olsthoorn, *Military*, p. 29; Peter Olsthoorn, 'Risks, Robots, and the Honorableness of the military Profession', in Bernhard Koch (ed.), *Chivalrous Combatants? The Meaning of Military Virtue Past and Present* (Baden-Baden: Nomos, 2019), p. 166.

42 Donald Kagan, *On the Origins of War and the Preservation of Peace* (New York: Doubleday, 1995), p. 8.

43 Hobbes, *Leviathan*, pp. 83; 113. See also Coker, *Barbarous*, p. 161; Pinker, *Angels*, p. 33. For a critical analysis of Thucydides' trinity of fear, honour and interest see Samuel Zilincik, 'Why the "Fear, Honour and Interest" Trinity Harms Our Understanding of War', *The RUSI Journal*, (2021), pp. 2–9.

44 Alternatively, it should be noted that honour is also a protected legal interest under the Fourth Geneva Convention belonging to International Humanitarian Law, but this version of honour is heavily gendered and arguably outdated. See Rachele Marconi, 'Between Outdated Morality and Evolutive Interpretation: The Concept of "Honour" under Article 27(2) of the Fourth Geneva Convention', *MPIL Research Paper Series*, No 2021–22.

military arguably inhabit what Larry May calls an 'honour community',[45] or what Appiah dubs a special 'honour world' in the sense that they constitute "a group of people who acknowledge the same codes, and whose respect is sought".[46] Such honour world, which can even transcend time as it connects people with their predecessors in the practice of honour,[47] shall be characterized here as a veritable *timopolis* (from the ancient Greek *timé* or honour) whose denizens are those belonging to the military profession across the world, as "an honor world needs not be limited to one's own society".[48]

To be sure, there are only a handful of militaries in the world that explicitly state honour as one of their core values. We may find it, for instance, in the motto of the U.S. Military Academy at Westpoint: "Duty, Honor, Country".[49] Further, the U.S. Army defines honour as "a matter of carrying out, acting, and living the values of respect, duty, loyalty, selfless service, integrity and personal courage in everything you do."[50] Similarly, the Chilean Army characterizes honour as the virtue that "leads to military rectitude and integrity, always acting with honesty and openness".[51] The Cadet's Pledge at the National Defence Academy of Japan undertakes to "realize the principles of honor, propriety and courage".[52] Finally, the *Code of Honor of an Officer of the Armed Forces of Ukraine* describes honour as the leading feature of a military officer,[53] as we saw in the Introduction.

But for the most part, honour in not included as such among the main stated values of militaries across the world.[54] This could stem from the fact that in

45 Larry May, *War Crimes and Just War* (Cambridge: Cambridge University Press, 2007), p. 6.

46 Appiah, *Honor*, p. 87. See also Aznar, 'Honor', p. 61.

47 David Cerdá, *Ética para Valientes. El honor en nuestros días* (Madrid: Rialp, 2022), p. 37.

48 Appiah, *Honor*, p. 88.

49 'Factsheet', https://www.westpoint.edu/about/public-affairs/news/fact-sheets, 4 October 2023.

50 U.S. Army, 'The Army Values', https://www.army.mil/values/, 23 February 2022.

51 Chilean Army, 'Military Values', https://www.ejercito.cl/our-commitment/military-values, 23 February 2022.

52 Japanese National Defence Academy, 'The National Defence Academy Cadets' Pledge', https://www.mod.go.jp/nda/english/about/pledge.html', 23 February 2022.

53 'Code of honor of an officer of the Armed Forces of Ukraine', https://sprotyvg7.com.ua/lesson/kodeks-chesti-oficera-zbrojnix-sil-ukraini, 16 October 2024.

54 Paul Robinson, 'Introduction: Ethics Education in the Military', in Paul Robinson, Nigel De Lee and Don Carrick (eds.), *Ethics Education in the Military* (New York: Routledge, 2016), p. 7. The fact that honour does not feature among the stated values of an institution does not mean that it may not become a value or standard cherished in practice by the members of said institution. Yet, this conceptual-normative inquiry is only concerned with official stated values, as it is not an empirical or sociological study on organizational culture.

some countries military honour has a rather dark history as it can be linked to the perpetration of atrocities in the past, such as in Nazi Germany, where the SS official motto was "My Honour is Loyalty" ("*Meine Ehre heißt Treue*").[55]

An additional reason for honour's lack of salience in contemporary lists of values could be that its contents may be absorbed by, or conflated with, similar values and virtues, such as honesty and integrity,[56] as evinced by the American and the Chilean cases. This might also explain why some influential works on PMEt do not explicitly include honour among the key virtues in the field.[57] This means that honour could manifest itself under different terminological guises, not unlike human dignity, as we shall see in the next chapter, whenever this core principle of international law appears to be working in all but name as a 'silent partner'[58] or as 'shadow human dignity'.[59]

Yet, lest honour be reduced to being just '*una parola*', 'a word', the need arises to endow this word with enough conceptual clarity that we may not only understand its meaning, but also be able to identify the instances where it might be operating in the background and, just as importantly, where it is definitely not there in either speech or spirit.

### 2.3 *Definitional Attempts in Contemporary Scholarship*

The main conceptual hurdle in this area is the fact that military honour admittedly lacks a fixed definition and, therefore, may accommodate any number of meanings and topics. Authors like Morris Janowitz, for instance, believe that old and modern notions of military honour comprise components as varied as gentlemanly conduct, personal fealty, self-regulating brotherhood, and the pursuit of glory.[60]

---

55 Philip McCormack, 'Case Study 1: Levels of Loyalty: Country, Service, Mission, Troops', in Michael Skerker, David Whetham and Don Carrick (eds.), *Military Virtues* (Havant: Howgate, 2019), p. 90.

56 James Cook, 'Honesty. Overview', in Michael Skerker, David Whetham and Don Carrick (eds.), *Military Virtues* (Havant: Howgate, 2019), pp. 149–157; Don Carrick, 'Integrity: Overview', in Michael Skerker, David Whetham and Don Carrick (eds.), *Military Virtues* (Havant: Howgate, 2019), pp. 171–176.

57 Michael Skerker, David Whetham and Don Carrick (eds.), *Military Virtues* (Havant: Howgate, 2019). Military honour is apparently assimilated to the virtues of honesty and integrity. See James Cook, 'Honesty. Overview', in Skerker, Whetham, and Carrick, *Military*, pp. 151–155.

58 Roger Brownsword, 'Human dignity from a legal perspective' in Düwell, Braarvig, Brownsword, and Mieth, *Cambridge Handbook*, pp. 8; 13.

59 Ginevra Le Moli, *Human Dignity in International Law* (Cambridge: Cambridge University Press, 2021), p. 137.

60 Janowitz, *Professional*, p. 218.

Taking up the semantic challenge this poses, in a monograph especially devoted to this concept Paul Robinson postulates that four main virtues constitute what he calls the 'unchanging core of military honour': prowess, courage, loyalty, and truthfulness. Among them, prowess – a combination of physical strength and skill with a weapon – is dominant. This needs to be complemented with courage and loyalty to colleagues, friends, and allies, as well as with truthfulness enabling soldiers to trust, not only each other, but also the enemy in the preservation of covenants.[61] Consequently, these virtues prompt soldiers to fight with honour, while at the same time showing mercy and respect for their enemies.[62]

Paraphrasing Hobbes, Sidney Axinn characterizes military honour as a veritable "relish for justice", or in his own words, "honour is honesty even when it hurts".[63] Further, for Axinn military honour refers to courage and fidelity in the performance of one's duties, as well as a sense of selflessness.[64] A very important consequence of this is that the enemy must be treated with respect. But for Axinn, the ultimate motivation behind respect is not a sense of common humanity or compassion; it is rather fear that commands respect, i.e. fear of the possibility that the enemy take my life.[65]

Michael Ignatieff posits that for centuries the warrior's honour has "implied an idea of war as a moral theater in which one displayed one's manly virtues in public. To fight with honor was to fight without fear, without hesitation, and, by implication, without duplicity."[66] Further, the code of honour is supposed to acknowledge the "moral paradox of combat: that those who fight each other bravely will be bound together in mutual respect; and that if they perish at each other's hand, they will be brothers in death".[67] Ultimately, he concludes, the warrior's code of honour encapsulates and ethic of responsibility that commands restraint and a need to spare non-combatants, lest war be reduced to mere slaughter.[68]

At this point, it is important to highlight that the term "warrior" has acquired a bad reputation of late, due to the deleterious effects of a misguided

61 Robinson, *Honour*, p. 3.

62 Ibid., p. 7.

63 Axinn, *Moral*, p. 40.

64 Ibid., pp. 42; 49.

65 Ibid., pp. 42; 186.

66 Michael Ignatieff, *The Warrior's Honor. Ethnic War and the Modern Conscience* (New York: Holt Paperbacks, 1997), p. 117.

67 Ibid. See also J.F. Verbruggen, *The Art of Warfare in Western Europe During the Middle Ages* (Rochester: The Boydell Press, 1997), p. 58.

68 Ignatieff, *Warrior's*, p. 117.

understanding of the military occupation as an unbridled "warrior-hero culture" or simply "warrior culture" like the one that was allowed to take root and fester in the Australian Special Forces units that were the object of an official inquiry known as the *Brereton Report*, as mentioned in the Introduction. The outcome of that investigation unequivocally states: "Special Forces operators should pride themselves on being model professional soldiers, not on being 'warrior heroes'".[69] On the other hand, there have been some calls to uphold a healthy version of the warrior culture, one that is grounded in the Just War Tradition and helps shaping military professionals who are reliable and humble,[70] as the term 'warrior' still seems to convey an elevated moral standing for combatants,[71] however aspirational. I shall return to the 'warrior-soldier' debate in the Conclusions of this work.

Now, some interesting contributions to the conceptualisation of military honour are the ones provided by Larry May and Shannon French, due to their potential to incorporate the notion of human dignity in the code of the warrior, as shall be seen in the next chapters.

Drawing on the works of Jeremy Bentham, May characterizes honour as "the combination of enhanced respect for normal moral rules plus the respect for special rules that require conscientious reflection and socialized motivation crucial for humanitarian law's requirement that soldiers act with restraint even when their lives are jeopardized on the battlefield".[72] The foregoing is arguably mirrored by the cardinal humanitarian principles of distinction, military necessity, and proportionality,[73] all of which contribute to normatively restrain the waging of war.

Interestingly, May proposes that military honour amounts to "a sense of being morally superior to others as scrupulous followers of moral rules" such that "the primary motivation for humane treatment comes from a sense of self-worth of the person who acts humanely".[74] In the same vein, French argues that the code of honour seems to hold the warrior to a higher ethical

69 Inspector-General of the Australian Defence Force, *Afghanistan Inquiry Report* (Canberra: Commonwealth of Australia, 2020), p. 330.

70 Andrew Hastie, 'SAS must put honour before glory', https://www.adso.org.au/andrew-hastie-sas-must-put-honour-before-glory/, 14 December 2022.

71 Rain Liivoja, 'Law and Honor: Normative Pluralism in the Regulation of Military Conduct', in Jan Klabbers and Touko Piiparinen (eds.), *Normative Pluralism and International Law: Exploring Global Governance* (Cambridge: Cambridge University Press, 2013), p. 145.

72 May, *Crimes*, p. 32.

73 Marco Sassòli and Antoine Bouvier, *How does law protect in war?* (Geneva: ICRC, 1999), p. 115.

74 May, *Crimes*, p. 32. Similarly, see Janowitz, *Professional*, p. 80.

standard than that required from an ordinary citizen. Thus "the code restraints the warrior. It sets boundaries on his behavior. It distinguishes honorable acts from shameful acts," both with reference to friends and foes, so that the warrior can be ultimately distinguished from murderers,[75] aided by the 'mechanisms of honour', i.e. shame and reputation,[76] as well as by a healthy amount of *amour propre* or *pundonor* in Spanish (from the French *point d'honneur*), that is, the satisfaction resulting from fulfilling one's duty and the desire to become a better version of ourselves,[77] which is mirrored by the Aristotelian virtue of "magnanimity", "greatness of soul" or "pride"[78] – a sentiment not unknown to knights as a class.[79] Conversely, moral injury would arguably amount to the deep dissatisfaction arising from the betrayal of our values by society and ourselves.

In other words, honour is a special sense of self-worth characterized by an enhanced respect for moral and legal standards, whose main consequence is the duty to treat others humanely even during combat, "as a way of displaying honor".[80] Christopher Coker has characterized this phenomenon of idiosyncratic self-worth as a new variant of aristocracy within meritocratic societies, as warriors belong to a distinctive minority therein.[81] Thereby, military honour seems to elicit an enhanced type of what Walzer calls self-respect,[82] which is grounded on a specific standard (in this case, the warrior's code), whereby, to paraphrase the author,[83] no self-respecting warrior would commit certain kinds of act even in the heat of battle. As we shall see in the next chapter, notions of rank and nobility do not only help to understand traditional

75 French, *Code*, p. 3.

76 Stefan Oeter, 'The (Non-)Importance of Chivalry in International Humanitarian Law', in Bernhard Koch (ed.), *Chivalrous Combatants? The Meaning of Military Virtue Past and Present* (Baden-Baden: Nomos, 2019), p. 48; Aznar, 'Honor', p. 62. See also on the need for an audience (real or imagined) for honour to make sense, Leo Braudy, *From Chivalry to Terrorism* (New York: Vintage Books, 2005), pp. 87–88; and on the importance of an enhanced capacity for embarrassment when failing to meet societal expectations to fuel bold behaviour, Tim O'Brien, *The Things They Carried* (London: 4th Estate, 2015), pp. 56–57.

77 Cerdá, *Ética*, p. 89.

78 Aristotle, *The Nicomachean Ethics* (New York: Oxford University Press, 2005), IV.3, p. 67.

79 James Turner Johnson, *Just War Tradition and the Restraint of War. A Moral and Historical Inquiry* (Princeton: Princeton University Press, 1984), p. 138.

80 May, *Crimes*, p. 67.

81 Coker, *Warrior*, p. 137.

82 Walzer, *Spheres*, pp. 274–275.

83 Ibid: "No self-respecting doctor would treat a patient like that. No self-respecting trade unionist would agree to such a contract".

concepts like military honour; they can also account for seemingly more contemporary categories such as human dignity.

## 2.4 *Towards a Working Definition of Military Honour*

Building on the foregoing, and before venturing into the theory of human dignity and its possible connections to honour that will be postulated in this investigation, the first analytical step required is the formulation of a working definition of military honour. Such a definition must refer to three distinct, yet connected, dimensions: nature, scope, and content.

### 2.4.1 Nature

First, regarding its nature, it becomes necessary to determine whether military honour is a virtue, a value, a principle, or something else. As indicated before, honour is not listed among the foremost military virtues that have been the subject of a recent collective volume in the specialized literature.[84] The volume lists the following core military virtues, complete with a theoretical introduction to each and practical applications in the form of brief case studies and anecdotes: justice, obedience, loyalty, courage, wisdom, honesty, integrity, perseverance, temperance, patience, humility, compassion, discipline, and professionalism. Military honour is admittedly assimilated by one or more of such virtues, including honesty and integrity.[85]

If treated as a virtue, military honour would have to be framed within the ethical tradition of virtue ethics. This is a point I will revisit in the chapter devoted to Professional Military Education (Chapter 5) in light of the importance virtue ethics is assigned in this subfield of moral philosophy. For now, it suffices to say a few words about virtue ethics.

As it is sufficiently known, virtue ethics is the strand of moral philosophy that focuses on the moral character of a person, rather than on the beneficial/deleterious consequences of an action (like consequentialism); or on the rightful/wrongful act performed by a person duty-bound to follow certain rules (such as the deontological approach).

Instead, virtue ethics centres the attention on a person's character, that is, the total sum of her dispositions to action, or her pattern of behaviour.[86] From such character stems that person's ability to lead a virtuous life throughout

84 Skerker, Whetham and Carrick, *Virtues*.

85 Cook, 'Honesty', pp. 151–155.

86 Simon Blackburn, *The Oxford Dictionary of Philosophy* (Oxford: Oxford University Press, 2005), p. 59.

time, in order to achieve the ultimate goal of human happiness or flourishing (*eudaimonia*).[87] Virtues are to be understood as habits of thought, feeling and action that enable us to choose what is right.[88] Qua habits, virtues can be acquired, trained and developed over time, a key feature for pedagogical processes such as military education and military training, as shall be seen in this inquiry.

Regarding their content, a virtue or *aretê* (ancient Greek for 'excellency') is the moderate middle ground or mean between two extremes, e.g. the virtue of courage amounting to the middle ground between the vicious extremes of cowardice and recklessness.[89]

Yet, if military honour is not considered as a virtue *per se* in the specialized literature, perhaps it could be construed as a reward for virtuous behaviour, much like Peter Olsthoorn has suggested,[90] and as Montesquieu himself saw honour originally.[91] As Aristotle puts it: "honour is the prize of virtue".[92] However, Olsthoorn concedes that this conceptualization of honour as a reward brings forth a problematic aspect of the concept, what he dubs the "inauthentic side" of honour insofar as it entails doing the right or honourable thing not for right's sake, but for the reward or prestige attached as a price – or perhaps as a decoration, such as the fabled *Légion d'honneur* or the famous *Congressional Medal of Honor*. In the end, he concludes, this side of honour still renders a service to morality inasmuch as it provides an additional motivation to do the right thing alongside our own conscience.[93] I shall return to honour as a reward in the Conclusions of this work.

If not a virtue or a reward for virtuous behaviour, perhaps honour can be considered as a *value*, like in the case of the U.S. Army and the Chilean Army, or as a *principle*, as it is conceived by the Japanese National Defence Academy. The U.S. Army indeed treats honour as a summative value of sorts that epitomizes all its other values (loyalty, duty, respect, selfless service, integrity, and

87 Aristotle, *The Nicomachean Ethics* (New York: Oxford University Press, 2005), I.4, p. 5.

88 David Fisher, 'Why morality matters to the military', in Don Carrick, James Connelly and David Whetham (eds.), *Making the Military Moral. Contemporary Challenges and Responses in Military Ethics Education* (New York: Routledge, 2018), p. 17.

89 Matt McCormick, 'Is it wrong to play violent video games?', *Ethics and Information Technology*, 3:4 (2001), pp. 277–287.

90 Olsthoorn, *Military*, p. 40.

91 Spector, 'Montesquieu'.

92 Aristotle, *Ethics*, IV.3, p. 68.

93 Olsthoorn, *Military*, pp. 15–16.

personal courage).[94] According to legal philosopher Robert Alexy, principles differ from values in that the former belong to the dimension of deontological imperatives whereby adherence to a rule or maxim is paramount (mainly within the legal domain); whereas values fall under the dominion of the axiological appraisal of what is to be considered *good* (i.e. the moral domain).[95] Now, military honour is a normative standard that belongs to both the ethical and the legal dimensions of the military professional. Consequently, military honour, as a normative concept, can be conceived of as either a moral value or a legal principle – in the latter case, being operationalized by such legal notions as the *lex artis* standard of behaviour that is expected of specific professionals such as lawyers or doctors when they perform their service to society.[96]

Further, from a philosophical standpoint, military honour can also be conceived of as an 'ideal rule' in the sense defined by Georg Von Wright. According to this author, the concept of 'norm' can be classified into six distinct types: (i) *prescriptions* guiding human behaviour under pain of punishment by the state; (ii) *rules* formally defining practices or systems such as languages, math or games; (iii) *directives* guiding us to achieve certain goals through the appropriate means; (iv) *customs* observed by a given community; (v) *moral principles* intrinsically connected to the value-notions of good and evil; and (vi) *ideal rules*.[97] Ideal rules are those standards concerned not with *doing*, but with *being*:

> Ideal rules are referred to for example when we say that a man ought to be generous, truthful, just, temperate, etc., and also when we say that a soldier in the army should be brave, hardy and disciplined; a schoolmaster patient with children, firm and understanding; a watchman alert, observant and resolute; and so forth (…).
>
> The person who has the properties of a good so-and-so in a supreme degree we often call an *ideal* so-and-so (…). The features which ideal

---

94 U.S. Army, 'ADRP-1: The Army Profession', https://irp.fas.org/doddir/army/adrp1.pdf, 25 May 2023, p. B-5. Similarly, see Jeremy Waldron's treatment of dignity as a status that abbreviates a 'package' of human rights. Jeremy Waldron, 'Is Dignity the Foundation of Human Rights?', *NYU Public Law and Legal Theory Research Paper Series*, 12–73 (2013), pp. 1–29.

95 Robert Alexy, *Teoría de los Derechos Fundamentales* (Madrid: Centro de Estudios Constitucionales, 1993), pp. 138–141.

96 Alejandro Pacheco Gómez, 'The incorporation of lex artis in the Law', *Mexican Bioethics Review ICSa*, 3:6 (2022), pp. 21–25.

97 Georg Von Wright, *Norm and Action* (London: Routledge & Kegan Paul, 1963), pp. 1–16.

> rules require to be present in good members of a class or kind of human beings can be termed the *virtues* characteristic of men of that class or kind (original emphasis).[98]

To be sure, the military profession is the quintessential occupation for the man and woman of *action*, so this type of norm associated with *being* instead of *doing* might not be entirely appropriate. Yet, Von Wright's characterization of ideal rules conveys the notion of an ideal every member of the armed forces should strive to achieve and emulate, as an aspirational archetype that inspires people to overcome difficulties and work on perfecting their character. In that sense, the 'honourable soldier', or the goal of 'becoming honourable'[99] could be an ideal rule or standard, enshrined in different codes of conduct, that many men and women in uniform are ready to live up to in order to become better professionals.

### 2.4.2 Scope

What about the scope of military honour? What relevant social universe should this 'honour world' or *timopolis* comprise? Since we are dealing with a value or principle that pertains to a specific professional group, the military honour world should include the members of the armed forces of states who have made of the 'management of violence' their trade.[100] That is, military professionals make up the relevant honour world or *timopolis* when it comes to military honour.

The term 'professional' here will be used to signify not only members of the commissioned officers class, but all of those belonging to the armed forces of states, from the rank and file to non-commissioned officers to the top brass – although the PMEt literature has not traditionally focused on the training and education of the lower ranks, a trend that is slowly starting to be reversed.[101]

---

98 Ibid., p. 14.

99 Janowitz, *Professional*, p. 215.

100 Samuel Huntington, *The Soldier and the State* (Cambridge: Harvard University Press, 2000), p. 11.

101 Janne Aalto, 'Challenges in combining ethical education for conscripts and professional military', Don Carrick, James Connelly and David Whetham (eds.), *Making the Military Moral. Contemporary Challenges and Responses in Military Ethics Education* (New York: Routledge, 2018), pp. 107–125.

It becomes necessary here to clarify that the honour world that will be the focus of this inquiry will not include non-state armed groups, despite their active engagement in most contemporary armed conflicts.[102]

Now, there are two main reasons for the exclusion of non-state actors in this study: (i) first, not all of these actors possess a body of principles or sources bearing on PMEt, since they are not technically 'professionals' offering a service that is of use to society.[103] They may be willing to abide by ethical standards for both strategic and principled reasons,[104] but access to the sources codifying such standards is much more difficult than state sources, which are public documents.[105] (ii) Second, respect for human dignity is, above all, a legal commitment entered to by states as the main subjects of international law, their militaries acting as 'agents or stewards of human dignity', as will be explained in subsequent chapters. Since non-sate armed groups cannot participate in international legal life to the same extent, they lack the ability to undertake such commitments with other legal subjects, unless in very exceptional circumstances limited to cease-fires and peace agreements. Should they prevail in an armed conflict and form a government within a state, then these non-state groups by definition cease to exist as such and become full-fledged subjects of international law.

The foregoing does not mean that non-state actors cannot strive to emulate the virtuous or honourable behaviour of the *timopolis* housing the group of professional military men and women across the world – and they are, in fact, encouraged to do so by civil society and by organisations such as the International Committee of the Red Cross and Geneva Call. Yet, the ethical and

102 SIPRI, 'Global developments in armed conflicts, peace processes and peace operations', https://www.sipri.org/yearbook/2021/02, 1 March 2022.

103 Huntington, *Soldier*, p. 9.

104 Francisco Lobo, 'Parody or deadly-serious commitment? Non-state armed groups upholding humanitarian standards in war', (https://www.kcl.ac.uk/parody-or-deadly-serious-commitment-non-state-armed-groups-upholding-humanitarian-standards-in-war), 08 June 2022; Olivier Bangerter, 'Reasons why armed groups choose to respect international humanitarian law or not', *International Review of the Red Cross*, 93:882 (2011), pp. 353–384; Hyeron Jo, Joshua K. Alley, Yohan Park, and Soren Jordan, 'Signaling restraint: international engagement and rebel groups' commitment to international law', *International Interactions*, 47:5 (2021), pp. 928–954. For an overview of some of the ethical dilemmas arising from the use of non-state actors to fight Ukraine's defensive war against Russia, see Thomas Gibbons-Neff, 'In Ukraine, Killings of Surrendering Russians Divide an American-Led Unit', https://www.nytimes.com/2024/07/06/world/europe/ukraine-russia-killings-us.html, 7 July 2024.

105 Although there is an impressive database curated by the Geneva Call organisation, titled "Their Words". See Geneva Call, 'Their Words', http://theirwords.org/, 1 March 2022.

political motivations of non-state actors to abide by legal and moral standards of behaviour are beyond the scope of this inquiry.[106]

### 2.4.3 Content

Finally, as for the content of military honour, it should be noted once again that it corresponds to what Ronald Dworkin calls an interpretive concept. It is worth reiterating that this entails: (i) the assumption that the practice in question has value, that is, it serves some interest or purpose or enforces some principle, and therefore there is a point to it; and (ii) that the requirements of the practice are not immutable but are sensitive to its point, such that the rules have to be applied, interpreted, extended or modified according to said point or purpose.

In that sense, according to the relevant literature, the contents required by military honour correspond to behaviour that satisfies the virtues of prowess, courage, loyalty, truthfulness, and mercy.

Under this light, it could arguably be said that the point or purpose of the notion of military honour is to endow the managers of professional violence with a normative standard especially tailored for their activity such that they are able to use force in the most restrained, effective, and rational way possible in any situation of armed conflict, thus being able to distinguish themselves from mere murderers.

From such a point or goal stem two major implications building on what has been explained in this chapter: (i) to the extent they abide by the particular code of honour bearing on their profession, the military get to experience the special type of self-worth described by May and French; and (ii) the code of military honour demands a particular kind of recognition respect, in the sense that the military belong to an institution that possesses a feature that society values and respects, and therefore they benefit from that recognition, becoming part of their identity and feeding the aforementioned sense of self-worth or self-respect. Conversely, the lack of such recognition due to the betrayal of moral beliefs shared by the soldier and society results in moral injury.

Further, regarding the kind of respect the military are not only owed but are expected to give, this is a special case of what Appiah calls 'positive recognition respect' whereby a positive attitude develops evincing that we esteem people highly as our 'honour peers'. As we shall see in the next chapters, human

106 For a brief reflection on this topic, see Francisco Lobo, 'Parody or deadly-serious commitment? Non-state armed groups upholding humanitarian standards in war', (https://www.kcl.ac.uk/parody-or-deadly-serious-commitment-non-state-armed-groups-upholding-humanitarian-standards-in-war), 08 June 2022.

dignity plays a particular role in the development and upholding of such positive recognition respect.

### 2.4.4 Proposed Working Definition of Military Honour

Based on the foregoing, a working definition of military honour is the following:

> Military honour is a normative standard, in the form of a principle, value or ideal, that is applicable to a particular honour world comprising all those professionals of arms belonging to state armed forces. The contents of this normative standard include the military virtues of prowess, courage, loyalty, truthfulness, and mercy. As a result of observing such contents, military honour can be construed as a reward for virtuous behaviour, while at the same time instilling a special sense of self-worth in the honourable individual and demanding a particular type of positive recognition respect from society.

•••

Equipped with this working definition, the next chapter will delve into the concept of human dignity to provide further analytical clarity for establishing the connection between the notions of military honour and human dignity that is the main focus of this conceptual-normative inquiry, after which the best pedagogical devices to instil said normative contents in the military are further explored.

CHAPTER 3

# Human Dignity

> That expression, dignity of man, once uttered by Kant, afterward became the shibboleth of all the perplexed and empty-headed moralists who concealed behind that imposing expression their lack of any real basis of morals, or, at any rate, of one that had any meaning.
>
> ARTHUR SCHOPENHAUER

∴

## 1 The Quest for the Holy Grail

Human dignity is a ubiquitous term. It is used so often and with so many different meanings that it would be only fair to pay the word 'extra' for all the work it is being put to do, to recall Humpty Dumpty's economics from Lewis Carroll's *Through the Looking Glass*.[1] Indeed, *pace* Schopenhauer and his proverbial bitterness, human dignity has become a household expression in our times. It has been characterized as the most fundamental legal concept.[2] Featuring in a growing number of constitutional texts,[3] human dignity is also mentioned in a plethora of preambles to international human rights treaties and instruments,[4]

1 "'When I make a word do a lot of work like that,' said Humpty Dumpty, 'I always pay it extra'". See Lewis Carroll, *Alice's Adventures in Wonderland & Through the Looking Glass* (London: MacMillam, 2016), p. 211.

2 Manuel Atienza, *Sobre la dignidad humana* (Madrid: Trotta, 2022), p. 11.

3 Qerim Qerimi, 'Dignity in *transition*: the constitutional and operational potential and limits of human dignity seen from the lens of post-conflict societies', *The International Journal of Human Rights*, No. 8 (2021), pp. 1211–1232.

4 Including the UN Charter, the Universal Declaration of Human Rights, the American Declaration of the Rights and Duties of Man, the International Covenants on Civil and Political Rights and on Economic, Social and Cultural Rights, the American Convention on Human Rights, the African Charter on Human and People's Rights, the Arab Charter on Human Rights, the Convention for the Protection of Human Rights and Dignity of the Human Being in Biomedicine, Protocol No. 13 to the European Convention on Human Rights, and the ASEAN Human Rights Declaration, among others.

 | DOI:10.1163/9789004754096_006

to the extent that it has even been recently used to ground a so-called "human right to friendship".[5]

Furthermore, as it is sufficiently known international law regulates war both directly, through the set of rules and principles known as International Humanitarian Law ('IHL') or the Law of Armed Conflict ('LOAC');[6] and indirectly, through the backdrop normative subsystem known as International Human Rights Law ('IHRL'), which does not cease to be applicable in times of war.[7] Both legal systems share the same bedrock value: human dignity.[8] Indeed, opinions by international human rights tribunals confirm the relevance of dignity as a cornerstone of that legal system.[9] International Humanitarian Law, on its part, enshrines respect for human dignity in Common Article 3 of the 1949 Geneva Conventions. This rule has been characterized by the International Court of Justice as reflecting customary law and as a 'minimum yardstick' by which the conduct of every state engaged in war must be measured.[10] Respect for human dignity under IHL extends even to those who have already seen the end of war, the dead.[11]

---

5 Jon Wittrock, 'A human right to friendship? Dignity, autonomy, and social deprivation', *The International Journal of Human Rights*, 26:9 (2022), pp. 1590–1607.

6 David Luban, 'Military Lawyers and the Two Cultures Problem', *Georgetown Public Law and Legal Theory Research Paper*, No. 12-057 (2012), pp. 1–55.

7 International Court of Justice (ICJ), *Legality of the Threat or Use of Nuclear Weapons, Advisory Opinion, I.C.J. Reports 1996*, p. 226, par. 25; ICJ, *Legal Consequences of the Construction of a Wall in the Occupied Palestinian Territory. Advisory Opinion, I.C.J. Reports 2004*, p. 136, par. 106; ICJ, *Armed Activities on the Territory of the Congo (Democratic Republic of Congo v. Uganda), Judgement, I.C.J. Reports 2005*, p. 168, par. 216; Human Rights Committee, 'General Comment No 36 (2018) on article 6 of the International Covenant on Civil and Political Rights, on the right to life', https://tbinternet.ohchr.org/Treaties/CCPR/Shared%20 Documents/1_Global/CCPR_C_GC_36_8785_E.pdf, 22 March 2022, par. 64; Philip Alston and Ryan Goodman, *International Human Rights* (Oxford: Oxford University Press, 2013), p. 412; Theodor Meron, *Standing Up for Justice* (New York: Oxford University Press, 2021), pp. 103–115.

8 International Criminal Tribunal for the Former Yugoslavia, Trial Chamber, *Prosecutor v. Anto Furundzija*, Judgment, 10 December 1998, Case No. IT-95-17/1-T, par. 183.

9 Inter-American Court of Human Rights, Case of the "Street Children" (Villagran-Morales et al) v. Guatemala, Judgment of November 19, 1999 (*Merits*), pars. 144; 191; European Court of Human Rights, Pretty v. The United Kingdom (*Application no. 2346/02*), Fourth Section, Judgment of 29 April 2002, par. 65.

10 ICJ, *Military and Paramilitary Activities in and against Nicaragua (Nicaragua v. United States), Merits, Judgment, I.C.J. Reports 1986*, p. 14, par. 218.

11 Edward Madziwa, 'Advancing honour and dignity in death for victims of armed conflicts: Exploring the challenges and opportunities of AI and machine learning in humanitarian forensic action under IHL', *International Review of the Red Cross*, 106: 926 (2024), pp. 760–794.

Beyond domestic and international law, and as a testament to its declared "amphibious" nature, dignity is also a familiar concept in political discourse,[12] as well as an essential component of contemporary international relations, as evinced by President Biden's pledge to uphold dignity and human rights, issued before his first international trip in June of 2021.[13] Over a year later, in the midst of the Russian invasion of Ukraine, President Zelensky would remark that his country and the EU share the same values, among them human dignity.[14] Accordingly, a few months later the head of the U.S. Agency for International Development ('USAID') would remark: "America and all who share our values – the world's democracies, allies in the private sector, civil society, multilateral institutions, religious and diaspora communities, everyday citizens – all of us must build on the unity that we have demonstrated in Ukraine to try to extend a broader *revolution of dignity* to people seeking to be free"[15] (emphasis added).

But what is human dignity exactly as a normative concept? As a term found in several international treaties, we may draw on the interpretive criteria used in international law to ascertain the meaning of such words, pursuant to Art. 31(1) of the Vienna Convention on the Law of Treaties, which sets forth the general rule of interpretation: "A treaty shall be interpreted in good faith in accordance with the *ordinary meaning* to be given to the terms of the treaty in their context and in the light of its object and purpose" (added emphasis). But can we really access the 'ordinary meaning' of such a protean word as 'dignity'? Is this interpretive legal rule enough to help us solve the puzzle of this compelling concept, or is an additional analytical endeavour required?

A theory that can successfully explain the notion of human dignity has been dubbed "the Holy Grail of human rights",[16] not least as dignity is also

---

12 Bearing on issues as diverse as refugees, poverty, abortion, suicide, bioethics, democracy, free speech, gay rights, torture, discrimination, privacy, forced labour, and religious freedom, among others. See Pablo Gilabert, *Human Dignity and Human Rights* (New York: Oxford University Press, 2018), pp. 114; 157.

13 Joe Biden, 'My trip to Europe is about America rallying the world's democracies', https://www.washingtonpost.com/opinions/2021/06/05/joe-biden-europe-trip-agenda/, 7 June 2021.

14 'We share common values – Zelensky after talks with von der Leyen', https://interfax.com.ua/news/general/822505.html, 9 April 2022.

15 'Samantha Power's democracy promotion plan', https://www.devex.com/news/devex-newswire-samantha-power-s-democracy-promotion-plan-103414?utm_campaign=wp_todays_worldview&utm_medium=email&utm_source=newsletter&wpisrc=nl_todayworld, 17 June 2022. On the 2013–2014 'Revolution of Dignity' in Ukraine, see Serhii Plokhy, *The Russo-Ukrainian War* (London: Allen Lane, 2023), p. 95.

16 Christopher McCrudden, "Human Dignity and Judicial Interpretation of Human Rights," *The European Journal of International Law* 19:4 (2008): 677.

considered to be "the moral heart of human rights".[17] This chapter aims to provide more conceptual clarity to a term that is readily used but not always well understood, as a required analytical step to bridge the gap between military honour and human dignity in the next chapter.

## 2 Human Dignity as an Essentially Contested Concept

### 2.1 *Theoretical Pedigree*

The core value of human dignity is admittedly hard to define, so much so that it has been characterized as an "essentially contested concept",[18] like "democracy", "art", "justice",[19] or "the rule of law".[20] The longstanding history of dignity as a normative category only adds complexity to the challenge of its conceptualization.[21] But what is an essentially contested concept?

The analytical distinction between 'concepts' and 'conceptions' entered the lexicon of legal theory arguably thanks to the work of Ronald Dworkin. In *Law's Empire*, Dworkin explains the difference in order to characterize the law itself as what he calls an 'interpretive concept',[22] as we saw in the previous chapter. Thus, Dworkin suggests that:

> The contrast between concept and conception is here a contrast between levels of abstraction at which the interpretation of the practice can be studied. At the first level agreement collects around discrete ideas that

17 Gilabert, *Dignity*, p. 113.

18 Philippe-André Rodriguez, 'Human dignity as an essentially contested concept', *Cambridge Review of International Affairs*, 28:4 (2015), pp. 743–756.

19 W.B. Gallie, 'Essentially Contested Concepts', *Proceedings of the Aristotelian Society*, 56 (1955–1956), pp. 167–198.

20 Jeremy Waldron, 'Is the Rule of Law and Essentially Contested Concept (in Florida)', *Law and Philosophy*, 21 (2002), pp. 137–164.

21 See Michael Rosen, *Dignity. It's History and Meaning* (Cambridge: Harvard University Press, 2012); Remy Debes (ed.), *Dignity. A History* (New York: Oxford University Press, 2017); Christopher McCrudden (ed.), *Understanding Human Dignity* (Oxford: Oxford University Press, 2015); McCrudden, 'Judicial', pp. 655–724; Marcus Düwell, Jens Braarvig, Roger Brownsword, and Dietmar Mieth (eds.), *The Cambridge Handbook of Human Dignity* (Cambridge: Cambridge University Press, 2014).

22 In his late works Dworkin would come to characterize dignity itself as such an interpretive concept. See Ronald Dworkin, *Justice for Hedgehogs* (Cambridge: Belknap Press, 2011), p. 204.

> are uncontroversially employed in all interpretations; at the second the controversy latent in this abstraction is identified and taken up.[23]

However, the distinction between concept and conception could be already found in the literature as early as 1971, when John Rawls published his seminal work *A Theory of Justice.* At the outset of his book Rawls remarks: "Thus it seems natural to think of the concept of justice as distinct from the various conceptions of justice and as being specified by the role which these different sets of principles, these different conceptions, have in common".[24] Thereby, Rawls' account would be one more among many other possible *conceptions* of the more abstract *concept* of justice.

Moreover, Rawls himself traces the pedigree of the distinction back to H.L.A. Hart's *The Concept of Law*, published a decade earlier. Indeed, after referring to the protean nature of the term 'justice' – which can be easily applied to distributions, compensations, judges, trials, and convictions – Hart states: "The general principle latent in these diverse applications of the idea of justice is that individuals are entitled in respect of each other to a certain relative position of equality or inequality".[25] Further on, Hart explains:

> There is therefore a certain complexity in the structure of the idea of justice. We may say that it consists of two parts: a uniform or constant feature, summarized in the precept 'Treat like cases alike' and a shifting or varying criterion used in determining when, for any given purpose, cases are alike or different. In this respect justice is like the notions of what is genuine, or tall, or warm, which contain an implicit reference to a standard which varies with the classification of the thing to which they are applied.[26]

At first glance, Hart obviously does not employ the concept-conception divide quite as literally as Rawls or Dworkin. However, the relevant structural difference is still recognizable in Hart's words – the 'uniform or constant feature' amounting to the uncontroversial 'concept', and the 'shifting or varying criterion' corresponding to the many 'conceptions' thereof.

Yet, what is still lacking in Hart's account is reference to the original author of the analytical distinction between concept and conceptions, Walter Bryce

23 Ronald Dworkin, *Law's Empire* (Oxford: Hart Publishing, 1998), p. 71.
24 John Rawls, *A Theory of Justice* (Cambridge: Belknap Press, 2005), p. 5.
25 H.L.A. Hart, *The Concept of Law*, 3rd edition (Oxford: Oxford University Press, 2012), p. 159.
26 Ibid., p. 160.

Gallie. In a rather obscure publication from 1956, titled *Essentially Contested Concepts*, Gallie for the first time introduced the distinction between concepts and contested uses thereof. Although concepts "usually carry with them an assumption of agreement",[27] Gallie contends:

> We find groups of people disagreeing about the proper use of the concepts, *e.g.*, of art, democracy, of the Christian tradition. When we examine the different uses of these terms and the characteristic arguments in which they figure we soon see that there is no one clearly definable general use of any of them which can be set up as the correct or standard use.[28]

Thus, the original account distinguished between 'concepts' and 'uses' thereof, which eventually became known – through the contributions of personalities such as Hart, Rawls and Dworkin – as the difference between 'concepts' and 'conceptions', however preserving intact the *structural* distinction between levels of abstraction throughout its uses in the literature.

Now, according to Gallie an essentially contested concept can be identified through the following traits: (i) it is 'appraisive' inasmuch as it entails judgments of value or achievement;[29] (ii) the referred value or achievement is 'internally complex', meaning that the positive judgment is assigned to the concept as a whole, not just to some of its parts; (iii) there are a number of possible rival descriptions of its total worth, which is also called 'ambiguity' by Gallie; (iv) the achievement must be adaptable to changing circumstances (not unlike Dworkin's 'interpretive concepts' as we saw in the previous chapter[30]), a trait which Gallie also labels 'openness' or 'persistent vagueness'; (v) essentially contested concepts – or rather conceptions or uses therefrom – are used both aggressively and defensively – i.e. to criticize and to reply to criticism vis-à-vis competing conceptions; (vi) the concept derives from an original exemplar or paradigm of uncontested authority among rival accounts; and (vii) the

---

27 W.B. Gallie, 'Essentially Contested Concepts', *Proceedings of the Aristotelian Society*, 56 (1955–1956), p. 167.

28 Ibid., p. 168.

29 It is in this appraisive sense that the term 'dignitarianism' as a normative stance may be better understood. According to Pablo Gilabert "Dignitarianism is a type of normative approach according to which at least some of the central norms concerning the treatment of individual entities depend on their inherent dignity". See Gilabert, *Dignity*, p. 191.

30 As I shall explain in the next chapter when I attempt to establish the connection between military honour and human dignity, an interpretive concept is not necessarily an essentially contested concept.

probability that the continuous competition between rival accounts will benefit rather than harm the original exemplar, so as to be "sustained and/or developed in optimum fashion".[31]

This last feature has been cast under a positive light by Jeremy Waldron. Reflecting on what he calls the "Florida debacle" referring to recounting of votes in the American presidential election of 2000, Waldron asks whether the notion of the 'rule of law', many a time invoked during that particular episode in American politics, could be labelled as an 'essentially contested concept'. At the core of these concepts, Waldron submits, lies contestation as their defining trait, not merely as an accidental feature of such concepts' penumbra.[32] Echoing John Stuart Mill's famous defence for pluralist debate so as to enhance freedom of speech and ultimately human knowledge,[33] Waldron believes that "the contestation between rival conceptions deepens and enriches all sides' understanding of the area of value that the contested concept marks out".[34] To illustrate this, Waldron holds that "we are sure we live under a Constitution in the United States, precisely because we argue so much about what the Constitution means".[35]

But what else can count as an essentially contested concept besides the examples given in their respective accounts by Gallie – i.e. art, democracy and Christianity – and Waldron – i.e. the rule of law and the Constitution? Waldron points out that a simple online search reveals a large list of concepts able to be characterized as 'essentially contested'. Among the foremost there is autonomy, citizenship, the Constitution, corruption, discrimination, equality, freedom, merit, popular sovereignty, power, proportionality, public interest, rights and sustainable development.[36] There has even been an attempt at characterizing politics itself as an essentially contested concept that is pragmatically

31 Gallie, 'Essentially', pp. 171–180.

32 Jeremy Waldron, 'Is the Rule of Law and Essentially Contested Concept (in Florida)', *Law and Philosophy*, 21 (2002), p. 149.

33 John Stuart Mill, *On Liberty* (New York: The Liberal Arts Press, 1956), p. 25.

34 Waldron, op. cit. (2002), p. 152.

35 Ibid., p. 163.

36 The rest of the list comprises alienation, author, bankruptcy, boycott, civil rights, coherence, community, competition, culture, diversity, equal protection, harm, justification, liberalism, motherhood, the national interest, nature, pornography, privacy, property, prosperity, prostitution, punishment, reasonable expectations, religion, republicanism, sovereignty, speech, and textuality. See Waldron, ob. cit. (2002), p. 149, at footnote 31. For an excellent account on how the concept-conception distinction is applied in human rights adjudication in the inter-American system of human rights, see Claudio Nash, *La concepción de derechos fundamentales en Latinoamérica* (Mexico D.F.: Fontamara, 2010).

self-replicating, whereby a particular political view is advanced to encourage similar political action congruent with it.[37]

What about human dignity? Could it be construed also as an essentially contested concept? Recent scholarship suggests that it can, a proposal I examine next.

### 2.2 *Human Dignity as an Essentially Contested Concept*

For all its conceptual hegemony, the notion of human dignity remains surprisingly ambiguous and contested. As Jacques Maritain admitted when asked about the philosophical debate preceding the Universal Declaration of Human Rights, a document that would enshrine human dignity as a foreground principle: "we agree about the rights but on condition no one asks us why".[38] It was Virginia Gildersleeve, the American delegate at the conference, who proposed replacing 'sanctity' with 'dignity' in the 1948 Declaration.[39] Admittedly, in this way human dignity acquired the kind of legal articulation that makes practical action possible despite there being disagreement.[40]

The above notwithstanding, recent scholarship has taken up the challenge of delving deeper into the conceptual density of human dignity.[41] In a publication titled *Human dignity as an essentially contested concept*,[42] Philippe-André Rodriguez has made a most remarkable effort to resurface the all but forgotten theoretical origins of the concept-conception divide by applying the framework originally devised by Gallie to the notion of 'human dignity'.

Despite Meir Dan-Cohen's recent propositions to the contrary – according to whom "there appear to be a number of concepts of dignity in circulation, too dissimilar even to be thought of as different conceptions of one concept"[43] – Rodriguez argues that the idea of human dignity can be readily described as an essentially contested concept from which different competing conceptions stem. After briefly explaining Gallie's seven conditions of essential

37 William E. Connolly, *The Terms of Political Discourse*. 3rd ed. (Princeton: Princeton University Press, 1993), pp. 12–22; 30.

38 James Griffin, *On Human Rights* (Oxford: Oxford University Press, 2013), p. 25.

39 Ginevra Le Moli, *Human Dignity in International Law* (Cambridge: Cambridge University Press, 2021), p. 123.

40 Jeremy Waldron, *Law and Disagreement* (Oxford: Clarendon Press, 1999).

41 For a practical application of such scholarship see Francisco Lobo, 'A conception of human dignity. The normative case against female genital mutilation', *Journal of Human Dignity and Wellbeing*, 7 (2019), pp. 80–98.

42 Philippe-André Rodriguez, 'Human dignity as an essentially contested concept', *Cambridge Review of International Affairs*, 28:4 (2015), pp. 743–756.

43 Meir Dan-Cohen. 'A Concept of Dignity', *Israel Law Review*, 44:9 (2011), pp. 9–23.

contestability, Rodriguez adds one of his own following Kenneth Ehrenberg, namely: (viii) the usefulness of conceiving a concept as essentially contested (the 'usefulness test').[44]

Applying the original 'Gallie's conditions' to the notion of human dignity, Rodriguez concludes that human dignity is an appraisive concept (condition i), which is used both aggressively and defensively (condition v).[45] Or as Andrea Gattini similarly suggests, human dignity is a two-edged sword capable of fostering either liberal or conservative views,[46] as each edge of the sword may be used to advance those respective agendas as appropriate. With its many iterations, human dignity has also proven undoubtedly open or persistently vague throughout history (condition iv).[47] It also seems straightforward enough to Rodriguez that dignity is an internally complex concept (condition ii), with regards to which different rival descriptions of its total worth have been set forth (condition iii), with some of them emphasizing rights, whereas others put stress on duties stemming from the concept. Rodriguez even provides examples of some of the foremost of those competing descriptions, including those of Jeremy Waldron, Ronald Dworkin, and Jürgen Habermas.[48]

As for condition vi, i.e. reference to an original exemplar of the concept of dignity, Rodriguez points out that in the Western tradition such exemplars are found in Cicero's account of human dignity as a higher standing of human beings as rational creatures, or in Kant's canonical characterization of dignity as inner worth.[49] Still, Rodriguez admits that the original exemplar criterion is much too open to criticism unless it can be widened from one single example into a tradition comprising a set of paradigmatic examples. The most recent of such examples in human history would be the heinous crimes committed during the 20th century, including the Holocaust and Rwanda, although Rodriguez admits that they actually provide examples of what human dignity is opposed

44 Rodriguez, 'Human', p. 746.

45 A good illustration of such dual use of the concept of dignity may be found in the U.S. Supreme Court's 2022 opinion overruling the *Roe v. Wade* and *Casey* precedents on abortion rights. In the decision, Justice Kavanaugh's concurring opinion recalls that pro-life activists uphold the human dignity of the foetus, whereas Justices Breyer's, Sotomayor's and Kagan's dissenting opinion point to the autonomy and dignity of the woman to make her own choices. See *Dobbs v. Jackson Women's Health Organization*, 597 U.S. __ (2022), Kavanaugh, J., concurring, p. 1; Breyer, Sotomayor, and Kagan, JJ., dissenting, pp. 40, 52.

46 Andrea Gattini, 'Setting the Scene: 100 Years of Human Dignity', in Andrea Gattini, Rosana Garciandia and Philippa Webb, *Human Dignity and International Law* (Leiden: Brill-Nijhoff, 2021), p. 7.

47 Rodriguez, 'Human', p. 746.

48 Ibid., p. 748.

49 Ibid., p. 749.

to, rather than a positive instantiation thereof.[50] Thus, as Hannah Arendt puts it reflecting on the horrors brought about by totalitarianism: "human dignity needs a new guarantee which can be found only in a new political principle, in a new law on earth".[51]

The last of Gallie's conditions, the 'progressive competition criterion' (condition vii), is put under suspicion by Rodriguez, since not every debate about an essentially contested concept would necessarily be of a high level thereby 'enriching and deepening' the concept. Rather, it is only from the eighth criterion proposed by Rodriguez, the 'usefulness test', that a concept's characterization as 'essentially contested' can be ultimately assessed.[52]

Thus, Rodriguez holds that there is still some value to the use of the concept of human dignity, however essentially contested, because "Affirming that people have an inherent dignity implies both that they will keep it regardless of whether they are respected or not and that their value will not fluctuate through their existence".[53] As soon as the competing descriptions of the concept of human dignity start cooperating with each other, Rodriguez concludes, the concept and the promise of protection for the human being that it holds will be enhanced. "For human dignity, however, this cooperation has yet to occur. From 1945 until the last decade or so, human dignity was not properly assessed in the academic literature, something that undermined the potential for decontestation. However, with the great revival of interest in the concept in the last few years, this process could be on its way".[54]

In what follows I will examine the academic output of such renewed interest in the form of four major conceptions of human dignity.

## 3 Competing Conceptions of Human Dignity

Upon examination, the relevant literature shows that there are at least four main competing conceptions of human dignity:[55] a) the welfare conception;

---

50 Ibid., pp. 749–750. See also Jürgen Habermas, 'The concept of human dignity and the realistic utopia of human rights', *Metaphilosophy* 41:4 (2010), p. 466.

51 Hannah Arendt, *The Origins of Totalitarianism*, 2nd ed. (Cleveland: Meridian Books, 1962), p. ix. See also Jeffrey C. Isaac, 'A New Guarantee on Earth: Hannah Arendt on Human Dignity and the Politics of Human Rights', *The American Political Science Review*, 90:1 (1996), pp. 61–73.

52 Rodriguez, 'Human', p. 750.

53 Ibid., p. 751.

54 Ibid., p. 753.

55 Francisco Lobo, 'A conception', pp. 80–98; Francisco Lobo, 'Aborto y Diversas Concepciones de Dignidad Humana', *Libertades Públicas, Colección Breviarios*, 8 (2017), pp. 1–19.

b) the autonomy conception; c) the *imago Dei* conception; and d) the rank conception. I shall examine each of them in this section.

### 3.1 *The Welfare Conception*

The welfare conception of dignity stresses the importance of the material conditions of a life of 'dignified existence'. It has been most beautifully epitomized by a Friedrich Schiller's epigram published in 1798: "give him food and shelter; When you have covered his nakedness, dignity will follow by itself".[56] A few years earlier, Schiller had defined dignity as resisting to natural instinct so as to acquire the necessary freedom for action, a task that can be undertaken only thanks to the power of the will. Schiller believed that "Mastery of instinct by moral force is *freedom of mind*, and *dignity* is the name of its epiphany".[57] Overall, we may say that Schiller's conception highlights the importance of material conditions of minimum wellbeing such that the will may undertake the Herculean task of resisting to natural inclinations.

The welfare conception of dignity also found its way from the German Romanticism of *Sturm und Drang* into political action in the 19th century. The European social revolutions at the time were concerned with the notion of the 'dignity of labour' as one of the linchpins of the struggle of working classes for equality of welfare – though Karl Marx himself promptly dismissed the idea of dignity as a mere 'refuge from history in morality'.[58] As we shall see, even Catholic doctrine at the time embraced the concept of the dignity of labour, albeit with characteristics of its own.[59]

Eventually, this materialistic conception of dignity made its way into positive law in the 20th century. It was first included under the phrasing "achieving a dignified life for everyone" in article 151 of the Weimar Republic's 1919 Constitution, an instrument rife with the *ethos* of social rights.[60] Later on, this conception was enshrined in the Universal Declaration of Human Rights issued in 1948. Article 23 of the Declaration sets forth the human right to work and to equal pay. In its third paragraph, this article establishes: "Everyone who works has the right to just and favourable remuneration ensuring for himself and his family an existence worthy of human dignity, and supplemented, if necessary, by other means of social protection".

---

56 McCrudden, 'Judicial', p. 660.

57 Friedrich Schiller, 'On Grace and Dignity', https://archive.schillerinstitute.com/educ/aesthetics/Schiller_On_Grace_and_Dignity.pdf, 7 April 2021, p. 374.

58 McCrudden, 'Judicial', p. 661.

59 Rosen, *Dignity*, p. 48.

60 Jürgen Habermas, 'Utopia', p. 468.

At the end of the 20th century, the Inter-American Court of Human Rights ruled against Guatemala in the case known as *Street Children* bearing on the kidnapping, torture and death of four minors by members of the security forces. In what matters here, the Court reasoned the following concerning the welfare conception of human dignity: "[i]n essence, the fundamental right to life includes, not only the right of every human being not to be deprived of his life arbitrarily, but also the right that he will not be prevented from having access to the conditions that guaranteed a dignified existence".[61]

Some years earlier, the Supreme Court of India ruled on a case along similar lines:

> We think that the right to life includes the right to live with human dignity and all that goes with it, namely, the bare necessaries of life such as adequate nutrition, clothing and shelter and facilities for reading, writing and expressing one-self in diverse forms, freely moving about and mixing and comingling with fellow human beings.[62]

This latter account is mirrored by what Pablo Gilabert characterizes as a continuum ranging from 'basic dignity', bearing on all the necessities of a decent life, to 'maximal dignity', referring to the conditions necessary to achieve a flourishing life.[63]

Further, the welfare conception has also been embraced in the canonical text of gender studies literature, Simone de Beauvoir's *The Second Sex*. There, de Beauvoir contends that "it is through labour that woman has conquered her dignity as a human being; but it was a remarkably hard-won and protracted conquest".[64]

Finally, it is worth noting that the surprising social upheaval during 2019 in one of Latin America's most developed, though socially unequal countries, Chile, made of the welfare conception of dignity a battle cry that eventually led to a referendum to draft a new constitution for the South American nation.[65] Another country where dignity has become a rallying cry for political mobilisation is Ukraine, where in 2023 its Constitutional Court declared that

61 Inter-American Court of Human Rights, 'Street Children', pars. 144; 191. See also on the right to health and a dignified existence, Inter-American Court of Human Rights, Vera Rojas et al v. Chile, Judgment of October 01, 2021 (*Merits*).

62 Supreme Court of India, 'Francis Coralie Mullin v. Dehli', AIR 1981 SC 746.

63 Gilabert, *Dignity*, p. 139.

64 Simone De Beauvoir, *The Second Sex* (London: Vintage, 1956), p. 135.

65 Francisco Lobo, 'Chile and a global revolution for dignity', https://www.openglobalrights.org/chile-and-a-global-revolution-for-dignity/, 12 May 2021.

"Human dignity will be denied if the state does not provide a person with at least minimal social benefits".[66]

### 3.2 *The Autonomy Conception*

Arguably, the autonomy conception of human dignity has enjoyed supremacy in the moral discourse for the last couple of centuries, ever since it was formulated by Immanuel Kant in his 1785 publication *Groundwork for the Metaphysics of Morals*. Given its hegemony in moral discourse, it is worth reproducing Kant's position *in extenso*:

> Now I say: a human being and generally every rational being *exists* as an end in itself, *not merely as a means* for the discretionary use for this or that will.
>
> (...) In the kingdom of ends everything has either a **price**, or a **dignity**. What has a price can be replaced with something else, as its *equivalent*; whereas what is elevated above any price, and hence allows of no equivalent, has a dignity.
>
> What refers to general human inclinations and needs has a *market price*; what, even without presupposing a need, conforms with a certain taste, i.e. a delight in the mere purposeless play of the powers of our mind, has a *fancy price*; but what constitutes the condition under which alone something can be an end in itself does not merely have a relative worth, i.e. a price, but an inner worth, i.e. *dignity* (emphasis in the original).[67]

Kant grounds dignity in 'autonomy', that is the state of affairs whereby the human being is subject only to the maxims or laws created by his or her own will, *auto* ('self') *nomos* ('rules'), as opposed to 'heteronomy' (i.e. rules imposed from the outside). Hence, Kant posits his famous 'principle of the autonomy of the will',[68] on which the notion of dignity ultimately rests.

66 Decision of the Second Senate of the Constitutional Court of Ukraine No. 3-r(II)/2023 dated March 22, 2023 in the case upon the constitutional complaint of Ihor Lazurenko regarding the conformity of the provisions of Articles 70.2.4 and 70.2.5 of the Law of Ukraine "On Enforcement Proceedings", Articles 50.2.3 and 50.2.4 of the Law of Ukraine "On General Compulsory State Pension Insurance" with the Constitution (constitutionality) (regarding guaranteed pension, which is the main source of living, not lower than the subsistence minimum).

67 Immanuel Kant, *Groundwork of the Metaphysics of Morals* (Cambridge: Cambridge University Press, 2012), pp. 40; 46.

68 Ibid., p. 51.

According to a Kant scholar, Oliver Sensen, there are three main paradigms of dignity that have been recognized and developed throughout history: (i) the archaic paradigm, which associates dignity with rank and elevated positions; (ii) the traditional paradigm, roughly corresponding to the Stoic idea of sublimity of human beings over nature and the potential for self-growth enclosed therein; and (iii) the contemporary paradigm, which belongs to the tradition of moral realism that postulates the existence of an objective normative substance that commands respect and recognition.

Although Kant is usually identified as the leading theorist of the latter paradigm, Sensen believes that his heavily duty-centred theory is actually more at home within the traditional paradigm.[69] Indeed, for all his rational liberalism, Kant tends to assign much more importance to the collective or 'kingdom' of rational beings than to the individual, as it is to morality that he attributes dignity in the first place, and only derivatively and contingently to humanity, insofar as it is capable of morality. By the time we reach the individual after all these transpositions, it seems they only benefit from a watered-down version of the dignity reserved for the original source of this fundamental trait, morality. Thus, the need arises for a more granular approach to complement Kant's.[70]

We also find references to dignity elsewhere in Kant's works, for instance, in the *Metaphysics of Morals* section titled *The Doctrine of Right*. There Kant alludes to "dignities" understood as a high estimation attached to a certain rank or office, such as nobility,[71] including the elevated position of a king[72] – what Sensen calls the archaic paradigm. This paradigm will become relevant again later on in this chapter, when I present Jeremy Waldron's modern thesis of dignity as rank.

We may also find representatives of the autonomy account following Kant's legacy in modern legal scholarship. In his canonical reconstruction of the rule of law tradition titled *The Morality of Law*, Lon Fuller argued in the 1960s that to respect the principles of the rule of law is to respect the dignity of the individual as a responsible agent capable of self-determination.[73] In a similar

69 Oliver Sensen, 'Kant's Conception of Human Dignity', *Kant-Studien*, 100 (2009), pp. 311–315.

70 Francisco Lobo, 'Kant's Conception of Human Dignity and the Importance of Singularity within Commonality', *International Journal of Law and Political Sciences*, 13:2 (2019), pp. 214–219.

71 Immanuel Kant, *The Metaphysics of Morals* (Cambridge: Cambridge University Press, 1996), p. 138; Michael Meyer, 'Kant's concept of dignity and modern political thought', *History of European Ideas*, 8:3 (1987), p. 320.

72 Sensen, 'Kant's', p. 310.

73 Lon Fuller, *The Morality of Law*. 2nd ed. (New Haven: Yale University Press, 1969), p. 162.

way, Joseph Raz would argue some years later that respecting people's dignity entails respecting their autonomy and their ability to plan their own future, which the rule of law should ideally enable.[74]

Also during the heyday of the Cold War, Harold Laswell and Myers McDougal postulated the so-called "New Haven school of international law", otherwise known as "policy-oriented jurisprudence," which held that, even amidst rising geopolitical tensions, human dignity remained a universal value shared by all powers.[75] In their variant of the autonomy conception, the value of human dignity is articulated as private choice, which is the main modality of power, rather than coercion.[76]

More recently, and after thoroughly reviewing the most relevant international and comparative case-law referring to such concept, Christopher McCrudden identifies what he calls the 'basic minimum content of human dignity', comprising the following elements: (a) the attribution of intrinsic worth to every human being (the 'ontological claim'); (b) the need for others to recognize and respect such worth (the 'relational claim'); and (c) the idea that the state must exist only for the sake of the human person (the 'limited-state claim'). These elements represent altogether what McCrudden suggests as the *concept* of human dignity endowed with a minimum core, from which several different *conceptions* may stem, an insight for which McCrudden acknowledges credit to Jeremy Waldron and Walter Gallie in a footnote.[77]

As for the themes commonly identified in the legal literature regarding the contents of dignity, and keeping the Kantian legacy alive, Gattini lists two main aspects of autonomy, namely self-determination and self-fulfilment, alongside the prohibition of inhumane treatment, the protection of group identity and culture, and the satisfaction of basic needs.[78]

Further, Dworkin proposed that there are two dimensions of human dignity: First, the principle of intrinsic value, meaning that "every human being

74 Joseph Raz, *The Authority of Law: Essays on Law and Morality* (Oxford: Oxford University Press, 1979), p. 221.

75 Myers McDougal and Harold Lasswell, 'The identification and appraisal of diverse systems of public order', *The American Journal of International Law*, 53 (1959), p. 5. See also John Norton, 'Prolegomenon to the jurisprudence of Myers McDougal and Harold Lasswell', *Virginia Law Review*, 54 (1968), pp. 662–688; Eisuke Suzuki, 'The New Haven School of international law: An invitation to a policy-oriented jurisprudence', *Yale Studies of World Public Order*, 1 (1974), pp. 1–48.

76 McDougal and Lasswell, 'The identification', p. 11.

77 McCrudden, 'Judicial', p. 679, at footnote 170.

78 Gattini, 'Setting', p. 5.

has a special kind of objective value".[79] Second, the principle of personal responsibility, whereby "every person has a special responsibility for realizing the success of his own life, a responsibility that includes exercising his judgment about what kind of life would be successful for him".[80] A few years later, Dworkin rephrased his conception of dignity as one comprising two ethical principles, i.e. the principle of self-respect – meaning that every person must take his or her own life seriously – and the principle of authenticity – namely that every person is responsible for living up to what they believe counts as a success in their lives.[81] Admittedly, Dworkin's somewhat protean conception of dignity can be said to have one cross-cutting linchpin, namely the Kantian idea of the autonomy of moral agents who must live up to their own freely chosen standards as to what counts as a good life.

Another author who has taken very seriously the characterization of human dignity as moral agency underlying the whole structure of human rights law is James Griffin, also one of Kant's heirs. Concerned about the lack of thorough theoretical development for the idea of human rights since the times of the Enlightenment – even denouncing the absence of a very concept, let alone a conception, of such rights[82] – Griffin contends that the hollow idea of dignity underpinning human rights needs to be filled with the notion of 'personhood'. According to Griffin, to be an agent in the relevant moral sense is to have autonomy so as to form our own conception of a worthwhile life, to count with a minimum provision of resources and capabilities – echoing Schiller's welfare account of dignity – and to have freedom from external interferences to pursue our life project.[83] Thus, "the sort of dignity relevant to human rights (...) is that of a highly prized status: that we are normative agents", thereby labelled by Griffin as 'dignity-conferring autonomy'.[84]

Now, the currency of the autonomy conception is not confirmed only by legal scholarship. It may be also observed in some contemporary case law. Indeed, in the *Omega* case, where the game of 'laser tag' was banned in Germany for infringing upon human dignity, the German Federal Administrative Court reasoned that this type of pastime awakens or strengthens in the player an attitude denying the fundamental right of each person to be acknowledged and

79 Ronald Dworkin, *Is Democracy Possible Here?* (Princeton: Princeton University Press, 2006), p. 9.
80 Ibid., p. 10. Similarly, Atienza, *Dignidad*, p. 65.
81 Ronald Dworkin, *Justice for Hedgehogs* (Cambridge: Belknap Press, 2011), pp. 203–204.
82 James Griffin, *On Human Rights* (Oxford: Oxford University Press, 2013), pp. 13; 17.
83 Ibid., p. 33.
84 Ibid., pp. 152–153.

respected. In other words, it denies their agency, and as a result, their dignity. This reasoning was later reaffirmed by the European Court of Justice.[85]

But the autonomy conception features most notably in the German Constitutional Court's decision of 2006 regarding the legality of the Aviation Security Act authorizing security forces to shoot down hijacked airplanes to prevent them from being used in terrorist attacks (the 'Airliner case'). Evidently drawing on Kant's terminology,[86] the Constitutional Court declared the Act to be unconstitutional, on the following grounds:

> Due to the circumstances, which cannot be controlled by them in any way, the crew and the passengers of the plane cannot escape this state action but are helpless and defenceless in the face of it with the consequence that they are shot down in a targeted manner together with the aircraft and as a result of this will be killed with near certainty. Such a treatment ignores the status of the persons affected as subjects endowed with dignity and inalienable rights. By their killing being used as a means to save others, they are treated as objects and at the same time deprived of their rights.[87]

As to the dignity of the hijackers who are killed, the Court contends that they are not used as means to an end, but on the contrary are reaffirmed in their status as moral agents whenever they are faced with the consequences of their freely chosen actions.[88] This conclusion bears out the legal principle enshrined in Art. 1 of the German Constitution or Basic Law according to which human dignity shall be inviolable, even when a life must be taken to protect it, and regardless of the existence of assaults against it.[89]

But how is it possible to claim that one has suffered an infringement upon human dignity and at the same time declare it is inviolable? Marcus Düwell

---

85 European Court of Justice (First Chamber), Case C-36/02, Omega Spielhallen- und Automatenaufstellungs-GmbH v. Oberbürgermeisterin der Bundesstadt Bonn, Judgment, 14 October 2004.

86 Habermas, 'Utopia', p. 465.

87 German Federal Constitutional Court, 1 BvR 357/07, 15 February 2006, par. 124. See also Tatjana Hörnle and Mordechai Kremnitzer, 'Human Dignity as a Protected Interest in Criminal Law', *Israel Law Review*, 44 (2011), p. 146; Dieter Grimm, 'Dignity in a Legal Context and as an Absolute Right', in Christopher McCrudden (ed.), *Understanding Human Dignity* (Oxford: Oxford University Press, 2015), p. 384; Le Moli, *Dignity*, p. 80.

88 German Federal Constitutional Court, 1 BvR 357/07, 15 February 2006, par. 141. See also Rosen, *Dignity*, pp. 104–107.

89 Grimm, 'Dignity', p. 389.

distinguishes between the categorical duty to treat others with respect as a result of their ontological status as bearers of human dignity, and the *claim* demanding that such a duty be discharged. Whenever dignity is actually violated, it is not dignity itself that is infringed upon, but rather this resulting claim to be treated with respect.[90] Similarly, Pablo Gilabert distinguishes between 'status-dignity' as a normative standing that can never be lost and 'condition-dignity' as the state of affairs resulting from respecting such status, respect which is contingent.[91] As Montaigne once put it, writing about rank (a concept we shall return to), "All forms of greatness are not brought low uniquely by a fall: some there are which allow you to stoop low without falling".[92]

Returning to case law, in a ruling coloured by the same Kantian overtones, the Chilean Supreme Court has ruled that crimes against humanity, like those committed under Pinochet's dictatorial regime, suppose the negation of the moral personality of the human being, which is manifested, in extreme circumstances, when the individual is treated as an object, thus constituting "a breach of and disregard for the dignity of the person".[93]

Down a more Dworkinian path – but always bearing the Kantian patina of this conception of human dignity – the Inter-American Court of Human Rights ruled in 2012 against Costa Rica for banning in vitro fertilization procedures in the country, due to alleged violations of the right to life and of human dignity of spare embryos. The Inter-American Court reasoned that:

> The protection of private life encompasses a series of factors associated with the dignity of the individual, including, for example, the ability to develop his or her own personality and aspirations (…). The concept of private life encompasses aspects of physical and social identity, including the right to personal autonomy, personal development and the right to establish and develop relationships (…).[94]

---

90 Marcus Düwell, 'Human dignity: Concepts, discussions, philosophical perspectives', in Marcus Düwell, Jens Braarvig, Roger Brownsword, and Dietmar Mieth (eds.), *The Cambridge Handbook of Human Dignity* (Cambridge: Cambridge University Press, 2014), pp. 42–43.

91 Gilabert, *Dignity*, p. 122.

92 Michel de Montaigne, *The Complete Essays* (London: Penguin, 2003), p. 1038.

93 Supreme Court of the Republic of Chile, Case CS No 921-09, 13 August 2009, par. 15.

94 Inter-American Court of Human Rights, Case of "In Vitro Fertilization" (Artavia Murillo et al.) v. Costa Rica, Judgment of November 28, 2012 (*Merits*), par. 143.

### 3.3 *The* imago Dei *Conception*

Although the welfare and the autonomy conceptions of human dignity are the ones we are most familiar with in our vernacular, there is an additional, older conception that has also been very influential in the philosophical development of the concept: the religious conception. This conception is sometimes mirrored by the works of secular philosophers when they elevate the value of "reverence for (human) life" to the highest place within their normative projects,[95] even postulating the idea of a "mystical value" of human beings.[96]As Michael Rosen underscores when reflecting on the archetypically Kantian German Basic Law: "the influence of religion (and of Catholicism in particular) on law and politics has always been great".[97]

Besides the well-known involvement of a Catholic philosopher in the drafting of the Universal Declaration of Human Rights, Jacques Maritain[98] who worked alongside scholars of different denominations and persuasions,[99] another interesting case in point is the Irish constitutional tradition. According to Samuel Moyn:

> Contrary to familiar beliefs, it was not West Germany that first constitutionalized dignity as a leading principle anyway. That distinction belongs to the Irish.
>
> In their 1937 constitution, the Irish gave it foundational placement, as a religiously inspired root concept connected (as in the later West German case) to the subordination of the otherwise sovereign democratic polity to God, and for many to the moral constraints of his natural law.[100]

95 Albert Schweitzer, *The Philosophy of Civilization* (New York: Prometheus Books, 1987), pp. 307–329.

96 Micah Lott, 'The Knowledge of Human Dignity', in Roger Teichmann (ed.), *The Oxford Handbook of Elizabeth Anscombe* (New York: Oxford University Press, 2022), pp. 292–307.

97 Rosen, *Dignity*, p. 91.

98 Ibid., p. 53.

99 John Loughlin, 'Introduction', in John Loughlin (ed.), *Human Dignity in the Judaeo-Christian Tradition. Catholic, Orthodox, Anglican and Protestant Perspectives* (London: Bloomsbury, 2021), p. 1; Hans Ingvar Roth, 'P.C. Chang and Charles Malik: The Two Philosophers of the Universal Declaration of Human Rights', *Human Rights Quarterly*, 45:4 (2023), pp. 545–567.

100 Samuel Moyn, 'The Secret History of Constitutional Dignity', in Christopher McCrudden (ed.), *Understanding Human Dignity* (Oxford: Oxford University Press, 2015), p. 96.

As we shall see in Chapter 6, the *imago Dei* conception of human dignity also informs, to an extent, the *ethos* of one of the selected militaries of this study, the Chilean Army.[101]

Further, as I will also argue, there are some continuities to be observed between the *imago Dei* conception and the modern rank conception, not least the impressive ability of both approaches to adapt and be refurbished with new contents as society evolves. As David Hollenbach has remarked: "the Catholic understanding of human dignity exists within a living tradition that is open to development and change".[102] Arguably, Kant's own conception is also reminiscent of Augustine's distinction between natural dignity and instrumental value,[103] which again bears out the influence of Catholic doctrine operating in the background of many philosophical developments familiar to us.

One of the earliest references to human dignity in Catholic thought can be traced back to the works of Pope Leo the Great in the 5th century AD. Leo contented that all humans possess dignity as a result of their being created in the "image of God".[104] Admittedly, in early Catholic thought the term *dignitas* was widely used as a descriptor, not only of human beings, but of the entire creation.[105] It should also be mentioned here that it was partly building on this conception of human dignity that the so called 'Iberian School of Peace' made some of its foremost contributions to the ethical assessment of European imperialism within the framework of the Just War Tradition.[106]

The concept of the image of God, or *imago Dei*, has been called "one of the most beautiful and valuable concepts of Old and New Testament theology",[107] and it has remained influential throughout the evolution of Catholic

101 "The Christian tradition is ingrained in the military ethos of the Chilean Army" ("La tradición cristiana está arraigada en el ethos militar del Ejército de Chile"). See Chilean Army, *Manual: Ethos del Ejército de Chile.* MOLD – 02005 (Santiago: Ejército de Chile, Comando de Educación y Doctrina, 2018), at 4–52.

102 David Hollenbach, 'Human dignity in Catholic thought', in Marcus Düwell, Jens Braarvig, Roger Brownsword, and Dietmar Mieth (eds.), *The Cambridge Handbook of Human Dignity* (Cambridge: Cambridge University Press, 2014), p. 255.

103 Bonnie Kent, 'In the Image of God. Human Dignity After the Fall', in Remy Debes (ed.), *Dignity. A History* (New York: Oxford University Press, 2017), p. 88.

104 Ibid., p. 74.

105 Ibid., p. 77.

106 Antônio Cançado Trindade, 'Prefacio', in Pedro Calafate and Ramón Emilio Mandado Gutiérrez (eds.), *Escuela Ibérica de la Paz* (Santander: Ediciones Universidad Cantabria, 2014), p. 45.

107 Vladimir Latinovic, 'Christ as *Imago Dei* – A Missed Opportunity of Ante-Nicene Christian Theology', in John Loughlin (ed.), *Human Dignity in the Judaeo-Christian Tradition. Catholic, Orthodox, Anglican and Protestant Perspectives* (London: Bloomsbury, 2021), p. 57.

doctrine.[108] It can arguably be elevated to the stature of an exemplar of the essentially contested concept of human dignity, from a Christian perspective.[109] It can be found at the outset of the most sacred book in Christianity, the Bible. In the Old Testament, the concept is introduced in the early chapters of the Book of Genesis, which recounts the tale of the creation of the world:

> And God said, 'Let us make humanity in our image, after our likeness; and let them have dominion over the fish of the sea and over the birds of the air, and over the cattle, and over all the earth, and over every creeping thing that creeps upon the earth'. So God created humanity in his own image; in the image of God he created them; male and female he created them.[110]

This passage has been interpreted traditionally in Christian theology as a description of that which makes humans special creatures participating in the divine through reason or spirituality. A less known reading was suggested by the second-century Church Father Irenaeus, who posed that 'image' refers to what is permanent in human beings and cannot be changed, such as our rationality, whereas 'likeness' of God has to do with all those divine qualities that humans used to possess before we fell from grace, but that are still attainable through Jesus Christ.[111] Put differently, while 'image' indicates a descriptive or ontological concept, 'likeness' entails a normative aspiration as to our ability to improve by nurturing the divine spark or scintilla within.[112] As Latinovic phrases it: "This is perhaps the most exciting part of (…) *imago Dei* anthropology – it encourages human beings to grow and 'provides a promising model to understand the mosaic evolution of human capacities'".[113]

---

108 John Loughlin, 'Human Dignity and Human Wretchedness from Iranaeus to Pico della Mirandola', in John Loughlin (ed.), *Human Dignity in the Judaeo-Christian Tradition. Catholic, Orthodox, Anglican and Protestant Perspectives* (London: Bloomsbury, 2021), p. 103.

109 Richard Conrad, 'The Holy Trinity as Source of Human Dignity according to St Thomas Aquinas', in John Loughlin (ed.), *Human Dignity in the Judaeo-Christian Tradition. Catholic, Orthodox, Anglican and Protestant Perspectives* (London: Bloomsbury, 2021), p. 80.

110 John Day, '"So God Created Humanity in His Own Image" (Genesis 1.27). What Does the bible Mean and What Have People Thought it Meant?', in John Loughlin (ed.), *Human Dignity in the Judaeo-Christian Tradition. Catholic, Orthodox, Anglican and Protestant Perspectives* (London: Bloomsbury, 2021), p. 16.

111 Ibid., p. 17.

112 John Milbank, 'The Dignity of the Ancients and the Dignity of the Moderns', in John Loughlin (ed.), *Human Dignity in the Judaeo-Christian Tradition. Catholic, Orthodox, Anglican and Protestant Perspectives* (London: Bloomsbury, 2021), p. 184.

113 Latinovic, 'Christ', p. 63.

In the event, the Catholic *imago Dei* doctrine would evolve over the centuries to acquire a particular physiognomy in the late nineteenth-century that moves in the direction of the welfare conception described above: the face of social justice.[114] Amidst the rise of socialism and Marxism across Europe, Pope Leo XIII issued in 1891 his famous encyclical aptly titled *Rerum Novarum* ("Of the New Things"). In that seminal document he laid the groundwork for what would become known as the Catholic Church's 'social doctrine', featuring the dignity of labour as a central aspect therein.

This type of dignity is connected to the mainstream concept of human dignity in a particular way, as Rosen points out: "For the Catholic Church in the nineteenth century, all members of society have dignity, but their dignity consists in their playing the role that is appropriate to their station within a hierarchical social order, one in which some are 'nobler than others'".[115] Rosen further underscores how impressive this Catholic turn to a more egalitarian conception of dignity after 1945 is when contrasted against this clearly anti-egalitarian, hierarchical reading on the concept.[116] Accordingly, Moyn calls this turn of the century Catholic doctrine a "corporatist version of dignity, in which it was family or labour that was dignified, not persons (and thus not persons with rights)".[117] In a more charitable interpretation, Hollenbach highlights how fraternity and solidarity are key in this view of dignity: "Human dignity is not realized by persons acting autonomously on their own but through collaboration and solidarity".[118] Moreover, John Milbank posits that corporatism and personalism are complementary within the Catholic tradition, as being human in the modern world means to act as an individual in several capacities and social functions.[119]

Ultimately, Rosen concludes that the Catholic conception of human dignity, from its origins as *imago Dei* through a hierarchical conception of the universe (and of human beings) to a more egalitarian brand of late, is, at the end of the day, incompatible with a Kantian conception where autonomy is pivotal.[120] This explains why contemporary views of dignity grounded on the Catholic tradition are determined to decry a so-called "culture of death," aiming to extend this special moral status to beings devoid of rational agency

---

114 Hollenbach, 'Catholic', p. 252.
115 Rosen, *Dignity*, pp. 49; 100.
116 Ibid., p. 51. See also Hollenbach, 'Catholic', p. 250.
117 Moyn, 'Secret', p. 98.
118 Hollenbach, 'Catholic', p. 254.
119 Milbank, 'Dignity', p. 176.
120 Rosen, *Dignity*, p. 93.

or autonomy, namely the foetus in the abortion debate,[121] and in bioethical discussions more broadly.[122] Accordingly, Pope John Paul II's case against the death penalty is based on analogous dignitarian concerns,[123] and this spirit of unfettered life affirmation was ultimately epitomized by the Instruction on certain bioethical questions issued in 2008 by Pope Benedict XVI to update Instruction *Donum vitae*, titled *Dignitas personae*.[124]

### 3.4 *The Rank Conception*

In a moral sense, ever since Kant dignity has been conceptualised in theory and practice as the inner worth that every rational agent enjoys, such that they are never to be treated merely as means and always as ends in themselves.[125] But beyond this household moral definition, in recent years some scholars have undertaken to rejuvenate dignity from a purely legal standpoint. Foremost among them is Jeremy Waldron with his 'dignitarian jurisprudence', according to which human dignity should be thought of as 'rank', that is, a privileged legal status commanding deference and respect, like nobility, only now universalized for every man and woman,[126] much like the once exclusive Roman citizenship was expanded in 212 AD and thus made available to every inhabitant of the empire.[127]

---

121 Ibid., pp. 94–96.

122 Atienza, *Dignidad*, p. 19.

123 Conrad, 'Trinity', p. 92.

124 'Instruction *Dignitas Personae* on Certain Bioethical Questions', https://www.vatican.va/roman_curia/congregations/cfaith/documents/rc_con_cfaith_doc_20081208_dignitas-personae_en.html, 6 September 2022.

125 Meir Dan-Cohen. 'A Concept of Dignity', *Israel Law Review*, 44:9 (2011), p. 13; Rosen, *Dignity*, pp. 19–31.

126 Jeremy Waldron, *Dignity, Rank and Rights. The Berkeley Tanner Lectures* (2009) (New York: Oxford University Press, 2012), p. 22. See also Jeremy Waldron, 'Dignity and Rank', *European Journal of Sociology*, 48:2 (2007), pp. 201–237; Gregory Vlastos, 'Justice and Equality', in Jeremy Waldron (ed.), *Theories of Rights* (New York: Oxford University Press, 1984), pp. 41–76; Stéphanie Hennette-Vauchez, 'A human *dignitas*? Remnants of the ancient legal concept in contemporary dignity jurisprudence', *I-CON*, 9:1 (2011), pp. 32–57. On "universal nobility" see also Ralf Stoecker, 'Three Crucial Turns on the Road to an Adequate Understanding of Human Dignity', in P. Kaufmann, H. Kuch, C. Neuhäuser, and E. Webster (eds.), *Humiliation, Degradation, Dehumanization. Human Dignity Violated* (New York: Springer, 2011), pp. 7–17; and Christian Neuhäuser and Ralf Stoekcer, 'Human dignity as universal nobility', in Marcus Düwell, Jens Braarvig, Roger Brownsword, and Dietmar Mieth (eds.), *The Cambridge Handbook of Human Dignity* (Cambridge: Cambridge University Press, 2014), pp. 298–309.

127 On the connection between citizenship and dignity see: Jeremy Waldron, 'Citizenship and Dignity', in Christopher McCrudden (ed.), *Understanding Human Dignity* (Oxford: Oxford University Press, 2015), pp. 327–343.

Cutting against the grain of the autonomy account,[128] Waldron intends to part from the reign of moral philosophy in order to analyse the idea of dignity from a different standpoint: the legal tradition. According to Waldron, "Dignity seems at home in law: law is its natural habitat",[129] so he undertakes the task of developing what he calls a true "jurisprudence of dignity".[130] Indeed, as already pointed out, the term 'dignity' features in a plethora of contemporary human rights legal instruments. Further, Waldron grapples with the idea that dignity could serve both as the foundation (one among others) and the content of (certain) human rights: "We may be able to distinguish between human dignity in general and certain particular rights that protect it explicitly and more or less directly".[131]

Waldron's jurisprudence of dignity postulates the reconstruction of the legal notion of 'rank' or 'status'. Some legal statuses are low (e.g. slavery and villeinage), whereas others are high (e.g. royalty and nobility).[132] A legal status is but "a particular package of rights, powers, disabilities, duties, privileges, immunities, and liabilities accruing to a person by virtue of the condition or situation they are in,"[133] and this package is epitomized by the corresponding status-term. In this sense, the status of human dignity may be better conceived of as an abbreviation or summary of a collection of (human) rights, rather than their *a priori* foundation.[134]

A high status further conveys the idea of uprightness of bearing, self-possession, self-control and self-presentation (including personal hygiene and its surprisingly high moral returns[135]) – all features that are relevant to the normative ideal of military honour, as we shall see in the next chapter. It is no different with the status we call dignity: "A good account of human dignity will explain it as a very general status. (…) That is what I am trying to do with an account of dignity as a high-ranking status, comparable to a rank of nobility – only a rank assigned to every human person, equally without discrimination: dignity as nobility for the common man".[136]

128 Meir Dan-Cohen, 'Introduction: Dignity and its (Dis)content' in Waldron, *Dignity*, pp. 4–5.
129 Waldron, *Dignity*, pp. 13–15.
130 Ibid., pp. 14–15.
131 Jeremy Waldron, 'Is Dignity the Foundation of Human Rights?', *NYU Public Law and Legal Theory Research Paper Series*, 12–73 (2013), pp. 3–5.
132 Waldron, *Dignity*, p. 21.
133 Waldron, 'Foundation', p. 24.
134 Ibid., p. 25.
135 Pinker, *Angels*, p. 170.
136 Waldron, *Dignity*, p. 22.

The rank conception can be observed, for example, in Judge Fitzmaurice's separate opinion in the case *Ireland v. United Kingdom* ruled by the European Court of Human Rights, when he reflected on the concept of "degrading treatment" in a specific paragraph and its accompanying footnote:

> In the present context it can be assumed that it is, or should be, intended to denote something seriously humiliating, lowering as to human dignity, or disparaging, like having one's head shaved, being tarred and feathered, smeared with filth, pelted with muck, paraded naked in front of strangers, forced to eat excreta, deface the portrait of one's sovereign or head of State, or dress up in a way calculated to provoke ridicule or contempt.
>
> (...) Footnote 17: Literally, "degraded" (de-graded) means reduced to a lower grade, rank, position or status; but the relevant meanings in the present context, as given in the dictionaries (see n. 15 supra) would be to "lower in estimation, character or quality" (Shorter Oxford); to "lower in dignity or estimation; bring into contempt" (Random House). Other descriptions used are "to debase" (ibid), "to humiliate" (Penguin). The relevant notions here are clearly those of humiliation, bringing into contempt, loss of esteem, and debasement, presumably from status as a human being.[137]

This status-based conception of dignity is arguably also found in exemplars from literature,[138] for instance, in the account Mr. Stevens offers of his role as a butler in Kazuo Ishiguro's renowned novel *The Remains of the Day*: "(...) 'dignity' has to do crucially with a butler's ability not to abandon the professional being he inhabits. (...) The great butlers are great by virtue of their ability to inhabit their professional role and inhabit it to the utmost; they will not be shaken out by external events, however surprising, alarming or vexing".[139] Thus, the professional butler (or civil servant, lawyer, soldier, etc.), will embrace 'person neutrality' by suspending all individual idiosyncrasies and preferences in order to properly fulfil a role.[140]

Consequently, and beyond what he terms the 'absolute worth' (i.e. Kantian or autonomy-based) account of human dignity, Waldron articulates a novel

---

137 European Court of Human Rights, Ireland v. The United Kingdom (*Application no. 5310/71*), Judgment of 18 January 1978, Separate Opinion of Judge Fitzmaurice, para. 27.

138 Francisco Lobo, 'A conception of human dignity. The normative case against female genital mutilation', *Journal of Human Dignity and Wellbeing*, 7 (2019), p. 89.

139 Kazuo Ishiguro, *The Remains of the Day* (London: Faber & Faber, 1989), p. 43.

140 Arthur Applbaum, *Ethics for Adversaries: The Morality of Roles in Public and Professional Life* (Princeton: Princeton University Press, 1999), pp. 64–65.

'ranking status' account.[141] But this fresh approach actually hinges on a pre-Kantian conception of human dignity dating back at least to Pico dellaMirandola's 15th century *Oration on the Dignity of Man*.[142]

According to dellaMirandola's constructivist view[143] human beings have been blessed with a protean nature, whereby they may decide to rise and become a 'heavenly' rational being and an intellectual 'angel', or rather descend into abject stations reserved for plants and beasts.[144] In use of such unique 'mutability', in Waldron's view human beings decided (in that "crucial moment" that was the year 1948[145]) to extend the highest station hitherto known to them, that of nobility, to every member of the species in the shape of the cardinal value of dignity, the latter operating as the legal fulcrum of such a momentous transvaluation.[146]

But Pico's constructivism is older than it seems, as there are some continuities to be found between the humanist tradition which he epitomizes and the Catholic conception of *imago Dei*.[147] At the very least the human ability to improve can be found already in Augustine's *City of God*,[148] the 'likeness' of God remaining ever retrievable for the fallen human being, as we saw in the previous section. Such a conception that harbours the belief in the ability of human beings to improve is called a "holistic view of the dignity of the human person".[149] The same tradition beginning with the Catholic view, through the contributions of humanist thinkers, would be continued later in the Enlightenment and beyond. Indeed, Rousseau makes a point of highlighting the capacity for self-perfection as one of the distinguishing qualities of human beings.[150] So does Max Scheler when postulating in his anthropological philosophy that human beings are able to resist biological impulses

141 Waldron, *Dignity*, p. 27.

142 For a challenge of the traditional view of Pico as a theorist of dignity, see Brian Copenhaver, 'Dignity, Vile Bodies, and Nakedness', in Debes, *History*, pp. 127–174.

143 Dan-Cohen, 'Introduction', p. 6.

144 Giovanni Pico dellaMirandola, *Oration on the Dignity of Man* (Chicago: Henry Regnery Company, 1956), pp. 8–9. Similarly, see Fernán Pérez de Oliva, 'Diálogo de la dignidad del hombre (1586)', http://www.cervantesvirtual.com/obra-visor/dialogo-de-la-dignidad-del-hombre--0/html/fedde6c2-82b1-11df-acc7-002185ce6064_2.html, 19 April 2021.

145 Gilabert, *Dignity*, p. 116.

146 Waldron, *Dignity*, p. 31; Jeremy Waldron, *One Another's Equals. The Basis of Human Equality* (Cambridge: Harvard University Press, 2017), p. 209.

147 Loughlin, 'Wretchedness', pp. 109, 113.

148 Kent, 'Image', p. 80.

149 Loughlin, 'Wretchedness', p. 117.

150 Jean-Jacques Rousseau, *Discourse on the Origins of Inequality* (*Second Discourse*) (Hanover: University Press of New England, 1992), p. 26.

when exercising self-consciousness, which allows them to model their lives as they please.[151]

Further, there is yet another resemblance between the Catholic conception and Waldron's that is more problematic: the idea of hierarchy. Admittedly, rank exhibits a distinctively non-egalitarian history. How could it be construed in an egalitarian way in modern times? 'Human dignity' may indeed refer to Cicero's idea of superiority of human beings over other creatures – what Sensen calls the traditional paradigm and what Waldron himself associates with 'distinctive equality'.[152] Yet, following Gregory Vlastos, Waldron at the same time attempts to update the old concept of rank through an analytical movement characterized as an 'upwards equalization' of every human being, resulting in equal empowerment.[153] Consequently, those societies embracing universal dignity today are 'castes societies' of sorts, only "with just one caste (and a very high caste at that). Every man a Brahmin. Every man a duke, every woman a queen".[154] As we shall see, Waldron refers to the way we pay attention to and respect (in terms of Darwall's recognition respect) the basic equality implied in human dignity as the "scintillation", in the sense that our understanding of this foundational moral idea fluctuates or "sparkles" between its theoretical possibility and the way it is actualized in each person we encounter, between humanity and the individual.[155]

Now, what does this upwards equalization actually entail from a legal standpoint? According to Waldron, this encompasses the universalization of all the erstwhile legal privileges and protections enjoyed by nobles in the past, through the body of norms we know as International Human Rights Law. Such privileges and protections, articulated today in the form of subjective legal rights, include: the right to have a hearing before a court of law and due process of law; the prohibition of imprisonment for debts; equality before the law; the right to legal counsel and representation; and the prohibition of torture.[156]

This last prohibition has been characterized by Waldron as a legal 'archetype'. Following Jung's definition of an archetype as a powerful image that becomes a sort of 'myth motif', Waldron contends that in a legal sense an archetype corresponds to a provision which "by virtue of its force, clarity and

151 Max Scheler, *El Puesto del Hombre en el Cosmos* (Buenos Aires, Losada, 1938), p. 82.

152 Waldron, *One*, p. 31.

153 Gilabert, *Dignity*, p. 182.

154 Waldron, *Dignity*, p. 34.

155 Jeremy Waldron, *One Another's Equals. The Basis of Human Equality* (Cambridge: Harvard University Press, 2017), pp. 157–167.

156 Waldron, *Dignity*, pp. 54–64; Jeremy Waldron, 'How Law Protects Dignity', *The Cambridge Law Journal*, 71:1 (2012), pp. 200–222.

vividness expresses the spirit that animates the whole area of law. It becomes a sort of emblem, token, or icon of the whole".[157]

Could human dignity be also conceived of as a legal archetype in this sense? To be sure, human dignity has been assigned the status of a 'right', a 'norm' or 'obligation', a 'protected interest' of criminal legislation, and a 'principle'.[158] Yet, beyond these traditional legal institutions, an archetype enjoys:

> a significance going beyond its immediate normative content, a significance stemming from the fact that it sums up or makes vivid to us the point, purpose, principle, or policy of a whole area of law. Like a Dworkinian principle, the archetype performs a background function in a given legal system. But archetypes differ from Dworkinian principles and policies in that they *also* operate as foreground provisions (…) in a way that expresses or epitomizes the spirit of a whole structured area of doctrine, and does so vividly effectively, publicly, establishing the significance of that area for the entire legal enterprise.[159]

More concretely, and as examples of such archetypes, Waldron points to some judicial precedents as epitomizing the English law of negligence (e.g. *Donohue v. Stevenson*), or the *habeas corpus* statutes as archetypal of the Western legal tradition upholding individual freedom.[160]

I believe it is in this same sense that Ginevra Le Moli has recently conceptualized dignity as a 'mother-right' of international law from which human rights derive, as indicated in the preambles to both the International Covenant on Civil and Political Rights and the International Covenant on Social, Economic and Cultural Rights.[161]

Accordingly, I contend that human dignity has become an archetype of the international legal system, and in particular of the sub-regimes of International Human Rights Law and International Humanitarian Law, for, as Waldron himself has pointed out: "There is an implicit commitment to dignity in the tissues

157 Jeremy Waldron, *Torture, Terror and Trade-offs. Philosophy for the White House* (New York: Oxford University Press, 2010), p. 227.

158 Düwell, 'Human', pp. 28–29; Le Moli, *Dignity*, p. 174; Hörnle and Kremnitzer, 'Protected'.

159 Waldron, *Torture*, p. 228.

160 Ibid., pp. 228–231.

161 "Recognizing that these rights derive from the inherent dignity of the human person". See Le Moli, *Dignity*, pp. 150–151; 191; 246. On the justificatory role of human dignity see also Gilabert, *Dignity*, p. 119.

and sinews of law".[162] Or in the unequivocal words of the Trial Chamber of the International Criminal Tribunal for the former Yugoslavia (ICTY):

> The essence of the whole corpus of international humanitarian law as well as human rights law lies in the protection of the human dignity of every person, whatever his or her gender. The general principle of respect for human dignity is the basic underpinning and indeed the very raison d'être of international humanitarian law and human rights law; indeed in modern times it has become of such paramount importance as to permeate the whole body of international law.[163]

Beyond being a merely doctrinal concept, the idea of a legal archetype carrying the weight of a value such as human dignity in a relatively simple form will prove crucial when it comes to instilling respect for this standard in practice, as we shall see in the chapter devoted to Professional Military Education.

Admittedly, although an archetype is according to Waldron's account both a background *and* a foreground legal concept, it may also be the case that dignity finds its way into the international legal system in all but name as a 'silent partner'[164] or as what Ginevra Le Moli has dubbed 'shadow human dignity', in the sense that, however absent in the text of a treaty, human dignity can still prompt, permeate and influence its preparatory works,[165] thus devolving into a traditional Dworkinian principle fulfilling a background role. Le Moli points to the European Convention on Human Rights and the Refugee Convention as two cases in point. None of these instruments mention human dignity by name. In the case of the former, the European Court of Human Rights regularly – albeit at times selectively – relies on the language of dignity to reinforce its judgments and as a powerful rhetorical/pedagogical device to exhort

162 Waldron, 'How', p. 222.

163 International Criminal Tribunal for the Former Yugoslavia, Trial Chamber, *Prosecutor v. Anto Furundzija*, Judgment, 10 December 1998, Case No. IT-95-17/1-T, par. 183. On the impact of the ad-hoc international criminal tribunals in the development of human dignity as a concept in international law see further Micaela Frulli, 'The Promise of International Criminal Justice: Achievements and Failures in Protecting Human Dignity', in Andrea Gattini, Rosana Garciandia and Philippa Webb, *Human Dignity and International Law* (Leiden: Brill-Nijhoff, 2021), pp. 52–70. On the cross-fertilisation between IHL and International Criminal Law more generally, see Gabriella Blum, 'The Shadow of Success: How International Criminal Law Has Come to Shape the Battlefield', *International Law Studies*, 100:133 (2023), pp. 133–185.

164 Roger Brownsword, 'Human dignity from a legal perspective' in Düwell, Braarvig, Brownsword, and Mieth, *Cambridge Handbook*, pp. 8; 13.

165 Le Moli, *Dignity*, p. 137.

states to comply with the Convention.[166] In the words of linguist John Firth: "You shall know a word by the company it keeps!".[167]

Indeed, a placeholder for dignity can sometimes be the germane idea of 'humanity' – sometimes keeping company to the former as '*human* dignity', sometimes making a solo appearance – particularly in the field of IHL, as a principle featuring in the famous Martens Clause which is to be used as an interpretive guidance within that regime.[168] Yet, 'dignity' is arguably a concept better suited for the military environment than 'humanity'. This is confirmed by the history of the concept of dignity, which was born as the *status*-based notion of *dignitas* in Roman times,[169] and to which *duties* and *hierarchies* were attached, all notions that are quite at home in the military milieu. Further, whilst humanity is usually concerned with the recipient of the respect owed to that normative category, dignity is more focused on the agent that is supposed to conduct themselves in a certain way and from whom certain behaviour is expected. Thereby, a status-based, agent-centred category such as dignity seems intuitively more appropriate for the military mindset than the more passive idea of humanity, considering that military honour is also an agent-based notion that defines the very identity of its bearer.[170] Nevertheless, as we shall see in Chapter 6, contemporary military doctrine is prone to combine (and even conflate) the concepts of dignity and humanity, thus confirming that the two notions are quite compatible at the end of the day.

Now, for all its originality, Waldron's account is admittedly still a work in progress that is not immune to a variety of critiques. One of his main critics is Michael Rosen, who highlights that Waldron does not properly acknowledge the Catholic roots of the concept of dignity.[171] Additionally, Don Herzog has recalled the infamous callousness of some nobles throughout history and thus proposes to follow the example of only 'the best aristocrats'.[172] Further, Wai Chee Dimock fairly raises the question about the tension between the welfare and the rank conceptions, in particular whether Waldron's account entails extending the same material life conditions of former nobles to every human being through so called 'social rights', with all the stress such a demand would

166 Veronica Fikfak and Lora Izvorova, 'Language and Persuasion: Human Dignity at the European Court of Human Rights', *iCourts Working Paper Series*, 287 (2022), pp. 5; 7.

167 John Firth, *Studies in Linguistic Analysis* (Oxford: Basil Blackwell, 1962), p. 11.

168 Sigrid Redse Johansen, *The Military Commander's Necessity. The Law of Armed Conflict and Its Limits* (Cambridge: Cambridge University Press, 2021), p. 72.

169 McCrudden, 'Judicial', p. 656.

170 Robinson, *Honour*, p. 3.

171 Michael Rosen, 'Dignity Past and Present', in Waldron, *Dignity*, pp. 79–98.

172 Don Herzog, 'Aristocratic Dignity?', in Waldron, *Dignity*, pp. 99–118.

put on national budgets worldwide, particularly in the developing world.[173] More recently Manuel Atienza has fairly raised the point about Waldron's account being too idealistic or 'fairy tale-like' when describing the evolution of the history of ideas under such a bright light – an optimism that may stem from Waldron's own religious views.[174]

Still, as it focuses on hierarchy, status, and the performance of social roles, the rank conception offers a lot of potential for the field of Professional Military Ethics.[175] In the next chapter I will explore this potential by revisiting the characterization of military honour as an interpretive concept such that it may coalesce with human dignity as an archetype of contemporary international law.

173 Wai Chee Dimock, 'High and Low', in Waldron, *Dignity*, pp. 119–129.

174 Atienza, *Dignidad*, pp. 120–124.

175 Hennette-Vauchez, 'Dignitas', p. 46.

CHAPTER 4

# Military Honour and Human Dignity

## 1 Introduction: a Tale of Two Dignities

The date is 12 March 2021. In the dead of night and with no civilians in sight due to the Covid-19 curfew still in force, a special 'exfil' mission is under way in downtown Santiago, the capital city of Chile. The package: an officer of the Chilean Army and his battle horse. A special detail of police and military personnel are deployed around the small square that houses the bronze statue of General Manuel Baquedano astride his mount, Diamante. Unveiled a little less than a century before, the statue was erected as an homage to Chile's victory after the War of the Pacific against Peru and Bolivia, between 1879 and 1884. Why did the statue have to be removed, and why under those circumstances?

Although it happened in early 2021, the removal of Baquedano's statue does not directly fall under the wider trend of historic revisionism originated with the 2020 *Black Lives Matter* movement that resulted in the toppling of several Confederate and slave-owner effigies in the United States and the United Kingdom.[1] It was rather the outcome of a home-brewed crisis.

Admittedly, already during the days of Baquedano himself a towering Chilean statesman and author, Vicente Pérez Rosales, began to question society's obsession with glorifying war instead of celebrating more productive endeavours, such as agriculture: "what reason may humankind have for erecting statues of those who apply themselves in the making and the use of machines that shorten life, rather than of those who exert themselves in making machines that prolong it?"[2]

Yet, the removal of Baquedano's statue was precipitated by the social crisis that began in Chile in October of 2019, and which was driven mainly by demands bearing on the welfare conception of dignity, as defined in the previous chapter. Baquedano's statue happened to be inconveniently located at the heart of the protesters' assembly area, *Plaza Baquedano* (also known as

---

1 Peio Riaño, 'La Guerra por la estatua del general Baquedano incendia Chile', https://www.eldiario.es/internacional/guerra-estatuas-general-baquedano-simbolo-incendia-chile_1_7322077.html, 6 April 2022.

2 Translated from the original: "¿qué razón tendrá la humanidad para erigir estatuas a los seres que se adiestran en hacer i en usar máquinas para acortar la vida, i no a aquellos que se desvelan en hacerlas para prolongarla?". See Vicente Pérez Rosales, *Recuerdos del Pasado. 1814–1860*. 3rd ed. (Santiago: Imprenta Gutenberg, 1886), p. 149.

 | DOI:10.1163/9789004754096_007

*Plaza Italia*), a place that has been symbolically rechristened since as *Plaza de la Dignidad* ('Dignity Square'). As an epitome of state-sponsored violence and militarism, Baquedano's effigy was periodically vandalized for over a year, until the Chilean authorities decided to relocate it.

The extraction was overseen by civilian and military authorities. A brief bugle call was heard as the men and women in uniform stood at attention saluting Baquedano and Diamante as they galloped, *ex machina*, through the air. A few days before, the Chilean Army had issued a press release condemning the actions of unknown individuals who had set the statue on fire. The communiqué describes the attack as an "indignity" and an affront on Chilean history. It also calls for the immediate relocation of the statue so it can be restored and "regain the *dignity* a figure so relevant in national history deserves" (emphasis added).[3] After being restored, the statue's final resting place is today the *Museo Histórico Militar* located in Santiago.

It seems, then, that the dignitarian rhetoric that pervades contemporary discourse has also made its way into the military camp. But this is not the first time the military have decried the existence of an attack on their dignity in that corner of the world. Right next door to Chile, in Argentina, similar words were heard once, albeit in much more dramatic fashion in the form of a military uprising in 1987.[4]

The military dictatorship that ruled Argentina since 1976 had to give power back to civilians in 1983, a year after the military fiasco of the Falklands/Malvinas War. Yet, still armed, well organised, and their pride wounded, the Argentinean military were adamantly opposed to judicial prosecutions of human rights violations committed during that military regime, as they saw themselves as fighters in a just, however 'dirty', war against communism. To have to face justice after risking life and limb for the motherland was considered a major humiliation.

The democratic government of President Alfonsín had to navigate the complexities of keeping heavily armed and ideologically committed armed forces in active duty for years, and as a result a law was passed that permitted to terminate all judicial prosecutions in Argentina by early 1987 ('*Ley de Punto Final*').

---

3 "*de manera que recupere ladignidad que merece una figura tan relevante en la historia nacional*". See Chilean Army, 'Comunicado Oficial / Ataque incendiario al Monumento del General Baquedano', https://www.ejercito.cl/prensa/visor/comunicado-oficial-ataque-incendiario-al-monumento-del-general-baquedano, 6 April 2022.

4 Jorge Saborido and Marcelo Borrelli, 'Por la "dignidad Militar": la revista Cabildo y el levantamiento carapintada en la Semana Santa de 1987', *La Trama de la Comunicación*, 18 (2014), pp. 293–311.

Yet, despite such generous concessions, the military were still not satisfied with the new administration's conduction of the country and the criminal cases that were still open against their ranks. As a culmination of protracted indiscipline, in April of 1987 different units in the provinces of Córdoba and Buenos Aires rose in arms against the established constitutional government, seriously threatening the success of one of the earliest examples in the world of the newly minted field of 'transitional justice'.

The rebellious units were eventually contained and neutralized by the bulk of the armed forces, who supported the democratically elected government. The uprising would go down in Argentinean history as the "rebellion of the painted-faces" ("*rebelión de los carapintadas*") as those who rose in arms were depicted in the media wearing their war paint. But the uprising is also known by another name in Argentina: "Operation Military Dignity" ("*Operativo Dignidad Militar*"), a name the rebels themselves reportedly adopted for an action they deemed necessary to restore their honour and dignity as the true defenders of an ungrateful nation.[5]

What these two South American tales of dignity on either side of the Andes suggest is that some military forces are not completely unfamiliar with the dignitarian rhetoric, as dignity is a concept as widespread as it is contested in normative discourse, as seen in previous chapters.

But what conception of human dignity is used by the military when they defend their legacy and reclaim what they believe to be their rightful place as defenders of the nation? Is it the welfare conception, the autonomy conception, the *imago Dei* conception, or the rank conception? Building on the theoretical scaffolding provided so far, this chapter will endeavour to problematize and clarify the possible connections between the concepts of military honour and human dignity.

## 2 What Killed the Duel? The Grammar of Equality in Dignity and War

In a commendable effort to ascertain the foundations of the normative concept of dignity as the basis for human rights, Pablo Gilabert introduces the notion of the 'circumstances of dignity', namely the states of affairs where dignitarian norms are practically relevant to achieve what he calls 'condition-dignity', or dignity as effectively respected:

5 Ibid., p. 303.

> In these circumstances, there are threats and obstacles to the achievement of condition-dignity, and they can be overcome. These threats and obstacles may have various sources. They may arise because of the presence of some disvaluable features of human beings, such as their greed or cruelty. Or they may result because of some deficits in people's exercise of some of their valuable human capacities, such as when they display insufficient sympathy. Or the key factor may be unfavorable external conditions, such as scarcity or material resources.[6]

In light of this characterization, we may ask: is war among those threats and obstacles that make up the circumstances of dignity? In times of war, often considerations about human rights and dignity come only as an afterthought in the form of criminal prosecution of atrocities and war crimes once the dust has settled. However, it is worth asking whether there is any room for dignitarian considerations on the battlefield during ongoing hostilities.

As we have seen, war has its own circumstances making it a permanent possibility in human interaction (the 'Circumstances of War'). Once that possibility materializes, war exhibits its own traits and has a nature of its own. According to one of the most canonical characterizations of war in the study of this phenomenon: "War is nothing but a duel on a larger scale. (…) *War is thus an act of force to compel our enemy to do our will*" (original emphasis).[7] Born in the womb of politics,[8] war is "simply a continuation of political intercourse with the addition of other means,"[9] unfolding as another form of communication among enemies, like speech or writing, endowed with its own 'grammar', albeit not with its own logic, as that logic remains ever political.[10]

What constitutes the grammar of the particular way of communication that is the duel, the basic pragmatic unit of warfare? Clausewitz, the author who fathered these renowned words, admittedly lived in a time when the duel was still popular among aristocratic men. Many officers who had served in the Napoleonic Wars came back home with a fancy for duelling as a way to uphold their honour at the slightest provocation.[11] This happened despite many attempts by governments over the centuries to outlaw such a colourful

6 Pablo Gilabert, *Human Dignity and Human Rights* (New York: Oxford University Press, 2018), p. 132.

7 Carl von Clausewitz, *On War* (New York: Oxford University Press, 2008), p. 13.

8 Ibid., p. 100.

9 Ibid., p. 252.

10 Ibid.

11 Kwame A. Appiah, *The Honor Code: How Moral Revolutions Happen* (New York: W.W. Norton & Company, 2010), p. 22.

and mystified challenge to the legitimate monopoly of force that the modern state had been trying to secure since the late Middle Ages.[12]

Indeed, just like a dialect being shaped by the passing of time and the practice of consecutive generations, duelling began acquiring a progressively formal articulation in medieval times before reaching the highly ritualised form it exhibited in Clausewitz's days. But it was not the only form of dispute settlement through violence that existed in the Middle Ages – and violence was, without a doubt, the common currency at the time.[13]

David Whetham has thoroughly documented the array of forms endemic violence acquired during the Middle Ages. Medieval society knew many forms of violence, both legal and illegal. In what matters here, legal violence could be pursued through three main avenues: (i) *self-defence*, as a matter of natural law not needing any prior authorization by a legitimate authority; (ii) a *feud* or a 'private war' between parties, that is, a permanent state of violence that becomes increasingly regulated over time, based on the principle of self-help and not aimed at the destruction of the adversary but to compel an agreement to reach peace (namely, a state of equilibrium of rights between the parties), eventually requiring the authorization of a prince to take place; and (iii) *war*, that is a sort of 'public feud' or feud between kings, with no superior authority to arbitrate the dispute and with all-out destruction allowed.[14]

An additional form of legalized violence in the Middle Ages came as 'trial by combat' or 'judicial duel', a subtype of ordeal within the context of a dispute before a court of law. This was a highly ritualised and regulated use of force with the consent of the authorities, such that: "By the thirteenth century, the formal proceedings had become increasingly exclusive with duels being bound up with the codes of chivalry and the *ius militare*".[15]

Nevertheless, the rising power of central government and its claim to the legitimate monopoly of force would eventually render the duel obsolete and redundant as a legal tool, for instance being finally abolished in England in 1818,[16] around the time Clausewitz chose to distil the essence of war precisely into this quaint form of violence.

Thereby, we may find an answer to Appiah's question "what killed the duel?"[17] in the historic process of increasing centralization of the use of force

12 Ibid., pp. 29–30.

13 Pinker, *Angels*, p. 66.

14 David Whetham, *Just Wars and Moral Victories. Surprise, Deception, and the Normative Framework of European War in the Later Middle Ages* (Leiden: Brill, 2009), pp. 71–113.

15 Ibid., p. 95.

16 Ibid., p. 101.

17 Appiah, *Honor*, p. 44.

by the modern state, culminating in the mass-army fuelled by industrial might during the 20th century[18] and to the detriment of the erstwhile atomization of violence that characterized the Middle Ages. It was the state who killed the duel, as modern military discipline displaced medieval chivalric morality.[19]

Indeed, according to Richard Kaeuper, the Middle Ages was a time when the phenomenon of violence was widespread in society, with those choosing to make of it their trade and creed, i.e. warriors and "thugs on horseback" (otherwise known as "knights"[20]), posing a constant threat to public order.[21] As Whetham has remarked: "For much of the early Middle Ages, the lack of any Leviathan entity and the consequent absence of centralised authority meant that there was something akin to the 'State of Nature' suggested by Hobbes."[22] Crucial to this "chronic sense of insecurity"[23] was the entitled attitude of knights towards violence as a prerogative integral to their social class: "The lay elite cherished as a defining privilege this right to violence in any matter touching their prickly sense of honour".[24] The fact that this was an hereditary class helped in perpetuating this worldview throughout time.[25] Admittedly, knightly armies also helped expand the boundaries of medieval society in Europe.[26]

Consequently, it does not come as a surprise that the warrior class resisted all attempts by kings and sovereigns to regulate and curtail violence in any of its many medieval guises, legal (including feuds and duels) or otherwise.[27] As Frantzen points out, knights created their own code of conduct to preserve their honour and not abuse their power.[28] As the modern state gradually achieved the monopoly of legitimate violence over the centuries, thus

18 Wilbur J. Scott, Karin Modesto De Angelis, and David R. Segal, *Military Sociology. A Guided Introduction* (New York: Routledge, 2023), p. 56.

19 James Turner Johnson, *Just War Tradition and the Restraint of War. A Moral and Historical Inquiry* (Princeton: Princeton University Press, 1984), p. 179.

20 Nancy Lindisfarne and Jonathan Neale, *Why Men? A Human History of Violence and Inequality* (London: Hurst & Co., 2023), p. 332.

21 Richard W. Kaeuper, *Chivalry and Violence in Medieval Europe* (New York: Oxford University Press, 1999), p. 2.

22 Whetham, *Just*, pp. 76–77.

23 Johan Huizinga, *The Autumn of the Middle Ages* (Chicago: The University of Chicago Press, 1996), p. 20.

24 Kaeuper, *Chivalry*, p. 8; see also p. 28.

25 J.F. Verbruggen, *The Art of Warfare in Western Europe During the Middle Ages* (Rochester: The Boydell Press, 1997), p. 27.

26 Ibid., p. 110.

27 Whetham, *Just*, p. 101.

28 Allen J. Frantzen, *Bloody Good. Chivalry, Sacrifice, and the Great War* (Chicago: University of Chicago Press, 2004), p. 3.

"cleansing" society of the bellicose relations that were rampant in the Middle Ages,[29] duelling was seen as a last stronghold of chivalrous uses of force. As Kaeuper remarks:

> Duelling certainly demonstrates at least a partial continuance into the early modern era of the old chivalric theme of a defence of honour through violence, and the old chivalric sense of political and even ethical autonomy as well. This survival of the chivalric obsession with honour and the perhaps even heightened assertion of personal independence seemed to the participants not so much an illegal as an extra-legal practice, a statement of their freedom from troublesome restraints in important matters of their own choosing.[30]

But whether perceived as illegal or extra-legal, duelling certainly represented a challenge to the state's purported monopoly of violence – admittedly, a Weberian notion that has become intuitive in present times but that was not always guaranteed as the modern state was taking shape – such that it could be construed as a veritable crime of *lèse majesté*,[31] an offence against the sovereign and the centripetal forces it wielded. Such defiance may be better understood by way of analogy if we consider the history of expropriations of private property from the Middle Ages to early modern times. If violence was previously 'privately owned' by knights, the advent of the modern state brought about a process of expropriation of such a particular preserve all in the name of the public good, which includes considerations bearing on the common defence of the polity.[32] It was the merit of Hugo Grotius, one of the greatest theorists of the modern state, to highlight the importance of the public good (*utilitas publica*) as a justification for expropriating private property.[33] Not surprisingly, Grotius also believed in limiting what he classified as 'private wars' (i.e. wars without the interference of public authority) to the maximum extent possible, always favouring judicial settlement,[34] again bolstering the case for the centripetal force of the modern state to advance the public good.

29 Michel Foucault, *Society Must Be Defended* (London: Penguin Books, 2003), p. 48.
30 Kaeuper, *Chivalry*, pp. 305–306.
31 Appiah, *Honor*, p. 29.
32 Susan Reynolds, *Before Eminent Domain. Toward a History of Expropriation of Land for the Common Good* (Chapel Hill: University of North Carolina Press, 2010), pp. 128–129.
33 Ibid., p. 95. See also Hugo Grotius, *The Right of War and Peace* (Indianapolis: Liberty Fund, 2005), Book I, I.VI.
34 Ibid., Book I, III.I–II.

Thus, the duel became a last pocket of medieval violence within Western modern society, as the result of a slow historic evolution of statecraft. A much swifter movement, but with similar political aims, may be observed in Japan as the feudal society imbued with a centuries-old warrior culture saw radical change being enacted by legal fiat supressing the special rights of the Samurai, all in the name of state-building in the fashion of Western nations in the late nineteenth century.[35] Coincidently, it was around the same time that the myth of the American cowboy in the wild west was being shaped, with his signature flair for duelling and disdain for central authority, as later immortalized in hundreds of films that would preserve it in the collective imagery until our days.[36]

The state, then, killed the duel, at least between private citizens, as war or the ultimate duel between sovereigns was pretty much in vogue still. That is perhaps why Clausewitz saw in the duel something so integral to warfare, in spite of is inexorable obsolescence in the domestic realm. The duel's allure among the aristocratic classes at the time, despite its increasing illegality, might have stemmed from an essential fact defining the very structure of the practice: equality. Indeed, according to Rule XXXVIII of the *Royal Code of Honour for the Regulation of Duelling*: "The parties (…) have, by the very act of meeting, made an acknowledgement of equality".[37]

Naturally, this did not mean that aristocrats were politically committed to the instauration of an egalitarian society, or that they participated in that passion for equality that, according to Tocqueville, was a quintessential feature of democratic centuries.[38] This aristocratic obsession with peer recognition might be better characterized as a 'sportsmanlike passion for symmetry', which was perfectly encapsulated by the duel in both its structure and spirit of fair play to be observed among those deemed equal. This quaint mentality even survived well into the 20th century, as evidenced by the British government's refusal to authorize the assassination of Adolf Hitler in 1938 on the grounds

---

35 Shannon E. French, *The Code of the Warrior. Exploring Warrior Values Past and Present* (Lanham: Rowman and Littlefield Publishers, 2005), pp. 226–227. See also Malcolm Vale, 'Chivalry and the Conduct of Warfare – Illusion and Reality', in Bernhard Koch (ed.), *Chivalrous Combatants? The Meaning of Military Virtue Past and Present* (Baden-Baden: Nomos, 2019), p. 30.

36 Leo Braudy, *From Chivalry to Terrorism* (New York: Vintage Books, 2005), p. 207; David Cerdá, *Ética para Valientes. El honor en nuestros días* (Madrid: Rialp, 2022), p. 182.

37 Appiah, *Honor*, p. 41.

38 Alexis De Tocqueville, *Democracy in America*, Vol. III (Indianapolis: Liberty Fund, 2010), pp. 872–879.

that such an act would be "unsportsmanlike",[39] as mentioned in the Prologue. This passion for symmetry arguably also made its way into the main legal regime governing armed conflict, International Humanitarian Law ('IHL'). Indeed, regardless of their *ad bellum* considerations to go to war, belligerents are to be considered equal before IHL,[40] as this regime governs an essentially horizontal or symmetrical relationship between allegedly co-equal parties.[41] Accordingly, when referring to irregular forces such as militias and resistance movements, the ICRC has pointed out in its 1960 Commentary to the Geneva Conventions that the legal requirement of "carrying arms openly" is intended to guarantee the "loyalty of the fighting"[42] even among seemingly asymmetrical forces. These legal institutions mirror the philosophical position known as traditionalism within the Just War tradition, as seen in Chapter 1.

Indeed, the sportsmanlike passion for symmetry, and its correlative unease around asymmetry, is arguably also relevant for contemporary debates on the ethics of killing, as it has usually been the case when novel means and methods of warfare, such as sniping and drones,[43] enter the battlefield. Accordingly, Gabriella Blum has classified the theories philosophers have formulated over the years to justify killing in war into three distinct categories: immunity theory, honour theory, and convention.[44] Immunity theory relies on a self-defence rationale whereby those who do not pose a threat should be immune from attack, and is embraced by the camp known as 'revisionists' within the Just War Tradition.[45] Convention theory basically deprives the rules of war of any moral content and grounds the principle of distinction between combatants and

39 Ward Thomas, 'Norms and Security: The Case of International Assassination', *International Security*, 25 (2000), p. 113.

40 Marco Sassòli, Antoine Bouvier, and Ann Quintin, *How does law protect in war?* 3rd ed. Vol. 1 (Geneva: ICRC, 2011), p. 19.

41 Jens David Ohlin, 'The Duty to Capture', *Minnesota Law Review*, 97 (2013), p. 1323; Asa Kasher, 'Combatant's Life and Human Dignity', *Israel Yearbook on Human Rights*, 24 (2014), pp. 219–246.

42 'Convention (III) relative to the Treatment of Prisoners of War. Geneva, 12 August 1949. Commentary of 1960. Article 4 – Prisoners of War', https://ihl-databases.icrc.org/en/ihl-treaties/gciii-1949/article-4/commentary/1960?activeTab=undefined, 2 May 2023. See also Redse Johansen, *The Military Commander's Necessity. The Law of Armed Conflict and Its Limits* (Cambridge: Cambridge University Press, 2021), p. 202.

43 Neil C. Renic, *Asymmetric Killing. Risk Avoidance, Just War, and the Warrior Ethos* (Oxford: Oxford University Press, 2020), pp. 24; 106; 158. See also Niklas Schörnig, 'Chivalry and Sniping – Simply Incompatible?', in Bernhard Koch (ed.), *Chivalrous Combatants? The Meaning of Military Virtue Past and Present* (Baden-Baden: Nomos, 2019), p. 194.

44 Gabriella Blum, 'The Dispensable Lives of Soldiers', *Journal of Legal Analysis*, 2:1 (2010), p. 133.

45 Ibid., pp. 133–134.

civilians on (more or less) arbitrary convention or agreement among states.[46] More relevant to our purposes in this chapter is the honour theory, which justifies non-combatant immunity and its correlative of combatant targetability by resorting to "medieval notions of honor and dignity".[47] Blum believes that this theory can be found in the writings of thinkers such as Thomas Nagel and Paul Kahn.

Reflecting on the war in Vietnam five decades ago, Nagel suggested that the hostility that characterizes war and conflict will always remain an interpersonal interaction between people, which need not dehumanize them, but on the contrary "extremely hostile behavior toward another is compatible with treating him as a person – even perhaps as an end in himself".[48] As a consequence of such a social reading of conflict, and mindful of the risk of romanticizing war, Nagel concludes that fighting fair entails an acknowledgement of agency even amidst the most hostile of interactions:

> There seems to be a perfect natural conception of the distinction between fighting clean and fighting dirty. To fight dirty is to direct one's hostility or aggression not at its proper object, but at a peripheral target which may be more vulnerable, and through which the proper object can be attacked indirectly.
>
> (...)
>
> It may seem paradoxical to assert that to fire a machine gun at someone who is throwing hand grenades at your emplacement is to treat him as a human being. Yet the relation with him is direct and straightforward. The attack is aimed specifically against the threat presented by a dangerous adversary, and not against a peripheral target through which he happens to be vulnerable but which has nothing to do with that threat.[49]

Writing at the dawn of the so called 'war on terror' and its predilection for targeted killings, Paul Kahn also reflected on what he called "the paradox of riskless warfare", which arises whenever the "structural reciprocal risk"[50] that has always characterized war is abandoned in pursuit of asymmetrical forms of violence, thus turning into policing, i.e. the application of force to the morally

46 Ibid., pp. 137–138.

47 Ibid., p. 137.

48 Thomas Nagel. "War and Massacre," Philosophy and Public Affairs, Vol. 1 no. 2 (1972), pp. 133–134.

49 Ibid., pp. 134; 138; 142.

50 Renic, *Asymmetric*, p. 35.

guilty.[51] Even though it seems to be the future of warfare, Kahn concludes that what is problematic about riskless war is that: "It is an image of warfare without the possibility of chivalry".[52] This is not necessarily an evil, he adds, but if war is to be transformed into police action, then the rules of engagement should be adjusted accordingly.[53]

Returning to Blum's account, the author posits that, even though medieval warfare was succeeded by conflicts characterized by reciprocity, professionalism and mass armies, some modern rules of war were still "driven by lingering remnants of medieval notions of honor and fairness on the battlefield",[54] of the kind Nagel and Kahn draw on to make the case for the honour theory, especially among the officer class.[55] As already seen in the Introduction, this medieval legacy is epitomized, for example, by the Canadian Law of Armed Conflict Manual, which includes chivalry among the "primary concepts" of this legal regime in the following terms:

> The concept of chivalry is difficult to define. It refers to the conduct of armed conflict in accordance with certain recognized formalities and courtesies. An armed conflict is rarely a polite contest. Nevertheless, the concept of chivalry is reflected in specific prohibitions such as those against dishonourable or treacherous conduct and against misuse of enemy flags or flags of truce. The concept of chivalry makes armed conflict slightly less savage and more civilized for the individual combatant.[56]

Thereby, inasmuch as it aims at benefitting not only the victims of war, but also its agents, it would appear more reflection on the normative connections between chivalry and modern IHL is needed if we are to fully understand the

51 Paul Kahn, 'The Paradox of Riskless Warfare', *Philosophy and Public Policy Quarterly*, 22:3 (2002), p. 2.

52 Ibid., p. 4.

53 Ibid.

54 Blum, 'Dispensable', p. 122; Helen M. Kinsella, *The Image before the Weapon. A Critical History of the Distinction between Combatant and Civilian* (Ithaca: Cornell University Press, 2011), p. 26.

55 Stefan Oeter, 'The (Non-)Importance of Chivalry in International Humanitarian Law', in Bernhard Koch (ed.), *Chivalrous Combatants? The Meaning of Military Virtue Past and Present* (Baden-Baden: Nomos, 2019), p. 52.

56 Canadian Armed Forces, 'Joint Doctrine Manual: Law of Armed Conflict at the Operational and Tactical Levels', https://www.fichl.org/fileadmin/_migrated/content_uploads/Canadian_LOAC_Manual_2001_English.pdf, 10 June 2022, par. 202.7. See also G. Corn, V. Hansen, R. Jackson, C. Jenks, E. Talbot Jensen and J. Schoettler, *The Law of Armed Conflict: An Operational Approach* (New York: Wolters Klumer, 2012), p. 202.

entirety of the phenomenon of armed violence that has been with us since times immemorial.

## 3 Chasing after Windmills

> We must remember that there never was a time when chivalry was perceived as other than in decline
>
> ALLEN J. FRANTZEN

In a study on the past and present of military virtues, Bernhard Koch underscores the normative importance of chivalry in the following terms:

> This volume concerns only aspects of the ethical side of the knighthood – that is, chivalry. This chivalric ethos is not simply a historical fact, but naturally also an outgrowth of literary fiction and idealization. However, virtues and values such as 'courage, honor and glory' undoubtedly play a role in this ethos, though they are often underexplored in the present-day discussion of legitimate use of force.[57]

At the outset, and before venturing any further into the potential connections that may be found between military honour and human dignity by resorting to the erstwhile code of chivalry and practices echoing its spirit, such as the duel or military manuals, a word of caution is needed. When looking into the past from the vantage point of the present it is very easy to succumb to one of two perils: we can either romanticize old practices, or we can dismiss them out of hand as quaint and absurd. Accordingly, the Scylla and Charybdis we should avoid in this exploration correspond to nostalgia and presentism.[58]

---

57 Bernhard Koch, 'Chivalry between History, Tradition and Obsolescence: Overcoming One-Dimensionality in the Ethics of War. An Introduction to this Volume', in Bernhard Koch (ed.), *Chivalrous Combatants? The Meaning of Military Virtue Past and Present* (Baden-Baden: Nomos, 2019), p. 7. On the etymological differences between 'knight' and 'chevalier', see Braudy, *From*, pp. 99–100.

58 A third danger that might arise when looking back into the past is that of historicism, as illustrated by the U.S. Supreme Court in its surprising 2022 opinion overruling the *Roe v. Wade* and *Casey* precedents on abortion rights, and thus depriving American citizens from a well-established constitutional right merely because it did not exist at a time when that particular legal system and society had not even been founded yet. Indeed, in its decision the Court looked into common-law sources dating back to the 13th century to conclude that "we are aware of no common-law case or authority, and the parties have not pointed to any, that remotely suggests a positive *right* to procure an abortion at any

In his own study of violence in the Middle Ages, Richard Kaeuper identifies these pitfalls at the beginning of his inquiry. Kaeuper uses Mark Twain's famous time-travel adventure *A Connecticut Yankee in King Arthur's Court* to illustrate how the eyes of the present – of any time in the present, whether Mark Twain's nineteenth century culture, or our own twenty-first century society – can easily forget to approach the past critically. In the words of Twain's protagonist when offering his first impressions on the early medieval society he found himself suddenly stranded in: "It was hard to associate them with anything cruel or dreadful; and yet they dealt in tales of blood and suffering with a guileless relish that made me almost forget to shudder".[59] Inspired by this approach, Kaeuper posits:

> For the great danger in the study of chivalry is to view this important phenomenon through the rose-tinted lenses of romanticism, to read chivalry in terms of what we want it to be rather than what it was. However glorious and refined its literature, however elevated its ideals, however enduring its link with Western ideas of gentlemanliness – and whatever we think of that – we must not forget that knighthood was nourished on aggressive impulses, that it existed to use its shining armour and sharp-edged weaponry in acts of showy and bloody violence. As Twain reminds us succinctly, we must not forget to shudder.[60]

Furthermore, the violence of this period, with all its "passionate intensity" and "fervent pathos",[61] was not only "showy and bloody"; it could resort to all kinds of tactics, manoeuvres, and even trickery and deception once the legal use of violence had been authorized, as documented by Whetham.[62] Accordingly, knights have been called "warlords" and "bloodthirsty marauders" by Steven Pinker,[63] as "Chivalry was in fact compatible with stark, ruthless slaughter" as indicated by H.J. Hewitt.[64] Or as Goethe puts it in his drama *Götz von*

stage of pregnancy". See *Dobbs v. Jackson Women's Health Organization*, 597 U.S. __ (2022), p. 20.

59 Mark Twain, *A Connecticut Yankee in King Arthur's Court* (New York: Barnes & Noble, 2005), p. 61.

60 Kaeuper, *Chivalry*, p. 2.

61 Huizinga, *Autumn*, pp. 1–9.

62 Whetham, *Just, passim*.

63 Pinker, *Angels*, pp. 66–67.

64 H.J. Hewitt, *The Black Prince's Expeditions of 1355–1357* (Manchester: Manchester University Press, 1958), p. 10.

*Berlichingen With the Iron Hand*: "Even the worthiest knights do more harm than good in their excursions".

The lesson to be drawn from such cautionary accounts of the Middle Ages is that we should tread carefully when looking into the past, lest our brains dry out as Don Quixote's from reading all those epic tales of chivalry that prompted the '*caballero de la triste figura*' ('knight of the sorrowful figure') to chase after all kinds of delusions and fantasies, when what he was really after were just windmills in the horizon.

This lesson becomes all the more compelling as the character of warfare has changed dramatically over the centuries, such that the kind of armed conflict that knights fought in is fundamentally different from what goes on in today's battlefields. Indeed, if the *nature* of war presupposes a political confrontation among equals encapsulated by the duel as its basic unit, the truth is that its *character*[65] or manifestation of this phenomenon in present-day conditions exhibits a marked asymmetric appearance, especially in the numerous conflicts fought between powerful state forces and non-state actors.[66]

On the other hand, we would not be doing justice to chivalry as a historically documented phenomenon if we were to dismiss it as obsolete due to presentism and forget it also espoused a normative dimension bearing on a plethora of ethical, religious, and legal standards governing the life and death of the knight and everyone around him. As Kaeuper himself points out: "The medieval world knew much violence, to be sure, but at least clerical ideas set the terms of the discourse and began to make a difference, to civilize the brutal warriors, and help them make their world a better place".[67] Such ambivalent violence, Frantzen further argues, "both built and destroyed communities" as chivalry was "at once war-making and peacemaking".[68] We do not need to adhere to that normative code to acknowledge that those partaking in the practices defined by such rules did actually believe in it.[69]

---

65 Rosa Brooks, 'Fighting words. Has the nature of "war" changed since the days of Clausewitz?', https://foreignpolicy.com/2014/02/04/fighting-words/, 04 February 2014. See also Michael P. Ferguson, 'The nature of war is not changing in Ukraine', https://thehill.com/opinion/national-security/3526558-the-nature-of-war-is-not-changing-in-ukraine/?fbclid=IwAR30UkkAy-DUdmhcrE90UjWXu1NzYxUbqoN07nr9YZkDjg7ZfY53Cp6myr4&fs=e&s=cl, 16 June 2022.

66 SIPRI, 'Global developments in armed conflicts, peace processes and peace operations', https://www.sipri.org/yearbook/2021/02, 1 March 2022.

67 Kaeuper, *Chivalry*, p. 84.

68 Frantzen, *Bloody*, p. 22.

69 Alasdair MacIntyre, *After Virtue*, 3rd ed. (Notre Dame: University of Notre Dame Press, 2007), p. 121.

Moreover, it was knights themselves who believed that the ideals of chivalry were something worth striving for, not out of purely pragmatic considerations bearing on their own survival as an elite group,[70] but because they genuinely believed that they could become better warriors and members of their respective communities by adhering to the code,[71] even if they did not always uphold such lofty standards in practice.[72]

What is, then, the best epistemological attitude to approach such historic normative standards and practices, in a way that they do not end up being mere romanticism or be dismissed altogether as useless and impractical, that is, to successfully navigate between nostalgia and presentism? In Chapter 2 we briefly introduced Alasdair MacIntyre's moral philosophy as a most notable attempt to account for the transformation of ethical standards in the transition between the late Middle Ages and Modernity, precisely the same period that is studied by scholars of chivalry such as Huizinga and Kaeuper. Thus, in order to make better sense of what MacIntyre would dub a 'simulacrum of morality' when talking about such practices as chivalry, two useful analytical tools for a critical approach to the period are the notions of interpretive concepts and essentially contested concepts, both of which have been used in previous chapters to describe military honour and human dignity, respectively.

We saw in Chapter 2 that military honour can be construed, like courtesy, as what Ronald Dworkin once called an "interpretive concept",[73] namely a concept that entails the following two main assumptions: (i) the practice has value, meaning that it serves some interest or purpose or enforces some principle, and therefore there is a point to it; and (ii) the requirements of the practice are not unchangeable but are sensitive to its purpose, such that the rules have to be applied, interpreted, extended or modified according the point of the practice.

When these assumptions are no longer observed, then the practice becomes mechanical and devoid of purpose,[74] as we saw with the example of the prefixes *Mister, Monsieur* and *Don*. It is arguably also what happens when traces of an erstwhile sophisticated language like Latin can be found in a modern language derived from it, for instance, Spanish. The average Spanish speaker inadvertently uses a variety of echoes of Latin to conveys ideas, without even

70 Verbruggen, *Art*, pp. 346–347.
71 Frantzen, *Bloody*, p. 3.
72 Verbruggen, *Art*, p. 273.
73 Ronald Dworkin, *Law's Empire* (Oxford: Hart Publishing, 1998), p. 47.
74 Ibid., p. 49.

having to set foot in a classics department or a law school.[75] This could be merely a mechanical invocation of an alien language, and it probably is so most of the time; yet, since they are used with meaning, they could otherwise provide an example as to an interpretive attitude that adapts and thus stands the test of time, even after 'vulgarization' takes place.

The same could be said of modern military honour as a direct descendant of the medieval code of chivalry,[76] after war and duelling were "vulgarized"[77] with the triumph of the modern state and its centripetal organization of social violence as the preserve of a new professional class.[78]

At the same time, we saw in Chapter 3 that human dignity has been characterized in the literature as an "essentially contested concept".[79] As such, human dignity is an appraisive concept, used both to assertively to make the case for a position or to defend it, while remaining vague or open-ended across time. It is further an internally complex concept around which revolve a number of different rival descriptions, with outstanding exemplars found in the accounts of Cicero and Kant, among others.

Since the contention here is that military honour is an interpretive concept and human dignity an essentially contested one, it is worth clarifying at this point that an interpretive concept is not the same as an essentially contested concept. Whereas an interpretive concept is sensitive to the practice's point and the attitudes people take towards it, it does not necessarily entail contention or rivalry. For instance, although social notions of courtesy or etiquette may evolve, this does not mean that people will always disagree about what courtesy or etiquette entail and actively engage in debate about it. They might not even articulate the reasons why they follow the rules of courtesy or etiquette. Debate might still happen around such practices, but this is not required for the practice to continue. In fact, the less contention, the more chances the practice will endure and perhaps flourish, provided its participants do not forget the point behind it. This is not the case with essentially contested concepts, like justice or dignity, where competition between rival

75 For example: *a priori, ad hoc, alter ego, conditio sine qua non, idem, in fragranti, lapsus, mea culpa, modus operandi, status quo, tabula rasa, vox populi*, etc.

76 Morris Janowitz, *The Professional Soldier* (New York: Free Press, 2017), p. 217; Allen J. Frantzen, *Bloody Good. Chivalry, Sacrifice, and the Great War* (Chicago: University of Chicago Press, 2004), p. 3.

77 Appiah, *Honor*, p. 47.

78 Kaeuper, *Chivalry*, p. 305.

79 Philippe-André Rodriguez, 'Human dignity as an essentially contested concept', *Cambridge Review of International Affairs*, 28:4 (2015), pp. 743–756; W.B. Gallie, 'Essentially Contested Concepts', *Proceedings of the Aristotelian Society*, 56 (1955–1956), pp. 167–198.

conceptions is key to the health of the concept and such rivalry is articulated as often as possible. To further illustrate this difference, we may think of interpretive concepts as a military parade advancing in one direction ceremoniously and unimpeded, whereas essentially contested concepts resemble more a pitched battle with clearly defined opposite sides struggling to dominate the field. Alternatively, interpretive concepts may be thought of as a symphony performed by an orchestra with a fixed structure and tempo, whereas essentially contested concepts are more akin to a disjointed jam session among jazz musicians.

Equipped with these analytical tools, we might stand a better chance at digging up the relics of the Middle Ages with the appropriate critical mindset to understand their lingering echoes and salvage what can be of use to make better sense of our practices in the present, especially as they might not live up to the challenge of justifying our behaviour beyond mere instrumental considerations.[80] In that sense, this is not merely a history of ideas, as pointed out in the Introduction, but an ethical exploration of normative standards whose contents might be in application until today.

## 4 Military Honour and Human Dignity in the Literature

In previous chapters I have summarized the foremost scholarly contributions pertaining to both military honour and human dignity. It is time now to ascertain whether those works have attempted to establish a connection between these two categories, or whether there is a conceptual gap in the literature that needs to be filled.

Admittedly, to some authors like Peter Olsthoorn dignity and honour are conceptually different since the former is universal, whereas the latter needs to be attributed to a limited range of people in order to make sense. Yet, he concedes that honour has experienced a similar evolution to dignity, when Roman classical honour is compared to a more egalitarian conception of democratic honour, a shift similar to the evolution from *dignitas* to universal dignity. Nevertheless, he ultimately discards human dignity as a possible content or touchstone for military honour as too abstract a notion.[81]

Similarly, Avishai Margalit famously argued in *The Decent Society* that, in order to combat humiliation, we must move from a traditional conception of

80 Bernhard Koch, '"God, How I hate the 20th Century". On Chivalry as a Myth and as an Ethical Virtue', *Ethics and Armed Forces*, 2 (2021), p. 31.

81 Peter Olsthoorn, *Military Ethics and Virtues* (New York: Routledge, 2011), pp. 13; 22; 40.

social honour (by definition reserved only to some), to a more egalitarian conception of honour for all, otherwise known as "human dignity". Although *dignitas* meant social honour for the Romans, Margalit contends that today dignity amounts to this type of "universalized honour" grounding respect for every single human being and shielding them from humiliation.[82] In this sense, Steven Pinker similarly remarks about this evolution: "A culture of honor, in which men were respected for lashing out against insults, became a culture of dignity, in which men were respected for controlling their impulses".[83]

We have already seen how, in a similar vein, Appiah believes that honour has been universalized such that we owe each other a special kind of what Darwall calls "recognition respect",[84] namely 'positive recognition respect' in the sense that not only we value a basic feature in others, but we also admire or esteem them as if they were our peers sharing in a specific quality with us. That quality is human dignity, which is how we designate honour in the age of universal human rights.[85] Similarly, Sidney Axinn treats honour and individual dignity as synonyms.[86]

Now, when it comes to the implications for *military* honour in particular, some authors have grappled with the idea that it bears certain relation to human dignity, however intuitively. For instance, Michael Rosen postulates that in a democratic society it is of the utmost importance for the state to display strict respect for dignity when exercising its most extreme power, including criminal punishment and the waging of war[87] – the latter being the kind of setting where military honour arguably is supposed to operate.

Some have attempted to connect military honour and human dignity more directly. James Whitman explains how notions of military honour have helped carving out a rich dignitarian jurisprudence in post-war Germany.[88] Eyal

82 Avishai Margalit, *The Decent Society* (Cambridge: Harvard University Press, 1996), pp. 57–58; see also Michael Rosen, *Dignity. It's History and Meaning* (Cambridge: Harvard University Press, 2012) p. 27, tracing this evolution back to Kant. On applying Margalit's thesis to the legal profession, see David Luban, *Legal Ethics and Human Dignity* (Cambridge: Cambridge University Press, 2009), p. 88.

83 Pinker, *Angels*, p. 592.

84 Stephen Darwall, 'Two Kinds of Respect', *Ethics*, 88:1 (1977), pp. 38–39.

85 Appiah, *Honor*, pp. 13–14; 128–130; 177.

86 Sidney Axinn, *A Moral Military*, 2nd ed. (Philadelphia: Temple University Press, 2009). pp. 55–56.

87 Rosen, *Dignity*, p. 75.

88 James Whitman, 'Enforcing Civility and Respect: Three Societies', *The Yale Law Journal*, 109 (2000), pp. 1339–1341.

Benvenisti draws on Kant to defend the dignity of enemy civilians in combat.[89] Shannon French highlights the importance for the warrior to respect their enemy's dignity, lest the former risk losing their humanity. Thus, respect for the warrior's moral code operates as a shield or "psychological armor" protecting the soldier from moral injury.[90] Larry May reaches the same conclusion when he explains how mercy, as a demand of military honour, is owed to every human being because of their equal dignity.[91]

Turning to the contributions by practitioners in the field of Professional Military Ethics ('PMEt'), human dignity as a value to be fostered and protected in times of war is also mentioned, albeit in a cursory way, in specific works on military virtues.[92] For instance, respect for the enemy's intrinsic dignity has been espoused by John Thomas, who highlights it as one of the main ethical challenges the modern military face.[93] Furthermore, dignity has also been associated with the military virtues of justice,[94] compassion,[95] and the discipline necessary to respect even the enemy's dignity.[96] Snider, Oh, and Toner point out international law and human rights as sources of professional military ethics,[97] thus indirectly relying on dignity as the bedrock value of those regimes. More so, according to these authors the U.S. Army's doctrine specifies that "preserving noncombatants lives and dignity is central to mission accomplishment".[98]

89 Eyal Benvenisti, 'Human dignity in combat: The duty to spare enemy civilians', *Israel Law Review*, 39:2 (2006), pp. 81–109.

90 Shannon E. French, *The Code of the Warrior. Exploring Warrior Values Past and Present* (Lanham: Rowman and Littlefield Publishers, 2005), pp. 10–11.

91 Larry May, *War Crimes and Just War* (Cambridge: Cambridge University Press, 2007), p. 81.

92 Olsthoorn, *Military*, pp. 5; 11. See also Juan Moliner, 'La educación y formación en ética militar', in Centro Conjunto de Desarollo de Conceptos, *Cuestiones sobre ética militar* (Madrid: Ministerio de Defensa, 2022), p. 26.

93 John Thomas, 'Ethical challenges for the modern military', in Don Carrick, James Connelly and David Whetham (eds.), *Making the Military Moral. Contemporary Challenges and Responses in Military Ethics Education* (New York: Routledge, 2018), pp. 102–104. See also Moliner, 'Educación', p. 37.

94 Edward Barrett, 'Justice. Overview: Just (and Unjust) Warriors: Nature and Causes', in Skerker, Whetham, and Carrick, *Military*, pp. 33, 34.

95 John Sattler and Michael Skerker, 'Case Study 1: Compassion toward Enemies', in Skerker, Whetham, and Carrick, *Military*, p. 299.

96 Benoit Royal, 'Case Study 1: The Necessity of Self Control and the Perils of Anger', in Skerker, Whetham, and Carrick, *Military*, p. 323.

97 Don Snider, Paul Oh and Kevin Toner, 'The Army's Professional Military Ethic in an Era of Persistent Conflict', https://catalog.hathitrust.org/Record/007099091, 7 April 2021, pp. 7–11.

98 Ibid., p. 18. See also Jeffrey Wilson, 'An Ethics Curriculum for an Evolving Army', in Robinson, De Lee and Carrick, *Ethics*, p. 38; 2006 COIN Manual: "preserving non-combatants lives

Paul Robinson further posits that respect for human life and dignity is a discrete military value, as evinced by the Canadian Armed Forces' and the Israeli Defense Forces' ethical doctrine,[99] both of which we shall revisit in Chapter 6. Accordingly, Asa Kasher has also defended respect for the dignity, not only of civilians, but of enemy soldiers as part of a code of professional military ethics.[100] Kasher's ideas are reflected in the doctrinal code of ethics famously known as the "Spirit of the IDF".[101] This code counts human dignity among its fundamental values, along with defence of the state, its citizens and residents; and patriotism and loyalty to the state. Dignity is understood therein as the inherent value of every human being, friend or foe.[102] The ethical doctrine of the IDF will be further analysed in Chapter 6.

## 5 Toward a New *Jus Armorum*

Building on the contributions listed above, I would like to offer additional reasons to bolster the case for respecting human dignity as an integral part of modern military honour. To that effect, I will revisit the idea of the 'sportsmanlike passion for symmetry' developed above to explain the persistence of the duel as an institution, a passion that has permeated both the moral and the legal regimes that govern the profession of arms, as evinced by what Blum calls the 'honour theory' and by the structure and rationale of IHL. I contend that such a passion indeed echoes the erstwhile code of chivalry, which can be refashioned in a way that reflects respect for modern human dignity such that invocations of chivalry and honour do not become mechanical or seem as mere 'simulacra of morality', as MacIntyre would say, but retain their 'point', namely, the interest, value or principle that they are supposed to serve. In the words of Bertrand Russell: "When the conception of honour is freed from aristocratic

and dignity is central to mission accomplishment. This imperative creates a complex ethical environment"; "remain faithful to basic American, Army and Marine Corps standards of proper behavior and respect for the sanctity of life", in H.R. McMaster, 'Preserving Soldiers' Moral Character in Counter-insurgency Operations', in Don Carrick, James Connelly and Paul Robinson (eds.), *Ethics Education for Irregular Warfare* (Cornwall: Ashgate, 2009), p. 17.

99 Paul Robinson, 'Integrity and Selective Conscientious Objection', *Journal of Military Ethics*, 8:1 (2009), p. 42.

100 Kasher, 'Combatant's', *passim.*

101 Tzvi Hauser, 'The Spirit of the IDF', *Azure*, 5757 (1997), p. 52.

102 Israel Defense Forces, 'The Spirit of the IDF', www.idfblog.com/2011/11/02/the-spirit-of-the-idf, 8 April 2021.

insolence and from proneness to violence, something remains which helps to preserve personal integrity and to promote mutual trust in social relations. I should not wish this legacy of the age of chivalry to be wholly lost to the world".[103]

This moves our notion of honour closer to what David Cerdá calls "ethical honour", that is, an updated version of honour that is the result of the evolution and interplay between ancestral notions of honour (i.e. tribal, merit-based, honorific, and privileged) and "integral honour" defined as the duty to respect universal human dignity, as "dignity works as a hinge between the individual and the collective, and it is its scintillating being that prompts the honourable task of combating its abuse".[104] It is worth noting that, according to Cerdá, the military originally adhere to tribal honour but are also able to espouse integral honour.[105]

We must begin, then, by exploring the point or purpose of chivalry in order to ascertain its importance in the present as an interpretive concept. Edmund Burke once lamented: "the age of chivalry is gone. That of sophisters, economists and calculators, has succeeded".[106] He was referring to the violent ending of the French monarchy, in particular of Queen Marie Antoinette, as a result of the 1789 Revolution. Burke's words touch upon one of the main dimensions of chivalry, that of courtly love and the adoration of the so called "fair sex".[107]

But there were more layers to this historic phenomenon than mere "generous loyalty to rank and sex",[108] bearing in mind that, as James Turner Johnson has pointed out, chivalry remains one of the most difficult to understand sources of the Just War tradition.[109] As observed in the Introduction, Kaeuper summarizes this complex social system which he dubs the "fusion of chivalric elements" as follows:

103 Bertrand Russell, *Human Society in Ethics and Politics* (London: Routledge, 1992), p. 43.

104 From the original: "La dignidad es bisagra entre lo individual y lo colectivo, y es su diamantina entidad la que suscita la tarea honorable de combater su abuso". See Cerdá, *Ética*, p. 41.

105 Ibid., pp. 20–31.

106 Edmund Burke, *Reflections on the Revolution in France* (New Haven: Yale University Press, 2003), p. 65.

107 Kaeuper, *Chivalry*, pp. 209 et seq. For a problematization of the shortcomings of chivalry from the perspective of gender equality, see Kinsella, *Image*, pp. 43–49.

108 Burke, *Reflections*, p. 65.

109 James Turner Johnson, *Just War Tradition and the Restraint of War. A Moral and Historical Inquiry* (Princeton: Princeton University Press, 1984), p. 123.

> Chivalry came into being as a powerful, mutually reinforcing fusion of several major functions, roles, and rights. Above all, the chivalrous defended honour through the violence of personal prowess; to this fusion they added a formal and rather independent piety, asserting God's blessing on their demanding and violent lives; they claimed an elite, usually noble, status and established their nobility by the practice of a chivalric way of life; they sought to regulate relationships between males and females on their own terms, exclusively linking love, too, with prowess and honour.[110]

Thereby, as discussed above, it is clear that violence was the common currency of chivalry in the Middle Ages. Yet, it was not unrestricted or unregulated violence by any means. As James Turner Johnson has remarked: "The chivalric code was the single most comprehensive statement of intentional limits on medieval warfare, and a great deal of what this professional ethic provided remains in Western tradition on war to this day".[111] Admittedly, as Helen Kinsella points out, the code would not always be honoured in practice as it would be "easily relinquished in times of stress".[112] This, however, is an issue pertaining more to rule-enforcement than to the existence or validity of said rules, of what *is* as opposed to what *ought to be*. Without grasping such a simple distinction, no normative language or practice (legal, ethical or otherwise) can ever be possible.[113]

Such intentional, normative limits were embodied in the erstwhile *Jus Armorum* or the 'Law of Arms',[114] a body of norms drawing on customary sources from Roman, Frankish, Germanic, Canon, and Civil Law, so important

110 Kaeuper, *Chivalry*, p. 302. Similarly, Braudy lists loyalty, prowess, *franchise* or largesse, and courtesy to women, children, and the elderly among the core values of chivalry. See Braudy, *From*, p. 118.

111 James Turner Johnson, 'Historical Tradition and Moral Judgment: The Case of Just War Tradition', *The Journal of Religion*, 64:3 (1984), p. 305; see also Christopher Greenwood, 'Historical Development and Legal Basis', in Dieter Fleck (ed.), *The Handbook of International Humanitarian Law*, 2nd ed. (Oxford: Oxford University Press, 2010), p. 18; Waldron, *Dignity*, p. 35. See also Johan Huizinga, *Homo Ludens* (London: Routledge and Kegan Paul, 1980), p. 96.

112 Kinsella, *Image*, p. 42.

113 Hans Kelsen, *Pure Theory of Law*, 2nd ed. (Clark: The Lawbook Exchange, 2005), pp. 75–81.

114 Theodor Meron, 'Shakespeare's Henry the Fifth and the Law of War', *The American Journal of International Law*, 86 (1992), pp. 1–45. See also Theodor Meron, *Bloody Constraint: War and Chivalry in Shakespeare* (New York: Oxford University Press, 1998); Oeter, '(Non-) Importance', p. 48; Clapham, *War*, p. 25, where the author traces the origins of *Jus Armorum* back to feudal, canon and Roman law.

as to be deemed constitutive of war, as "rules and the law are absolutely central to the whole idea of medieval warfare itself",[115] such that these standards "became formative for the practices of medieval war, and helped the warriors to make sense of violence and war".[116]

The *Jus Armorum* eventually acquired a more defined legal articulation over the centuries in the form of International Humanitarian Law ('IHL') or the Law of Armed Conflict ('LOAC') through customary law and treaty law. As a result of this evolution, the cardinal principle of distinction between combatants and non-combatants in IHL is understood to be based on considerations of chivalry.[117] As Jens David Ohlin notes "the core elements of the law of war are (…) a set of prohibitions that emerge from pre-legal norms that are then formative as legal constraints. (…) The best way of expressing those ethical norms is 'chivalry'".[118] Further, Ohlin highlights the symbiotic relationship between chivalry and the law:

> The chivalric code is effective because it is more than just a mere code – it is codified in a legal system that brings the chivalric code into a system of legal adjudication, as rudimentary as it might be. The chivalric code is embodied in formal rules of engagement, in professional training, in legal conventions, in decisions of international criminal courts, and even decisions of domestic courts. What the legal system adds to the chivalric code is clarity, precision, reality. Without the legal system, the chivalric code is just a system of inchoate regulations without form and definition. The law of war needs the chivalric code for its robustness, while the chivalric code needs the law to fulfill its promise.[119]

Similarly, Terry Gill poses that chivalry is a longstanding legal and ethical principle underpinning IHL and guiding the conduct of professional soldiers to this day,[120] resulting in a mutual reinforcement between the two normative

115 Whetham, *Just*, pp. 251; 246.

116 Oeter, '(Non-)Importance', p. 46.

117 Oona Hathaway and Scott Shapiro, *The Internationalists. How a Radical Plan to Outlaw War Remade the World* (New York: Simon & Schuster, 2017), p. 76. See also Koch, 'Chivalry', p. 19; Oeter, '(Non)Importance', p. 65.

118 Jens David Ohlin, 'War's Rustic Code of Honor', https://ssrn.com/abstract=4931591, 12 September 2024, p. 42.

119 Ibid, p. 50.

120 Terry Gill, 'Chivalry: A Principle of the Law of Armed Conflict?', in Mariëlle Matthee, Brigit Toebes, and Marcel Brus (eds.), *Armed Conflict and International Law: In Search of the Human Face* (The Hague: Asser Press, 2013), pp. 33–51. See also Clapham, *War*,

systems of law and ethics in this field, as evinced by some domestic LOAC manuals.[121]

The prohibition of perfidy in IHL further evidences such chivalrous legacy.[122] Indeed, perfidy is a term of art in IHL that essentially amounts to deliberately betraying an adversary's trust.[123] According to Whetham: "The laws on perfidy can be seen as a vestigial sense of chivalry, demanding a minimum level of fairness in attack and defence, based upon the idea of mutual respect between antagonists. In this principle there remains some sense of past honour (...)".[124]

---

301; Federico Aznar, '¿Qué es el honor militar?', in Centro Conjunto de Desarollo de Conceptos, *Cuestiones sobre ética militar* (Madrid: Ministerio de Defensa, 2022), p. 57. On the works of Christine de Pizan as a crucial precedent for this normative development see Gregory Reichberg, Henrik Syse and Endre Begby (eds.), *The Ethics of Wat. Classic and Contemporary Readings* (Oxford: Blackwell, 2006), p. 212. On a moral history of chivalry, see Braudy, *From*.

121 Rain Liivoja, 'Law and Honor: Normative Pluralism in the Regulation of Military Conduct', in Jan Klabbers and Touko Piiparinen (eds.), *Normative Pluralism and International Law: Exploring Global Governance* (Cambridge: Cambridge University Press, 2013), pp. 147; 157. See also Rain Liivoja, 'Chivalry Without a Horse: Military Honour and the Modern Law of Armed Conflict', *ENDC Proceedings*, Vol. 15 (2012), p. 76.

122 Liivoja, 'Law', p. 159. See also Gerhard Werle, *Principles of International Criminal Law*, 2ª ed. (The Hague: TMC Asser Press, 2009), p. 476; Meron, *Bloody*, pp. 12–13; Evan Wallach, 'Pray Fire First Gentlemen of France: Has 21st Century Chivalry Been Subsumed by Humanitarian Law?', *Harvard National Security Journal*, 3 (2012), p. 433; Mike Madden, 'Of Wolves and Sheep: A Purposive Analysis of Perfidy Prohibitions in International Humanitarian Law', *Journal of Conflict and Security Law*, 17:3 (2012), p. 441; Kinsella, *Image*, p. 154.

123 See Additional Protocol I to the Geneva Conventions, Art. 37: "Prohibition of perfidy:

1. It is prohibited to kill, injure or capture an adversary by resort to perfidy. Acts inviting the confidence of an adversary to lead him to believe that he is entitled to, or is obliged to accord, protection under the rules of international law applicable in armed conflict, with intent to betray that confidence, shall constitute perfidy. The following acts are examples of perfidy:
   (a) the feigning of an intent to negotiate under a flag of truce or of a surrender;
   (b) the feigning of an incapacitation by wounds or sickness;
   (c) the feigning of civilian, non-combatant status; and
   (d) the feigning of protected status by the use of signs, emblems or uniforms of the United Nations or of neutral or other States not Parties to the conflict.
2. Ruses of war are not prohibited. Such ruses are acts which are intended to mislead an adversary or to induce him to act recklessly but which infringe no rule of international law applicable in armed conflict and which are not perfidious because they do not invite the confidence of an adversary with respect to protection under that law. The following are examples of such ruses: the use of camouflage, decoys, mock operations and misinformation".

124 Whetham, *Just*, p. 5.

But nowhere in IHL is the spirit of honour that defines chivalry better encapsulated than in the so-called 'Martens Clause' mentioned in the Introduction, which today reads: "In cases not covered by this Protocol or by other international agreements, civilians and combatants remain under the protection and authority of the principles of international law derived from established custom, from the principles of humanity and from the dictates of public conscience".[125] The Martens Clause has been described as the legal yardstick which codifies the principle of humanity in IHL,[126] and which bears out the standing of human dignity as a legal archetype of that sub-regime of international law, as suggested in the previous chapter. Indeed, according to the 2004 British *Joint Service Manual of the Law of Armed Conflict*, the Martens Clause "incorporates the earlier rules of chivalry that opposing combatants were entitled to respect and honour. From this flowed the duty to provide humane treatment to the wounded and those who had become prisoners of war".[127] According to the architect of said clause, this standard of behaviour originally appealed to the professionalism of soldiers as the practitioners of an activity regulated by the laws of war,[128] as "military forces are a common class of professionals who have undertaken to comport themselves honorably".[129]

This normative lineage suggests that there is a relation between the ancient code of chivalry and modern military honour that is more than merely accidental, anecdotal or poetic; it is constitutive of our understanding of war and our attitudes toward it, as encapsulated in what Michael Walzer once called the "war convention", namely "the set of articulated norms, customs, professional codes, legal precepts, religious and philosophical principles, and reciprocal arrangements that shape our judgments of military conduct".[130]

---

125 Additional Protocol I to the Geneva Conventions (1977), Art. 1(2).

126 Ginevra Le Moli, *Human Dignity in International Law* (Cambridge: Cambridge University Press, 2021), p. 177.

127 Ministry of Defence of the United Kingdom of Great Britain and Northern Ireland, 'The Joint Service Manual of the Law of Armed Conflict', https://assets.publishing.service.gov.uk/government/uploads/system/uploads/attachment_data/file/27874/JSP3832004Edition.pdf, 20 June 2022, pp. 23–24. See also Ohlin, 'Duty', p. 1270; Oeter, '(Non)Importance', pp. 54–55; Kinsella, *Image*, p. 105; Francisco Lobo, 'The "capture or kill" debate revisited: Putting the "human" back in "human enhancement of soldiers"', *The Military Law and the Law of War Review*, 58:1 (2020), p.109.

128 Rotem Giladi, 'The Enactment of Irony: Reflections on the Origins of the Martens Clause', *The European Journal of International Law*, 25(3) (2014), p. 854.

129 US Department of Defense, *Law of War Manual* (Washington D.C.: DoD, 2023), p. 69.

130 Michael Walzer. *Just and Unjust Wars. A Moral Argument with Historical Illustrations.* 4th ed. (New York: Basic Books, 2006), p. 44.

Indeed, these norms or standards, however old, can be thought of as both *regulative* of a specific activity, i.e. the waging of war, as well as *constitutive* of a particular identity,[131] in this case the warrior's identity as a veritable "sociological descendant of the feudal knight".[132] As the managers of the outcome of the Circumstances of War, soldiers need these codes not only to define their social role, but to protect their moral integrity and humanity,[133] thus preventing moral injury. In Walzer's words: "Though chivalry is dead and fighting unfree, professional soldiers remain sensitive (or some of them do) to those limits and restraints that distinguish their life's work from mere butchery".[134] Or as recently pointed out by the International Committee of the Red Cross: "Every day, armed forces implement IHL to reduce war's cost to humanity. For many, respect for the rules is a matter of professional identity and core values".[135]

Thus, these standards become part of modern military honour as a direct descendant of the medieval code of chivalry, as honour was "the veritable currency of chivalric life,"[136] such that chivalry was truly "honour in its medieval guise"[137] – and conversely, military honour can be said to be chivalry in its modern guise, or, to paraphrase Theodore Meron 'chivalry reinvigorated'.[138] As Liivoja affirms: "to speak of chivalry is to speak of a military code of honour, which already sounds far less archaic".[139] It would appear as though the same material making up such currency of chivalric life has been refashioned into a newly minted notion of military honour as an aspect of Professional Military Ethics, which arguably amounts to a new *Jus Armorum* or Law of Arms echoing chivalry in the mind of the modern military professional.

---

131 Peter J. Katzenstein, 'Introduction: Alternative Perspectives on National Security', in Peter J. Katzenstein (ed.), *The Culture of National Security: Norms and Identity in World Politics* (New York: Columbia University Press, 1996), p. 5. On constitutive rules more generally see Georg Von Wright, *Norm and Action* (London: Routledge & Kegan Paul, 1963), pp. 3–7; and John Rawls, 'Two Concepts of Rules', *The Philosophical Review*, 64:1 (1955), pp. 3–32.

132 Walzer, *Just*, p. 34.

133 French, *Code*, pp. 10–11.

134 Walzer, *Just*, p. 45.

135 ICRC, *International Humanitarian Law and the Challenges of Contemporary Armed Conflicts* (Geneva: ICRC, 2019), p. 10.

136 Kaeuper, *Chivalry*, p. 129. See also Verbruggen, *Art*, p. 54.

137 Meron, *Bloody*, p. 11. See also on chivalry as the erstwhile version of honour, Jody Prescott, *Empirical Assessment in IHL Education and Training* (London: Anthem Press, 2021), p. 68; and Whetham, *Just*, pp. 174–177.

138 Meron, *Bloody*, p. 204.

139 Liivoja, 'Chivalry', p. 75.

## 6 Chivalry Reappraised: Military Honour as Respect for Human Dignity

How can this reconstruction of modern military honour as an interpretive concept belonging to a new *Jus Armorum* be connected to human dignity as an essentially contested concept? I believe that the answer lies in one of the competing conceptions of human dignity reviewed in the previous chapter, a conception that can effectively shed some light on the point or purpose of the idea of military honour as chivalry in modern guise.

As we saw in the previous chapter, Jeremy Waldron's account of dignity allows for a reconstruction of the status of nobility that universalizes, not only those privileges formerly reserved to aristocrats in times of peace, but also in times of war, including the right not to be tortured or mistreated while in captivity.[140] Waldron describes this moral evolution thusly:

> In ages past, chivalry might require that noble warriors, such as knights, be treated with dignity when they fell into the hands of hostile powers; but this was hardly expected in the treatment of the common soldier; they were abused and probably slaughtered. (…) But modern prohibitions on degrading treatment are oriented specifically to the common soldier, the ordinary detainee, solicitous of their dignity in ways that would have been inconceivable in times past for anyone but officers and gentlemen.[141]

In a similar vein, Ignatieff has characterized the Geneva Conventions (from the first one in 1864 onwards) as "an attempt to refurbish older military traditions of honour for a new age of democratic battle, and to extend the decencies of nurture and memorial beyond the aristocratic warrior elite to the common man",[142] in particular when accorded prisoner of war status.[143] In this sense,

---

140 Kaeuper, *Chivalry*, pp. 169–170; Braudy, *From*, p. 120; Liivoja, 'Law', p. 158; Liivoja, 'Chivalry', p. 78.

141 Jeremy Waldron, *Dignity, Rank and Rights. The Berkeley Tanner Lectures* (2009) (New York: Oxford University Press, 2012), p. 35. See also Jeremy Waldron, *Torture, Terror and Trade-offs. Philosophy for the White House* (New York: Oxford University Press, 2010), p. 309. Admittedly, officers are still entitled to privileged treatment when compared to NCOs and enlisted personnel according to the Third Geneva Convention. See Oeter, '(Non)Importance', p. 64.

142 Ignatieff, *Warrior's*, p. 114. Against see Henry Shue, 'Torture', *Philosophy and Public Affairs*, 7:2 (1978), p. 129. See also Torsten Meireis, 'Chivalry and Law-sustaining Force', in Bernhard Koch (ed.), *Chivalrous Combatants? The Meaning of Military Virtue Past and Present* (Baden-Baden: Nomos, 2019), p. 129.

143 Vale, 'Chivalry', p. 42.

it has been argued that respecting a prisoner of war's honour – which entails an acknowledgment of their physical and moral integrity, sense of self-worth, and rank – is a way of respecting their inherent human dignity,[144] as well as of acknowledging their particular professional status intrinsically tied to the sovereign state.[145]

Yet, even though human dignity arguably had its first legal expression in the laws of war,[146] neither Waldron nor Ignatieff develops further what those privileges and decencies were for the erstwhile aristocratic warrior.[147] If dignity is a status, as we saw in the previous chapter, then it becomes necessary to ascertain those aristocratic privileges of war that "describe and motivate the package of entitlements and obligations that distinguish the status".[148]

The expansion or universalization of privileges described by Ignatieff and Waldron became necessary as the erstwhile code of chivalry arguably "had next to nothing to do with ordinary people at all".[149] Or did it? We have already seen how chivalry was an intricate social system amounting to a mélange of such elements as violence, honour, prowess, piety, status, and courtly love.[150] But as a code of behaviour, it had to do with the exercise of violence as much as it did with its restraint and rightful use. Medieval society being characteristically communitarian and intertwined in ways that are hard to fathom from our modern, individualistic point of view, this code of behaviour had to touch upon all members of society, not just the privileged classes. Even Twain's cynical account of medieval life cannot but acknowledge that to help those who are defenceless, regardless of their social class, and risking one's own health and life while doing so, is to be "great, now; sublimely great".[151]

---

144 Jemma Arman, Jean-Marie Henckaerts, Heleen Hiemstra, and Kvitoslava Krotiuk, 'The Updated ICRC Commentary on the Third Geneva Convention', in Michael N. Schmitt and Christopher J. Koschnitzky (eds.), *Prisoners of War in Contemporary Conflict* (Oxford: Oxford University Press, 2023), pp. 356–357.

145 Derek Jinks, 'Protecting Prisoners of War in Contemporary Conflicts', in Michael N. Schmitt and Christopher J. Koschnitzky (eds.), *Prisoners of War in Contemporary Conflict* (Oxford: Oxford University Press, 2023), p. 163.

146 Le Moli, *Dignity*, p. 88.

147 An attempt to unpack those privileges in light of a current debate in IHL today can be found in Lobo, 'Capture', pp. 85–120.

148 Charles Beitz, 'Human Dignity in the Theory of Human Rights: Nothing But a Phrase?', *Philosophy and Public Affairs*, 41:3 (2013), p. 285.

149 Kaeuper, *Chivalry*, p. 185; Kinsella, *Image*, p. 42.

150 Kaeuper, *Chivalry*, p. 302.

151 Twain, *Connecticut*, p. 394.

International in character and scope, manuals of chivalry and knightly piety covered behaviour on and off the field of battle.[152] Perhaps one of the greatest accounts of the chivalrous code from the time when it was still alive and well is Christine de Pizan's *Book of Deeds of Arms and of Chivalry*, a work that, although it was published in the early 15th century, has only recently been rightfully acknowledged as part of the Just War canon.[153] Pizan's contribution is endowed with a unique concern for the victims of war,[154] while at the same time not neglecting the agency that warriors have and retain even in the heat of battle. On either end of the 'deed', whether the agent's or the recipient's, ethical standards remain of the utmost importance to her, as war and conflict are "great and weighty matters that touch the lives, the blood, and the honor and the fortunes of an infinite number of peoples".[155] Compassion is pivotal in this account.[156]

Accordingly, at the *jus ad bellum* dimension she argued in favour of aiding defenceless people, including widows, orphans, and "all who are unjustly trampled under foot by another power".[157] As for *jus in bello*, prisoners of war must be spared and treated well.[158] Further, since common folk are not actively involved in war and do not make of it their profession, they should be immune to the extent possible from all the damage and destruction of war, just like members of the clergy were similarly spared.[159]

An additional component of the code of chivalry highlighted by Pizan refers to showing due respect for the enemy, a reciprocity-based, proto-professional virtue of courtesy.[160] This tradition of respect for the rights of one's opponents, which can trace its roots back to the Roman notion of *hostis iustus*,[161] is reminiscent of the aforementioned sportsmanlike passion for symmetry that

152 Frantzen, *Bloody*, pp. 77–79.

153 Reichberg, Syse and Begby, *Ethics*, pp. 210–226; Cian O'Driscoll, 'Christine de Pizan', in Daniel R. Brunstetter and Cian O'Driscoll (eds.), *Just War Thinkers* (New York: Routledge, 2018), pp. 64–76.

154 Reichberg, Syse and Begby, *Ethics*, p. 210; O'Driscoll, 'Pizan', p. 73.

155 Christine de Pizan, *The Book of Deeds of Arms and of Chivalry* (Pennsylvania: The Pennsylvania State University Press, 2003), p. 18.

156 Frantzen, *Bloody*, p. 109.

157 Pizan, *Book*, pp. 16–17.

158 Ibid., p. 169.

159 Ibid., p. 171. See also Renic, *Asymmetric*, p. 68.

160 James Turner Johnson, *Just War Tradition and the Restraint of War. A Moral and Historical Inquiry* (Princeton: Princeton University Press, 1984), p. 134.

161 Beatrice Heuser, *War. A Genealogy of Western Ideas and Practices* (New York: Oxford University Press, 2022), p. 282.

characterized the knight's behaviour and that survived in the form of the modern duel and the legal prohibition of perfidy. In Pizan's own words:

> It should also be remembered that according to the customs of gentility and true nobility a leader must observe in the conduct of arms in any circumstance that may arise all that good breeding requires, if he wishes to gain due honor and praise, meaning that even to his enemies he must be upright and truthful in act and judgment wherever required. Along with this, he will honor those who are good and meritorious as he would wish to be honored by them.[162]

Such respect for the enemy – which is arguably enhanced by considerations of compassion once symmetry is lost[163] – is born out of what Ignatieff calls the "moral paradox of combat": "that those who fight each other bravely will be bound together in mutual respect; and that if they perish at each other's hand, they will be brothers in death".[164] Accordingly, Dragan Stanar has denounced drone warfare as a form of outrage upon human dignity of those forbidden by IHL, since it risks dehumanizing soldiers as the reciprocal threat that is essential to war is removed, effectively resulting in a 'hierarchy of dignity' among warriors. This is morally unacceptable as, even amidst the heat of battle, soldiers retain their equal right to (live and die with) dignity.[165]

Admittedly, considerations of dignity in conditions of modern warfare featuring targeted killings and other forms of dehumanizing violence seem quaint or even "silly".[166] To talk of chivalry may sound even quainter today. In this sense, it is worth recalling the question: is chivalry effectively dead, as Burke

162 Pizan, *Book*, pp. 25; 163.

163 Merkl, 'Meaning', p. 119.

164 Ignatieff, *Warrior's*, p. 117. See also Verbruggen, *Art*, p. 58.

165 Dragan Stanar, 'The right to die with dignity: Soldiers in post-modern warfare', *Yearbook of Human Rights Protection: The Right to Human Dignity*, 3 (2020), pp. 519–531.

166 Waldron himself has in more recent years come to deem considerations of chivalry as "silly" when applied to the debate about drone warfare and targeted killings. His main concern here, however, is the "casting-off of some very old constraints," which is arguably proof that he still believes in the normative content carried within the quaint vessel we call 'chivalry'. See Jeremy Waldron, 'Against', in Tamar Meisels and Jeremy Waldron, *Debating Targeted Killing* (New York: Oxford University Press, 2020), p. 163. Further, perceptions of dignity are still relevant when it comes to targeted killings using drones, as recently documented by Ilse Verdisen. See Ilse Verdiesen, *Agency Perception and Moral Values Related to Autonomous Weapons* (Leiden: Brill-Nijhoff, 2022), p. 120. Indeed, drone warfare has prompted a revival of discussions around the theme of chivalry in Germany. See Koch, 'Chivalry', p. 16.

laments, or as Walzer matter-of-factly states? And if so, are we all the better for it, as Mary Wollstonecraft suggests in her pro-Enlightenment rebuttal to Burke, postulating that "probably the spirit of romance and chivalry is in the wane; and reason will gain by its extinction"?[167]

Perhaps chivalry is dead, at least under its old, medieval guise. And yet, its point or purpose of limiting violence and sparing the innocent, weak and helpless,[168] of protecting "those who are neither powerful nor strong"[169] in the name of honour[170] still carries weight in our discussions about war to this day, as borne out by the "moral reality of war" and its value laden language.[171] As IHL specialists Louise Doswald-Beck and Sylvain Vité have remarked: "If the chivalry of earlier times cannot be resurrected, it would be a positive development if the military could be encouraged to take a certain pride in the professionalism shown when behaving in accordance with humanitarian law".[172] Thus, following Torsten Meireis, chivalry could be repurposed in modern times as the ethos of a *miles protector* ("defender soldier") tasked with protecting civilians, and thus become embedded in the modern notion of a "law-sustaining force" that fosters respect for human dignity and human rights.[173]

Military honour as an essential component of contemporary PMEt plays a key role in giving continuity to that noble legacy, as tradition and a sense of belonging is arguably a key dimension of any honour world. As Simone Weil once remarked, honour "has to do with a human being considered not simply as such, but from the point of view of his social surroundings. This need is fully satisfied where each of the social organisms to which a human being belongs allows him to share in a noble tradition enshrined in its past history and given public acknowledgement."[174] Thus, as Leo Braudy has also suggested: "The most lasting cultural mediator between the individual soldier and his social group, between violence and civility, between war and peace, is the concept

---

167 Mary Wollstonecraft, *A Vindication of the Rights of Men* (London: J. Johnson, 1790), pp. 64–65.

168 Johnson, *Just*, pp. 132–136.

169 Heuser, *War*, p. 348.

170 Frantzen, *Bloody*, p. 3.

171 Walzer, *Just*, p. 15.

172 Louise Doswald-Beck and Sylvain Vité, 'International Humanitarian Law and Human Rights Law', *International Review of the Red Cross*, 293 (1993), pp. 118–119.

173 Meireis, 'Chivalry', pp. 121; 129. See also Anna Simons, 'The Military and Society: A Refresher', *2024 Index of U.S. Military Strength* (2024), pp. 65; 70.

174 Simone Weil, *The Need for Roots* (New York: Routledge, 2002), p. 19.

of honor. Honor serves as a justification for the professional as well as for the conscript, for the warrior hero as much as for the ordinary soldier".[175]

Ultimately, we can distil the essence of the interpretive practice of chivalry into the restriction of violence (out of social, religious, and ethical considerations) and the extension of a protective blanket to an increasing number of beneficiaries who are vulnerable to violence due to contingent or permanent reasons[176] – not unlike what the modern state purported to do with its own ambition to centralize violence – "in order to protect, defend, and preserve tranquility for the people"[177] against the scourge of war. Such a humanitarian aspiration can be said to be readily at home within the rank conception of dignity, as both military honour and this conception of human dignity aim at rejuvenating our best traditions, thus "interpreting old virtues in new ways"[178] even when we find ourselves far from our finest hour due to the tragedy of war.

By applying what Waldron calls the "scintillation"[179] or our moral ability to move back and forth between understanding the theoretical possibility of human dignity as worthy of our respect and recognizing its actualization in every individual we encounter – including on the battlefield – this scintillation becomes a way to reignite that ember of chivalry we call honour, which has remained burning slowly for centuries, such that, paraphrasing Mahler, we may keep tradition alive by preserving the fire instead of merely worshiping the ashes.

Further, updating the content of a traditional notion such as military honour, endowing it with a renewed humanitarian spirit, becomes all the more important as "In a democratic society it is highly inappropriate for honor to be the sole, or even the dominant, value of the professional military cadre. Honor

175 Braudy, *From*, p. 79.

176 Contingent reasons may refer to race and gender, both traits that might render someone particularly vulnerable in a situation of political violence or armed conflict depending on the motivations and/or the means through which violence is carried out. Permanent reasons refer to the natural condition of vulnerability affecting special groups of people, such as children and the elderly. The UN has made a point of protecting particularly vulnerable populations in times of armed conflict, for example, through a special UNGA Declaration (1974) and UNSC Resolution 1325 (2000) on "Women, Peace and Security" ("WPS"). See also Kinsella, *Image*, p. 150.

177 Johan Huizinga, *The Autumn of the Middle Ages* (Chicago: The University of Chicago Press, 1996), p. 70.

178 Peter Olsthoorn, 'Educating for Restraint', in Eric-Hans Kramer and Tine Molendijk (eds.), *Violence in Extreme Conditions. Ethical Challenges in Military Practice* (Cham: Springer, 2023), p. 123.

179 Jeremy Waldron, *One Another's Equals. The Basis of Human Equality* (Cambridge: Harvard University Press, 2017), pp. 157–167.

comes to be combined with and dependent upon public prestige and popular recognition. The military must be afforded sufficient prestige and respect to insure a sense of self-esteem".[180] By upholding human dignity the military can rest assured that civil society will recognize and reward its contributions.

Now, there is still a major logical obstacle we need to overcome if the rank conception of dignity is to serve as a philosophical device for refashioning chivalry and old notions of honour. This has to do with the egalitarian essence of dignity in contradistinction to the anti-egalitarian record of honour and chivalry. Indeed, societies organized around the idea of honour are highly competitive, as everyone is striving to attain or preserve the honour coveted by others.[181] Since honour is originally a relative or positional good that is enjoyed as others do not possess it in the same amount, the easiest way to gain praise is by putting others down, as honour is left "without meaning when equally distributed".[182] As James Turner Johnson puts it: "A code [of] morality, such as that of chivalry, tends to erect a wall between those having the code and those not having it".[183]

Thus, if honour is "inevitably comparative and invidious (…) the chivalric tradition is irrevocably anti-egalitarian".[184] Furthermore, chivalry as a social phenomenon suffered from a double form of exclusionary nature: not only was it a code reserved for nobility (notwithstanding certain humanitarian benefits afforded to common folk),[185] it was also only to be applied among Christians, excluding every other creed.[186] How to reconcile such an anti-egalitarian tradition with the quintessential egalitarianism that lies at the heart of human dignity?

The truth is that chivalry had less to do with inherited status than with a universal ethical standard that could be achieved by all.[187] Further, chivalry has also gone through a process of universalization throughout history, such that "The trappings of chivalry were at least in part appropriated by increasing

180 Janowitz, *Professional*, p. 225.
181 Kaeuper, *Chivalry*, p. 149.
182 Olsthoorn, *Military*, p. 13; Olsthoorn, 'Risks', p. 171.
183 Johnson, *Just*, p. 135.
184 William Hunt, 'Civic Chivalry and the English Civil War', in Anthony Grafton and Ann Blair (eds.), *The Transmission of Culture in Early Modern Europe* (Philadelphia: University of Pennsylvania Press, 1990), p. 208.
185 Johnson, *Just*, p. 137.
186 Amin Maalouf, *The Crusades through Arab Eyes* (London: Saqi Books, 2012); Kinsella, *Image*, p. 25; Huizinga, *Autumn*, p. 92. Exceptionally it would be honorarily extended to other warriors in recognition of their prowess in battle, such as Muslims. See Heuser, *War*, p. 133.
187 Meron, *Bloody*, pp. 12; 119.

numbers of people from non-noble social levels".[188] But not only its trappings, but the heart of its ethos, honour, also underwent a process of universalization. As we saw before, Appiah points out how honour in the age of universal human rights comes with a special sort of "positive recognition respect" which entails an attitude of respect towards everybody as our "honour peers" and participants in that modern guise of honour that we call dignity.[189] In the same vein, Margalit talks of dignity as "universalized honour".[190]

This historic and ethical progression has been possible since honour, the beating heart of chivalry, is not necessarily attained by blood, but by virtuous behaviour,[191] a key feature to which we shall return in the chapter devoted to Professional Military Education. Such an evolution is perfectly epitomized by what William Hunt calls "urban militarism", a political movement of citizens during the English Civil War that fostered "civic chivalry" and "citizen honour" as an affirmation of the collective and personal dignity of the bourgeoisie and of the working classes.[192] For, as Cervantes wrote a few decades before, "blood is inherited, whereas virtue is acquired, and virtue is by itself more precious than blood".[193] And, as confirmed by Montaigne, the exercise of virtue always comes with effort and struggle,[194] which means anyone willing to work hard enough can achieve this lofty goal.

## 7 Holding High the Banner of Human Dignity

The duel writ large that we call war is waged by human beings charged with representing a political view that is purported to prevail against that of a different community. Since the twilight of the Middle Ages, around the same time chivalry was in decline, the political body people have favoured for organizing

188 Kaeuper, *Chivalry*, p. 308.

189 Appiah, *Honor*, pp. 13–14; 128–130; 177. For an account of dignity as a replacement rather than a continuation of honour, see Peter Berger, 'On the Obsolescence of the Concept of Honor', *European Journal of Sociology*, 11:2 (1970), p. 340.

190 Margalit, *Decent*, pp. 57–58.

191 Kaeuper, *Chivalry*, p. 308.

192 Hunt, 'Civic', pp. 208–209; 213. On a similar evolution during the Great War see also Vale, 'Chivalry', p. 40. For a study of a similar evolution as observed in Spain, see Alberto Cañas de Pablos, '"Worth More Than Life Itself": Military Honour and the Birth of Its Courts in Spain (1810–1870)', *Journal of Military Ethics*, 21:3–4 (2022), pp. 304–319.

193 "*la sangre se hereda, y la virtud se aquista, y la virtud vale por sí sola lo que la sangre no vale*". Miguel de Cervantes, *El Ingenioso Hidalgo Don Quijote De La Mancha* (Barcelona: Editorial Planeta, 2022), p. 698.

194 Michel de Montaigne, *The Complete Essays* (London: Penguin Books, 2003), p. 472.

their lives both in times of peace and of war has been the modern state. And it has been states, as the foremost subjects of public international law for the past centuries, the ones who have committed to upholding the normative archetype of human dignity through the different instruments and sources of International Humanitarian Law and International Human Rights Law, as we saw in Chapter 3.

Like we also saw in Chapter 1, professional soldiers are public agents that represent their respective states, holding a special commission issued by them,[195] in what Benvenisti and Cohen describe as a "principal-agent" rationale.[196] As one of the characters in the 1982 film *L'Honneur d'un capitaine* (which is sometimes used for ethical training by some militaries[197]) puts it: "Captain Carion is dead. The functionary Marcel Carion has fulfilled his contract".[198] Therefore, as a public official tasked by virtue of this unique contract[199] with honouring their principal's international commitments and representing their community,[200] the soldier could be said to be, not only a *miles protector*, but a veritable *agent or steward of human dignity* in times of war,[201] as the rules of IHL "are binding not only upon States but also upon every protected individual".[202] As Benbaji and Statman put it: "soldiery is shaped by treaty-based positive and customary international law, as well as by informal rules and widely shared attitudes. By enlisting in the military, combatants commit themselves to these rules".[203]

Indeed, if the military sometimes think of themselves as 'guardians' of the societies they fight for, then safeguarding one of the foremost contemporary values embraced by modern societies, human dignity, should be a matter of

195 John Fabian Witt, *Lincoln's Code* (New York: Free Press, 2012), p. 206.

196 Eyal Benvenisti and Amichai Cohen, 'War is Governance: Explaining the Logic of the Laws of War From a Principal-Agent Perspective', *Michigan Law Review*, 112:8 (2014), pp. 1363–1415.

197 Henri Hude, 'Reshaping the Ethical Training of Future French Commissioned Officers', in Paul Robinson, Nigel De Lee and Don Carrick (eds.), *Ethics Education in the Military* (New York: Routledge, 2016), p. 113. On the use of films for ethical education in the military more broadly see Moliner, 'Educación', p. 44.

198 "*Le capitaine Carion est mort. Le fonctionnaire Marcel Carion a rempli son contrat*".

199 John Hackett, *The Profession of Arms* (London: Sidgwick & Jackson, 1983), p. 140.

200 Moliner, 'Educación', p. 28.

201 Janne Aalto, 'Challenges in combining ethical education for conscripts and professional military', in Carrick, Connelly, and Whetham, *Making*, p. 116; Asa Kasher, 'Teaching and Training Military Ethics: An Israeli Experience', in Robinson, De Lee and Carrick, *Ethics*, p. 140.

202 Le Moli, *Dignity*, p. 194.

203 Yitzhak Benbaji and Daniel Statman, *War by Agreement. A Contractarian Ethics of War* (New York: Oxford University Press, 2019), p. 117.

professional importance to the man and woman in uniform.[204] This is also consistent with the view of military honour as an agent-based notion defining the very identity of its bearer.[205] To paraphrase Ishiguro,[206] soldiers can choose to 'inhabit the role' of stewards of human dignity to the utmost, as an expedient of the highest possible form of professionalism.

Moreover, if professional soldiers are public officials charged with applying a specific branch of the law, then they would have to share an "internal aspect of (humanitarian) rules", drawing on H.L.A. Hart's terminology, that is, a reflective critical attitude towards the correctness of the given standard.[207] Thus, *military honour*, as a conscientious reflection of special self-worth,[208] could be construed as an *enhanced internal aspect of rules* wherein standards of professional ethics and legal standards merge in a single normative agent who is constituted by said rules.[209] Such martial *lex artis* becomes even more stringent in the case of higher ranks (the "top brass"), who should comply with the standard of care of a "reasonable military commander".[210]

Lastly, the chivalric code has been characterized as an ethos or an ideology,[211] in the sense that it has historically been more of an aspiration guiding human action than an incontrovertible fact. Thus, if chivalry is nothing but honour in its medieval guise, then chivalry, like honour can also be described as what Georg Von Wright calls an 'ideal rule',[212] that is, a role model or abstract stand-

204 Janowitz, *Professional*, p. 249.

205 Robinson, *Honour*, p. 3.

206 Kazuo Ishiguro, *The Remains of the Day* (London: Faber & Faber, 1989), p. 43.

207 H.L.A. Hart, *The Concept of Law*, 3rd ed. (Oxford: Oxford University Press, 2012), pp. 56–57.

208 May, *Crimes*, p. 84.

209 Katzenstein, 'Introduction', p. 5.

210 Ian Henderson and Kate Reece, 'Proportionality under International Humanitarian Law: The "Reasonable Military Commander" Standard and Reverberating Effects', *Vanderbilt Journal of Transnational Law*, 51:835 (2018), pp. 835–855; Johansen, *Military*, pp. 76–77; 'Final Report to the Prosecutor by the Committee Established to Review the NATO Bombing Campaign Against the Federal Republic of Yugoslavia', http://www.icty.org/x/file/Press/nato061300.pdf, 8 April 2021, par. 50; International Committee of the Red Cross. 'IHL Database. Customary IHL. Practice Relating to Rule 14. Proportionality in Attack', https://ihl-databases.icrc.org/customary-ihl/eng/docs/v2_rul_rule14, 13 July 2021; High Court of Justice of Israel, HCJ 2056/04, *Beit Sourik Vill. Council v. Gov't of Israel*, 58(5) PD 817, para. 46; High Court of Justice of Israel, HCJ 769/02, *Pub. Comm. against Torture in Israel v. Gov't of Israel*, 62(1) PD 507 (2006) (Isr.), reprinted in 46 I.L.M. 375, para. 57. See similarly on the use of an abstract reasonableness test International Criminal Tribunal for the Former Yugoslavia, Trial Chamber, *Prosecutor v. Galić*, Judgment, 5 December 2003, Case No. IT-98-29-T, para. 58.

211 Vale, 'Chivalry', p. 29.

212 Von Wright, *Norm*, p. 14.

ard to which people in uniform strive to live up to. And since it is an ideal standard, it is bound to be breached in practice, and such a violation calls for appropriate consequences. In other words, soldiers should be held accountable whenever they fail to discharge their duties as stewards of human dignity, for instance, by committing war crimes.

Indeed, even though the code of chivalry was originally anti-egalitarian, reserving humanitarian treatment to only a lucky few and meting out brutality for all the rest,[213] it is also a matter of historical record that breaches of the code of chivalry and the punitive reactions they prompted helped to shape the modern regime of International Criminal Law.[214] Most famously, the trial of Sir Peter von Hagenbach in 1474 for crimes committed against the people of Breisach was an affair that congregated knights from all over the Holy Roman Empire to constitute what is considered to be the first international criminal tribunal. As a result of his appalling offences, and before being executed, Hagenbach was stripped of his knighthood, such a degradation being extremely rare at the time and only warranted as punishment for the most atrocious acts.[215]

## 8 Concluding Remarks: Moving Past the Windmills

> Honor is a bubble that can be inflated by some parts of human nature, such as the drive for prestige and the entrenchment of norms, and popped by others, such as a sense of humor.
>
> STEVEN PINKER

This last tale of chivalry suggests that the knights that answered the call to judge the conduct of one of their peers followed Mark Twain's advice, as they did not forget to shudder in the face of the brutality they were summoned to redress. And rightly so, since any criminal law system is indicative of the character of the society where it was created.[216] In other words, the offences we punish – and how we punish them – tell us plenty about the type of society we live in, the values we cherish and the breaches we are not willing to tolerate.

213 Whetham, *Just*, p. 109.

214 Le Moli, *Dignity*, p. 157; Corn et al, *Law*, p. 467.

215 Gordon Gregory, 'The Trial of Peter von Hagenbach', in Kevin Heller and Gerry Simpson (eds.), *The Hidden Histories of War Crimes Trials* (Oxford: Oxford University Press, 2013), pp. 13–49.

216 Günther Jakobs, *Sociedad, norma y persona en una teoría de un Derecho penal funcional* (Bogotá: Universidad Externado de Colombia, 1996), p. 14.

In the days of Peter von Hagenbach, the late medieval society where he lived still appreciated the code of chivalry enough to mete out justice in its name, while at the same time planting the seed for International Criminal Law to sprout and flourish centuries later.

But it is not only through crime and punishment that we can get a glimpse into the soul of society. Comedy and humour work in a similar way, in the sense that, just like criminal law upholds our most important beliefs and values, humour can lay bare those same societal standards in a harmless way. We can learn as much about a society by looking at what they laugh about as by looking at what they cry about.

This can be achieved by using such comedic devices as caricatures, parody and satire. For instance, we can make fun of the code of chivalry by resorting to a caricature like the stubborn Black Knight from *Monty Python and the Holy Grail*, or satires and parodies like Shakespeare's Falstaff and Cervantes' Don Quixote, all of which we have encountered throughout this investigation. For similar reasons, it might prove difficult to conceal a smile when hearing about the above-mentioned Mexican drug cartel self-styled as the 'Knights Templar of Michoacán' ('*Caballeros Templarios de Michoacán*'), however serious their intentions might have been when they adopted such a fabled moniker.[217]

Such humorous devices are parasitic of the realities they aim to portray and mock, without which they would not produce the intended comedic effect. This can be observed even in times of war.[218] Cervantes' Don Quixote exemplifies this heuristic aptitude of humour in canonical fashion, as the renowned *Hidalgo* "embodies a half-mocking, half-serious nostalgia for the age of the knight".[219] In the words of David Cerdá, Cervantes "Satirizes about chivalry and lays bare its mistakes; but no one has sung about its poetry and magnificence like he has".[220]

We set out on this analytical journey mindful of the dangers of presentism and nostalgia for the past. But nostalgia, properly administered when mediated by sensible idealism, can also be used as a reminder of the things that used to matter to us and that have now been lost,[221] although perhaps not irretrievably.

---

217 Francisco Lobo, 'Parody or deadly-serious commitment? Non-state armed groups upholding humanitarian standards in war', (https://www.kcl.ac.uk/parody-or-deadly-serious-commitment-non-state-armed-groups-upholding-humanitarian-standards-in-war), 08 June 2022.

218 Liane Hartnett and Cian O'Driscoll, 'Sad and laughable and Strange: At War with Just War', *Global Society*, 35:1 (2021), p. 35.

219 Braudy, *From*, p. 192. See also Oeter, '(Non-)Importance', p. 50.

220 "Ironiza sobre la caballería y desnuda sus errores; pero nadie ha cantado como él su poesía y magnificencia". See Cerdá, *Ética*, p. 340.

221 Braudy, *From*, p. 81.

And this is precisely what Don Quixote – that key to the "universal meaning of life"[222] – epitomizes as a reminder of our best traditions, that the wealth of the "Golden Age" of chivalry may be revived in this, "our age of iron".[223] It is in this sense that Peter Berger concludes that honour and dignity are not necessarily antithetical, but their respective institutional and humanist natures can be reconciled, once we move past the windmills of delusion:

> A return to institutions will, *ipso facto*, be a return to honor. It will then be possible again for individuals to identify themselves with the escutcheons of their institutional roles, experienced now not as self-estranging tyrannies but as freely chosen vehicles of self-realization. The ethical question, of course, is what these institutions will be like. Specifically, the ethical test of any future institutions, and of the codes of honor they will entail, will be whether they succeed in embodying and in stabilizing the discoveries of human dignity that are the principal achievements of modern man.[224]

•••

Thus far, this investigation has introduced us to the code of chivalry and explored the factual background conditions leading to the possibility of war in order to take what the military do seriously. In an attempt to answer the main research questions motivating this work, the last three chapters have further delved into the normative contents that may be found beyond mere instruction in the laws of war in order to ensure combatants behave appropriately on the battlefield, thus reducing unjustified harm to civilians and avoiding moral injury to themselves. Consequently, a new doctrine of *Jus Armorum* combining the powerful normative contents of military honour and human dignity has emerged. But it is not enough that philosophers alone grasp the message. It also needs to be communicated to those who go to war in ways that resonate

---

222 José Ortega y Gasset, *Meditaciones del Quijote y otros ensayos* (Madrid: Alianza, 2014), p. 89.

223 "Sancho, my friend, you may know that I was born, by Heaven's will, in this our age of iron, to revive what is known as the Golden Age. (…) I am he for whom are reserved the perils, the great exploits, the valiant deeds". See Braudy, *From*, p. 191. From the original: "*Sancho amigo, has de saber que yo nací, por querer del Cielo, en esta nuestra edad de hierro, para resucitar en ella la de oro.* (…) *Yo soy aquél para quien están guardados los peligros, las grandes hazañas, los valerosos hechos*". Miguel de Cervantes, *El Ingenioso Hidalgo Don Quijote De La Mancha* (Barcelona: Editorial Planeta, 2022), p. 145.

224 Berger, 'Obsolescence', pp. 346–347.

with their own shared practices and codes of behaviour, in the 'language of lions' as it were. Equipped with such robust normative contents, it is time now to move on to the next logical step, namely those pedagogical efforts characterized as Professional Military Education and training aimed at instilling said normative contents in our professional men and women at arms. The last two chapters of this inquiry will address this fundamental issue.

CHAPTER 5

# Professional Military Ethics Education

> You who wish to win honour in arms, put into practice what training in youth teaches you in order to be a master of the skills of chivalry in maturity, for it is better to be able to say 'I know' than to say 'Why did I not learn?'
>
> VEGETIUS

∵

## 1 Introduction: Enter Sandman

The climax of the prescient film *Outbreak* (1995) depicts a dramatic exchange between one of the main characters, Colonel Sam Daniels, MD, and the pilot – callsign 'Sandman' – in charge of executing 'Operation Clean Sweep', which entails bombing the small town of Cedar Creek to contain a lethal virus. A momentous showdown ensues between Colonel Daniels aboard his small helicopter and the bomber carrying the deadly payload:

> Cl. Daniels: We have an antiserum being administered as we speak.
> Every infected person will have their dosage, so you must abort the mission.
> This is urgent. Do you read me?
> You cannot bomb this town. You must abort.
> I'm talking to the bomber pilots.
> Do you read me?

His co-pilot, Major Salt, tells Colonel Daniels that it is of no use, as the pilots have "been trained not to" answer him. Nevertheless, given the stakes, Colonel Daniels perseveres, making a final desperate appeal to Sandman's ethical sense:

> Cl. Daniels: What you do in the next thirty seconds will be your testimony to life.

 | DOI:10.1163/9789004754096_008

It works. He somehow gets through to the pilot, who finally decides to drop the bomb into the ocean. "It might have been wind shear, over", Sandman explains to his commanding officer with a self-satisfied smirk.

However miraculous this turn of events, is Major Salt right overall? Is there any room for ethics inside the pilot's cockpit,[1] and the soldier's battle station more generally? Are pilots and other military professionals trained not to give it a second thought on whether or not they should follow orders? Is Sandman the exception, perhaps the serendipitous result of defective training and education that have proved ineffective in rooting civilian morality out of him?

Alternatively, could Sandman be considered as the archetype of a properly trained soldier who knows when to do the right thing, the product of a process of socialization specifically tailored to enhance what is human in all of us? The expression 'human enhancement' of soldiers is one increasingly being used in the literature.[2] Yet, it is a phrase which strikes one as distinctively question-begging: What is it exactly that is supposed to be enhanced? The adjective 'human' gives us our first clue, although not a very helpful one considering it is already difficult to define what makes us human in the first place,[3] without adding the complexities of warfighting to the mix. If being human entails possessing a set of distinctive traits – including rationality, speech, sociability, ingenuity, a sense of morality, a (variable) capacity for laughter, for cooking, for dancing, and so forth – does this mean that the expression 'human enhancement of soldiers' amounts to the endeavours to improve such traits in the fighting individual? In other words, does it mean that we aim at producing soldiers that are more rational, articulate, sociable, inventive, ethical, and who also have a better sense of humour, are more skilled in the kitchen, and are better dancers?

This is probably not what armies have in mind when they invest millions in research for the human enhancement of soldiers. What is meant by it, then? Counterintuitive as it may sound, 'human enhancement' is actually aimed at improving the underlying biology of soldiers, that is, the animal part of Aristotle's proverbial *zoon logon ekhon* ('rational animal').[4] Indeed, 'human

1 Juan Moliner, 'La educación y formación en ética militar', in Centro Conjunto de Desarollo de Conceptos, *Cuestiones sobre ética militar* (Madrid: Ministerio de Defensa, 2022), p. 41.

2 Ioana Maria Puscas, 'Military Human Enhancement', in William H. Boothby (ed.), *New Technologies and the Law in War and Peace* (Cambridge: Cambridge University Press, 2018), pp. 182–229.

3 Joanna Bourke, *What it means to be human* (Berkeley: Counterpoint, 2011).

4 Hannah Arendt, *The Human Condition*, 2nd ed. (Chicago: University of Chicago Press, 1998), p. 27.

enhancement' is defined as "a medical or biological intervention introduced into the body designed to improve performance, appearance, or capability besides what is necessary to achieve, sustain or restore health."[5] The ultimate goal is to produce "super-soldiers"[6] that are stronger, smarter, who eat and sleep less, and are able to endure more pain, as the human element is deemed the "weakest link" in defence systems.[7]

To be sure, enhancing cognitive abilities might push soldiers one step closer to the ideal of rationality that inspired Aristotle's anthropological definition of human beings *per genus et differentiam*. Yet, exclusively enhancing rationality or 'dianoetic virtues' while neglecting 'ethical virtues' might result in an impoverished version of the Aristotelian ideal,[8] closer to the creature created by Mary Shelley's Dr. Frankenstein than to the virtuous, thinking, sociable individual Aristotle envisaged. After all, as Walzer once aptly remarked: "Until wars are really fought with pawns, inanimate objects and not human beings, warfare cannot be isolated from moral life".[9] Thus, human enhancement is, and should remain, an area "beset with ethical complexities".[10]

Accordingly, Ingmar Persson and Julian Savulescu believe that a veritable "moral enhancement"[11] can be achieved by adopting different strategies. On the one hand, the possibility to use "biomedical means of moral enhancement – *moral bioenhancement*",[12] namely drugs, is increasingly available. On the other, traditional moral education remains a time-honoured method of instilling values in people, which, nevertheless, is admittedly falling short given the formidable challenges posed by technological innovations and climate change.[13] This chapter will focus on this type of traditional moral instruction as applied

---

5 Patrick Lin, Maxwell J. Mehlman and Keith Abney, *Enhanced Warfighters: Risk, Ethics, and Policy* (San Luis Obispo: California Polytechnic States University, 2013), p. 11.

6 Jon Harper, 'How Technology Could Create 'Super Soldiers'', http://www.nationaldefensemagazine.org/articles/2016/8/1/2016august-how-technology-could-create-super-soldiers, 01 August 2016; Adam Henschke, "Supersoldiers': Ethical concerns in human enhancement technologies', http://blogs.icrc.org/law-and-policy/2017/07/03/supersoldiers-ethical-concerns-human-enhancement-technologies-2/, 03 July 2017.

7 Puscas, 'Military', p. 182.

8 Aristotle, *The Nicomachean Ethics* (New York: Oxford University Press, 2005), 1.13, pp. 19–22.

9 Michael Walzer, *Just and Unjust Wars*, 4th ed. (New York: Basic Books, 2006), p. 64.

10 Henschke, 'Supersoldiers'.

11 Ingmar Persson and Julian Savulescu, *Unfit for the Future: The Need for Moral Enhancement* (Oxford: Oxford University Press, 2012).

12 Ibid., p. 2.

13 Ibid.

to military training and education, such that we may find the best ways to put the 'human' – that is, the ethical – back in 'human enhancement' of soldiers,[14] that they may acquire a sense of military honour that is respectful of human dignity and that shields them from moral injury.

## 2 Playing Soldier: the Military Profession and Soft Role-Morality

In a previous chapter we saw that the main traits informing the concept of a profession like the military career are expertise, responsibility, and corporateness.[15] According to Morris Janowitz, author of *The Professional Soldier*: "A professional group develops a sense of group identity and a system of internal administration. Self-administration – often supported by state intervention – implies the growth of a body of ethics and standards of performance".[16] How does this particular brand of professionalism fare in democratic societies?

In his masterpiece *Democracy in America*, Alexis de Tocqueville explains how the passion for equality that perfuses democratic societies, including the way they wage war, results in a curious paradox when it comes to the type of mindset cultivated within their militaries:

> In democratic armies, all the soldiers can become officers, which generalizes the desire for advancement and extends the limits of military ambition almost infinitely.
>
> (…)
>
> All of the ambitious men contained in a democratic army therefore wish vehemently for war, because war empties places and finally allows violation of the right of seniority, which is the only privilege natural to democracy.
>
> We thus arrive at this singular consequence that, of all armies, the ones that most ardently desire war are democratic armies, and that, among peoples, those who most love peace are democratic peoples; and what

14 Francisco Lobo, 'The "capture or kill" debate revisited: Putting the "human" back in "human enhancement of soldiers"', *The Military Law and the Law of War Review*, 58:1 (2020), pp. 85–120.

15 Samuel Huntington, *The Soldier and the State* (Cambridge: Harvard University Press, 2000), pp. 8–10.

16 Morris Janowitz, *The Professional Soldier* (New York: Free Press, 2017), p. 6.

really makes the thing extraordinary is that it is equality which produces these opposite effects simultaneously.[17]

Further, Tocqueville warns of the risks of democratic armies driving away the best citizens from their ranks, not only in the sense of having a diminished public debate surrounding the use of force,[18] but leading up to the danger of the "military family"[19] becoming "a small uncivilized nation [which] possesses the weapons, and it alone knows how to use them".[20] Such is the peril of "the military's social isolation"[21] in democratic societies, a situation that can be exacerbated by "tribal cultures" developing within the ranks[22] and which can arguably account for the proverbial mistrust of standing armies since the rise of the modern state.[23] Admittedly, as has been argued throughout this investigation, the military can also amount to a "spiritual freezer" of sorts, in the sense of becoming a reservoir of moral values that society may no longer deem important as time passes by,[24] a place where the echoes of chivalry can still be heard centuries later.

Now, the solution to such perils and disconnects, and to 'the Tocqueville Paradox' in general is, unsurprisingly, more civil-military integration as more virtuous citizens decide to go into the military career. Thus, Tocqueville himself prescribes: "The general spirit of the nation, penetrating the particular spirit of the army, tempers the opinions and the desires that arise from the military state, or by the omnipotent force of public opinion, it suppresses them. Have enlightened, well-ordered, steady and free citizens, and you will have disciplined and obedient soldiers".[25]

If the foregoing is true; if "war is too serious a matter to entrust to military men";[26] and if indeed military virtues (such as courage, fortitude, and loyalty)

---

17 Alexis de Tocqueville, *Democracy in America* (Indianapolis: Liberty Fund, 2010), Vol. 4, Part III, Ch. 22, pp. 1155; 1157.

18 Andrew Milburn, *When the Tempest Gathers* (Bransley: Pen & Sword, 2020), p. 16.

19 Janowitz, *Professional*, p. xxxvi.

20 Tocqueville, *Democracy*, p. 1159.

21 N. Fotion and Gerard Elfstrom, *Military Ethics. Guidelines for Peace and War* (New York: Routledge, 2021), pp. 50; 85.

22 Sönke Neitzel, 'Tribal Cultures and *Innere Führung* – A Contradiction?', *Ethics and Armed Forces*, 2 (2021), p. 9.

23 Beatrice Heuser, *War. A Genealogy of Western Ideas and Practices* (New York: Oxford University Press, 2022), p. 231.

24 Federico Aznar, '¿Qué es el honor militar?', in Centro Conjunto de Desarollo de Conceptos, *Cuestiones sobre ética militar* (Madrid: Ministerio de Defensa, 2022), p. 53.

25 Tocqueville, *Democracy*, p. 1163.

26 Harald Høiback, *Understanding Military Doctrine* (New York: Routledge, 2017), p. 52.

are virtues that can be applied "in every walk of life",[27] then the need for a soft role-morality as applied to the military becomes apparent. In this sense, military honour becomes a social mechanism to ensure not just allegiance to the law, but also to promote virtuous behaviour that is beneficial for society at large, as well as for the military that live (and die) by the same values as the former.[28] As remarked by Arthur Applbaum when arguing against what he calls the "mediated moralization" (i.e. the view that role prescriptions are nonmoral prescriptions): "Something important is missed if a physician's commitment to heal the sick or a journalist's commitment to inform the public is accounted for by saying that role occupants are morally obligated to perform the nonmoral commands of their roles".[29] Something is also missing if we explain a soldier's willingness to sacrifice his or her life (their embrace of unlimited liability) by leaving out their commitment to protecting those who cannot protect themselves.[30] As General MacArthur famously stated during Yamashita's trial: "The soldier, be he friend or foe, is charged with the protection of the weak and unarmed. It is the very essence and reason for his being".[31]

As explained in Chapter 1, soft-role morality[32] espouses the principle that, although professionals have ethical standards of their own, they are never completely isolated from the society or community they serve and, as a result, they are answerable to the public according to the standards and principles set by general morality. As Daryl Koehn eloquently puts it:

> We must also remember that professionals become such as adults. For the years before professionals make their profession, they develop character and principles as members of a public. If a professional ethic is to have any practical effect, it must somehow 'hook' into the public ethic. While a professional ethic might extend and develop one dimension of

27 John Hackett, *The Profession of Arms* (London: Sidgwick & Jackson, 1983), p. 141.

28 Peter Olsthoorn, *Military Ethics and Virtues* (New York: Routledge, 2011), pp. 14–15.

29 Arthur Applbaum, *Ethics for Adversaries: The Morality of Roles in Public and Professional Life* (Princeton: Princeton University Press, 1999), p. 54.

30 Dave Grossman and Loren W. Christensen, *On Combat. The Psychology and Physiology of Deadly Conflict in War and Peace*. 4th ed. (New York: Open Road Media, 2022), pp. xx–xi; 176.

31 Kelly Ashkin, 'Treatment of Sexual Violence in Armed Conflicts: A Historical Perspective and the Way Forward', in Anne-Marie Brouwer et al (eds), *Sexual Violence as an International Crime: Interdisciplinary Approaches* (Cambridge: Intersentia, 2013), p. 48.

32 Bradley Wendel, 'Legal Ethics as Political Moralism or the Morality of Politics', *Cornell Law Review*, 93:6 (2008), pp. 1413–1436; Daryl Koehn, *The Ground of Professional Ethics* (New York: Routledge, 1994), pp. 153–154; Paul Camenisch, 'On the Matter of Good Moral Character', *The Linacre Quarterly*, 45:3 (1978), pp. 273–283.

> an agent's existing morality, such an ethic will not replace the prior ethic wholesale.[33]

Conversely, society can also be held accountable by the professional, especially the military professional who is liable to moral injury as this phenomenon amounts to the betrayal of the values shared between the soldier and the society he or she fights for.[34] Soft role-morality is, admittedly, a two-way street.

As also pointed out in Chapter 1, Koehn further attempts to distil the essence of professional ethics into one single concept, that of trust, which is also an important component of normal life:

> To the extent that professional roles are, as I have been arguing, public expectations originating in and coalescing around professions so construed, occupying a professional role is a moral act binding the occupier to observe the conditions for genuine trustworthiness. Conceived in this manner, professional ethics and roles are clearly extensions of ordinary morality. Professionals have not invented trust nor the conditions under which vulnerable clients will reasonably extend trust.
>
> But to say that professionals have invented neither trust nor client vulnerability is not to claim that they have simply conformed their behavior to societal expectations. Their ethic is properly understood as an intensification of the value of trust in interpersonal relations.[35]

Koehn's point about trust being at the heart of professional ethics is echoed by the doctrinal publication titled *The Army Profession* issued by the U.S. Army in 2015, which characterizes societal trust as the "bedrock" of the military profession.[36] Or as Christopher Coker has remarked, "a soldier's covenant is not restricted to his friends or to the service. In a democratic society he has a covenant with those he serves – the rest of us".[37]

In the same vein, Tocqueville reflects on the "conservative element" involved in soldiering, namely, the preservation of social values even as individuals go into the profession of arms – a task growing in difficulty as the technical means

---

33 Koehn, *Ground*, p. 153.

34 Brad Allenby and Tom Frame, 'Moral Injury', in Center on the Future of War, Arizona State University, *Moral Injury: Towards an International Perspective* (Tempe: Arizona State University, 2017), p. 6.

35 Ibid., p. 154.

36 U.S. Army, 'ADRP-1: The Army Profession', https://irp.fas.org/doddir/army/adrp1.pdf, 25 May 2023, Ch. 3.

37 Coker, *Warrior*, p. 135.

of warfare evolve at a faster pace than societal views and practices.[38] In the case of democratic countries, citizens "bring into the army the spirit of the society and preserve it there. (...) The soldier will bring to the military career the strength or the weakness of the national mores; there he will manifest the faithful image of the nation".[39]

Now, as they go into the military, citizens agree to a set of standards and rules devised to govern their behaviour in that particular field. This is an integral aspect of the contractarian account within the Just War Tradition ('JWT') as explained in Chapter 1. According to that branch of JWT, the moral duty to respect the fundamental rights of others sometimes needs to be qualified in light of the social rules applicable to a specific situation, including the standards defining specific roles.[40] Drawing on the example of a police officer whose job is not to prove that a suspect is actually guilty of a criminal charge, contractarian authors Yitzhak Benbaji and Daniel Statman argue that there exists a "moral division" of labour as defined by said social rules and the roles they set forth, such that "role-holders might have a moral right to follow the package of social rules that define their role, and (*qua* holders of such roles) to disregard moral reasons that pertain to their actions".[41] Accordingly,

> [a]s a social role, soldiery is shaped by treaty-based positive and customary international law, as well as by informal rules and widely shared attitudes. By enlisting in the military, combatants commit themselves to these rules – a commitment that is morally effective if the agreement that constitutes soldiery is almost universally accepted, and also mutually beneficial and fair.[42]

Regardless of their personal motivations and states of mind when they join, what matters, according to the contractarian view, is the normative sources defining the military role (both domestic and international), the act of enrolling constituting tacit consent to the package of duties making up the social role in question.[43] However, this contractarianism must always be moderated or tempered by general social mores as soft-role morality suggests.

38 According to Janowitz this is indeed the main dilemma of the military profession. See Janowitz, *Professional*, p. 258.

39 Tocqueville, *Democracy*, pp. 1166; 1169.

40 Yitzhak Benbaji and Daniel Statman, *War by Agreement. A Contractarian Ethics of War* (New York: Oxford University Press, 2019), p. 38.

41 Ibid., p. 51.

42 Ibid., p. 117.

43 Ibid., p. 125.

Such tacit consent raises some questions, however, as to what is required for the role to become activated. "The nature of his contract sets the man-at-arms apart. But how apart? That is an important question today"[44] as Hackett puts it. Are we in the presence of an actual contract to which more than one party need to consent? And if so, who else should be involved in the process other than the individual joining the armed forces?

As to the first question, Koehn believes that taking on a profession is not a *quid pro quo* exchange: "unlike a contract which must be explicitly accepted by both parties in order to be binding, the profession binds the speaker upon utterance. A profession no one ever spoke would not be a profession at all. Speakers make these pledges or professions in order to encourage others to trust them".[45]

Yet, it would still be plausible to understand the military profession within the framework of the contractarian tradition to the extent that, although a formal contract may or may not be involved, the soldier publicly undertakes to provide a service to a community[46] by embracing a role entrusted to them as defined by social rules and including a set of duties and expectations – with the addition of an expectation of unlimited liability on the soldier's part to offset the exceptional power entrusted to them, as Hackett claims.[47] Such a community may, but needs not, be organised politically in the form of a modern nation-state. This is a point often neglected in the JWT literature, as this tradition spans across a period of time vastly superior to the historical existence of the modern state. As Nicholas Melgaard and David Whetham remark: "the just war tradition predates the modern, state-based system by some two thousand years. Its criteria have evolved over that time and have been applied to the wars of nation-states just as they were applied to the conflicts of city states, princedoms and empires in the middle ages".[48]

---

44 Hackett, *Profession*, p. 73.

45 Koehn, *Ground*, p. 59.

46 Aznar, 'Honor', p. 58.

47 Hackett, *Profession*, p. 202. See also Juan Moliner, *La ética militar como como marco de reflexión sobre la guerra y la profesión militar* (Madrid: Ministerio de Defensa, 2022), p. 31; British Army, 'Values and Standards of the British Army', https://www.army.mod.uk/media/5219/20180910-values_standards_2018_final.pdf, 24 May 2023, p. 3; Canadian Armed Forces, 'The Canadian Armed Forces Ethos – Trusted to Serve', https://www.canada.ca/en/department-national-defence/corporate/reports-publications/canadian-armed-forces-ethos-trusted-to-serve.html, 21 March 2023, p. 34.

48 Nicholas Melgaard and David Whetham, 'Jus ad vim. War, peace and the ethical status of the in-between', in Seumas Miller, Mitt Regan and Patrick F. Walsh (eds.), *National Security Intelligence and Ethics* (London: Routledge, 2021), p. 193. See also Christian

Nevertheless, as argued in a previous chapter, the modern state is the form of political organization that communities have favoured over the past centuries and it has been within its midst that the role of the military professional has flourished, as the service of collective security has been entrusted to their expertise by said states,[49] soldiers becoming stewards or agents charged with honouring their state's commitments.

## 3 Professional Military Ethics ('PMEt') and Ethical Schools of Thought

Advocating for a more active involvement of the military in society does not amount to an apology of the militarization of politics or making the case for a military state. In acknowledging the dangers of the military becoming an "ethical cocoon"[50] of its own, while at the same time fostering a soft-role morality approach, the aim is to accept that the military are a legitimate part of society that is porous to all the cultural changes within it, as pointed out by Fotion and Elfstrom.[51]

Among such changes, for instance, we find the so-called "secular revolution" in morality taking place during the 1960s in many Western countries, as stressed by Stephen Deakin.[52] According to this author: "The new ethics were individualistic, materialistic, egalitarian, morally relativistic, and secular".[53]

However, this does not necessarily mean that ethics in the military profession experimented a full overhaul or that traditional values were discarded overnight. On the contrary, the three main schools of ethical thought, namely virtue ethics, deontological ethics, and utilitarian ethics, remain strongly influential in the military profession,[54] evidencing the permeability between

Nikolaus Braun, *Limited Force and the Fight for the Just War Tradition* (Washington, DC: Georgetown University Press, 2023), p. 33.

49 Max Weber, *The Vocation Lectures* (Indianapolis: Hacket, 2004), p. 33; Michel Foucault, *Society Must Be Defended* (London: Penguin Books, 2003), pp. 48–49; James C. Scott, *Seeing Like a State* (New Haven: Yale University Press, 2020), pp. 2; 15; 55.

50 Fotion and Elfstrom, *Military*, p. 90.

51 Ibid., pp. 62; 91.

52 Stephen Deakin, 'Education in an Ethos at the Royal Military Academy Sandhurst', in Paul Robinson, Nigel De Lee and Don Carrick (eds.), *Ethics Education in the Military* (New York: Routledge, 2016), p. 19.

53 Ibid.

54 James Connelly, 'On making the military moral', in Don Carrick, James Connelly and David Whetham (eds.), *Making the Military Moral. Contemporary Challenges and Responses in Military Ethics Education* (New York: Routledge, 2018), pp. 10–11.

civilian and military ethics. It is also important to bear in mind that, as pointed out by James Connelly, these theories are not rivals among which we need to pick a winning side, for "actual moral reasoning always combines concerns for consequences with concern for the rightness or wrongness of certain actions as such".[55]

### 3.1 *Utilitarianism and PMEt*

As to the specific schools of thought, according to Peter Olsthoorn "In most military ethics training and education programmes (…) it is virtue ethics and deontological or rule-based ethics (…) that are used more often".[56] He adds that there seems to be general agreement that utilitarian ethics do not work well in military settings.[57] Such a claim is arguably borne out by the Australian Defence Forces' ('ADF') most recent manual of military ethics, which counts consequentialism – of which utilitarianism is one of the main subtypes[58] – among the ethical theories that do not align with the ADF's approach to ethics (which amounts to an admixture of natural law, deontological ethics and virtue ethics).[59]

Nevertheless, prior to venturing too swiftly into the main ethical schools percolating the military *ethos*, i.e. virtue ethics and deontological ethics, it is worth scrutinizing the value of utilitarianism more closely before dismissing it as a useful approach to military ethics.[60] The ADF manual itself concedes that "The concept of 'the greatest good for the greatest number' has broad appeal within the conduct of military operations".[61] This arguably includes the policy of winning over the 'hearts and minds' so integral to counterinsurgency

55 Ibid., p. 10; Peter Olsthoorn, 'Educating for Restraint', in Eric-Hans Kramer and Tine Molendijk (eds.), *Violence in Extreme Conditions. Ethical Challenges in Military Practice* (Cham: Springer, 2023), p. 128. On a proposal to combine deontological ethics with virtue ethics in the military see Hilliard Aronovitch, 'Good Soldiers, A Traditional Approach', *Journal of Applied Philosophy*, 18:1 (2001), p. 16.

56 Peter Olsthoorn, 'The Ethics Curriculum at the Netherlands Defence Academy, and Some Problems with its Theoretical Underpinnings', in Paul Robinson, Nigel De Lee and Don Carrick (eds.), *Ethics Education in the Military* (New York: Routledge, 2016), p. 119. Similarly, Moliner, 'Educación', p. 33.

57 Olsthoorn, 'Curriculum', p. 119.

58 Simon Blackburn, *The Oxford Dictionary of Philosophy* (Oxford: Oxford University Press, 2005), p. 377.

59 Australian Defence Forces, 'Military Ethics', https://theforge.defence.gov.au/sites/default/files/2021-12/ADF-P-0%20Military%20Ethics%20Ed%201_0.pdf, 10 December 2022, pp. 14–18.

60 Moliner, *Ética*, p. 94.

61 Australian Defence Forces, 'Military', p. 18.

('COIN') doctrine during the 20th century,[62] a policy clearly imbued with a consequentialist rationale. In that sense, the 'greatest number' would also include those whose hearts and minds are trying to be so captivated.

Further, the other side of the coin of such a consequentialist calculus may be found articulated within the main *desideratum* of International Humanitarian Law or the Law of Armed Conflict: to alleviate human suffering.[63] Indeed, whether it is about maximizing the happiness *of all*, or minimizing the suffering *of all*,[64] consequences are certainly important in the main normative regime governing the conduct of hostilities. This allows us to plausibly characterize IHL as a normative body informed by the type of consequentialism known as 'restricted utilitarianism'[65] or 'rule utilitarianism',[66] i.e. the form of utilitarianism that assesses an action focusing not on its consequences *per se*, but on whether or not it complies with a prior rule itself factoring in utilitarian considerations.

Beyond actual warfighting, it is also worth mentioning at this point that sometimes the military can be at the forefront of social change and evolution, and therefore can become instrumental in the attainment of socially desirable outcomes bringing about the greatest good for the greatest number. A case in point is the gradual retreat of racial segregation in the United States. Indeed, President Truman signed an executive order to end racial inequality in the US armed forces as early as 1948, thus foreshadowing civilian policies on this crucial ethical issue,[67] including the landmark *Brown v. Board of Education* decision by the US Supreme Court in 1954 and the Civil Rights Act of 1964.[68] Admittedly, gender inequality remains an entrenched problem in

62 David Fisher, 'Why morality matters to the military', in Don Carrick, James Connelly and David Whetham (eds.), *Making the Military Moral. Contemporary Challenges and Responses in Military Ethics Education* (New York: Routledge, 2018), p. 15.

63 Frits Kalshoven and Liesbeth Zegveld, *Constraints on the Waging of War. An introduction to International Humanitarian Law*, 3rd ed. (Geneva: ICRC, 2001), p. 12. Similarly, Yoram Dinstein, *The Conduct of Hostilities under the Law of International Armed Conflict*, 2nd ed. (Cambridge: Cambridge University Press, 2010), p. 17.

64 Olsthoorn, 'Educating', p. 127.

65 J.J.C. Smart, 'Extreme and Restricted Utilitarianism', *The Philosophical Quarterly*, 6:25 (1956), pp. 344–354.

66 Dale E. Miller, 'Rule utilitarianism', in Ben Eggleston and Dale E. Miller (eds.), *The Cambridge Companion to Utilitarianism* (Cambridge: Cambridge University Press, 2014), pp. 146–165.

67 Janowitz, *Professional*, pp. xxxvi; 203.

68 Wilbur J. Scott, Karin Modesto De Angelis, and David R. Segal, *Military Sociology. A Guided Introduction* (New York: Routledge, 2023), p. 100.

the US armed forces (and elsewhere, including IHL[69]) that urgently needs to be addressed to catch up with civil society standards.[70] If the military manages to bring about more gender equality, however, that will arguably result in an increase of the overall happiness of any society.

Finally, it is worth pointing out that authors like Fotion and Elfstrom have advocated a "utilitarian military ethics"[71] in part due to the formidable challenge that war poses to a rights-based system such as deontological ethics on account of the mass violation of rights that armed conflicts entail.[72] Yet, an enforcement failure, however widespread, is not enough to disregard an entire school of thought. Otherwise, virtue ethics and utilitarian ethics would also have to be dismissed during war, considering these are admittedly not the best of times for displays of virtue or for the advent of happiness on earth.

### 3.2 *Deontological Ethics and PMEt*

Deontological ethics is of great value in the exercise of the military profession considering its proverbial love of rules and the premium it places on duty. Since the normative standards, both moral and legal, of what the JWT calls the 'war convention' are incorporated into the professional *ethos* of the military, as seen in previous chapters, a rules-based or deontological approach is a key component of the understanding and exercise of this 'rule-enforcement' profession of sorts that aims at securing compliance with a set of rules previously agreed upon by states.[73]

Moreover, deontological ethics has earned a place of its own in the military profession. Thus, as Olsthoorn explains, the works of liberal deontological

---

69 Rachele Marconi, 'Between Outdated Morality and Evolutive Interpretation: The Concept of "Honour" under Article 27(2) of the Fourth Geneva Convention', *MPIL Research Paper Series*, No 2021–22; Helen M. Kinsella, *The Image before the Weapon. A Critical History of the Distinction between Combatant and Civilian* (Ithaca: Cornell University Press, 2011), p. 122.

70 Kate Germano and David Smith, 'Case Study 2: Gender Equity as Fairness in the Military Institution', in Skerker, Whetham, and Carrick, *Military*, pp. 51–61; Scott, Modesto De Angelis, and Segal, *Sociology*, pp. 107–124.

71 Fotion and Elfstrom, *Military*, p. 22.

72 Ibid., pp. 12–13.

73 Yitzhak Benbaji and Daniel Statman, *War by Agreement. A Contractarian Ethics of War* (New York: Oxford University Press, 2019), p. 73. See also from a revisionist perspective David Rodin, *War and Self-Defense* (Oxford: Oxford University Press, 2002), pp. 180–181. On the soldier as an 'agent of the law' under a theological view of the Just War Tradition, see Cian O'Driscoll, *Victory. The Triumph and Tragedy of Just War* (New York: Oxford University Press, 2020), p. 28; and see further a critical approach on the law-enforcement analogy in pp. 82–83; 87–89 therein.

thinkers such as John Rawls and Lawrence Kohlberg are deemed important and useful within the military, particularly when it comes to moral development,[74] as we shall see in the last section of this chapter. Reflecting on the Kantian notion of autonomy as applied to soldiers, Olsthoorn concludes that "moral duties are to be followed, not because they are imposed from the outside and are backed by sanctions, but because they [the military professionals] accept them by choice, requiring quite an amount of altruism and a universalistic outlook".[75]

Lastly, there are two further ways in which deontological ethics is interwoven with contemporary military ethics within the conceptual framework set forth in this investigation on military honour and human dignity. First, as suggested in a previous chapter, military honour is an agent-based concept that bears on the subject's own identity,[76] so a system predicated on the very notion of normative agency, such as deontological ethics, should be easily accommodated in that particular professional setting. Secondly, as also indicated before, the military can further be seen as veritable agents or stewards of human dignity insofar as they are tasked with honouring their countries' commitments to that value under international law, dignity undoubtedly representing the epitome of Kantian deontological ethics, as we saw in a previous chapter.

### 3.3 *Virtue Ethics and PMEt*

Now, virtue ethics seems to be a popular school of thought among the military, especially after that school's revival in the 1980s,[77] despite having been "snowed under by deontological and consequentialist approaches to ethics".[78] This is so despite the fact that one of the leading authors of that revival, Alasdair MacIntyre,[79] has more recently said that military ethics is a discipline in crisis due to the advent of rhetorical, technological and political changes in the seemingly outdated 19th century conceptions of war upon which military ethics was built. He thus calls for a re-examination of contemporary military

---

74 Olsthoorn, 'Curriculum', p. 124.

75 Ibid.

76 Paul Robinson, *Military Honour and the Conduct of War. From Ancient Greece to Iraq* (New York: Routledge, 2006), p. 3.

77 Michael Skerker, 'Preface', in Michael Skerker, David Whetham and Don Carrick (eds.), *Military Virtues* (Havant: Howgate, 2019), p. xxv; Michael Sandel, *Justice. What's the Right Thing to Do?* (New York: Farrar, Straus and Giroux, 2010); Braun, *Limited*, p. 61.

78 Jan Klabbers, *Virtue in Global Governance* (Cambridge: Cambridge University Press, 2022), p. 95.

79 Alasdair MacIntyre, *After Virtue*, 3rd ed. (Notre Dame: University of Notre Dame Press, 2007).

ethics allowing room for justice and prudence to play a special role.[80] It is worth noting that authors like Philip McCormack have drawn on MacIntyre's theoretical framework precisely to shore up contemporary military ethics with a solid foundation.[81]

Further, Olsthoorn accounts for the increasing interest in virtue ethics as applied to military training and education as follows:

> What makes virtue ethics especially interesting for the military is its concern with character formation. It assumes that character can be developed, and that virtues are not to be understood as inborn or God-given qualities, but as dispositions that can be acquired through training and practice. Such an approach also fits the tendency of many Western militaries to move away from a largely functional approach towards a more aspirational approach that aims at making soldiers better persons, mainly based on the view that bad persons are not likely to form morally good soldiers – although they could still be effective ones.[82]

But what exactly is virtue ethics and why is it so popular with the military? Virtue ethics is the school of moral philosophy that focuses on the moral character of a person, rather than on the consequences of an action (like utilitarianism); or on the rightful/wrongful act performed by a person duty-bound to follow certain rules (such as the deontological approach).

A person's *character* amounts to the total sum of her dispositions to action, or her pattern of behaviour.[83] Character defines a person's ability to lead a virtuous life across time, in order to achieve the ultimate goal of human happiness or flourishing (*eudaimonia*).[84] *Virtues* are defined as habits of thought, feeling and action that enable a person to make the right decisions.[85] As to their content, a virtue or *aretê* stands halfway between two opposite extremes,

80 Alasdair MacIntyre, 'Military Ethics: A Discipline in Crisis', in George Lucas (ed.), *Routledge Handbook of Military Ethics* (New York: Routledge, 2015), pp. 3–14.

81 Philip McCormack, 'Virtues or Values?', in Michael Skerker, David Whetham and Don Carrick (eds.), *Military Virtues* (Havant: Howgate, 2019), pp. 15–30.

82 Peter Olsthoorn, 'Introduction. Military Virtues and Moral Relativism', in Michael Skerker, David Whetham and Don Carrick (eds.), *Military Virtues* (Havant: Howgate, 2019), p. 2. See also Olsthoorn, 'Educating', p. 121.

83 Blackburn, *Dictionary*, p. 59.

84 Aristotle, *Ethics*, 1.4, p. 5.

85 Fisher, 'Why', p. 17.

for instance the virtue of courage being the middle ground between the vicious extremes of excessive fearlessness and cowardice.[86]

An important feature of virtues is the fact that, *qua* habits, they can be acquired, trained, and developed over time, a key feature for pedagogical processes such as military education and military training, as we shall see in the last section. Thus, character can be truly 'sculpted' with the right instruction, such that "the virtuous person will immediately know how to act in a specific set of circumstances",[87] much like honour is obtained, not by blood, but by consistent virtuous behaviour according to the chivalric tradition.[88] In the immortal words of Cervantes' *Don Quixote*: "if you take the path of virtue, and you can claim to do virtuous deeds, you shall envy no prince or lord; for blood is inherited, whilst virtue is conquered, and virtue is worth by itself what blood can never be worth".[89]

## 4 Military Doctrine and Rules of Engagement ('ROE')

However much is imported by citizens coming from civil society when they go into the military, including ideas of right and wrong pursuant to soft-role morality and articulated in the language of either utility, duty, or virtue, the fact remains that they enter a unique institutional milieu with characteristics of its own that are shaped by the specific service it provides to society. As Srđan Starčević has remarked:

> Since the basic social role of the military presupposes its use in armed conflict and since many long-term activities of the military (but its everyday activities also) revolve around this presumed use and the imperative of victory in combat, it is not surprising that many characteristics of the military, especially those that constitute *differentia specifica* of this institution, have been determined precisely by the nature of war combat and

86 Aristotle, *Ethics*, III.7, pp. 50–51.

87 Klabbers, *Virtue*, pp. 129; 256.

88 Richard W. Kaeuper, *Chivalry and Violence in Medieval Europe* (New York: Oxford University Press, 1999), p. 308.

89 Translated from the original: "si tomas por medio a la virtud, y te precias de hacer hechos virtuosos, no hay para qué tener envidia a los que los tienen de príncipes y señores; porque la sangre se hereda, y la virtud se aquista, y la virtud vale por sí sola lo que la sangre no vale". See Miguel de Cervantes, *El Ingenioso Hidalgo Don Quijote De La Mancha* (Barcelona: Editorial Planeta, 2022), Part II.42, p. 698.

> the imperative of victory (…). A command relationship in the military is one of them.[90]

In other words, 'the job maketh the military man'. Accordingly, a veritable "political-military culture" develops around the defensive function of the armed forces, in the sense that these professionals make up a "subset of the larger political culture that influences how members of a given society view national security, the military as an institution, and the use of force in international relations".[91] Such sub-culture is expected to be informed by the main features defining the military profession, which stem from the very nature of their stock in trade, war. Indeed, if war is characterized by uncertainty and danger,[92] with an ever-present possibility of things going terribly wrong,[93] then this particular culture will be modelled accordingly, resulting in a social group unsurprisingly prone to secrecy and hierarchical structures.

As a result of this sub-culture, over time the military develop their own views on what is most effective to achieve their purpose, otherwise known as 'military doctrine'. Military doctrine is defined by Harald Høiback as "institutionalized beliefs about what works in war and military operations".[94] That is, doctrine amounts to the "logic" of professional behaviour in the military, comprising both scientific knowledge and expertise, as well as traditions and political assumptions.[95]

Thus, doctrine could be further conceived of as a forge of sorts where the social aspects of military personnel are welded into professional conceptions, operating on three specific levels corresponding to the main elements of doctrine: theory, authority, and culture.[96] Theory comprises the assumptions about what works best in warfighting, supported by arguments and reason. But the persuasiveness of a theoretical argument is not enough, as it needs to be backed up by the power of authority in a hierarchical environment such as the military. Finally, cultural elements providing a sociological explanation of

---

90 Srđan Starčević, 'Military Command and the Right to Human Dignity', *Yearbook of Human Rights Protection. The Right to Human Dignity*, 3 (2020), p. 135.

91 Thomas Berger, 'Norms, Identity, and National Security in Germany and Japan', in Peter J. Katzenstein (ed.), *The Culture of National Security: Norms and Identity in World Politics* (New York: Columbia University Press, 1996), p. 325.

92 Carl von Clausewitz, *On War* (New York: Oxford University Press, 2008), pp. 26–27; 61.

93 Charles Perrow, *Normal Accidents. Living with High-Risk Technologies* (Princeton: Princeton University Press, 1999), p. 97.

94 Høiback, *Understanding*, p. 1.

95 Janowitz, *Professional*, p. 257.

96 Høiback, *Understanding*, p. 10.

the type of individuals we are purposely putting in harm's way is key to understanding their motivations, their abilities, as well as their own limitations. It might also explain dissent within the military, as in the end "internal differences over doctrine reflect civilian dilemmas".[97]

This last cultural aspect is sometimes referred to as '*ethos*', that is "the characteristic spirit and the prevalent sentiment, taste or opinion of a people, institution, or a system".[98] *Ethos* is even taken as a synonym with doctrine itself. Yet, according to Høiback, doctrine differs from *ethos* in that the former is articulated (preferably on paper), it is backed up by authority, and it is supposed to guide action and to anticipate possible scenarios.[99] In short, doctrine could be said to be 'formalized *ethos*'. Doctrine and *ethos* coexist in a symbiotic relationship, such that doctrine can cultivate *ethos* and *ethos* can lubricate doctrine. *Ethos* is also relevant as a fall-back position when doctrine fails in light of the new realities of the battlefield, for instance, trench warfare for which armies were not really prepared in 1914.[100]

Indeed, one risk entailed in military doctrine is its tendency to "ossify",[101] to become so entrenched as to be considered axiomatic or dogma that can never be challenged or updated, thus becoming divorced from the realities of contemporary armed conflict. This is where the concept of 'Rules of Engagement' ('ROE'), in addition to a living *ethos* keeping doctrine fresh, becomes of critical importance. Normative an activity as the military profession is, ROE are key to understanding how it is performed in the real world. ROE are understood as military directives or orders informed by the Law of Armed Conflict, which set out practical criteria for identifying targets and regulating the use of force against them.[102]

J.F.R. Boddens Hosang defines ROE as "rules governing the use of force and actions which can (potentially) influence or regulate the escalation of the use of force or hostilities in the area of operations".[103] As informed by law, ROE can never be more permissive than the legal framework (both domestic and international) governing armed conflict.[104] In addition, ROE can be modelled

97 Janowitz, *Professional*, p. 343.
98 Høiback, *Understanding*, p. 22; Moliner, *Ética*, p. 90.
99 Høiback, *Understanding*, p. 23.
100 Ibid., pp. 24; 41; 185.
101 Ibid., p. 12.
102 Craig Jones, *The War Lawyers. The United States, Israel, and Juridical Warfare* (Oxford: Oxford University Press, 2020), p. 30.
103 J.F.R. Boddens Hosang, *Rules of Engagement and the International Law of Military Operations* (Oxford: Oxford University Press, 2020), p. 19.
104 Ibid., p. 31.

by domestic military doctrines reflecting the national practices of the state implementing the laws of war.[105]

The fact that the formal status of ROE varies from country to country (whether they be executive orders, deployment orders, operational plans, or standing directives[106]) bears out their "fluid" nature,[107] not only regarding their structure but also their content. Indeed, ROE are more than just mere technical norms or directives, that is, teleological devices indicating the most appropriate means to achieve certain ends,[108] what Kant called "hypothetical imperatives"[109] – although admittedly such teleological considerations have always been important within the JWT,[110] and military doctrine is sometimes conceptualized as such hypothetical imperatives.[111]

ROE are in actuality an admixture of several elements that go beyond military exigencies, such as law and politics.[112] Thus, following Roach, Boddens Hosang postulates that ROE are at the intersection of different overlapping areas, including policy, diplomacy, operational interests, and law.[113] Arguably, ethics also plays an important role in this alloy, on account of the premium ROE usually place on the natural or inherent right of self-defence,[114] which is a quintessential institution of the ethics of war – and of general social morality, it should be added.

At the end of the day, as Boddens Hosang underscores, the goal should be to instil in military professionals such an understanding and respect for the rules of war such that observance of these standards "becomes second nature".[115] He thus concludes: "The humanitarian goals of IHL can only be achieved through a combination of proper drafting and review of the rules on the use of force and proper training and education in IHL for all military forces. Humanity is, after all, not a rule in the rule book, but a higher principle and goal that

105 Ibid., p. 20.

106 International Institute of Humanitarian Law, *Sanremo Handbook on Rules of Engagement* (Sanremo: IIHL, 2009), p. 1.

107 Jones, *Lawyers*, p. 30.

108 Georg Von Wright, *Norm and Action* (London: Routledge & Kegan Paul, 1963), pp. 9–11.

109 Immanuel Kant, *Groundwork of the Metaphysics of Morals* (Cambridge: Cambridge University Press, 2012), p. 28.

110 David Whetham, *Just Wars and Moral Victories. Surprise, Deception, and the Normative Framework of European War in the Later Middle Ages* (Leiden: Brill, 2009).

111 Høiback, *Understanding*, p. 94.

112 Jones, *Lawyers*, p. 30.

113 Boddens Hosang, *Rules*, p. 31.

114 Ibid., pp. 73 et seq. See also IIHL, *Sanremo*, p. 3.

115 Boddens Hosang, *Rules*, p. 183.

transcends such documents".[116] It is to such processes of training and education that we must finally turn.

## 5 Professional Military Ethics Training and Education

> Among democratic peoples, military discipline must not try to obliterate the free impulse of souls; it can only aspire to direct it; the obedience that it creates is less exact, but more impetuous and more intelligent. Its root is in the very will of the man who obeys; it rests not on his instinct alone, but on his reason.
>
> ALEXIS DE TOCQUEVILLE

The scandal prompted in the Australian Defence Forces by the 2020 *Brereton Report*, bearing on alleged misconduct and potential criminal acts by Special Forces deployed in Afghanistan since 2005,[117] laid bare the need to probe the way the military are being taught to distinguish between what is morally and legally acceptable and what is not. Despite receiving the best possible training, these soldiers still committed atrocities even when there was no 'heat of battle' to justify it or real moral dilemmas to excuse their behaviour. Killing the unarmed is plainly wrong, and those soldiers' inability to live up to that simple truth despite their advanced preparedness lends credence to Sebastian Junger's reminder that a military unit can be both the best-trained and the worst-disciplined at the same time.[118]

But preparation, training, and education, do help in *reducing* misconduct and war crimes, a point that has been empirically proved in the past decades.[119] This prompts the question: how can we instil in the military respect for all the rules that govern their activity, be they part and parcel of general social morality (and its main schools of thought) or the more technical standards articulated in the form of military doctrine and ROE? If respect for human dignity

116 Ibid., p. 184.

117 Inspector-General of the Australian Defence Force, *Afghanistan Inquiry Report* (Canberra: Commonwealth of Australia, 2020).

118 I would like to thank Cian O'Driscoll for pointing out this nuance to me. See Sebastian Junger, *War* (New York: Twelve, 2011), p. 13.

119 Cristopher H. Warner et. al., 'Effectiveness of Battlefield-Ethics Training During Combat Deployment: A Programme Assessment', *The Lancet*, 378: 9794 (2011), pp. 915–924; Andrew Bell, 'Combatant socialization and norms of restraint: Examining officer training at the US Military Academy and Army ROTC', *Journal of Peace Research*, 59:2 (2022), pp. 180–196.

as a matter of military honour is one of our main concerns in the 21st century, how can we teach this?

Answering this question is the preserve of the subfield known as 'Professional Military Education' ('PME'),[120] sometimes referred to as "military education and enculturation".[121]

The importance of PME cannot be overstated. As episodes like the *Brereton Report* illustrate, it is crucial to train soldiers in moral standards *before* they face the dilemmas on the battlefield to avoid atrocities,[122] that they may draw on what Grossman calls the "Well of Fortitude" when they need it the most.[123] After all: "Whatever is drilled in during training comes out the other end in combat – no more, no less",[124] and keeping in mind that "You do not rise to the occasion in combat, you sink to the level of your training".[125] Or as David Rodin has recently pointed out concerning the ethics of standing armies in periods *between* wars, i.e. *jus inter bellum*:

> Like Olympic athletes, soldiers spend far more time and energy on preparation than they do on the main event, and in both cases, their performance depends critically on how they are equipped, prepared, and trained. If you want a theory of how athletes can compete competitively and ethically, you will not get very far if you focus on the competition and ignore everything the athlete does to prepare before the opening ceremony. Similarly, if we want to understand how soldiers and officials can perform ethically in war, we will need a comprehensive view of the activities undertaken to train and prepare between wars, and this view will need to be fully integrated with our view of the ethics of combat.[126]

120 Sally Rohan, 'An organic professional military ethic and the educational challenge', in Don Carrick, James Connelly and David Whetham (eds.), *Making the Military Moral. Contemporary Challenges and Responses in Military Ethics Education* (New York: Routledge, 2018), p. 87; Roger Wertheimer, 'Preface', in Roger Wertheimer (ed.), *Empowering our Military Conscience. Transforming Just War Theory and Military Moral Education* (New York: Routledge, 2010).

121 Høiback, *Understanding*, p. 42.

122 Moshe Halbertal, 'The Goldstone Illusion', https://newrepublic.com/article/70956/the-goldstone-illusion, 7 April 2021.

123 Dave Grossman, *On Killing. The Psychological Cost of Learning to Kill in War and Society* (New York: Back Bay Books, 1996), p. 83.

124 Dave Grossman and Loren W. Christensen, *On Combat. The Psychology and Physiology of Deadly Conflict in War and Peace*. 4th ed. (New York: Open Road Media, 2022), p. 75.

125 Ibid., p. 76.

126 David Rodin, 'Justice between Wars', *Ethics and International Affairs*, 35:3 (2021), pp. 438–439.

### 5.1 *'Training' and 'Education'*

The *Brereton Report* includes a unique Annex on PME drafted by the Director of the Centre for Military Ethics at King's College London, Professor David Whetham.[127] Prof. Whetham introduces a conceptual distinction between "training" and "education" that is worth mentioning at the outset:

> While the two terms are often used interchangeably, training and education are both vital and represent different processes which are aimed at creating different outcomes. Training equips one to deal with the specifics; education that leads to reflective, deliberative thinking is required to allow the flexibility to adapt to the uncertainties of the real world.[128]

In a follow-up publication to his report, Whetham further clarifies: "Ethics education needs to deal with complexity and ambiguity as opposed to values and standards training and/or law of armed conflict briefs, which focus very much upon right and wrong answers in specific black and white situations".[129] Additionally, one of Whetham's main recommendations included in his contribution to the *Brereton Report* is to foster routine, healthy ethical discussions across all ranks at all times, which is arguably a key aspect of the process of continuous education that every professional needs.[130] On account of the importance of soft-role morality for the profession of arms, such routine discussions should be expanded so as to engage also with those very societies that task soldiers to fight their wars for them. To this end, the chivalric tradition can be once again of assistance in the visualization of the kinds of discussion soldiers and their societies are expected to have, as noted by Frantzen: "Knights talked about knighthood and about the doings of knights. This lore, which included public evaluation of the knight's conduct, formed and endlessly reformed the chivalric tradition".[131]

Furthermore, Andrew Bell sums up the difference as follows: "training" is the acquisition of military skills, whereas "education" amounts to the acquisition

127 David Whetham, 'Special Operations Command: Leadership and Ethics Review', in Inspector-General of the Australian Defence Force, *Afghanistan Inquiry Report* (Canberra: Commonwealth of Australia, 2020), pp. 504–531.

128 Ibid., p. 507.

129 David Whetham, 'Ethics and the Special Forces', *In-Depth Briefing-CHACR*, 55 (2023), p. 2.

130 Whetham, 'Special', pp. 527–528.

131 Allen J. Frantzen, *Bloody Good. Chivalry, Sacrifice, and the Great War* (Chicago: University of Chicago Press, 2004), p. 78.

of knowledge.[132] Fotion and Elfstrom further illustrate this distinction when they describe a US Army manual used to "teach officers how to deal critically with problems rather than feeding them answers to these problems already examined critically by others",[133] words which arguably capture the *Sapere aude* ("Dare to know") spirit that according to Kant is the very definition of enlightenment.[134] This arguably also reflects the change of organizational authority that reportedly has taken place in modern militaries since the second half of the 20th century, featuring a shift from a paradigm of "authoritarian domination" into one based on persuasion and reason.[135]

Fotion and Elfstrom conclude that these ethical notions should be "drilled into" military personnel, time permitting.[136] The danger remains, as Høiback points out, that instruction may turn into "corrupt indoctrination", that is, making people believe blindly without grounding such beliefs in rationality. On the contrary, instruction "is educational if it appeals to your rationality, even if you don't agree with everything you read, and, even if you are obliged to act according to a doctrine you do not wholeheartedly support".[137]

## 5.2 *Stages of Moral Development*

Now, as mentioned above, the theories of a particular deontological scholar on moral development, Lawrence Kohlberg, have great appeal within the field of PME.[138] This is not surprising considering that Kohlberg sets out a process that can be described as a moral progression across increasingly sophisticated stages of moral development,[139] an analytical framework that is of value to any field where actors need to undergo a series of trials and tests in order to

---

132 Andrew Bell, 'Combatant socialization and norms of restraint: Examining officer training at the US Military Academy and Army ROTC', *Journal of Peace Research*, 59:2 (2022), p. 183.

133 Fotion and Elfstrom, *Military*, p. 81.

134 Immanuel Kant, 'What is Enlightenment?', http://www.columbia.edu/acis/ets/CCREAD/etscc/kant.html, 19 December 2022.

135 Janowitz, *Professional*, p. 8; Fotion and Elfstrom, *Military*, pp. 61–62; Hackett, *Profession*, p. 199.

136 Fotion and Elfstrom, *Military*, p. 83.

137 Høiback, *Understanding*, p. 158.

138 Olsthoorn, 'Curriculum', p. 124; Peter Bradley and Allister MacIntyre, 'Solving the military moral bystander problem with ethics instruction', in Don Carrick, James Connelly and David Whetham (eds.), *Making the Military Moral. Contemporary Challenges and Responses in Military Ethics Education* (New York: Routledge, 2018), p. 45.

139 Lawrence Kohlberg, *The Philosophy of Moral Development. Moral Stages and the Idea of Justice* (San Francisco: Harper and Row, 1981), pp. 17 et seq.

achieve their goals, including naturally the military profession where education is by definition progressive and continuous.[140]

Kohlberg's stages of moral development can be divided into three main levels: preconventional, conventional, and postconventional. The *preconventional level* refers to the stage where the agent (usually a child) is responsive to cultural rules and labels of good and bad but can only interpret them in terms of their physical or hedonistic consequences. It is further divided into two sub-stages: 1. The Punishment and Obedience Orientation, where avoidance of punishment is the main concern; 2. The Instrumental Relativist Orientation, in which the agent seeks to gain advantages based on *quid pro quo* considerations.

Subsequently, the *conventional level* is that in which the agent satisfies the expectations of a larger group they belong to, such as family, the nation, etc. This level is further divided into: 3. The Interpersonal Concordance or "Good Boy-Nice Girl" Orientation, which aims at obtaining approval from others; 4. Society Maintaining Orientation, amounting to respect for authority and fulfilling one's duty to maintain the social order.

Finally, the *postconventional level*, otherwise referred to as the 'autonomous' or 'principled' level, is the one where the individual engages with moral values for their own sake, beyond fear or punishment or the desire to please others or uphold a heteronomous social order. It is divided into: 5. The Social Contract Orientation, whereby individual legal rights are recognized and upheld as a result of a social agreement; 6. The Universal Ethical Principle Orientation, where ethical principles are freely chosen by the individual based on reason, universality and consistency. They are universal principles of justice, including respect for human rights and for the dignity of the individual.[141] It is worth mentioning here that for some authors like David Traven entire nations may also experience a similar evolution leading to this postconventional level, the modern laws of war being the result of such a feat of collective moral progress.[142]

Although Kohlberg is classified as a deontological thinker,[143] and despite the evident Kantian overtones found across his theory of moral development and his early dismissal of Aristotelianism with its focus on what he calls "a bag of virtues",[144] his sequential system can still be said to accommodate certain

140 Hackett, *Profession*, p. 197.

141 Ibid., pp. 17–19; 409–412.

142 David Traven, *Law and Sentiment in International Politics. Ethics, Emotions, and the Evolution of the Laws of War* (New York: Cambridge University Press, 2021), p. 280.

143 Olsthoorn, 'Curriculum', p. 124.

144 His reliance on the concept of autonomy is telling, as well as the indication of the categorical imperative as an example of a Stage 6 ethical principle. See Kohlberg, *Philosophy*, p. 19.

elements of virtue ethics. Indeed, progression throughout a period of time in which character is wrought and honed by habit is a keystone of virtue ethics, as illustrated by Macintyre:

> If a human life is understood as a progress through harms and dangers, moral and physical, which someone may encounter and overcome in better and worse ways and with a greater or lesser measure of success, the virtues will find their place as those qualities the possession and exercise of which generally tend to success in this enterprise and the vices likewise as qualities which likewise tend to failure.[145]

Now, Olsthoorn believes that in most cases, including within the military, individuals are "stuck" at the second level, the conventional stage. More specifically, the military are likely to function at the first sub-stage of the conventional level, the Interpersonal Concordance Orientation seeking approval from peers within the group.[146] Similarly, Janowitz believes that it is difficult – yet not impossible – for the military professional to reach anything resembling the postconventional level:

> The forms of military social life, plus the social origins of the profession, make the development of a cosmopolitan outlook difficult. One who is well traveled is not necessarily cosmopolitan. Where cosmopolitanism does develop in the military, it results from educational experiences and conscious personal effort rather than from the social life or protocol of the military community.[147]

But however challenging, it is admittedly not impossible for military personnel and warriors more broadly to exhibit such progress in socialization and internalization of normative standards. So much has been documented by Brian McQuinn, Fiona Terry, Oliver Kaplan, and Francisco Gutiérrez-Sanin, all authors commenting on the relevance of the International Committee of the Red Cross ('ICRC') 2018 study on *The Roots of Restraint in War*.[148] In what matters here regarding moral development, the authors illustrate how members

145 MacIntyre, *After*, p. 144.
146 Peter Olsthoorn, *Military Ethics and Virtues* (New York: Routledge, 2011), p. 32.
147 Janowitz, *Professional*, p. 211.
148 ICRC, *The Roots of Restraint in War* (Geneva: ICRC, 2018).

of armed groups are socialized, or welcomed into the "military culture",[149] to increasingly internalize normative values, mirroring the moral progression that can be observed in Kohlberg's own model:

> Socialization is another key element of promoting restraint. Socialization is the process by which people adopt the norms and rules of a given community (…). A first type of socialization that can affect restraint (Type 0) involves only temporary norm adoption following instrumental calculations of punishment or reward. The other two types involve differing degrees of internalization: learning and following a norm in order to conform to group expectations and behavior (Type 1); and fully internalizing the norm, so that it becomes part of the individual's identity, i.e., that it is the 'right thing to do because it is who I am' (Type 2).[150]

Roughly speaking, Type 0 socialization would amount to Kohlberg's preconventional level, with Type 1 corresponding to the conventional level, and Type 2 reflecting the postconventional level. At this point it is important to highlight that Type 2/Stage 6 entail respecting universal human dignity as the right thing to do, something that can better be instilled in soldiers if at the same time their own dignity is acknowledged and respected during the educational and training process. This is what Starčević means when he classifies military discipline into "mechanical" and "conscious", where the former entails humiliation and corporal punishment while the latter respects the dignity of the soldier as it aims at explaining the purpose of their activities and to uphold societal values, while at the same time making for a more effective chain of command as it reasserts authority.[151] Thus, as Ohlin remarks, "The warrior ethos means that soldiers think of discipline as a necessary element of being a good soldier".[152]

Thereby, by training and educating military professionals in the practice and respect for human dignity – both their own and everyone else's, including

149 Scott, Modesto De Angelis, and Segal, *Sociology*, p. 46.

150 Brian McQuinn, Fiona Terry, Oliver Kaplan, and Francisco Gutiérrez-Sanin, 'Introduction: promoting restraint in war', *International Interactions*, 47:5 (2021), pp. 810–811. See also ICRC, *The Roots of Restraint in War* (Geneva: ICRC, 2018), p. 25.

151 Starčević, 'Military', pp. 139–141.

152 Jens David Ohlin, 'War's Rustic Code of Honor', https://ssrn.com/abstract=4931591, 12 September 2024, p. 55.

the enemy's[153] – a veritable set of 'dignitarian virtues' emerges, understood as "dispositions to think, feel, and act in tune with dignitarian norms".[154]

## 5.3 *Storytelling to Develop Compassionate Leadership*

Now, there is still something to be said for a more 'mechanical', or 'intuitive' way of instilling respect for values such that Type 2 socialization or Stage 6 Orientation may be achieved. It does not relate to fear of punishment, but to a more inspirational way of conveying a message that is both effective and simple: storytelling, more specifically what Høiback calls "military storytelling"[155] using role models or heroes as exemplars,[156] as "people are moved by good stories"[157] and "perhaps the best doctrines are those that are presented within a greater story".[158] Stories recounting the great deeds of honourable soldiers can go a long way as tools of "formative ethics",[159] much more so than IHL instruction, in shaping the military's professional identity.[160] Admittedly, even fictional or mythical heroes can help in shaping the modern soldier's identity.[161]

Indeed, as remarked by thinkers of the calibre of Hannah Arendt,[162] Alasdair MacIntyre,[163] and Yuval Noah Harari,[164] human beings are narrative, storytelling creatures. The heroes or role models[165] featuring in those stories are highly effective vehicles for conveying a message such as the promotion

153 Fotion and Elfstrom, *Military*, p. 16; Benoit Royal, 'Case Study 1: The Necessity of Self Control and the Perils of Anger', in Michael Skerker, David Whetham and Don Carrick (eds.), *Military Virtues* (Havant: Howgate, 2019), p. 323; Sherman, *Stoic*, pp. 70; 75.

154 Pablo Gilabert, *Human Dignity and Human Rights* (New York: Oxford University Press, 2018), p. 137.

155 Høiback, *Understanding*, p. 122. See also Scott, Modesto De Angelis, and Segal, *Sociology*, p. 47.

156 On the use of exemplars to teach virtue ethics see Nancy E. Snow, 'Teaching Virtues in the Military', *Journal of Military Ethics*, 22:3–4 (2023), pp. 185–199.

157 Høiback, *Understanding*, p. 128.

158 Ibid., p. 123.

159 Heinrich Dickerhoff, '"We Must Also Reach the Soul"', *Ethics and Armed Forces*, 2 (2021), p. 60.

160 Rain Liivoja, 'Chivalry Without a Horse: Military Honour and the Modern Law of Armed Conflict', *ENDC Proceedings*, Vol. 15 (2012), p. 94. Conversely, for an uncompromising scepticism about the moral or instructional value of true war stories, see Tim O'Brien, *The Things They Carried* (London: 4th Estate, 2015), p. 72.

161 Shannon E. French, *The Code of the Warrior. Exploring Warrior Values Past and Present*. 2nd ed. (Lanham: Rowman and Littlefield Publishers, 2017), p. 254.

162 Hannah Arendt, *The Human Condition*, 2nd ed. (Chicago: University of Chicago Press, 1998), p. 97.

163 MacIntyre, *After*, pp. 121–130.

164 Yuval Noah Harari, *Nexus* (New York: Random House, 2024), pp. 18 et seq.

165 Aronovitch, 'Good', p. 20.

of a certain set of values and virtues, as such role models epitomize the ideal rules or standards[166] we aspire to put into practice. Such role models are like so many mirrors in which we can have a look and aspire to be reflected back.[167]

For this, historical cases (both good and bad) can be a helpful tool to train soldiers,[168] preferably by using "case studies drawn from military personnel 'from the same services and country as themselves' so that they understand that they too could become torturers or murderers – that the 'good guys' can also do bad things",[169] since admittedly "under the right circumstances, almost anyone is capable of committing a war crime".[170] As Klabbers also reminds us: "Bad examples can be as educational as good ones".[171] In this sense, Mathias Thaler contends that thought experiments and works of fiction also have a potential for addressing the imagination such that it can better visualize even the most atrocious of acts, such as torture or genocide.[172]

In teaching the lessons such exemplars have to offer the notion of leadership is of the utmost importance, as leaders are expected to, precisely, lead by example. Indeed, military leaders are expected, like a good shepherd, not only to use troops effectively as tools to achieve a goal, but in completing the mission, also to preserve their integrity as human beings, ideally preventing moral injury in the process.[173] In the poignant words of a US Army officer during the Vietnam War:

> I had to do more than keep them alive. I had to preserve their human dignity. I was making them kill, forcing them to commit the most uncivilized of acts, but at the same time I had to keep them civilized. That was my duty as their leader. (…) A leader has to help them understand that there are lines they must not cross. He is their link to normalcy, to order, to humanity.[174]

---

166 Von Wright, *Norm*, pp. 13–15.

167 David Cerdá, *Ética para Valientes. El honor en nuestros días* (Madrid: Rialp, 2022), pp. 148; 332.

168 Høiback, *Understanding*, p. 79.

169 Whetham, 'Special', p. 526. See also on negative moral exemplars as pedagogical tools: Snow, 'Teaching', pp. 192–193.

170 Andrew Milburn, *When the Tempest Gathers* (Bransley: Pen & Sword, 2020), p. 340.

171 Klabbers, *Virtue*, p. 166.

172 Mathias Thaler, *Naming Violence. A Critical Theory of Genocide, Torture, and Terrorism* (New York: Columbia University Press, 2018).

173 Jonathan Shay, *Achilles in Vietnam. Combat Trauma and the undoing of Character* (New York: Scribner, 2003), p. 312.

174 G. Corn, L. Blank, C. Jenks and E. Talbot Jensen, 'Belligerent Targeting and the Invalidity of a Least Harmful Means Rule', *International Law Studies*, 89 (2013), pp. 621–622. See

Admittedly, in combat situations to lead by example can be extremely difficult, as one's own sense of self-preservation can indeed become overwhelming.[175] That is why one of the 'aristocratic' virtues that Jeremy Waldron identifies in his reconstruction of dignity, self-control,[176] becomes so important for military leadership and the military profession in general. A case in point, as we will see in the final chapter, is the concept used in the German armed forces for ethics education and training, namely that of "leadership development and civic education" (*Innere Führung*, literally "inner leadership").[177]

But good leadership requires more than just self-control. It must also be infused with empathy[178] and compassion. Compassion is counted among the main military virtues,[179] the sentiments of moral horror it fosters in the military and civilians alike arguably being one of the main drivers behind the moral revolution represented by International Humanitarian Law.[180] Compassion has been defined by Paul Gilbert as "a sensitivity to suffering in self and others with a commitment to try to alleviate and prevent it".[181] It is arguably one of humankind's earliest traits and one of the key abilities to our evolutionary success.[182] Compassion is also a fundamental component of "transformational

---

also Francisco Lobo, 'The "capture or kill" debate revisited: Putting the "human" back in "human enhancement of soldiers"', *The Military Law and the Law of War Review*, 58:1 (2020), p. 120.

175 Milburn, *Tempest*, p. 245.

176 Jeremy Waldron, *Dignity, Rank and Rights. The Berkeley Tanner Lectures* (2009) (New York: Oxford University Press, 2012), p. 22.

177 Alexander Merkl, 'The Meaning of Military Virtues for Peace – a Moral Theological Approach', in Bernhard Koch (ed.), *Chivalrous Combatants? The Meaning of Military Virtue Past and Present* (Baden-Baden: Nomos, 2019), p. 112; Matthias Gillner, 'Ethical Education in the German Armed Forces: Embraced Values and Moral Judgment', *Ethics and Armed Forces*, 2 (2019), p. 23.

178 Traven, *Law*, pp. 47–48. See also Maria Varaki, 'The Quest for *Phronesis* in the Holy Land', in Jan Klabbers, Maria Varaki, and G.V. Vilaça, *Towards Responsible Global Governance* (Helsinki: Unigrafia, 2018), pp. 131–142.

179 Philip McCormack, 'Compassion. Overview', in Michael Skerker, David Whetham and Don Carrick (eds.), *Military Virtues* (Havant: Howgate, 2019), pp. 287–295; John Sattler and Michael Skerker, 'Case study 1: Compassion toward Enemies', in Michael Skerker, David Whetham and Don Carrick (eds.), *Military Virtues* (Havant: Howgate, 2019), pp. 298–300.

180 Traven, *Law*, pp. 218; 263.

181 Paul Gilbert, 'Compassion: Definitions and controversies', in Paul Gilbert (ed.), *Compassion. Concepts, Research and Applications* (New York: Routledge, 2017), p. 11.

182 Penny Spikins, 'Prehistoric origins. The compassion of far distant strangers', in Paul Gilbert (ed.), *Compassion. Concepts, Research and Applications* (New York: Routledge, 2017), pp. 16–30.

leadership", that is, the type of leadership that promotes a consideration for the good and welfare of others.[183]

This is something that every leader undertaking the task of moral education should put into practice if it is to become effective, considering the kind of beings humans are and the way they respond positively to compassion as evidenced by practice. Indeed, it is the lack of consideration for compassion and caregiving in the process of moral development that prompted, in part, Carol Gilligan's compelling feminist critique of Kohlberg's overly abstract and individualistic categories.[184] But within the collectivist milieu that is the 'military family', admittedly, caregiving and compassion should also be taken into account. As Nancy Sherman puts it: "the task for the individual, whether civilian or military, youth or adult, is to temper control with forgiveness, soldierly strength with tolerance for human frailty".[185]

Naturally, in a line of work such as warfighting, there are practical limitations to what compassion can accomplish, considering that war is about breaking things and hurting people, up to and including taking their lives, as we saw in Chapter 1. But death and compassion are not necessarily mutually exclusive, as evinced by the phenomenon of mercy killings on the battlefield, which, although not a legal defence against criminal charges, can have a potential impact on a jury in a Court Martial procedure, as we saw in the Introduction.[186] Further, even in war killing another human being can be done by acknowledging their agency and dignity as they pose a symmetrical threat to us, thus targeted killings representing a characteristically undignified way of taking a fellow human being's life.[187]

## 5.4 *Entering the Game: When the Legal Language Is Not Enough*

The main research question motivating this investigation refers to the importance of additional normative standards besides the mere instruction in the laws of war for the military. Its main hypothesis is that the law is not enough,

183 Daniel Martin and Yotam Heineberg, 'Positive leadership, power and compassion, in Paul Gilbert (ed.), *Compassion. Concepts, Research and Applications* (New York: Routledge, 2017), p. 221.

184 Carol Gilligan, *In a Different Voice* (Cambridge: Harvard University Press, 2003).

185 Nancy Sherman, *Stoic Warriors. The Ancient Philosophy Behind the Military Mind* (New York: Oxford University Press, 2005), p. 12.

186 'Maynulet testifies in own defense, says killing wounded Iraqi "right thing to do"', https://www.stripes.com/news/maynulet-testifies-in-own-defense-says-killing-wounded-iraqi-right-thing-to-do-1.31154, 20 December 2022.

187 Dragan Stanar, 'The right to die with dignity: Soldiers in post-modern warfare', *Yearbook of Human Rights Protection: The Right to Human Dignity*, 3 (2020), pp. 519–531.

and that said additional normative standards can be found in established concepts such as military honour and human dignity insofar as such echoes of chivalry may resonate with military professionals through appropriate training and education. These are reflected in their shared practices and codes of behaviour as members of a community where such experiences make sense beyond what is simply stated in black-letter regulations. As stated in the Introduction, we need to learn the language of lions.

Indeed, in one of his latest works on global governance, Jan Klabbers remarks that "Just as the competent linguist speaks a language (i.e. applies the rules of the language) without always realizing how and why or actively knowing the grammar, the competent moral agent will behave in ethical fashion by disposition and training".[188] As he later clarifies, Klabbers is precisely relying here on Wittgenstein's theory of "language games".[189] As also seen in the Introduction, for Wittgenstein, speaking a language equals engaging in such a "game" in the sense that "language is part of an activity, or a form of life".[190] Such a form of life can be further conceptualized as "the underlying consensus of linguistic and nonlinguistic behaviour, assumptions, practices, traditions, and natural propensities which humans, as social beings, share with one another, and which is therefore presupposed in the language they use".[191]

It is to this underlying consensus that Wittgenstein refers when he talks about that "system of reference"[192] that is needed in order to interpret and understand a language game, such that "Uttering a word is like striking a note on the keyboard of the imagination".[193] Could words like 'honour', 'duty', 'courage', or 'dignity' have this effect? Arguably so, as language games as a form of life also extend to the parcel of society that is the military, for "The military profession is more than an occupation; it is a complete style of life",[194] with its own codes, traditions and understandings. Can a war story strike such a cord in the military? A truly compelling war story, after all, "makes the stomach believe" in Tim O'Brien's poignant account.[195] And for words to have such a moving effect a shared form of life is essential.

---

188 Klabbers, *Virtue*, p. 9.

189 Ibid., p. 47.

190 Ludwig Wittgenstein, *Philosophical Investigations* (Croydon: Blackwell Publishing, 2009), p. 15.

191 A.C. Grayling, *Wittgenstein. A Very Short Introduction* (New York: Oxford University Press, 2001), p. 97.

192 Wittgenstein, *Investigations*, p. 88.

193 Ibid., p. 7.

194 Janowitz, *Professional*, p. 175.

195 O'Brien, *Things*, p. 80.

A core component of this "system of reference" as applied to the military is what has been described here as the war convention, comprising both moral and legal standards of behaviour. And as the ideals of chivalry declined, as also seen in a previous chapter, the need for upholding legal rules has become proportionately greater, as pointed out by Janowitz.[196] Thus, instruction for the armed forces bearing on the basic contents of International Humanitarian Law ('IHL') becomes key "to develop an awareness of what is right and what is wrong".[197]

Further, instruction in IHL is important for two additional legal considerations. First, such an awareness becomes all the more relevant as IHL is a field where the phenomenon known as 'self-application' of the law[198] is particularly acute due to the lack of courts or law-enforcement agencies on the battlefield,[199] rule-enforcement being mostly left to soldiers' sense of professionalism.[200] For this to be effective, in addition, clear and workable legal concepts are essential for the military to be able to apply them in practice, under what Jens David Ohlin dubs "War's Rustic Code of Honor", in the sense that the law of war is "simple, uncomplicated, robust, distilled to its core, and ultimately effective because it is tailored, in bespoke fashion, for its unique context".[201] In this sense, Waldron's concept of a legal archetype discussed in Chapter 3 can prove especially helpful, for instance, by summarizing the spirit of a whole body of law in one simple concept such as military honour as respect for human dignity. As we shall see in the last part of this investigation, some official documents issued for military training and education purposes arguably enshrine such an archetype.

Second, IHL instruction is a legal obligation of states parties to the Geneva Conventions, who are under a conventional duty to disseminate their

196 Janowitz, *Professional*, p. 219.

197 Christopher Greenwood, 'Historical Development and Legal Basis', in Dieter Fleck (ed.), *The Handbook of International Humanitarian Law*, 2nd ed. (Oxford: Oxford University Press, 2010), p. 40.

198 Henry Hart and Albert Sacks, *The Legal Process. Basic Problems in the Making and Application of Law* (New York: Westbury, 1994), pp. 120–121.

199 Jeremy Waldron, 'Deep Morality and the Laws of War', in Seth Lazar and Helen Frowe (eds.), *The Oxford Handbook of Ethics of War* (Oxford: Oxford University Press, 2018), p. 81; Marcela Prieto Rudolphy, *The Morality of the Laws of War: War, Law, and Murder* (Oxford: Oxford University Press, 2023), p. 89.

200 Jens David Ohlin, 'War's Rustic Code of Honor', https://ssrn.com/abstract=4931591, 12 September 2024, p. 57.

201 Ibid., p. 1.

contents,[202] so as to "bring IHL home".[203] This obligation, likewise grounded in International Human Rights Law,[204] must be discharged both in times of peace and war, and according to the ICRC commentary on this particular provision, it includes the entirety of the Geneva Conventions, including Common Article 3 therein safeguarding human dignity. In addition, the ICRC further clarifies:

> the scope of Article 127 must not be reduced to an obligation to post and distribute the text of the Convention. The formulation 'disseminate … so that the principles thereof may become known' has a wider meaning than 'publish the text' or 'make it available'. Dissemination aims at making the spirit of the Geneva Conventions understood by all people and to have their content *internalized* rather than their text simply publicized. As such, Article 127 obliges States to 'include the study thereof in their programmes of military and, if possible, civil instruction' (emphasis added).[205]

Nevertheless, it is worth pointing out that not even the highest possible quality of military education and training can prevent the commission of war crimes with absolute efficacy, as the findings of the *Brereton Report* on the Australian Defence Forces in Afghanistan bear out. For now, it will suffice to conceptualize this particular duty to disseminate as an "obligation of conduct" and not one of "result". According to the International Court of Justice, an obligation of conduct is one of due diligence that entails using "all means reasonably available" and all measures within the state's power, but without a guaranteed result.

---

202 III Geneva Convention of 1949, Art. 127:
The High Contracting Parties undertake, in time of peace as in time of war, to disseminate the text of the present Convention as widely as possible in their respective countries, and, in particular, to include the study thereof in their programmes of military and, if possible, civil instruction, so that the principles thereof may become known to all their armed forces and to the entire population.
Any military or other authorities, who in time of war assume responsibilities in respect of prisoners of war, must possess the text of the Convention and be specially instructed as to its provisions.

203 ICRC, *International Humanitarian Law and the Challenges of Contemporary Armed Conflicts* (Geneva: ICRC, 2019), p. 72.

204 Inter-American Court of Human Rights, Case of "Masacre de Mapiripán" v. Colombia, Judgment of September 15, 2005, para. 316.

205 International Committee of the Red Cross, 'Convention (III) relative to the Treatment of Prisoners of War. Geneva, 12 August 1949. Commentary of 2020. Article 27 – Dissemination of the Convention', https://ihl-databases.icrc.org/en/ihl-treaties/gciii-1949/article-127/commentary/2020?activeTab=undefined#_Toc42507340, 07 March 2023.

Such was the opinion of the Court with regards to the prevention of the crime of genocide.[206] In order to assess a state's endeavours to prevent similar atrocities that also violate peremptory norms of general international law or *jus cogens*, namely grave breaches of the basic rules of IHL or war crimes,[207] the same rationale should apply, as according to an ancient legal maxim 'where the same reason applies the same legal provision should apply' ('*ubi est eadem ratio, ibi eadem dispositio iuris esse debet*').

It is also important to bear in mind that legal rules, like any other standard of behaviour, must be applied using personal judgment and discretion, as Klabbers underscores.[208] Further, they are to be applied using what Aristotle calls *phronesis*, namely 'practical wisdom' or 'prudence' amounting to carefully pondering the consequences of our decisions and avoid acting out of pure impulse.[209] It has also been equated to 'common sense', particularly by Hannah Arendt, for whom the appalling record of the 20th century is explained by an absence of such worldly wisdom or 'sixth sense'.[210]

Transposing this to the occupation of warfighting, we may call the practical wisdom or *phronesis* that every military profession should cultivate a true

---

206 International Court of Justice (ICJ), *Application of the Convention on the Prevention and Punishment of the Crime of Genocide (Bosnia and Herzegovina v. Serbia and Montenegro), Judgment, I.C.J. Reports 2007*, p. 43, para. 430.

207 International Law Commission (2022). 73rd Session. A/CN.4/L.967. Texts of the draft conclusions and Annex adopted by the Drafting Committee on second reading. International Law Commission, Geneva, p. 6:
Conclusion 23 Non-exhaustive list
Without prejudice to the existence or subsequent emergence of other peremptory norms of general international law (jus cogens), a non-exhaustive list of norms that the International Law Commission has previously referred to as having that status is to be found in the annex to the present draft conclusions.
Annex
(a) The prohibition of aggression;
(b) The prohibition of genocide;
(c) The prohibition of crimes against humanity;
(d) The basic rules of international humanitarian law;
(e) The prohibition of racial discrimination and apartheid;
(f) The prohibition of slavery;
(g) The prohibition of torture;
(h) The right of self-determination.

208 Klabbers, *Virtue*, p. 73. See also on the importance of virtue ethics in the application of rules, Christian Nikolaus Braun, *Limited Force and the Fight for the Just War Tradition* (Washington, DC: Georgetown University Press, 2023), p. 62.

209 Ibid., p. 118.

210 Jonathan Peter Schwartz, *Arendt's Judgment: Freedom, Responsibility, Citizenship* (Philadelphia: University of Pennsylvania Press, 2016), p. 122.

'military-prudence', or 'milisprudence' in the learning and the application of the Law of Armed Conflict, not unlike the type of judgment that the military have always applied in the form of a "skilful caution" or "expert prudence" in the art of war, as stressed by Clausewitz himself,[211] such that they can calibrate[212] how much force to use on account of the circumstances. Prudence will be further analysed in the final chapter on military virtues.

This kind of judgment arguably remains the preserve of human beings for the time being, as only they can show a "detailed understanding of the social and ethical landscape to which they pertain" as opposed to Autonomous Weapons Systems.[213] As the ICRC pointed out in a recent report, when assessing the challenge of autonomous weapons systems: "combatants must make context specific *judgments* to comply with IHL"[214] (emphasis added). This becomes particularly relevant when it comes to the discretionary judgment or 'assessment' that is required of a military commander when applying the IHL principle of military necessity.[215]

But knowing the applicable law is not enough,[216] as the ICRC has admitted after initially favouring a mainly legalistic approach, at present complementing it with the ethical dimension needed for a successful socialization in a true "culture of restraint" while using force,[217] an approach reaffirmed by ethicists a year into the Gaza war in Israel.[218] In the same vein, Jody M. Prescott, a legal adviser himself, has recently championed a multidisciplinary approach to military training that includes more than just IHL experts (with their predilect pedagogical tool, PowerPoint slides), adding mental and behavioural health specialists, statisticians, ethicists, and counsellors into the mix.[219]

---

211 Clausewitz, *War*, p. 41. See also Moliner, *Ética*, p. 136.

212 Grossman and Christensen, *Combat*, p. 18.

213 Maciek Zając, 'AWS compliance with the ethical principle of proportionality: three possible solutions', *Ethics and Information Technology*, 25:13 (2023), p. 6.

214 ICRC, *International Humanitarian Law and the Challenges of Contemporary Armed Conflicts* (Geneva: ICRC, 2019), p. 29.

215 Sigrid Redse Johansen, *The Military Commander's Necessity. The Law of Armed Conflict and Its Limits* (Cambridge: Cambridge University Press, 2021), pp. 1; 64 et seq.

216 Moliner, 'Educación', p. 27.

217 ICRC, *The Roots of Behaviour in War* (Geneva: ICRC, 2004); ICRC, *Restraint*; Brian McQuinn et al. 'Introduction'. See also Yoram Dinstein, 'Legal Advisers in the Field During Armed Conflict', *International Law Studies*, 97 (2021), p. 920; Theodor Meron, *Bloody Constraint: War and Chivalry in Shakespeare* (New York: Oxford University Press, 1998), p. 204.

218 Elke Schwarz and Neil Renic, 'Beyond Law: Reaffirming the Centrality of Ethics in War', https://www.justsecurity.org/103464/beyond-law-reaffirming-the-centrality-of-ethics-in-war/, 8 October 2024.

219 Jody Prescott, *Empirical Assessment in IHL Education and Training* (London: Anthem Press, 2021), pp. 2; 38.

This multi-disciplinary approach could further bolster the process of routine, healthy ethical discussions recommended by Whetham in the *Brereton Report*,[220] as military professional engage with a number of experts and practitioners throughout their careers.

Furthermore, this complementary approach combining law and ethics is well suited for the military and their conceptions of honour amidst the hardships of the battlefield, as discussed in a previous chapter, especially since "honour systems often flourish where official legal protection of rights is poor",[221] and bearing in mind that on the battlefield there cannot be "a legal expert alongside each rifleman".[222] Accordingly, Olsthoorn posits that the concept of honour can be useful to reinforce rules and virtues alike, and he concludes that: "it seems to make sense (...) to see honor as something that is especially apt not so much to promote obedience to the law, but much more to encourage the practicing of virtues that are not backed by legal sanctions yet are important in people's private lives and for the functioning of society as a whole (or the military)".[223]

### 5.5 *Getting the Message Across: Military Manuals and Codes of Ethics*

Finally, as for the question about the most effective methods for delivering Professional Military Ethics Education, in recent years distance learning has experienced a significant boost – not least thanks to the Covid-19 pandemic – such that today "integrating media, facsimiles of original documental, video footage, etc. in a way that would be less usual in a classroom can be done with very effective results using web-based technology",[224] as pointed out by Whetham. He further remarks: "The best of these packages are developed with a huge amount of input from education psychologists, military personnel and ethicists working together",[225] thus echoing Prescott's defence of a multi-disciplinary approach to PME. At the forefront of this effort today is the new application for mobile devices titled *Cards for Humanity*, jointly developed

220 Whetham, 'Special', pp. 527–528.

221 Robinson, *Honour*, p. 2. See also Christopher Coker, *Barbarous Philosophers. Reflections on the Nature of War from Heraclitus to Heisenberg* (London: Hurst & Company, 2010), pp. 161; 188.

222 Moliner, *Ética*, p. 136.

223 Olsthoorn, *Military*, pp. 14–15.

224 David Whetham, 'Challenges to the professional military ethics education landscape', in Don Carrick, James Connelly and David Whetham (eds.), *Making the Military Moral. Contemporary Challenges and Responses in Military Ethics Education* (New York: Routledge, 2018), p. 152.

225 Ibid., p. 153.

by the Centre for Military Ethics at King's College London and Case Western Reserve University.[226]

Prescott himself additionally highlights the advantages of more advanced technological mediums for delivering these contents, including incorporating IHL training in war video game play at the initiative of the ICRC.[227] This is part of a wider trend that sees in "military entertainment" or "militainment" a useful tool for instilling respect for the rules of war in active military personnel.[228] This is not surprising, considering that, as once remarked by Johan Huizinga, author of *Homo Ludens*, "Ever since words existed for fighting and playing, men have been wont to call war a game".[229] With their in-built narrative structure and their aptness for repetition and progression, video games can indeed be useful tools for instilling the habits needed for character development,[230] such that, in the case of soldiers, "militainment" may effectively become "enter-training".[231]

But more traditional, tangible means of positive reinforcement are usually preferred in the military for instilling respect for values – medals and citations representing the epitome of those "marks of honour" that signify the worth of a soldier's character and prowess[232] – marking the culmination of a successful process of moral socialisation. And in order to achieve those high honours, the way is usually paved by codes and manuals indicating the standards of behaviour that military professionals are expected to observe.

As we saw in a previous section, doctrine differs from a more informal *ethos* in that the former is articulated in written form.[233] Codes of ethics become especially relevant after events or scandals that represent manifest moral failure on the part of a group or an institution.[234] Thereby, codes of ethics can

---

226 'New App Helps Military Service Members Consider Issues of Ethics In and Out of War', https://www.kcl.ac.uk/news/new-app-helps-military-service-members-consider-issues-of-ethics-in-and-out-of-war, 21 December 2022.

227 Prescott, *Empirical*, pp. 92 et seq.

228 Ben Clarke, Christian Rouffaer and François Sénéchaud, 'Beyond the Call of Duty: why shouldn't video game players face the same dilemmas as real soldiers?', *International Review of the Red Cross*, 94:886 (2013), pp. 711–737.

229 Johan Huizinga, *Homo Ludens* (London: Routledge and Kegan Paul, 1980), p. 89.

230 Matt McCormick, 'Is it wrong to play violent video games?', *Ethics and Information Technology*, 3:4 (2001), pp. 277–287.

231 Francisco Lobo, 'Training and war games', https://www.euroisme.eu/index.php/en/events/past-conferences/berlin-2020, 9 October 2023.

232 Robinson, *Honour*, p. 5; Sherman, *Stoic*, p. 69.

233 Høiback, *Understanding*, p. 23.

234 Klabbers, *Virtue*, p. 137.

become "display windows for the services"[235] for society to understand and keep abreast of what their defence forces are up to. Further, codes of ethics and military manuals are also an important way to implement international legal standards in the domestic system, such codes and manuals amounting to "official publications" or "verbal acts" providing evidence of the existence of a potential *opinio juris* (legal conviction) underpinning a customary rule of IHL,[236] and therefore amounting to an informal codification of said *lex lata* standards for practical purposes.[237]

Fotion and Elfstrom add that codes of ethics face challenges coming both from sceptics and idealists, each expecting too little or too much from them, respectively.[238] They further classify codes into four categories: 1. The internal code governing relations within the military organisation, namely an administrative set of organisational regulations and procedures; 2. The creedal code, a normative set of values and virtues that provides the moral contents or spirit underlying the internal code; 3. The fighting code referring to the conduct of hostilities and the treatment of the enemy and civilian population; and 4. The prisoner's code to be applied in case of captivity.[239]

The important thing to know about codes is that they provide guidance by summarising standards of behaviour that we would otherwise have to figure out by ourselves, much like J.S. Mill's metaphor about moral rules resembling the nautical almanack the mariner uses to help them navigate the agitated waters of life.[240] In the words of Fotion and Elfstrom:

---

235 Høiback, *Understanding*, p. 51.

236 UN International Law Commission, 'Draft conclusions on identification of customary international law', https://legal.un.org/ilc/texts/instruments/english/draft_articles/1_13_2018.pdf, 11 January 2023, Conclusion 10(1): "Forms of evidence of acceptance as law (*opinio juris*) include, but are not limited to: public statements made on behalf of States; official publications; government legal opinions; diplomatic correspondence; decisions of national courts; treaty provisions; and conduct in connection with resolutions adopted by an international organization or at an intergovernmental conference".

See also International Committee of the Red Cross. 'IHL Database. Customary IHL. Sources', https://ihl-databases.icrc.org/en/customary-ihl/sources, 11 January 2023: "III. Military Manuals. This category of practice includes all types of instructions to armed and security forces such as manuals, directives and teaching booklets (...)". See further Jean-Marie Henckaerts and Louise Doswald-Beck, *Customary International Humanitarian Law. Vol. I: Rules* (New York: Cambridge University Press-ICRC, 2009), p. xxxviii.

237 Yoram Dinstein, 'Law of Armed Conflict Manuals', *Yearbook of International Humanitarian Law*, 23 (2020), pp. 5–6.

238 Fotion and Elfstrom, *Military*, p. 66.

239 Ibid., pp. 77–79.

240 J.J.C. Smart, 'Extreme and Restricted Utilitarianism', *The Philosophical Quarterly*, 6:25 (1956), p. 349.

> Codes are paradigm examples of sets of ready-made rules. In addition to being useful in educating children (or raw recruits in military settings) and during emergencies, they save time by keeping us from having to think through what we are supposed to do on every occasion when we are faced with a problem. Without such rules, we would be kept so busy doing critical thinking as to be paralyzed into inaction.[241]

This need for clear, actionable rules becomes all the more acute on account of the proverbial military aversion for theory and excessively intellectual endeavours.[242] Consequently, whatever their contents may be, for codes to be effective they need to be "so ingrained into the consciences of military personnel as to be unforgettable".[243] For this the process of PME becomes essential.

Yet, it is also important to be mindful of the general limitations of codes of ethics, as "no professional code can replace the individual's sense of what to do and what not to do",[244] namely, their own personal judgment as a moral agent, which confirms the importance of distinguishing between education and training. After all, doctrine cannot do wonders: "reiterations of doctrine cannot transform human nature or 'change cockroaches into butterflies'".[245]

Bearing in mind these limitations, as well as the functions and educational potential of code of ethics in the process of PME, we must finally turn to the study of concrete examples of such documents for the remainder of this investigation.

---

241 Fotion and Elfstrom, *Military*, p. 67.

242 Høiback, *Understanding*, p. 63; Sophy Antrobus and Hannah West, '"This Is All Very Academic": Critical Thinking in Professional Military Education', *RUSI Journal*, 167:3 (2022), pp. 78–86.

243 Fotion and Elfstrom, *Military*, p. 73.

244 Klabbers, *Virtue*, p. 144.

245 Høiback, *Understanding*, p. 186.

CHAPTER 6

# Military Virtues Revisited

> The knightly character is art not nature, something that needs to be achieved, not something that can be relied upon to happen.
>
> C.S. LEWIS

∴

## 1 Introduction

Thus far I have described the main factual premise of this conceptual-normative inquiry as all the factors amounting to the 'Circumstances of War' ('CoW'), namely three main theses that, as they interact with each other, make the possibility of war (but not necessarily its actualization) a permanent feature of the world we live in: the interest thesis (T1), the mortality thesis (T2), and the technology thesis (T3) (Chapter 1). An earnest inquiry into the stock in trade of the military professional, namely war, allows us to take what they do and who they are seriously. Accordingly, the specific type of professional that is tasked with the successful management of the outcome of said circumstances is expected to behave in a certain way that is informed by normative standards tailored to the profession ('Professional Military Ethics' or 'PMEt'), as well as by general societal standards following a soft role-morality approach. In this sense, I have developed the ideas of military honour (Chapter 2) and human dignity (Chapter 3), as well as the way their normative propositions may be merged under the banner of a new *Jus Armorum* or Law of Arms whose echoes of chivalry rejuvenate our best traditions refurbished with a modern humanitarian content (Chapter 4). Upon ascertaining the philosophical meaning of these normative categories, the next logical step is to find the best possible ways to convey that message through appropriate pedagogical devices that resonate with the shared practices and codes of behaviour of those who go to war. Thus, I have explained the importance of 'Professional Military Education' ('PME') in the effective communication and socialization of the standards making up the body of PMEt and of general morality, including the importance of new methods and technologies to get the message across, as well as the power of

 | DOI:10.1163/9789004754096_009

tried and trusted pedagogical devices such as military manuals and codes of ethics (Chapter 5).

In this final chapter I intend to apply these contents to empirical examples of normative standards of behaviour as found in different military manuals and codes of ethics around the world. The main research questions of this investigation refer to the sufficiency of the instruction in the laws of war to ensure appropriate behaviour by soldiers on the battlefield, as well as to potential additional normative sources found in ethics. The main hypothesis driving the research posits that such legal instruction is not enough, and that additional normative standards are indeed needed in order to avoid unjustified harm to civilians and moral injury to soldiers, as recognised by authoritative voices in the humanitarian field in times of armed conflict.[1] It is the moral argument of this work that said additional normative standards can be found in the echoes of chivalry known as military honour and human dignity and their interplay. Accordingly, this final chapter will provide illustrations or examples of additional normative concepts of the kind the main puzzle and hypothesis of this investigation rely on as they are found in contemporary military doctrine from different forces around the world.

In short, and to paraphrase JWT scholars like Michael Walzer[2] or Daniel Brunstetter,[3] this chapter amounts to *a moral argument with doctrinal illustrations*. As pointed out in the previous chapter, virtue ethics is the most popular school of thought among military professionals today, and therefore it is appropriate to scrutinize and assess the argumentative quality of these official documents through the prism of that moral tradition that seems to thrive within the military milieu.

Yet, however popular and time-honoured, virtue ethics is also in need of examination in the military profession, as recently proposed by Peter Olsthoorn. This author is concerned that contemporary military virtues are more functional than aspirational, meaning that they admittedly primarily serve the interests and aims of the organization, at the risk of not providing restraint to the behaviour of individuals at war, especially vis-à-vis civilians. He concludes that "we need to look for virtues that are better suited for today".[4]

1 ICRC, *The Roots of Restraint in War* (Geneva: ICRC, 2018), p. 32.

2 Michael Walzer. *Just and Unjust Wars. A Moral Argument with Historical Illustrations*. 4th ed. (New York: Basic Books, 2006).

3 Daniel Brunstetter, *Just and Unjust Uses of Limited Force. A Moral Argument with Contemporary Illustrations* (New York: Oxford University Press, 2021).

4 Peter Olsthoorn, 'Military Virtues for Today', *Ethics and Armed Forces*, 2 (2021), p. 25.

But we need not navigate the waters of contemporary PMEt without a compass, nor is there any need to break new ground when it comes to the study of such a longstanding moral tradition as applied to one of the oldest occupations in human history. Indeed, for this analytical endeavour we may draw on the most comprehensive compilation that can be found today in the field of PMEt, the volume edited in 2019 by Michael Skerker, David Whetham, and Don Carrick under the title *Military Virtues* ('MV').[5] This book offers a unique trove of knowledge combining the theoretical understanding and the experience of 38 scholars and practitioners, resulting in a journey spanning across 14 virtues identified as central to the practice of the military profession: justice, obedience, loyalty, courage, wisdom or prudence, honesty, integrity, perseverance, temperance, patience, humility, compassion, discipline, and professionalism.

In this final chapter I will focus on four virtues from said list (in no particular order), otherwise known in the field of ethics as the four "cardinal virtues", namely justice, prudence, courage, and temperance.[6] These virtues have been part of the canon of moral philosophy ever since Plato included them in Book IV of *The Republic*,[7] and they are drawn on as a direct source in the military doctrine of some militaries, such as the Chilean Army.[8] Yet, not all of them have received the attention they deserve in the PMEt literature.[9] As Olsthoorn remarks:

> although there is evidently still an important role for the conventional soldierly virtues [e.g. courage], it is equally evident that, however instrumental in attaining the objectives of the military, they are not particularly helpful to military personnel confronted with 'morally and culturally critical situations' such as corruption or child abuse. Because military personnel today have to deal with more than just opposing forces, that is a cause for some concern. The virtues we teach military personnel should

5 Michael Skerker, David Whetham and Don Carrick (eds.), *Military Virtues* (Havant: Howgate, 2019).

6 See Philip McCormack, 'Virtues or Values?', in Michael Skerker, David Whetham and Don Carrick (eds.), *Military Virtues* (Havant: Howgate, 2019), pp. 16–17.

7 Plato, *The Republic* (Luton: Andrews UK Limited, 2012), pp. 233 *et seq.*

8 Chilean Army, *Manual: Ethos del Ejército de Chile. MOLD – 02005* (Santiago: Ejército de Chile, Comando de Educación y Doctrina, 2018), pp. 4–5 et seq.

9 A notable recent exception can be found in Chaplain (Lt. Col.) Jared L. Vineyard, 'Cardinal Virtues as Warrior Virtues', https://www.armyupress.army.mil/journals/military-review/online-exclusive/2025-ole/cardinal-virtues/, 09 June 2025.

> suit their task, and today they are not only the more martial ones [e.g. wisdom, patience, temperance, humility and compassion].[10]

Accordingly, in this chapter I shall focus only on the four cardinal virtues as applied to the military profession in order to fill this gap. By doing so, this inquiry purports not only to contribute to the literature on said four virtues in particular, but more importantly, its main goal as stated in the Introduction is to find those additional normative standards that are needed to complement and enhance the baseline legal instruction received by the military. Such additional normative standards are an integral part of the hypothesis underlying the main research questions motivating this investigation. Part of those additional standards have already been found in the core notions of military honour and human dignity explored in this thesis. In this last chapter, the four cardinal virtues as they are codified in the official practice of different militaries around the world will provide the rest of the answer, insofar as they represent a vehicle through which theoretical notions like dignity and honour, among others, find an explicit articulation in military doctrine.

Thus, by using the cardinal virtues as a framework, I shall apply the substantive contents elaborated thus far in this inquiry, namely military honour and human dignity, to assess how they are incorporated into the canon of military virtues in both the specialized literature and the manuals and codes of different militaries across the world. If military manuals and codes of ethics are useful pedagogical devices for conveying the message of additional normative standards to strengthen the ethical behaviour of soldiers on the battlefield beyond mere legal instruction, as it has been argued here, then references to said additional standards as found in such official publications become worthy of analysis, insofar as their inclusion in such instruments makes them categories of contemporary military doctrine, regardless of whether or not they are defined or the depth with which they are treated therein. Since doctrinal materials can be extensive and difficult to navigate, the use of the four cardinal virtues provides a useful navigation tool or argumentative thread to guide us in this hermeneutic task. Ultimately, by problematising words like 'honour' and 'dignity' as found on official publications, we may promote those healthy routine ethical discussions that are much needed in the military.

Consequently, the brief overview offered in this chapter is meant to be a contribution to the applied fields of PMEt and PME and thus will not provide

10 Peter Olsthoorn, 'Introduction. Military Virtues and Moral Relativism', in Michael Skerker, David Whetham and Don Carrick (eds.), *Military Virtues* (Havant: Howgate, 2019), pp. 8–9.

a comprehensive philosophical analysis of the full list of virtues, for which the aforementioned volume *MV* provides a thorough analysis. This chapter will only offer a brief conceptualization of each virtue, followed by examples of their doctrinal articulation in different military manuals, in the following contingent order: a) Justice; b) Prudence; c) Courage; and d) Temperance.

Two further analytical caveats need to be stated before venturing into the contents of each of the cardinal virtues. The first caveat refers to the core concepts of this inquiry, namely military honour and human dignity. With regards to military honour, even though some armed forces around the world include it in their lists of virtues and values (see Chapter 2), the PMEt volume here consulted does not mention it as part of the list of military virtues, neither is it included among the traditional cardinal virtues. This could be due to the fact that honour has been conceptualized more as a reward for virtuous behaviour than as a virtue in and of itself,[11] or because it is sometimes absorbed by germane concepts such as integrity and loyalty, as explained in Chapter 2. I shall revisit in the Conclusions one of the contemporary virtues from the catalogue found in *MV*, namely 'professionalism', in order to examine whether it should be likewise considered as a reward for virtuous behaviour, or whether it should be understood as the summation and actualization of all the military virtues such that a virtuous behaviour for the military will equal a professional behaviour, which would be at the same time an honourable one.

As for human dignity, it has been conceptualized in Chapter 3 as a legal archetype[12] that may at times feature in normative documents as a foreground provision, and it may be found in such capacity in some military manuals and codes of ethics as we shall see. Yet, it may also be the case that a form of "shadow human dignity"[13] is doing the justificatory work in the background, even if not mentioned by name, for instance, when germane concepts such as 'humanity' or 'intrinsic value' are invoked. Regardless of its inclusion by name, if dignity is somehow present with regards to its contents, namely as a demand for universal respect for the intrinsic value of human life and human agency, then it can be said to be satisfied as a normative category, whether the label 'dignity' is used or not.

The second caveat refers to the concept of 'virtue' and its conflation with that of 'values'. We already saw in Chapter 2 how values and principles differ in

11 Peter Olsthoorn, *Military Ethics and Virtues* (New York: Routledge, 2011), p. 40.

12 Jeremy Waldron, *Torture, Terror and Trade-offs. Philosophy for the White House* (New York: Oxford University Press, 2010), p. 228.

13 Ginevra Le Moli, *Human Dignity in International Law* (Cambridge: Cambridge University Press, 2021), p. 137.

that the former belong in the axiological level of analysis referring to 'goods' for human life, whereas the latter refer to deontological imperatives that demand adherence to a certain rule.[14] Values and principles further differ from virtues in that, while the first two correspond to a level of abstraction that may or may not resonate with the individual, virtues begin with the moral agent and his or her capacity for ethical reasoning and character development, which is why they are a popular pedagogical tool among the military.[15]

## 2 The Cardinal Virtues and the Military

### 2.1 *Justice*

Given the popularity of virtue ethics among the military, it is perhaps appropriate to begin our survey of the virtue of justice by drawing on the works of one of the most famous representatives of that school, Aristotle. In the *Nicomachean Ethics* Aristotle identified two main types of justice: distributive and rectificatory. The first type applies to relations of geometrical distribution of goods between the whole and its parts, whereas the second refers to arithmetical transactions between individuals.[16]

A main challenge posed to Aristotle's theory of justice as a virtue that can be predicated of individuals is the philosophy of John Rawls, to which contemporary readers of Aristotle (for instance, the military) should pay heed. In his canonical work *A Theory of Justice*, Rawls introduces the first chapter with the following thesis: "Justice is the first virtue of social institutions, as truth is of systems of thought".[17] As for individuals, since justice can only be predicated of institutions, Rawls reserves for them the idea of the "goods" they can attain, namely the rational means to achieve certain goals in life, including the primary goods of liberty, opportunity, income, wealth, and self-respect.[18] Thus, individuals cannot be said to be "just" *simpliciter*, but they can and should develop the fundamental good known as a "sense of justice"[19] such that they show a personal commitment to just institutions, eventually arriving at the most honed moral state of "purity of heart" whereby the individual is mindful

14 Robert Alexy, *Teoría de los Derechos Fundamentales* (Madrid: Centro de Estudios Constitucionales, 1993), pp. 138–141.

15 McCormack, 'Virtues', pp. 25–26.

16 Aristotle, *The Nicomachean Ethics* (New York: Oxford University Press, 2005), v.3, pp. 84–88.

17 John Rawls, *A Theory of Justice* (Cambridge: Harvard University Press, 2005), p. 3.

18 Ibid., p. 433.

19 Ibid., pp. 567–577.

of the fact that the principles of justice transcend time and space so long as they can be agreed upon among reasonable beings, that they may "act with grace and self-command from this point of view".[20]

This form of "dualism", i.e. the separation of the spheres of institutions and individuals to reserve the principles of justice only to the former, has been criticized in the moral philosophy literature, most notably by supporters of a monist or unified approach whereby individuals can also be called out whenever they do not live up to the expectations of (distributive) justice.[21]

It is beyond the scope of this inquiry to venture into the monism-dualism debate within moral philosophy. Yet, it is worth mentioning that the structural similarities between that argument and the ongoing debate between traditional Just War theory and revisionism have been highlighted by Yitzhak Benbaji, according to whom the "moral division of labour" espoused by traditional JWT clearly delineating *jus ad bellum* and *jus in bello* is unacceptable to revisionists.[22] For the latter, an unjust war in *jus ad bellum* terms automatically renders every single combatant from the wrong side an unjust warrior.

But is it possible for even a combatant fighting for an unjust cause to behave justly? This is perfectly possible according to traditionalism, provided that all combatants abide by the *jus in bello* standards of behaviour making up the war convention, regardless of the (just or unjust) causes of the war.[23] If we accept, *pace* Rawls, that justice is a virtue that can be predicated also of individuals even as the moral division of labour characteristic of traditional JWT is at work, then we need a definition of justice in that particular context.

The definition provided by Edward T. Barrett in the cited *Military Virtues* volume that structures this chapter may assist us in this quest: "Clarifying the underpinning of the just war criteria illuminates exactly what the virtue of justice entails for soldiers. Most fundamentally, it requires *sensitivity to the dignity of all persons*, and a disposition to respect the rights of those associated with military operations"[24] (emphasis added). This attitude entails protecting

---

20 Ibid., p. 587.

21 G.A. Cohen, *If You're Egalitarian, How Come You're So Rich?* (Cambridge: Harvard University Press, 2001).

22 Yitzhak Benbaji, 'The War Convention and the Moral Division of Labour', *The Philosophical Quarterly*, 59:237 (2009), p. 608.

23 Michael Walzer. *Just and Unjust Wars. A Moral Argument with Historical Illustrations*. 4th ed. (New York: Basic Books, 2006), p. 21.

24 Edward Barrett, 'Justice. Overview: Just (and Unjust) Warriors: Nature and Causes', in Michael Skerker, David Whetham and Don Carrick (eds.), *Military Virtues* (Havant: Howgate, 2019), p. 34.

the lives of one's own nationals (civilians and combatants), as well as additional "cosmopolitan duties to respect the rights of adversary combatants and bystanders, duties that are embodied in the *in bello* discrimination, necessity and due care criteria".[25] This corresponds to what in a previous chapter was characterized as Kohlberg's final stage of moral development whereby universal principles of justice , including respect for human rights and human dignity, are freely chosen by the moral agent.[26]

Thus, according to this account the military virtue of justice explicitly calls for respecting the dignity of everyone involved in a situation of armed conflict. It is not entirely clear which conception of human dignity Barrett espouses, but it arguably combines the autonomy and the rank conceptions, as borne out by the Kantian language employed when referring to the rights people have, as well as the criteria underpinning the universal duties of respect, including non-discrimination, which are based on assigning a special normative status to individuals.

Furthermore, as explained in Chapter 3, human dignity has become a legal archetype in international law, meaning that it is the kind of provision that captures the spirit of a whole normative body or bodies, for example, International Human Rights Law and International Humanitarian Law.[27] Thus, respect for human dignity amounts to respect for the law through honouring one of its main archetypes, a respect which has been of old a defining aspect of the virtue of justice.[28]

When it comes to the application of the law in war, far from being what Clausewitz once dismissed as "imperceptible limitations hardly worth mentioning",[29] the fact is that law is considered today an integral part of the war enterprise under such labels as "juridical warfare"[30] or "lawfare", and integrated into the regular process of some militaries under the concept of "operational

25 Ibid., p. 35.

26 Lawrence Kohlberg, *The Philosophy of Moral Development. Moral Stages and the Idea of Justice* (San Francisco: Harper and Row, 1981), pp. 17–19; 409–412.

27 Jeremy Waldron, *Torture, Terror and Trade-offs. Philosophy for the White House* (New York: Oxford University Press, 2010), pp. 227–228; Jeremy Waldron, 'How Law Protects Dignity', *The Cambridge Law Journal*, 71:1 (2012), p. 222; International Criminal Tribunal for the Former Yugoslavia, Trial Chamber, *Prosecutor v. Anto Furundzija*, Judgment, 10 December 1998, Case No. IT-95-17/1-T, par. 183.

28 Aristotle, *Ethics*, V.1, p. 81.

29 Carl von Clausewitz, *On War* (New York: Oxford University Press, 2008), p. 13.

30 Craig Jones, *The War Lawyers. The United States, Israel, and Juridical Warfare* (Oxford: Oxford University Press, 2020), pp. 37; 281.

law".[31] In particular, lawfare has been defined as "the strategy of using – or misusing – law as a substitute for traditional military means to achieve an operational objective".[32] Whether it is misused or not is a matter of prudence or judgment, as we shall see in the next section. For now, it is conceivable to say that a responsible use of legal institutions today should entail not only applying legal provisions to achieve victory or for facilitating effective statecraft,[33] but also taking into account the legal archetype that encapsulates the spirit of that very system, namely human dignity.

•••

But respect for human dignity is not only a theoretical concern within the PMEt literature. This value has been enshrined in different military manuals and codes of ethics as an integral part of the doctrine of some militaries around the world.

As early as 1957[34] the doctrinal concept of *Innere Führung* (literally "inner guidance" or "inner leadership" and officially translated as "leadership development and civic education") has operated as the authoritative moral compass of the German *Bundeswehr*. It is presently codified in the Central Service Regulation A-2600/1, known as "*Innere Führung – Selbstverständnis und Führungskultur*" ("*Innere Führung – Self-Image and Leadership Culture*"), which states: "Soldiers in the Bundeswehr accomplish their mission when, out of personal conviction, they actively defend human dignity, freedom, peace, justice,

---

31 "Operational Law" or "OPLAW" is defined as "that body of law, both domestic and international, affecting legal issues associated with the deployment of U.S. forces overseas in peacetime and combat environments". See Jones, *Lawyers*, p. 93. Such legal issues may include rules of engagement, criminal jurisdiction, claims, displaced persons, riot control agents, command and control, and fiscal law. See LCDR Rachel Mangas JAGC, USN and MAJ Matthew Festa, USAR (eds.), *Operational Law Handbook*, 16th ed. (Charlottesville: JAGC Legal Centre and School, 2016), p. 513.

32 Charles Dunlap, 'Lawfare Today: A Perspective', *Yale Journal or International Affairs*, 3 (2008), pp. 146–154. For a thorough study of the epiphenomenon of lawfare see Orde Kittrie, *Lawfare. Law as a Weapon of War* (New York: Oxford University Press, 2016).

33 Francisco Lobo, 'From "Lawfare" to "Lawcraft": Law in the Service of Contemporary Statecraft and Foreign Policy', https://blogs.kcl.ac.uk/warcrimes/2021/08/12/from-lawfare-to-lawcraft-law-in-the-service-of-contemporary-statecraft-and-foreign-policy/, 12 August 2021. Conversely, on the risks of the law humanizing or sanitizing immoral acts of violence see Samuel Moyn, *Humane* (New York: Farrar, Straus and Giroux, 2021), p. 260.

34 Sönke Neitzel, 'Tribal Cultures and *Innere Führung* – A Contradiction?', *Ethics and Armed Forces*, 2 (2021), p. 4.

equality, solidarity and democracy as the guiding values of our country".[35] These normative contents, which lie at the heart of a unique conception of military professionals as "citizens in uniform",[36] are directly derived from the Basic Law for the Federal Republic of Germany,[37] which sets forth its cardinal principle in Article 1 therein as follows: "Human dignity shall be inviolable. To respect and protect it shall be the duty of all state authority".[38] As mentioned in Chapter 3, this provision has been construed by the German Constitutional Court in unequivocally Kantian terms.[39]

Another vanquished power of the Second World War, Japan, similarly embraces justice as respect for humanity as part of its modern military doctrine, drawing on the particular chivalric tradition of the fabled samurai warrior. In the 1961 *Ethos of Self Defence Force Personnel*, we find that this force's declared main objective is to "contribute to a global peace that is founded on justice and order".[40] An indirect reference to respect for human dignity is included therein under the phrasing "love of others and concern for the motherland and its people".[41]

The South African Defence Forces also include dignity in its 2000 *Code of Conduct for Uniformed Members of the SANDF*, wherein members of that organisation pledge to, among other things, "serve and defend my country and its people in accordance with the Constitution and the law and with honour, dignity, courage and integrity" and to "treat all people fairly and respect their rights and dignity at all times, regardless of race, ethnicity, gender, culture, language or sexual orientation".[42] The first sentence admittedly refers to dignified behaviour as a way of conducting oneself with self-control and aplomb (the rank conception), whereas the second allusion conveys the idea of equal treatment based on inherent worth beyond accidental individual traits (the

35 Eva Högl, 'Civil courage in the military – not a contradiction in terms!', *Ethics and Armed Forces*, 2 (2021), p. 46.

36 Ibid., p. 47; Jens O. Koltermann, 'Citizen in Uniform: Democratic Germany and the Changing "Bundeswehr"', *Parameters*, 42:2 (2012), pp. 108–126.

37 Högl, 'Civil', p. 46.

38 Federal Ministry of Justice, 'Basic Law for the Federal Republic of Germany', https://www.gesetze-im-internet.de/englisch_gg/englisch_gg.html, 6 July 2023.

39 German Federal Constitutional Court, 1 BvR 357/07, 15 February 2006, par. 124.

40 Fumio Ota, 'Ethics Training for the Samurai Warrior', in Paul Robinson, Nigel De Lee and Don Carrick (eds.), *Ethics Education in the Military* (New York: Routledge, 2016), p. 157.

41 Ibid.

42 South African National Defence Forces, 'Code of Conduct', https://www.resdal.org/Archivo/d0000124.htm#:~:text=I%20accept%20personal%20responsibility%20for,risk%20of%20my%20own%20life., 10 July 2023.

autonomy conception). Furthermore, according to K.I. Theletsane, who echoes the rank conception in his own account:

> Respect and dignity are the fundamental values of every military (...). In the African culture, it is even considered as one of its building blocks.
>
> (...) From childhood, Africans learn that behaviour towards those in authority, such as the king, the elders and other members of the community, should always be respectful and these members of society become dignified through respect. Respect and dignity, together with survival, a spirit of solidarity and compassion, constitute the African value system of *Ubuntu* that must form the core in ethics education in the SANDF.[43]

Also interestingly, the *Spirit of the IDF* ('Israel Defense Forces' or 'IDF') expanded its original catalogue of values to include a more universal concern for human dignity in 2001,[44] which is phrased in characteristically Kantian wording as follows: "The IDF and its soldiers are obligated to preserve human dignity. All human beings are of inherent value regardless of race, faith, nationality, gender or status".[45] Accordingly, the derived principle of 'Purity of Arms' (formulated originally in 1994) is explained therein as follows:

> The IDF servicemen and women will use their weapons and force only for the purpose of their mission, only to the necessary extent and will maintain his human image even during combat. IDF soldiers will not use their weapons and force to harm human being who are not combatants or prisoners of war, and will do all in their power to avoid causing harm to their lives, bodies, dignity and property.[46]

This is all consistent with the foundational values of the Israeli legal system, as found in the ersatz constitution known as the Basic Law, whereby dignity means "the value of the human being, the sanctity of his life, and his being a free person" (Art. 1).[47] Accordingly, the Supreme Court of Israel – reportedly

---

43 K.I. Theletsane, 'Form and Content of the Ethics Programme in the South African National Defence Force', *African Journal of Public Affairs*, 11:1 (2019), pp. 88–89.

44 James Eastwood, *Ethics as a Weapon of War. Militarism and Morality in Israel* (Cambridge: Cambridge University Press, 2020), p. 57.

45 Israel Defense Forces, 'The Spirit of the IDF', https://www.idf.il/en/mini-sites/spirit-of-the-idf/, 6 July 2023.

46 Eastwood, *Ethics*, p. 261.

47 Knesset, 'Basic Law: Human Dignity and Liberty', https://m.knesset.gov.il/EN/activity/documents/BasicLawsPDF/BasicLawLiberty.pdf, 13 July 2023.

the only tribunal in the world willing to adjudicate law-of-war issues in real time[48] – referred to human dignity in one of its landmark decisions on targeted killings in the following terms: "Needless to say, unlawful combatants are not beyond the law. They are not 'outlaws'. (...) [T]heir human dignity as well is to be honored; they as well enjoy and are entitled to protection, even if most minimal, by customary international law".[49]

This global trend may be also observed in the *Indian Army Doctrine* published in 2004, which opens with an inclusion of the "Code of the Warrior" taken from the *Bhagavad Gita* which includes a pledge to always protect the weak, be humane, cultured and compassionate.[50] Moreover, the section specifically devoted to professionalism and the military *ethos* bases the legitimacy of the profession of arms in the observance of the Law of Armed Conflict and its underpinning moral values, including references to chivalry with a refurbished humanitarian dimension, as clear example of shadow human dignity drawing on the rank conception as seen in Chapter 4. Thus, two of the main principles governing the military ethos are: "The conduct of military operations within prescribed norms such as the laws of armed conflict and the concept of military chivalry" and "The requirement for members of the profession to uphold a high standard of discipline to protect the weak and defenceless and to always act for the common good".[51]

In the same vein, in 2015 the United States Army issued a new version of its doctrinal publication *ADRP-1: The Army Profession*, which unpacks what it means to be a "Trusted Army Professional". Among other traits of character, this includes recognizing "the intrinsic dignity and worth of all people, treating them with respect" in times of war and peace,[52] in what seems to be a clear application of the autonomy conception of human dignity.

Analogously, the 2018 document titled *Values and Standards of the British Army* features among its values that of 'Respect for Others', which is predicated on the belief that "everyone is born free and equal in dignity. It follows that everyone must be treated fairly and with dignity and respect regardless of: gender; ethnicity (including nationality); sexual orientation; age; disability; gender reassignment; marriage or civil partnership; pregnancy and maternity;

48 Luban, 'What', p. 48.

49 High Court of Justice of Israel, HCJ 769/02, *Pub. Comm. against Torture in Israel v. Gov't of Israel*, 62(1) PD 507 (2006) (Isr.), reprinted in 46 I.L.M. 375, para. 25.

50 Headquarters Army Training Command, *Indian Army Doctrine* (Shimla: Headquarters Army Training Command, 2004).

51 Ibid., para. 7.16.

52 U.S. Army, 'ADRP-1: The Army Profession', https://irp.fas.org/doddir/army/adrp1.pdf, 25 May 2023, pp. 2-6–2-7.

religion; belief or non-belief; rank and position".[53] This wording arguably combines both the autonomy conception and the rank conception, as it refers to dignity as an inborn trait that is to be respected regardless of rank or station.

Following the same trend, the document titled *Ethos del Ejército de Chile* ('*Ethos of the Chilean Army*') issued in 2018 codifies the ethical principle of respecting and protecting 'human integrity', which is clearly a case of shadow human dignity combining both the Kantian and the *imago Dei* conceptions:

> The Chilean Army recognizes the universal nature of the person and their intrinsic dignity. That is to say, it considers that the person has a dignity that is a fact, not a right, which stems from the idea of man created in God's image, endowed with intelligence and will. (...) human dignity is the basis of natural law and of human rights, which are previous to the positive laws of states.
>
> (...) Such foundational considerations referring to the person enable the military to respect, in times of peace and of war, every human being, as required by international humanitarian law which is to be known to them. Thus, every human being and military must be considered and treated based on their status as a person, rigorously demanding they fulfil their duties and respecting their rights. Their education in this topic includes fostering and practicing the values of inclusion, respect for diversity, as well as due concern for all those who are vulnerable during armed conflict, starting with women, children and innocent elderly citizens, as well as the wounded, sick and prisoners of war and the entire civilian population. For the same reasons, every soldier is to treat with dignity all enemies who have surrendered, assisting them as needed and bound to respect medical care and facilities, as recognized by their symbols and emblems.[54]

Respect for human dignity is thus an integral part of Chilean Military Law.[55] Accordingly, the Supreme Court of Chile has also relied on the concept of human dignity to define what counts as crimes against humanity, in particular when addressing actions committed by agents of the Pinochet regime, including the murder of a notorious constitutionalist member of the armed forces,

---

53 British Army, 'Values and Standards of the British Army', https://www.army.mod.uk/media/5219/20180910-values_standards_2018_final.pdf, 24 May 2023, p. 15.

54 Free translation from Spanish. See Chilean Army, *Ethos*, pp. 3-5–3-6.

55 Sergio Cea and Ricardo Coronado, *Derecho Militar. Parte General* (Santiago: Legal Publishing, 2011), pp. 17–18.

General Carlos Prats.[56] According to the Court crimes against humanity are outrages upon human dignity,[57] as they entail treating individuals as objects by depriving them of moral agency.[58]

It is worth noting that also in 2018 the Spanish Land Army, whose influence over the Chilean Army is explicitly acknowledged by the latter,[59] issued a similar doctrinal document, *Values of the Land Army*, linking respect for human dignity with honour, in the following terms: "Honour is based and grounded in a well-formed conscience, in which several other values are thoroughly cultivated such as integrity, chivalry, justice, integrity and respect for the dignity of others as well as our own".[60]

In 2020 the French Army issued an updated version of its code of ethics under the title '*Honneur, courage et dignité*' ('*Honour, courage and dignity*'), otherwise known as the '*Livre orange*' or the '*Orange book*'. Article 2 of the *Code of Honour of the French Soldier* contained therein reads: "in all circumstances I shall conduct myself with honour, courage and dignity".[61] Dignity appears to be used here in the sense of dignified behaviour or self-control that is characteristic of the rank conception. Nevertheless, a more Kantian definition of the concept is provided in the *Orange book* as follows: "Dignity: the certainty that each person has intrinsic value, which demands respect for others as well as for oneself". It also entails avoiding degrading treatment, corruption and addiction.[62] A form of shadow dignity in the guise of humanity can further

56 A similar nobility at the time could be found in the lifework of General Guillermo Pickering, who concludes his memoirs about the same agitated times in Chilean history as follows: "I will never submit to the thought that everything must end like in the jungle, where the law of the strongest will always prevail" (free translation from Spanish). See Guillermo Pickering, *Profesión soldado. Apuntes de un general del Ejército de Chile* (Santiago: LOM Ediciones, 2022), p. 212.

57 Supreme Court of the Republic of Chile, Case CS No 2182-98, 08 July 2010, para. 14.

58 Supreme Court of the Republic of Chile, Case CS No 921-09, 13 August 2009, para. 15.

59 Chilean Army, *Ethos*, p. 2–3.

60 Free translation from Spanish. See Spanish Army, 'Los Valores en el Ejército de Tierra', https://ame1.org.es/wp-content/uploads/2018/03/EME-Valores-del-Ejercito-de-Tierra-2018.pdf, 31 July 2023, p. 23.

61 Free translation from French. See État-major de l'armée de Terre, 'Honneur, courage et dignité. Le comportement du soldat de l'armée de Terre', https://www.info-reglement.terre.defense.gouv.fr/images/multimedia/photo/illustrations/livre_orange-Comportement_du_soldat-web-VD.pdf, 7 July 2023, p. 13; Comité d'éthique de la défense, 'Avis sur l'éthique dans la formation des militaires', https://www.defense.gouv.fr/sites/default/files/tronc_commun/20220413_Comit%C3%A9%20d%27%C3%A9thique%20de%20la%20d%C3%A9fense%20-%20Avis%20sur%20l%27%C3%A9thique%20dans%20la%20formation%20des%20militaires.pdf, 7 July 2023, p. 20.

62 Free translation from French. See État-major, 'Honneur', pp. 18–19.

be observed in Article 8 of the soldier's code, which reads: "During combat, I will not abandon my weapon, nor my wounded or deceased comrades. Master of my strength, I act with humanity and respect my enemy". Accordingly, the French Code of Defence also sets forth the ethical duties and responsibilities of military commanders and their subordinates, including "honour and dignity in behaviour" and "humanity and respect for the rules of the law of armed conflict".[63]

Similarly, the Australian Defence Forces' 2021 publication *Military Ethics* includes among its sources some ethical principles emanating from the Just War Tradition, such as "Humanity", as yet another case of shadow human dignity as it is supposed to mean "treating everybody with respect and acknowledging their inherent dignity and right to life, even the adversary we may be fighting".[64] It further sets forth its defence values, among which we find that of 'Respect', namely "The humanity of character to value others and treat them with dignity",[65] as respect for human dignity "is, and will always be, our best defence against ethical failure in war or peace".[66]

More recently, the 2022 doctrinal document under the name *The Canadian Armed Forces Ethos – Trusted to Serve* states that the first ethical principle of that organisation, in lexicographical importance, is to "Respect the Dignity of All persons", which refers to treating people with respect and humanity in all places such that people always feel included. Thus, "those who respect the dignity of all persons demonstrate humility, empathy and compassion and give credit where it is due".[67] Such a call for fair treatment is also echoed in the literature regarding the specific challenge of gender equality within the military more generally.[68]

Finally, in 2022 a battle-tested Ukrainian military issued an updated version of its *Code of Conduct for Military Personnel of the Armed Forces of Ukraine*. In what matters here, the new version of the AFU *Code of Conduct* includes the following reminder for the Ukrainian soldier of today's battlefields: "REMEMBER:

---

63 Free translation from French. See Comité, 'Avis', p. 5.

64 Australian Defence Forces, 'Military Ethics', https://theforge.defence.gov.au/sites/default/files/2021-12/ADF-P-0%20Military%20Ethics%20Ed%201_0.pdf, 10 December 2022, p. 24.

65 Ibid., p. 30.

66 Ibid., p. 39.

67 Canadian Armed Forces, 'The Canadian Armed Forces Ethos – Trusted to Serve', https://www.canada.ca/en/department-national-defence/corporate/reports-publications/canadian-armed-forces-ethos-trusted-to-serve.html, 21 March 2023, pp. 16–18.

68 Kate Germano and David Smith, 'Case Study 2: Gender Equity as Fairness in the Military Institution', in Michael Skerker, David Whetham and Don Carrick (eds.), *Military Virtues* (Havant: Howgate, 2019), pp. 51–61.

The armed forces are a part of society, and as defenders of society, we have to win people's respect; by protecting human dignity, we win people's support".[69] Human dignity is an established principle protected under Ukrainian constitutional law.[70] It is also a value espoused within the country's military,[71] including in the 1999 *Statute of the Internal Service of the Armed Forces of Ukraine*, which imposes certain duties on military personnel, inter alia "to respect the honor and dignity of every person".[72] The *Code of Conduct* also refers to Order No. 164 issued in 2017 by the Ukrainian Ministry of Defence,[73] which itself includes an Annex 4 reminding Ukrainian soldiers of the IHL prohibition on torture, inflicting bodily harm, mutilation, and mocking or disrespecting human dignity.[74] These documents preserve the core contents of the *Code of Conduct for Combatants* issued by the Ministry of Defence of Ukraine already in 1998,[75] and, under the reconstruction of the code of chivalry proposed in this book, they also arguably continue the tradition established in the 1999 *Code of Honor of an Officer of the Armed Forces of Ukraine*, which also underscores the values of service to the people and respect for human dignity, not only with regards to civil society, but among officers and their subordinates as well.[76] Further, as mentioned in the Introduction, the *Code of Honor* includes a provision that epitomizes this chivalric tradition imbued with a modern humanitarian content:

---

69 Armed Forces of Ukraine, 'Кодекс поведінки військовослужбовців Збройних Сил України', https://www.mil.gov.ua/content/pdf/Code_of_Conduct_for_Military_Personnel.pdf , 08 November 2024, p. 13.

70 Svitlana Melnychuk, Ivan Zagorui, Liudmyla Zagorui, Ihor Kravchenko, and Nadiia Kuderska, 'Freedom and Human Dignity as Fundamental Constitutional Values: The Challenge of Modernity', *Lex humana*, 15:3 (2023), pp. 424–437.

71 Ihor Prykhodko et al., 'Army Values of the Ukrainian Soldier: Its Contents and Its Assessment by Combatants', https://doi.org/10.1080/15027570.2025.2468015, 12 May 2025.

72 Verkhovna Rada of Ukraine, 'Law of Ukraine on the Statute of the Internal Service of the Armed Forces of Ukraine', https://zakon.rada.gov.ua/laws/show/548-14#Text, 07 May 2025, Art. 11.

73 Armed Forces of Ukraine, 'Кодекс', p. 3.

74 Ministry of Defence of Ukraine, 'Наказ 23.03.2017 No. 164', https://zakon.rada.gov.ua/laws/show/z0704-17#Text, 08 November 2024, Annex 4.

75 Ministry of Defence of Ukraine, *Кодекс поведінки учасників бойових дій* (Kyiv: Ministry of Defence of Ukraine, 1998), p. 17.

76 "The officer corps of the Ukrainian army is not a closed caste of military men, but blood from blood, flesh from flesh of the Ukrainian people. This is the nobility of our officers, and this is why the Ukrainian people entrusted them with the defense of their homeland". See 'Code of honor of an officer of the Armed Forces of Ukraine', https://sprotyvg7.com.ua/lesson/kodeks-chesti-oficera-zbrojnix-sil-ukraini, 16 October 2024.

> 3.9 Knightly spirit.
> Under no circumstances can an officer be forced to change his or her beliefs, faith, or to betray the military oath. An officer considers it beneath his dignity to disregard the spiritual values of others. An officer is a model of chivalrous attitude towards the sick, wounded, and civilians.[77]

Interestingly, and in keeping with the national doctrine, the "Warriors of Light" initiative in Ukraine calls on soldiers to respect the rules of war as a way of preserving their honour, dignity and humanity.[78]

This cursory review of the text of the aforementioned doctrinal documents indicates that in most cases the archetype of human dignity is used as a foreground provision in many normative documents, i.e. it is mentioned explicitly therein, with some instances of shadow human dignity also doing some of the philosophical work (e.g. as 'humanity'). As for its contents, the Kantian autonomy conception of dignity is often relied on as it pertains to the intrinsic worth or value of human beings *qua* human, with some cases clearly drawing also on other notions such as the *imago Dei* conception in the case of the Chilean Army, or the rank conception in the case of the Indian Army, the British Army, the Canadian Armed Forces, and the Ukrainian Armed Forces insofar as they draw explicitly on chivalry, or promote equal, fair and judicious treatment regardless of status, rank or position.

These doctrinal manifestations of dignity bear out the importance of the virtue of justice understood in the terms previously defined by Barrett and Kohlberg, that is, as a virtue evincing an advanced stage of moral development that entails showing universal respect for the human rights and dignity of every human being, friend or foe, whether in times of war or peace.

## 2.2 *Prudence*

Next on the list of cardinal virtues we find prudence, also referred to in *MV* as 'wisdom'. It was once characterized by Plato as the cure for a certain deprivation or inanition of the soul caused by ignorance.[79] Wisdom is defined by Rick Rubel as "the quality of having experience, knowledge and *good judgment* to make the best decision in a given situation"[80] (original emphasis). Rubel draws

77 Ibid.

78 Code of Warriors of Light, 'Welcome to the LOAC learning platform', https://www.armedconflict.law/, 23 April 2025.

79 Plato, *Republic*, p. 358.

80 Rick Rubel, 'Wisdom. Overview', in Michael Skerker, David Whetham and Don Carrick (eds.), *Military Virtues* (Havant: Howgate, 2019), p. 127.

on Aristotle's conceptualization of '*phronesis*', or 'practical wisdom', namely "*the habit of making the right decisions and taking the right actions in the context of relentless pursuit of excellence for the common good*"[81] (original italics).

Indeed, Aristotle lists *phronesis* or practical wisdom among the intellectual virtues (acquired through study and reasoning) that are needed in order to acquire all the other virtues of character (which in turn happens through habitual exercise).[82] He characterizes a person of practical wisdom as someone who is "able to deliberate well about what is good and expedient for himself, not in some particular respect, e.g. about what sorts of thing conduce to health or to strength, but about what sorts of thing conduce to the good life in general".[83] Following in Aristotle's footsteps, Stoic philosophers also conceived of wisdom as the ultimate ethical state for a good life.[84]

This classical understanding of practical wisdom has admittedly been neglected in political philosophy since at least the times of the Enlightenment with its characteristic predilection for scientific knowledge or *episteme* over *phronesis*.[85] But in recent times there have been calls for a rejuvenation of the concept of *phronesis* as applied to global governance.[86] This echoes Hannah Arendt's efforts to rehabilitate prudence in political philosophy during the second half of the 20th century. Arendt's works draw not only on classical Aristotelian doctrine, but also on Kant's philosophy.

According to Kant judgment is a higher cognitive faculty that links reason and understanding.[87] He defines judgment as "the ability to think the particular as contained under the universal. If the universal (the rule, principle, law) is given, then judgment, which subsumes the particular under it, is *determinative*"[88] (original emphasis). Reflecting on aesthetic judgment in particular, Kant then explains the idea of "common sense" or *sensus communis*, which can mean either: (i) the "vulgar" or ordinary understanding that can be found in all human beings; or (ii) a higher form of common sense, namely

81 Ibid.

82 Alasdair MacIntyre, *After Virtue*, 3rd ed. (Notre Dame: University of Notre Dame Press, 2007), p. 154.

83 Aristotle, *Ethics*, VI.5, p. 106.

84 Nancy Sherman, *Stoic Wisdom. Ancient Lessons for Modern Resilience* (New York: Oxford University Press, 2021), p. 79.

85 Jürgen Habermas, *Theory and Practice* (Boston: Beacon Press, 1974), p. 42.

86 Jan Klabbers, *Virtue in Global Governance* (Cambridge: Cambridge University Press, 2022), p. 118; Maria Varaki, 'The Quest for *Phronesis* in the Holy Land', in Jan Klabbers, Maria Varaki, and G.V. Vilaça, *Towards Responsible Global Governance* (Helsinki: Unigrafia, 2018), pp. 131–142.

87 Immanuel Kant, *Critique of Judgment* (Indianapolis: Hackett, 1987), p. 16.

88 Ibid., p. 18.

a shared "power to judge that in reflecting takes account (a priori), in our thought, of everyone else's way of presenting [something], (...) and [thus] put ourselves in the position of everyone else, merely by abstracting from the limitations that [may] happen to attach to our own judging".[89]

Kant's conceptualization of common sense as an enlarged mentality of sorts – which is evocative of Rawls's own concept of an "Original Position" enabling us to ascertain the principles of justice[90] – is accordingly used by Arendt to build her own argument on judgment,[91] which she applies primarily to political thought:

> Political thought is representative. I form an opinion by considering a given issue from different viewpoints, by making present to my mind the standpoints of those who are absent; that is, I represent them. (...) this is a question neither of empathy, as though I tried to be or to feel like somebody else, nor of counting noses and joining a majority but of being and thinking in my own identity where actually I am not. The more people standpoint's I have present in my mind while I am pondering a given issue, and the better I can imagine how I would feel and think if I were in their place, the stronger will be my capacity for representative thinking and the more valid my final conclusions, my opinion.[92]

What about military judgment or wisdom? What does it demand of the military professional? Clausewitz famously stated that war involves the maximum use of force, as "war is an act of force, and there is no logical limit to the application of that force".[93] Consequently, war leads, in theory, to extremes, "a clash of forces freely operating and obedient to no law but their own".[94] In practice, however, war never reaches such extremes due to the limitations of the real world, including human fallibility, material calculations, and the ultimate political goals of war.[95] "Warfare thus eludes the strict theoretical requirement that extremes of force be applied. Once the extreme is no longer feared or aimed at, it becomes a matter of *judgment* what degree of effort should be

89 Ibid., p. 160.

90 Rawls, *Theory*, Ch. III.

91 Jonathan Peter Schwartz, *Arendt's Judgment: Freedom, Responsibility, Citizenship* (Philadelphia: University of Pennsylvania Press, 2016), pp. 122–148.

92 Hannah Arendt, *Between Past and Future* (New York: Penguin Classics, 1993), p. 241.

93 Clausewitz, *War*, p. 15.

94 Ibid., p. 16.

95 Ibid., pp. 17–18.

made"[96] (emphasis added). Admittedly, Clausewitz also envisions the theoretical possibility of a passion-less (i.e. a human-less) war, or "war by algebra" governed by pure logic,[97] not by human judgment and common sense.

Now, the kind of judgment or practical wisdom that is particular to the profession of arms is called by Aquinas "military prudence" (i.e. prudence as it pertains to the direction of military service, not its execution),[98] or we may simply refer to it as '*milisprudence*'. Just as common sense and a set of "background conditions" enabling communication[99] tell us that in order to "cut" the cake we merely need a knife and not a lawn mower, it is by applying milisprudence that we know it is not (militarily) necessary to "shoot a bird with a cannon" when a smaller calibre weapon will produce the same result.[100] It may also alert us to the inconvenience – beyond the glaring immorality – of attacking civilians or not mitigating harm done to them thus creating the conditions for future insurgency.[101]

This concept of milisprudence further raises two questions: how can we know the content of our decision is wise or prudent? And, who is supposed to exercise this kind of military judgment?

In order to ascertain what the requirements of military prudence are, we may draw on the notion of military necessity. According to Sigrid Redse Johansen, a Judge Advocate General for the Norwegian Armed Forces, all the

96 Ibid., p. 19.

97 Ibid., p. 14. In this sense, an interesting testing ground located at the frontier between human judgment and pure logic, between *phronesis* and *episteme* as it were, may be found in Artificial Intelligence (AI), a field growing in notoriety, not least due to its potential military applications. Some scholars believe that with its capability for programmable precision, autonomous weapons systems using AI could uphold the IHL principle of distinction better than humans can, given the latter's cognitive biases. See 'The AI Arms Race is Changing Everything', https://time.com/6255952/ai-impact-chatgpt-microsoft-google/?utm_campaign=wp_todays_worldview&utm_medium=email&utm_source=newsletter&wpisrc=nl_todayworld, 26 July 2023; John Gray, 'The human era is ending', https://www.newstatesman.com/ideas/2023/08/the-end-of-the-human-era?, 13 August 2023; George R. Lucas, *Law, Ethics and Emerging Military Technologies. Confronting Disruptive Innovation* (Oxon: Routledge, 2023); Kevin Jon Heller, 'The Concept of the "Human" in the Critique of Autonomous Weapons', *Harvard National Security Journal*, 14 (2023), pp. 1–73; Christof Heyns, 'Report of the Special Rapporteur on extrajudicial, summary or arbitrary executions', https://digitallibrary.un.org/record/755741?ln=en, 25 July 2023, pp. 10–11.

98 Gregory Reichberg, Henrik Syse and Endre Begby (eds.), *The Ethics of War. Classic and Contemporary Readings* (Oxford: Blackwell, 2006), pp. 186–187. See also Braun, *Limited*, p. 110.

99 John Searle, *The construction of social reality* (New York: The Free Press, 1995), p. 130.

100 Johansen, *Military*, p. 269.

101 Maj. J. David Thompson, 'Military Reasons for Civilian Harm Mitigation', *Liaison*, 13:2 (2021), p. 55.

principles governing International Humanitarian Law (i.e. distinction, the prohibition of unnecessary suffering and wanton destruction of property, proportionality, and precautions in attack) contain in-built or explicit considerations of military necessity.[102] Thus, understanding the often misunderstood[103] and neglected[104] principle of military necessity becomes a crucial first step to grasp the importance of military prudence.

For the purposes of this brief review, we may rely on the definition of military necessity usually cited in the literature[105] as found in the *Manual of the Law of Armed Conflict* issued by the United Kingdom in 2004:

> Military necessity permits a state engaged in an armed conflict to use only that degree and kind of force, not otherwise prohibited by the law of armed conflict, that is required in order to achieve the legitimate purpose of the conflict, namely the complete or partial submission of the enemy at the earliest possible moment with the minimum expenditure of life and resources.[106]

Given its conceptual normative constraints (i.e. the prohibitions of the Law of Armed Conflict in-built in this definition), military necessity does not amount to a calculation that operates at the level of utility, convenience or expediency, but at a normative level.[107] In other words, it corresponds not to what Kant calls a "hypothetical imperative" – namely teleological devices indicating the most appropriate means to achieve a given goal[108] – but to a "categorical imperative" indicating the right thing to do.[109]

---

102 Sigrid Redse Johansen, *The Military Commander's Necessity. The Law of Armed Conflict and Its Limits* (Cambridge: Cambridge University Press, 2021), pp. 4; 41.

103 Michael Schmitt, 'Military Necessity and Humanity in International Humanitarian Law: Preserving a Delicate Balance', *Virginia Journal of International Law*, 50:4 (2010), p. 796.

104 Patterson, 'Returning', p. 1.

105 Gabriella Blum, 'The Dispensable Lives of Soldiers', *Journal of Legal Analysis*, 2:1 (2010), p. 78; Melzer, *Interpretive*, p. 79; Johansen, *Military*, p. 30.

106 Ministry of Defence of the United Kingdom of Great Britain and Northern Ireland, 'The Joint Service Manual of the Law of Armed Conflict', https://assets.publishing.service.gov.uk/government/uploads/system/uploads/attachment_data/file/27874/JSP3832004Edition.pdf, 20 June 2022, pp. 21–22.

107 Johansen, *Military*, p. 56.

108 Georg Von Wright, *Norm and Action* (London: Routledge & Kegan Paul, 1963), pp. 9–11.

109 Immanuel Kant, *Groundwork of the Metaphysics of Morals* (Cambridge: Cambridge University Press, 2012), p. 28. It is worth noting here that such external normative constraints can be similarly found in the original version of the *Kriegsraison* doctrine, which alluded to the commander's "subjective freedom and arbitrary judgment" that was to be guided by "the precepts of civilization, freedom and honour, the traditions prevalent in

In this received formulation, however, military necessity is defined somewhat tautologically as all it states is that what is militarily *necessary* is that which is *required* to achieve the purpose of the conflict, which makes military necessity a clear example of teleological reasoning.[110] Hence the need for additional qualifiers to circumvent the glaring tautology, including both considerations of expediency (i.e. the minimum expenditure of life and resources) and of principle (i.e. legal prohibitions).

Such additional legal limitations include the principle of humanity, a standard that is supposed to temper or rein in military necessity,[111] such that the latter does not become unchained *Kriegsraison*. Yet, conceptual tautology re-emerges in the analysis of humanity as a vector of military necessity,[112] as the usual definitions of this second principle orbit around the notion of military necessity merely stating that what is not militarily necessary is contrary to humanity.[113] For example, the UK *Manual of the Law of Armed Conflict* defines it as the principle that "forbids the infliction of suffering, injury, or destruction *not actually necessary* for the accomplishment of legitimate military purposes"[114] (emphasis added). Similarly, Nils Melzer explains that "considerations of humanity require that, within the parameters set by the specific provisions of IHL, no more death, injury, or destruction be caused than is actually *necessary* for the accomplishment of a legitimate military purpose in the prevailing circumstances"[115] (emphasis added).

the army and the general usages of war". Accordingly, two types of limitations to the military commander's judgment were conceived in this original version of the *Kriegsraison* doctrine: the normative (ethical and legal) convictions of the warrior as such, as well as considerations of reciprocity. This moderate version of the *Kriegsraison* may find some parallels in legal theory, for example, what Dworkin calls "discretion" in some of its meanings, as well as what Norberto Bobbio calls "moderate ethical positivism". See Johansen, *Military*, p. 111; Ronald Dworkin, *Taking Rights Seriously* (Cambridge: Harvard University Press, 1977), pp. 32–33; Norberto Bobbio, *El problema del positivismo jurídico* (Mexico D.F.: Fontamara, 1991), pp. 46–47.

110 Johansen, *Military*, p. 28.

111 Schmitt, 'Military', p. 802.

112 Johansen, *Military*, p. 105.

113 Francisco Lobo, 'The "capture or kill" debate revisited: Putting the "human" back in "human enhancement of soldiers"', *The Military Law and the Law of War Review*, 58:1 (2020), p. 106.

114 Ministry of Defence of the United Kingdom of Great Britain and Northern Ireland, 'The Joint Service Manual of the Law of Armed Conflict', https://assets.publishing.service.gov.uk/government/uploads/system/uploads/attachment_data/file/27874/JSP383 2004Edition.pdf, 20 June 2022, p. 23.

115 Melzer, *Interpretive*, p. 80.

In other words, the category we call 'humanity' is assigned the logical negative value of 'not-military necessity', such that it does not contribute any new content thus remaining what Kant calls an analytic judgment as opposed to a synthetic one.[116] In order to turn the principle of humanity into a synthetic proposition with a content of its own as separate from military necessity the concept of human dignity as understood here in the sense of rejuvenating the idea of chivalry and military honour might be of help, as I have argued elsewhere[117] as well as in previous sections of this work (Chapters 3 and 4).

Of the many definitions of "humanity",[118] the idea of compassionate or humane treatment towards one another is the one most relevant for understanding the body of law known as the International Humanitarian Law, and therefore, apposite to the military profession. As Larry May posits: "Humane treatment in both humanitarian and human rights law promotes the minimum amount of compassionate and merciful treatment that humans characteristically do, and should, display toward fellow humans".[119]

For that, the imaginative capabilities enabled by the virtue of compassion can indeed hone the military judgment that is entailed in the idea of milisprudence. Compassion, which is rooted in the theological virtue of charity,[120] is counted among the military virtues in *MV*.[121] It is defined by Paul Gilbert as "*a sensitivity to suffering in self and others with a commitment to try to alleviate and prevent it*" (original italics).[122] Compassion can arguably play an important role in prudence or the faculty of judgment as applied to the military profession in light of the main objective of the Law of Armed Conflict, i.e. to alleviate human suffering in times of war by sparing those who do not directly participate in hostilities and by restricting violence to the strict amount needed.[123]

116 Immanuel Kant, *Critique of Pure Reason* (New York: Cambridge University Press, 1998), p. 130.

117 Lobo, 'Capture', p. 109.

118 David Luban lists three main definitions: Humanity understood as 'humankind', as 'humaneness', or as 'humanness' (philosophical or existential condition of being human). See David Luban, 'A Theory of Crimes Against Humanity', *Yale Journal of International Law*, 29 (2004), p. 87.

119 Larry May, *War Crimes and Just War* (Cambridge: Cambridge University Press, 2007), p. 89.

120 Christian Nikolaus Braun, *Limited Force and the Fight for the Just War Tradition* (Washington, DC: Georgetown University Press, 2023), p. 108.

121 Philip McCormack, 'Compassion: Overview', in Michael Skerker, David Whetham and Don Carrick (eds.), *Military Virtues* (Havant: Howgate, 2019), pp. 287–295.

122 Paul Gilbert, 'Compassion: Definitions and controversies', in Paul Gilbert (ed.), *Compassion. Concepts, Research and Applications* (New York: Routledge, 2017), p. 11.

123 Yoram Dinstein, *The Conduct of Hostilities under the Law of International Armed Conflict*, 2nd ed. (Cambridge: Cambridge University Press, 2010), p. 17; Marco Sassòli, Antoine

In this sense, a professional soldier who understands the main purpose of the body of law governing his or her trade should be a compassionate one.

But who is the subject of this type of judgment, the *milisprudente* called upon to apply it? In the law it is common to assess the behaviour of a person by measuring it against an abstract standard or yardstick, what an ideal archetype would or should do in a given situation, for example, a 'reasonable businessman' or a 'good *paterfamilias*', and of course common sense – the latter largely dependent on who allegedly shares such a common capability.[124] In the case of military judgment, as we saw in Chapter 4, the accepted standard of behaviour is that of a 'reasonable military commander'.[125]

As indicated in Chapter 4, professional soldiers are public officials charged with applying a specific branch of the law, International Humanitarian Law or the Law of Armed Conflict. *Qua* legal rules, the standards integrating IHL exhibit an "internal aspect of (humanitarian) rules" drawing on H.L.A. Hart's terminology.[126] Thus, as suggested in Chapter 4, *military honour*, understood

---

Bouvier, and Ann Quintin, *How does law protect in war?* 3rd ed. Vol. I (Geneva: ICRC, 2011), p. 1; Françoise J. Hampson, 'The relationship between international humanitarian law and international human rights law', in Scott Sheera and Sir Nigel Rodley, (eds.), *Routledge Handbook of International Human Rights Law* (New York: Routledge, 2014), p. 193. Compassion can be further reassessed in the context of war considering that the need for care has been coded into our evolutionary biology for longer than violence. See Penny Spikins, 'Prehistoric origins. The compassion of far distant strangers', in Paul Gilbert (ed.), *Compassion. Concepts, Research and Applications* (New York: Routledge, 2017), pp. 16–30.

124 Patricia Cochran, *Common Sense and Legal Judgment. Community Knowledge, Political Power, and Rhetorical Practice* (Montreal: McGill-Queen's University Press, 2017), pp. 15–19.

125 Ian Henderson and Kate Reece, 'Proportionality under International Humanitarian Law: The "Reasonable Military Commander" Standard and Reverberating Effects', *Vanderbilt Journal of Transnational Law*, 51:835 (2018), pp. 835–855; Johansen, *Military*, pp. 76–77; 'Final Report to the Prosecutor by the Committee Established to Review the NATO Bombing Campaign Against the Federal Republic of Yugoslavia', http://www.icty.org/x/file/Press/nato061300.pdf, 8 April 2021, par. 50; International Committee of the Red Cross. 'IHL Database. Customary IHL. Practice Relating to Rule 14. Proportionality in Attack', https://ihl-databases.icrc.org/customary-ihl/eng/docs/v2_rul_rule14, 13 July 2021; High Court of Justice of Israel, HCJ 2056/04, *Beit Sourik Vill. Council v. Gov't of Israel*, 58(5) PD 817, para. 46; High Court of Justice of Israel, HCJ 769/02, *Pub. Comm. against Torture in Israel v. Gov't of Israel*, 62(1) PD 507 (2006) (Isr.), reprinted in 46 I.L.M. 375, para. 57. See similarly on the use of an abstract reasonableness test International Criminal Tribunal for the Former Yugoslavia, Trial Chamber, *Prosecutor v. Galić*, Judgment, 5 December 2003, Case No. IT-98-29-T, para. 58.

126 Hart, *Concept*, p. 56.

a conscientious reflection of special self-worth,[127] could be construed as an *enhanced internal aspect of rules* wherein standards of professional ethics and legal standards merge in a single normative agent called upon to apply such martial *lex artis.*

As Klabbers remarks, every legal rule must be applied using personal judgment and discretion.[128] According to Johansen, the standard of expected reasonableness for the military commander must be assessed with all the available information at the time a decision is made, not with the benefit of perfect hindsight *ex post facto*.[129] Just like with any other instance of *phronesis*, some doubt will inevitable be a part of the decision-making process by the military, and this is why they are afforded certain margin of appreciation to make the best possible decision given the known facts and circumstances at the time and on account of the inevitable 'fog of war' surrounding the entire process,[130] as "at its core, wisdom involves the adept balancing of both knowing and doubting".[131]

Johansen clarifies that the reasonable military commander standard actually applies to the entire chain of command,[132] a point well-made if we consider the phenomenon of the 'strategic corporal' in contemporary armed conflict whereby even the lower ranks must make decision that will impact operations not only at the tactical, but at the strategic level as well.[133] However, the importance of officers in leading by example to help keep the humanity of their troops should never be underestimated.[134]

•••

Now, all these theoretical elucubrations about military judgment are not necessarily reflected by the practice of armies as documented in the different doctrinal manuals under assessment in this inquiry. Yet, some of those instruments

---

127 May, *Crimes*, p. 84.

128 Klabbers, *Virtue*, p. 73.

129 Johansen, *Military*, pp. 76–77.

130 Ibid., pp. 66; 80; 87.

131 Steven M. Kleinman, 'Case Study 2: Operationalizing Wisdom: aggressive Restraint in the global War on Terror', in Michael Skerker, David Whetham and Don Carrick (eds.), *Military Virtues* (Havant: Howgate, 2019), p. 147.

132 Johansen, *Military*, p. 83.

133 David Fisher, 'Why morality matters to the military', in Don Carrick, James Connelly and David Whetham (eds.), *Making the Military Moral. Contemporary Challenges and Responses in Military Ethics Education* (New York: Routledge, 2018), p. 18.

134 G. Corn, 'Contemplating the meaning of "responsibility" in responsible command', https://papers.ssrn.com/sol3/papers.cfm?abstract_id=2546594, 1 October 2020.

indeed touch upon the subject of prudence and judgement, however briefly or obliquely, which are worth mentioning to end this section.

An early recognition of prudence can be found in the last part of the list of virtues included in the concept of *Innere Führung* informing the ethical doctrine of the German *Bundeswehr* since the late 1905os. Indeed, the above-mentioned Central Service Regulation A-2600/1, otherwise known as "*Innere Führung – Selbstverständnis und Führungskultur*", lists the virtues a soldier of the *Bundeswehr* is expected to cultivate, thus becoming "brave, loyal and conscientious, comradely and considerate, disciplined, competent and willing to learn, truthful to themselves and to others, fair, tolerant and open to other cultures, and *able to distinguish right from wrong conduct*" (No. 507, emphasis added).[135] Discernment of the type described therein is arguably a manifestation of good judgment.

Similarly, the Japanese *Ethos of Self Defence Force Personnel* issued in 1961 highlights the importance of individual development, explicitly pledging therein: "We will strive to make ourselves into positive and upstanding members of society who are free from prejudice, and cultivate sound judgment".[136] This echoes the precepts already codified in the 1887 *Imperial Precepts to Soldiers and Sailors*, which encouraged service members to cultivate "sound discrimination of right and wrong".[137]

The 2001 *Spirit of the IDF* includes a value of "Responsibility", whereby it instructs its service members to "carry out their duties at all times with initiative, involvement and diligence with common sense and within the framework of their authority, while prepared to bear responsibility for their conduct" (emphasis added).[138] The 1994 version of the *Spirit* also included a reference to wisdom as combined with courage: "In every encounter with the enemy, the soldier will use the force at his disposal bravely and *wisely*"[139] (emphasis added).

The 2004 *Indian Army Doctrine* refers to the art of command in battle by stating: "Effective battle command demands timely and correct decisions based on the accurate and *skilful judgement* of battle situations. Effective decision-making combines *judgement* with information *as an element of combat power*"[140] (emphasis added).

135 Matthias Schwarzbauer, 'Make *Innere Führung* Attractive Again! A Personal Essay', *Ethics and Armed Forces*, 2 (2019), p. 52.

136 Ota, 'Ethics', p. 158.

137 Ibid., p. 154.

138 Eastwood, *Ethics*, p. 260.

139 Ibid., p. 255.

140 Headquarters Army Training Command, *Indian*, Ch. 3, p. 32.

Similarly, the 2015 *The Army Profession* issued in the U.S. remarks:

> When applying military expertise, Army professionals repetitively make *discretionary judgments*, often with high moral implications and consequences. Whether we are Soldiers or Army Civilians, in war or peace, we make decisions accepting prudent risk and take action with disciplined initiative under mission command. In all cases, we are guided by the moral principles of the Army Ethic.[141] (emphasis added)

In the same vein, the 2018 *Values and Standards of the British Army* unpack what the standard of "Lawfulness" entails: "Rules of Engagement set out when, and how, force may be used against an enemy. In some circumstances, they limit a soldier's ability to use force and demand greater restraint than the law would permit. This requires self-discipline and *judgement*, often in circumstances of danger"[142] (emphasis added).

The 2018 *Ethos of the Chilean Army* also expounds on the cardinal virtue of prudence as applied to the military profession:

> Given that danger, uncertainty and luck constitute the climate of war, prudence is essential in the military preparation of combat and is part of the essential qualities of a commander in the decision-making process. (…) The *prudent course of action* is always exercised in the right time, that is, it addresses the weight of circumstances and the adequate timing.[143] (emphasis added)

Analogously, the 2020 *Way of the New Zealand Warrior* stresses that "Those who show *good judgment* and stand up for what is right, who look after their teams and respect people, who are loyal to those around them and are honest, are the leaders people look to when things get tough"[144] (emphasis added).

Linking this virtue explicitly to the IHL principle of proportionality, the 2021 *Military Ethics* Australian publication states:

141 U.S. Army, 'ADRP-1', pp. 5–2.
142 British Army, 'Values', p. 25.
143 Free translation from Spanish. See Chilean Army, *Ethos*, pp. 4–14.
144 New Zealand Army, 'The Way of the New Zealand Warrior', https://www.nzdf.mil.nz/assets/Uploads/DocumentLibrary/Way-of-the-New-Zealand-Warrior-2020.pdf, 23 May 2023, p. 47.

> Proportionality requires weighing the military advantage gained from prosecuting legitimate military targets against the foreseeable (but not intended) collateral deaths among non-combatants, as well as damage to civilian property. It compares the expected cost to the expected benefit. It requires *ethical judgement* as to the reasonableness of the planned use of force.[145] (emphasis added)

More recently, the 2022 *Canadian Armed Forces Ethos* remarks that: "The CAF Ethos does not define standards of behaviour in minute detail. The CAF is a values-based organization that depends on self-discipline and *sound judgement* to uphold its high standards of conduct and performance"[146] (emphasis added).

Finally, the 2022 *Code of Conduct for Military Personnel of the Armed Forces of Ukraine* includes a prohibition that arguably reflects the concept of military prudence described above, to wit: "DO NOT DESTROY. Do not cause excessive destruction, more than is required to perform a combat mission".[147] Curiously enough, the 1999 *Code of Honor of an Officer of the Armed Forces of Ukraine* explicitly favours action over judgment ("An officer's ability is proved not by judgment, but by actions"[148]). Yet, this particular provision is part of a broader section bearing on readiness and reliability that does value "intelligence, skill and will"[149] as well as "the unity of word and deed",[150] all provisions that in the end bear out the importance of prudence in the execution of military duties.

In sum, prudence is recognized in some doctrinal instruments whether as judgment, wisdom, common sense or discernment (including a proper understanding of what military necessity may or may not require), such that the military professional is expected to manage the outcome of the Circumstances of War in the most conscientious manner possible on behalf of the society they are tasked to protect.

### 2.3 *Courage*

Contrary to what Goethe wrote in his *Götz von Berlichingen With the Iron Hand* to the effect that valour can never be forgotten since it cannot be learned, courage or valour is also considered a virtue that can be acquired and developed, especially in war. In fact, courage is deemed the most distinctly martial

145 Australian Defence Forces, 'Military', p. 23.
146 Canadian Armed Forces, 'Trusted', p. 16.
147 Armed Forces of Ukraine, 'Кодекс', p. 15; Ministry of Defence of Ukraine, *Кодекс*, p. 19.
148 'Code of honor'.
149 Ibid.
150 Ibid.

of the cardinal virtues.[151] It is a concept that is naturally at home in the military profession, tasked as this is with the management of the inherently perilous outcome of the Circumstances of War. Its importance in Professional Military Ethics is borne out by its ubiquitous presence in the doctrine of several armed forces around the world, as we shall see in this section.

Already in *The Republic* Plato characterized courage as one of the virtues more easily found among the class of soldiers. He explains its essence by using a metaphor:

> Courage may be defined as a sort of salvation – the never-failing salvation of the opinions which law and education have prescribed concerning dangers. You know the way in which dyers first prepare the white ground and then lay on the dye of purple or of any other colour. Colours dyed in this way become fixed, and no soap or lye will ever wash them out. Now the ground is education, and the laws are the colours; and if the ground is properly laid, neither the soap of pleasure nor the lye of pain or fear will ever wash them out. This power which preserves right opinion about danger I would ask you to call 'courage,' adding the epithet 'political' or 'civilized' in order to distinguish it from mere animal courage and from a higher courage which may hereafter be discussed.[152]

Thus, courage is connected to intention and knowledge that enable an adequate assessment of risk.[153] And if courage is salvation concerning dangers as it instils in us the right opinion about those perils, then fear amounts to the wrong opinion in the face of the same dangers. In other words, without danger or peril there would be no opportunity for either courage or fear to arise. Indeed, as John Rawls stresses when explaining the importance of certain negative circumstances or conditions of scarcity for a virtue such as justice to arise: "Unless these circumstances existed there would be no occasion for the virtue of justice, just as in the absence of threats of injury to life and limb there would be no occasion for physical courage".[154] Or as William Ian Miller puts it in his monograph on *The Mystery of Courage*: "Courage is a virtue that depends on scarcity, danger, death, and pain".[155]

---

151 Olsthoorn, 'Introduction', p. 8.

152 Plato, *Republic*, p. 43.

153 Pauline Shanks Kaurin, 'Courage. Overview', in Michael Skerker, David Whetham and Don Carrick (eds.), *Military Virtues* (Havant: Howgate, 2019), p. 103.

154 John Rawls, *A Theory of Justice* (Cambridge: Harvard University Press, 2005), p. 128.

155 William Ian Miller, *The Mystery of Courage* (Cambridge: Harvard University Press, 2000), p. 204.

It is not unusual to think about courage from the concept of fear as a starting point.[156] Early on, Aristotle listed courage among the main virtues, one that can be better understood in terms of its relationship with two different feelings, fear and confidence. Interestingly, he does not equate courage with the total absence of fear, as some degree of this feeling may be acceptable and even advisable, for example, fear of disgrace. In this sense, the virtues of courage and practical wisdom are intrinsically related, "for the brave man feels and acts according to the merits of the case and in whatever way reasons directs".[157] Aristotle thus concludes that the brave man is the one "who faces and who fears the right things and from the right motive, in the right way and at the right time, and who feels confidence under the corresponding conditions".[158] Accordingly, courage is a mean between two extremes: excessive fear and excessive rashness or misguided confidence.[159]

When it comes to war, Aristotle believes that the highest form of courage is that displayed by the citizen-soldier in battle, as this is virtuous courage grounded in a noble desire for honour. Furthermore, this separates the citizen-soldier from the mercenary or sellsword who might appear brave at first:

> Professional soldiers turn cowards, however, when the danger puts too great a strain on them and they are inferior in numbers and equipment; for they are the first to fly, while citizen-soldiers die at their posts (…) For to the latter flight is disgraceful and death is preferable to safety on those terms; while the former from the very beginning faced the danger on the assumption that they were stronger, and when they know the facts they fly, fearing death more than disgrace; but the brave man is not that sort of person.[160]

Miller explains that, as a martial virtue, courage is needed to defend oneself, one's family and nation, thus securing the space necessary for other virtues to develop. Furthermore, construed as fortitude, courage amounts to "a certain firmness of mind" that becomes essential for the virtuous life.[161] In this sense, courage tolerates certain amount of failure so long as it helps in developing

156 Scott Cooper, 'Case Study 2: Moral Courage', in Michael Skerker, David Whetham and Don Carrick (eds.), *Military Virtues* (Havant: Howgate, 2019), p. 118.

157 Aristotle, *Ethics*, III.7, p. 50.

158 Ibid.

159 Ibid., p. 51.

160 Ibid., p. 53.

161 Miller, *Mystery*, p. 5.

the habit that is the building block of virtue ethics: "This kind of wise endurance means that some acts will be cowardly, but it accepts that you will not be a coward if you resolve to do better the next time and then in fact do better enough next times to show a proper respect for the virtue".[162]

But what is fear exactly in the context of war and the 'unlimited liability' that the outcome of the Circumstances of War entails? What makes a coward during combat? Ernest Hemingway once wrote: "Cowardice, as distinguished from panic, is almost always simply a lack of ability to suspend the functioning of the imagination. Learning to suspend your imagination and live completely in the very second of the present minute with no before and no after is the greatest gift a soldier can acquire".[163]

This negative account of courage, or the absence of cowardice, arguably clashes with the virtue of prudence explained above since it requires to discard the very imaginative faculties of judgment that make a wise soldier. Indeed, as Aristotle remarks, without the guidance of other virtues such as justice and prudence, an act identified as brave may be no different from those of the "wild beasts rushing at those who have wounded them".[164]

Another interesting account of fear in combat is provided in Tim O'Brien's Vietnam war memoir *The Things They Carried.* He writes about soldiers:

> They carried all the emotional baggage of men who might die. Grief, terror, love, longing – these were intangibles, but the intangibles had their own mass and specific gravity, they had tangible weight. They carried shameful memories. They carried the common secret of cowardice barely restrained, the instinct to run or freeze or hide, and in many respects this was the heaviest burden of all, for it could never be put down, it required perfect balance and perfect posture. They carried their reputations. They carried the soldier's greatest fear, which was the fear of blushing. Men killed, and died, because they were embarrassed not to.[165]

These words echo Aristotle's view of the citizen-soldier as the archetype of courage, in that they are more afraid of shame or disgrace vis-à-vis their peers than they are in the face of mortal danger.

162 Ibid., p.46.

163 Ernest Hemingway (ed.), *Men at War* (New York: Berkeley Publishing, 1958), p. 17. Similarly, see Miller, *Mystery*, p. 171.

164 Aristotle, *Ethics*, III.8, p. 53.

165 Tim O'Brien, *The Things They Carried* (London: 4th Estate, 2015), p. 19.

Now, as a military virtue, courage comprises three dimensions: physical, moral, and existential.[166] Physical courage corresponds to feats of physical strength, including overcoming the warrior's own fatigue, weakness and fear, alongside the main objective of physically subduing the enemy. "Martial courage" would thus be a subtype of physical courage.[167] Existential courage refers to metaphysical pressures that "threaten one's sense of authentic selfhood and fulfilment".[168] Finally, moral courage refers to "mental and spiritual perseverance and commitment to principles in the face of outside pressure".[169] Due to its relevance in relation to contemporary military honour as rejuvenated chivalry for the promotion of human dignity, as well as its strong connection to the other cardinal virtues, moral courage shall be examined in the remainder of this section. Indeed, moral courage has been said to be the defining soldierly virtue, more so than physical courage.[170]

But what is moral courage exactly? As a type of prosocial behaviour, moral courage is defined as "the expression of personal views and values in the face of dissention and rejection".[171] Unlike heroism, which is another kind of prosocial behaviour that is met with praise and approval, the morally courageous person knows they will have to suffer condemnation, or even violence, from society for standing up for what they believe is right.[172]

As applied to military virtues, "moral courage has come to mean the capacity to overcome the fear of shame and humiliation in order to admit one's mistakes, to confess a wrong, to reject evil conformity, to denounce injustice, and also to defy immoral or imprudent orders".[173] The difference between physical and moral courage is further explained by Miller as follows: "[p]hysical courage decays under the intense and relentless demands of combat while moral courage needs its daily constitutional; it grows by the doing of deeds that require its mobilization. Standing up for what we think is right is not easy, but it may well get easier if we cultivate the habit of doing so".[174]

The need for this kind of perseverance that characterizes moral courage becomes particularly acute, Miller concludes, in the midst of totalitarian

166 Kaurin, 'Courage', pp. 104–105.
167 Ibid., p. 104.
168 Ibid., p. 105.
169 Ibid., p. 104.
170 Cooper, 'Courage', p. 124.
171 Silvia Osswald, Dieter Frey and Bernhard Streicher, 'Moral Courage', in E. Kals and J. Maes (eds.), *Justice and Conflicts* (Berlin: Springer-Verlag, 2012), p. 392.
172 Ibid., p. 394.
173 Miller, *Mystery*, p. 254.
174 Ibid., p. 65.

regimes,[175] an assessment with which Primo Levi would agree as for him cowardice becomes part of the mores of a society under those conditions enabling the most horrible excesses.[176]

Another important feature of moral courage is that, even if it is not innate behaviour, as a virtue it can be trained and practised.[177] This is a point of the utmost importance if we want to draw on courage when it is actually needed, lest we find out we are not as brave as we thought in the face of danger or social disapproval. In Tim O'Brien's poignant account:

> All of us, I suppose, like to believe that in a moral emergency we will behave like the heroes of our youth, bravely and forthrightly, without thought of personal loss or discredit. (...) If the stakes ever became high enough – if the evil were evil enough, if the good were good enough – I would simply tap a secret reservoir of courage that had been accumulating inside me over the years. Courage, I seemed to think, comes to us in finite quantities, like an inheritance, and by being frugal and stashing it away and letting it earn interest, we steadily increase our moral capital in preparation for that day when the account must be drawn out. It was a comforting theory. It dispensed with all those bothersome little acts of daily courage; it offered hope and grace to the repetitive coward; it justified the past while amortizing the future.[178]

O'Brien's point is of the highest importance considering that, as Miller puts it bluntly, cowardice is the expected baseline for the modern bureaucratized army, but it can nonetheless draw on different techniques for engendering courage when it is required.[179] It is through training and education, including the instillation of those "little acts of daily courage", that such baseline can be turned into the trove that is valour. For this, as we have pointed out consistently, the articulation of this virtue in different military manuals and doctrinal documents across the world is a fundamental first step.

•••

175 Ibid.
176 Primo Levi, *The Drowned and the Saved* (London: Abacus, 2013), p. 6.
177 Osswald, Frey and Streicher, 'Moral', p. 401.
178 O'Brien, *Things*, pp. 41; 244.
179 Miller, *Mystery*, p. 133.

As mentioned in a previous section, the concept of *Innere Führung* has been the backbone of the German *Bundeswehr* since the second half of the 20th century. In that view, soldiers are conceived of as veritable "citizens in uniform",[180] and this cross-fertilization between the military and the civilian worlds is also reflected in the concept of "civil courage", which is historically rooted in military tradition. "In Germany, civil courage in the military is therefore not a contradiction in terms, but rather a synonym for the concept of the citizen in uniform".[181] This archetypal character is supposed to stand up for what is right, championing humane and democratic values even in the face of harsh backlash or criticism from society.[182] Indeed, as pointed out by Osswald, Frey and Streicher, moral courage is synonym with civil courage, or in its German expression *Zivilcourage*, calling for a morally courageous intervention in the face of injustice, discrimination, abuse or corruption.[183] This expectation colours the entire social fabric and follows citizens wherever they may be found, whether they don a *Bundeswehr* uniform or not.

Similarly, the 1961 *Ethos of Self Defence Force Personnel* states very clearly that in the fulfilment of their responsibilities, the Japanese forces will discharge their duties at risk to themselves "*with courage and perseverance*".[184] This modern document builds on the Japanese imperial tradition as crystalized in the 1887 *Imperial Precepts to Soldiers and Sailors*, which introduce an important distinction regarding courage or valour by drawing on the virtue of prudence analysed above:

> there is true valour and false. To be incited by mere impetuosity to violent action cannot be called true valour. The soldier and sailor should have sound discrimination of right and wrong, cultivate self-possession, and form their plans with deliberation. Never to despise an inferior enemy or fear a superior, but to do one's duty as soldier or sailor, this is true valour. Those who thus appreciate true valour should in their daily intercourse set gentleness first and aim to win the love and esteem of others.[185]

In the case of the South African 2000 *Code of Conduct for Uniformed Members of the SANDF*, courage is included at the forefront of its stated values:[186]

180 Koltermann, 'Citizen'.
181 Högl, 'Civil', p. 47.
182 Ibid.
183 Osswald, Frey and Streicher, 'Moral', p. 392.
184 Ota, 'Ethics', p. 158.
185 Ibid., pp. 154–155.
186 Theletsane, 'Form', p. 85.

"I pledge to serve and defend my country and its people in accordance with the Constitution and the law and with honour, dignity, *courage* and integrity (…) I will carry out my mission with courage and assist my comrades-in-arms, even at the risk of my own life" (emphasis added).[187] These seemingly more traditional articulations of courage are complemented with moral courage commitments, such as "I will refuse to obey an obviously illegal order"; "I will treat all people fairly and respect their rights and dignity at all times, regardless of race, ethnicity, gender, culture, language or sexual orientation"; and "I will report criminal activity, corruption and misconduct to the appropriate authority".[188]

The 2001 *Spirit of the IDF* is not as explicit as other doctrinal documents when it comes to the codification of courage as a military value,[189] although there are traces of this virtue to be found in the official wording. In its original 1994 formulation, under the section "*Guiding Principles – In Military Service*" we find the following statement bearing on physical courage: "4. The soldier will be prepared to endanger his life when encountering the enemy, and to save human life (to the extent necessary), but will do everything possible to preserve his life and that of his comrades in any other military activity".[190] Accordingly the subsection titled *Encountering the Enemy* therein contains the following wording:

> 19. In every encounter with the enemy, the soldier will use the force at his disposal *bravely* and wisely, while demonstrating tenacity, and with on-going readiness to fulfil all his duties, notwithstanding danger to his life or any other obstacle.
>
> 20. The soldier will be prepared to do whatever is necessary, even risk his life, in order to rush to the aid of his comrades and not to abandon wounded troops on the battlefield.[191] (emphasis added)

At the same time, moral courage could be also identified therein: "16. The soldier participating in a discussion or argument connected with IDF activity, before, during or after implementation, will take a stand and express his opinion in line with his knowledge and professional belief, honestly, *bravely* and fairly" (emphasis added).[192]

---

187 South African National Defence Forces, 'Code'.
188 Ibid.
189 Israel Defense Forces, 'Spirit'.
190 Eastwood, *Ethics*, p. 254.
191 Ibid., p. 255.
192 Ibid.

The 2001 version of the *Spirit of the IDF* is much more succinct than its predecessor. Beyond its three "Fundamental Values" (namely "Defense of the State, its Citizens and Residents"; "Patriotism and Loyalty to the State"; and "Human Dignity"),[193] the subsection "Values" includes at the forefront: "Pursuit of the Mission and Drive to Victory – IDF servicemen and women will fight and conduct themselves with *courage* in the face of all dangers and obstacles. They will persevere in their mission resolutely and thoughtfully even to the point of endangering their lives" (emphasis added).[194]

The 2004 *Indian Army Doctrine* also lists courage among the core values making up the military *ethos* of the institution.[195] Moral courage may also be found in this doctrinal body, under the description on "Basic Morality" contained therein:

> Professional honesty, *courage of conviction*, integrity, tolerance to accept reality and differing points of view are some of the essential qualities which should be always encouraged. The higher the position in the hierarchy, the greater should be the commitment to moral values. In addition, a commander should possess *the courage to take hard decisions*.[196] (emphasis added)

Likewise, the 2015 U.S. Army *ADRP-1: The Army Profession* includes the following hybrid account of physical and moral courage under the section titled *Honorable Servants of the Nation – Professionals of Character*:

> Leadership demands *courage*. Our mission, our duty, and life itself require we reject cowardice – we accept risk, overcome adversity, and face our fears. Our desired outcome, regardless of our best efforts in making decisions, planning, and leading, is not assured. We realize that we may be harmed in performing our duty and accomplishing the mission. The harm we fear may be physical, emotional, or spiritual. To carry on requires *courage*, an attribute of our character and an Army Value. We communicate with candor and tact, seeking shared understanding and demonstrating *courage by doing what is right* despite risk, uncertainty, and fear. A decision and action is right if it is ethical (consistent with the moral principles of the Army Ethic), effective (likely to accomplish its

193 Israel Defense Forces, 'Spirit'.
194 Eastwood, *Ethics*, p. 260.
195 Headquarters Army Training Command, *Indian*, Ch. 7, p. 17.
196 Ibid., Ch. 3, p. 36.

> purpose, accepts prudent risk), and efficient (makes disciplined use of resources).[197] (emphasis added)

As an Army Value, personal courage entails to:

> Face fear, danger or adversity (physical or moral). Personal courage has long been associated with our Army. With physical courage, it is a matter of enduring physical duress and at times risking personal safety. Facing moral fear or adversity may be a long, slow process of continuing forward on the right path, especially if taking those actions is not popular with others. You can build your personal courage by daily *standing up for and acting upon the things that you know are honorable.*[198] (emphasis added)

The 2018 *Values and Standards of the British Army* lists courage, both physical and moral, among the values of that institution, as a quality needed by every soldier, one that is "especially important for those placed in positions of authority".[199] It then goes on to unpack moral and physical courage, assigning the highest importance to the former:

> Moral courage is the characteristic on which the other Values and Standards depend. It provides the resolve to do what is right even when it may be unpopular, risk ridicule or appear dangerous by insisting on the maintenance of the highest standards of decency and behaviour at all times.
>
> (...) Physical courage is the readiness to confront and overcome fear and fatigue. Physical courage on the battlefield must be complemented by moral courage if we are to maintain the highest standards of behaviour and therein our ability to deliver operational success.[200]

The 2018 *Ethos of the Chilean Army* defines courage ("*valor*") as "The moral and physical force that leads to undertake great challenges with resolve, knowingly facing danger and adversity".[201] Such 'moral force' is one oriented by superior principles and aimed at valuable or just goals.[202] In perfectly Aristotelian fashion, the *Ethos* then proceeds to clarify the difference between the virtue of

197 U.S. Army, 'ADRP-1', pp. 2–7.

198 Ibid., p. B-5.

199 British Army, 'Values', p. 11.

200 Ibid.

201 Free translation from Spanish. See Chilean Army, *Ethos*, pp. 4–31.

202 Ibid.

courage and the extremes of cowardice and excessive temerity. While fear is a normal feeling in the face of danger, cowardice is a conscious choice to avoid pain. Recklessness amounts to lack of reflection and pleasure derived from danger. Interestingly from a virtue ethics approach, the *Ethos* concludes that "the cardinal virtue of prudence seeks the mean between temerity and cowardice, it decides with intelligence in the face of danger and assesses the risks and consequences of the decisions made. Only a prudent man can show the true virtue of courage without falling into these extremes".[203]

In the same tradition, the 2018 *Values of the Land Army* from Spain includes a '*Values Card*' that defines courage as a "Wilful act that leads to rationally face the risks and dangers derived from fulfilling duty, overcoming the instinct of survival".[204]

The 2020 *Orange book* for the French Army also sets forth in Article 2 of the *Code of Honour of the French Soldier* contained therein: "in all circumstances I shall conduct myself with honour, courage and dignity".[205] Further, courage is defined therein as follows: "Force of character and firmness in the face of risk both in daily life as in the presence of danger. Mastery of self, physical, intellectual, and *moral* that enables a calm and reflective attitude in adversity and uncertainty" (emphasis added).[206]

The 2020 *Way of the New Zealand Warrior* similarly lists courage ('*Tū Kaha*') among the core values of the New Zealand Army. It specifically introduces the distinction between physical and moral courage, whereby:

> Physical courage gives a soldier the strength and drive to do what has to be done, no matter how difficult or dangerous the task. Physical courage involves overcoming fear so you can still operate effectively in spite of the danger or risks. Moral courage is the strength of character to do what you know is right in spite of pressure. Pressure can take the form of peer pressure, bribes or, on operations, illegal orders contrary to the Law of

---

203 Free translation from Spanish. Ibid., pp. 4-32–4-33.

204 Free translation from Spanish. See Spanish Army, 'Valores', p. 77.

205 État-major de l'armée de Terre, 'Honneur, courage et dignité. Le comportement du soldat de l'armée de Terre', https://www.info-reglement.terre.defense.gouv.fr/images/multimedia/photo/illustrations/livre_orange-Comportement_du_soldat-web-VD.pdf, 7 July 2023, p. 13; Comité d'éthique de la défense, 'Avis sur l'éthique dans la formation des militaires', https://www.defense.gouv.fr/sites/default/files/tronc_commun/20220413_Comit%C3%A9%20d%27%C3%A9thique%20de%20la%20d%C3%A9fense%20-%20Avis%20sur%20l%27%C3%A9thique%20dans%20la%20formation%20des%20militaires.pdf, 7 July 2023, p. 20.

206 État-major, 'Honneur', p. 18.

> Armed Conflict. Moral courage also allows a leader to make decisions, which may be unpopular but still have to be enforced. Those with moral courage make difficult decisions and stand by their principles in the face of adversity.[207]

Also interestingly, the 2021 *Military Ethics* document for the Australian Defence Forces defines courage focusing mainly on the moral dimension of this virtue: "The strength of character *to say no and do the right thing, always, especially in the face of adversity*" (original emphasis).[208] More specifically, when dealing with "normalised deviance" moral courage becomes of particular import according to this doctrinal publication: "Dealing with normalised deviance demands strong leadership from all levels of the ADF. It requires the *moral courage* to question group processes; call out transgressions, changed practices and behaviour; hold people to account; and recalibrate the group back to the expected behaviours of our profession of arms" (emphasis added).[209]

Further, the 2022 *Canadian Armed Forces Ethos – Trusted to Serve* includes courage among its *Military Values*, a concept that is developed therein in both its physical and moral facets:

> Courage is a quality that allows a military professional to overcome fear and pain in pursuit of the mission, and to do what is right in the face of adversity. Courage is both physical and moral; it allows us to confront danger such as physical risk to life and limb. It also allows us to confront the moral anguish of taking actions that may cause injury or death to those around us, or the moral courage to do the right thing despite social pressures. (…) Moral courage enables us to speak the truth to our superiors and teammates.[210]

Finally, the 2022 *Code of Conduct for Military Personnel of the Armed Forces of Ukraine* incorporates moral courage insofar as is instructs military personnel not only to refrain from committing violations of the laws of war, but also to report all violations to the respective commanding officer,[211] which is arguably a somewhat formalized version of moral courage. In addition, the 1999 *Code of Honor of an Officer of the Armed Forces of Ukraine* further qualifies this virtue

207 New Zealand Army, 'The Way', p. 22.
208 Australian Defence Forces, 'Military', p. 29.
209 Ibid., p. 35.
210 Canadian Defence Forces, 'Trusted', p. 25.
211 Armed Forces of Ukraine, 'Кодекс', p. 5; see also Ministry of Defence of Ukraine, *Кодекс*, p. 21.

by stating that "The courage of a combat officer is his bold decisions and ability to *take responsibility*" (emphasis added).[212]

Summing up, these doctrinal documents evidence the salience of courage in different military forces across the world, as courage has of old been deemed a quintessentially martial virtue. Yet, it is not only physical courage that is espoused in said instruments, but, just as importantly (or perhaps even more so), moral courage is likewise a virtue required of the modern military professional who is thus expected to stand up for what is right even against pressure from within or without.

### 2.4 *Temperance*

The ancient Greeks called *sōphrosunē* the virtue whereby excess is checked by an adequate amount of self-control, such as when powerful people do not abuse their power. As such, it is "the quality of knowing how far to go on a particular occasion and when to pause or temporarily draw back".[213]

Aristotle more specifically characterizes temperance as a virtue concerned with pleasure, more specifically bodily pleasure, "the kind of pleasures that the other animals share in, which therefore appear slavish and brutish; these are touch and taste".[214] Its corresponding vice would be self-indulgence.

When dealing with the intellectual virtues, however, Aristotle again mentions temperance or *sōphrosunē*, this time not restricting it to bodily pleasure but as the marker of a truly wise person, for practical wisdom entails being able to deliberate about the good life for people in general: "we consider that those can do this who are good at managing households or states (This is why we call temperance (*sōphrosunē*) by this name; we imply that it preserves one's practical wisdom (*sōzousa tēn phronēsin*) (...))".[215]

Indeed, as Stephen Deakin remarks:

> The virtue of temperance is traditionally viewed as one of moderation and self-control in the use of alcohol, food and sex, although it has a much wider application than this. It is associated with *good judgment*, a sound mind, practical intelligence, restraint, patience, self-discipline, balance, discretion and control of addictive and negative human passions, while

212 'Code of honor'.
213 MacIntyre, *After*, p. 136.
214 Aristotle, *Ethics*, III.10, p. 56.
215 Ibid., p. 106.

> being active and purposeful rather than passive. (...) Temperance is the virtue of 'enough'[216] (emphasis added).

It is due to this functional connection between temperance and other virtues such as wisdom that Deakin concludes: "Temperance is an *enabling virtue*, for the other virtues each require self-control, discipline, sound judgment, personal mastery, a commitment to and a knowledge of what is good and a willingness to make sacrifices for the common good to achieve them" (emphasis added).[217]

In the context of military virtues, the 'virtue of enough' amounts to restraint and self-control bearing on the unique destructive power that is at the disposal of the military professional. As we have seen, self-control is one of the defining features of the rank conception of dignity that now is expected of every human being as the lofty station becomes universal,[218] including in times of war when the rights, privileges and duties of the knights of old are today extended to every soldier. As Deakin contends:

> In the West, ideas about temperance emerge from an amalgam of the ancient Greek thinkers and Christianity, and these find expression in the Just War Tradition [JWT]. For a millennium or more the chivalric tradition celebrated these virtues. Medieval knights were to use their strength for the good; with forbearance, self-control and moderation, to oppose evil. Showing temperance was a quality of a good knight. (...) Such beliefs came to shape the virtues of military behaviour in the West.[219]

Indeed, we find the footprints of this legacy in modern military thinking at least with relation to two notions: leadership and lawfulness. With regards to leadership, some militaries incorporate this notion as an integral part of their ethical doctrine not only in the sense of being able to lead troops into battle, but also including the capability of self-control and firm commitment to moral values.[220] As for lawfulness, the *temperantia in bello* that is quintessential to

216 Stephen Deakin, 'Temperance. Overview: The Virtue of Temperance', in Michael Skerker, David Whetham and Don Carrick (eds.), *Military Virtues* (Havant: Howgate, 2019), pp. 215–216.

217 Ibid., pp. 216–217.

218 Jeremy Waldron, *Dignity, Rank and Rights. The Berkeley Tanner Lectures (2009)* (New York: Oxford University Press, 2012), p. 22.

219 Deakin, 'Temperance', p. 216.

220 Ibid., p. 217.

the JWT, as illustrated by the principles of military necessity and humanity, also requires a particular disposition in military professionals:

> Temperate soldiers will obey the laws of war. Just war requires temperate fighters who will act with restraint and moderation. Just War thinking accepts that wars will occur, it seeks to limit war and its effects through the Law of Armed Conflict (LOAC). (…) LOAC cannot codify everything and cover every eventuality. It requires ethically and legally aware soldiers and their temperate judgement for it to succeed. Temperance is at the heart of the law of armed conflict.[221]

Furthermore, temperance can ground strategies such as that of "courageous restraint",[222] ideally extending to entire units beyond individuals,[223] such that approaches like "Civilian Harm Mitigation" ('CHM') may help prevent today's tactical victories from turning into tomorrow's strategic defeats due to the perpetuation of insurgency.[224]

•••

Now, in practice it is arguably more common to find temperance in military manuals articulated not as such, but under the name of 'discipline'. Although this latter term is treated as a military virtue in its own right, one intuitively associated with rule-enforcement and punishment, the truth is that it may also refer to a defining aspect of temperance, that of *sōphrosunē* or self-control, which in turn becomes the key to access today the kind of restraint that characterized the erstwhile code of chivalry. As James Turner Johnson notes: "the common soldier of the modern period had not been schooled for knighthood; he had no opportunity to internalize chivalric norms in his upbringing. For him discipline took the place of this process".[225] Accordingly, Paul Robinson further remarks:

221 Ibid., pp. 220–221.

222 Ibid., p. 222.

223 David M. Barnes, 'Case Study 2: Unit Temperance and the Haditha Case', in Michael Skerker, David Whetham and Don Carrick (eds.), *Military Virtues* (Havant: Howgate, 2019), pp. 231–239.

224 Thompson, 'Military', p. 58.

225 James Turner Johnson, *Just War Tradition and the Restraint of War. A Moral and Historical Inquiry* (Princeton: Princeton University Press, 1984), p. 185.

> On the other hand, discipline refers to what Volkov calls a 'phenomenon of individual self-consciousness.' Discipline of this sort is often called 'self-discipline' and may be seen as a moral or spiritual characteristic, which manifests itself in behaviour. Discipline of this second sort overlaps to some degree with various other virtues, such as obedience, *self-control, restraint*, and promptness.[226] (emphasis added)

In this sense, one manifestation of temperance in contemporary military doctrine can be found in the aforementioned Central Service Regulation A-2600/1 codifying the concept of *Innere Führung* for the German Armed Forces. As mentioned before, soldiers of the *Bundeswehr* are expected to be "brave, loyal and conscientious, comradely and considerate, *disciplined*, competent and willing to learn, truthful to themselves and to others, fair, tolerant and open to other cultures, and able to distinguish right from wrong conduct" (No. 507, emphasis added).[227] Unit cohesion and discipline are reiterated elsewhere in *Innere Führung* as values to be fostered in that institution (No. 401).[228]

As indicated above, the Japanese 1887 *Imperial Precepts to Soldiers and Sailors* underscored the importance of cultivating self-possession among the members of the armed forces.[229] This is further expanded in the 1961 *Ethos of Self Defence Force Personnel*, in which service members pledge to "develop into well-balanced individuals with regard to qualities such as intellect, initiative, trustworthiness and physical fitness",[230] as discipline is deemed "the lifeblood of a unit".[231]

The South African *Code of Conduct for Uniformed Members of the SANDF* of 2000 includes some phrasing conveying the idea of self-control or restraint that is integral to discipline, as its member pledge to do the following: "I will not abuse my authority, position or public funds for personal gain, political motive or any other reason. (…) I will strive to improve the capabilities of the SANDF by maintaining *discipline*, safeguarding property, developing skills and knowledge, and performing my duties diligently and professionally" (emphasis added).[232] More directly connected to the conduction of hostilities, members of the SANDF also commit to self-restraint in the following terms: "I will employ

226 Paul Robinson, 'Discipline. Overview', in Michael Skerker, David Whetham and Don Carrick (eds.), *Military Virtues* (Havant: Howgate, 2019), p. 313.

227 Schwarzbauer, 'Make', p. 52.

228 Ibid., p. 53.

229 Ota, 'Ethics', p. 154.

230 Ibid., p. 158.

231 Ibid.

232 South African National Defence Forces, 'Code'.

methods of attack to achieve the military objective with the least amount of harm to civilian life and property. I will not attack or harm enemy personnel who surrender. I will disarm them and treat them as prisoners of war".[233]

The original formulation of the value of Purity of Arms in the *Spirit of the IDF* also included discipline as a value entailing the challenging of manifestly illegal orders,[234] something that is preserved in the 2001 version of the doctrine.[235] Furthermore, temperance or self-control as a guiding standard in the conduction of hostilities is also fostered in the IDF's military doctrine under the unique concept of Purity of Arms, originally formulated as follows: "The soldier will use his weapon and his power to vanquish the enemy only to the degree required, and will exercise *self-restraint* in order to prevent unnecessary harm to human life, body, honour and property"[236] (emphasis added). In its 2001 version, as we have seen, *Purity of Arms* continues to require self-restraint in the use of weapons and force y soldiers "only for the purpose of their mission, only to the necessary extent".[237]

The 2004 *Indian Army Doctrine* similarly includes a quote from *Ramayana* by Lord Rama highlighting the importance of temperance.[238] It also lists self-discipline or "self-regulating discipline" as a fundamental value of the Indian military *ethos*.[239]

As mentioned above, the 2015 U.S. Army *ADRP-1: The Army Profession* lists discipline as a dimension of courage, under the rubric Honorable Servants of the Nation – Professionals of Character: "A decision and action is right if it is ethical (consistent with the moral principles of the Army Ethic), effective (likely to accomplish its purpose, accepts prudent risk), and efficient (makes *disciplined* use of resources)"[240] (emphasis added). Furthermore, the same document highlights what it means to serve following the "Army Ethic": "Our ethic provide strategic leaders with moral guidance when considering prudent

233 Ibid.

234 Eastwood, *Ethics*, p. 252.

235 Ibid., p. 261.

236 Ibid., p. 251.

237 Ibid., p. 261.

238 "*O friend, behold my chariot through which I am always decidedly victorious. Courage and tenacity are its wheels, immutable truth and character are its flags. Strength, discrimination,* self-control *and charity are its horses. Forgiveness, mercy and equanimity are the reins and devotion to the Lord is its charioteer. O friend, whoever possesses such a chariot can never be defeated*" (emphasis added). See Headquarters Army Training Command, *Indian*, Ch. 2, p. 14.

239 Ibid., Ch. 7, p. 17.

240 U.S. Army, 'ADRP-1', pp. 2–7.

risk, *disciplined initiative*, and the consequences of military operations"[241] (emphasis added). The concept of discipline is further developed therein: "With discipline, we choose the harder right over the easier wrong in the face of temptation, obstacles and adversity".[242] Accordingly, the Annex titled "Norms of Conduct" also refers to discipline as temperance: "Soldiers who manage violence under the stress and ambiguity of combat require the highest level of individual and organizational discipline".[243] This has strategic repercussions, as mentioned above, since a restrained exercise of military power may mitigate harm to civilians and shape more friendly environments in the long run.[244]

The 2018 *Values and Standards of the British Army* likewise list discipline among its core values. It defines it by incorporating a normative element:

> Discipline is a defining characteristic of the professional soldier and is an essential quality in combat. (…) For officers and soldiers, discipline instils self-control, fosters self-confidence, helps overcome fear and enables trust. (…) It requires that officers and soldiers adhere to military conventions and act in compliance with legal orders, even under the worst conditions of war. (…) The best discipline is *self-discipline*.[245] (emphasis added)

Interestingly, the 2018 *Ethos of the Chilean Army* explicitly refers to the cardinal virtue of temperance ("*templanza*"). Bearing on material pleasures, the *Ethos* remarks the importance of this cardinal virtue for the military: "In order to cultivate temperance in today's world, the military person must be fully aware of their condition as a civil servant and of the deleterious influence that the media can have, when they often lead to materialism, greed, mass consumption of created needs, debt and immediate pleasures (hedonism)".[246] More directly connecting temperance to discipline, the document further adds:

> In matters of the service, *temperance* is important because it allows to maintain the correct functioning of discipline and hierarchy. (…) At every level of the hierarchy, the military person must keep moderation and avoid showing off their authority, as limited as it might be. (…) The

241 Ibid., pp. 3–5; 5–2.
242 Ibid., pp. 7–2.
243 Ibid., p. B-4.
244 Thompson, 'Military', p. 55.
245 British Army, 'Values', p. 13.
246 Free translation from Spanish. See Chilean Army, *Ethos*, pp. 4–8.

> adequate use of power and authority normally determine the existence of leadership in the exercise of command.[247] (emphasis added)

As a military virtue in its own right, discipline is defined therein as "The self-mastery that prompts a person to fulfil their duty, subordinating their will to the collective good" and as a "psychological power of self-possession, or *self-control*, enabling the soldier to fulfil military duties related to the rational use of force"[248] (emphasis added). The *Ethos* adds that "given the faculty to wield arms, it is precisely discipline that which allows to differentiate between a professional army and a violent horde".[249]

In the same tradition, the 2018 *Values of the Land Army* from Spain incorporates discipline among its main values, defined therein as "To rationally assume and practice, out of a sense of duty, the Army rules, in order to secure the purpose of the mission".[250]

The 2020 *Orange book* of the French Army likewise defines discipline as "the set of rules of conduct and obligations that, on the one hand, govern certain groups or collectives, and on the other hand are *self-imposed*"[251] (emphasis added). It also requires not to obey manifestly illegal orders or orders contrary to honour.[252]

The 2020 *Way of the New Zealand Warrior* also includes demonstrating self-control as a manifestation of the military value of integrity.[253] It also incorporates a notion of self-discipline bearing on hardening oneself physically,[254] though not necessarily as a manifestation of temperance.

More recently, the 2021 *Military Ethics* Australian doctrinal publication connects temperance with the notion of unlimited liability analysed previous chapters: "Unlimited liability requires from us the highest standards of behaviour, ethical reasoning and *self-restraint*. It may involve putting ourselves at risk to make sure that the force we use is restrained and proportionate"[255] (emphasis added). Besides promoting the disciplined use of force, the document also

---

247 Free translation from Spanish. See Ibid., pp. 4–9.
248 Free translation from Spanish. See Ibid., pp. 4–34.
249 Free translation from Spanish. See Ibid., pp. 4–35.
250 Free translation from Spanish. See Spanish Army, 'Valores', p. 12.
251 Free translation from French. See État-major, 'Honneur', p. 22.
252 Ibid., p. 23.
253 New Zealand Army, 'The Way', p. 51.
254 Ibid., p. 50.
255 Australian Defence Forces, 'Military', p. 4.

highlights the importance of self-control and "slow thinking" to ponder all the consequences of our actions.[256]

The 2022 *Canadian Armed Forces Ethos – Trusted to Serve* document also lists discipline among the "Professional Expectations" of these forces, underscoring the importance of both individual and collective discipline. Thus, it concludes:

> Those who are disciplined are critical of their own conduct and behaviour first, and challenge unacceptable behaviour in others. They enforce discipline and uphold professional standards, they take ownership and do what is right without incentive or reward, they demonstrate *self-control* in the face of adversity, and they cultivate cohesion through teamwork.[257] (emphasis added)

Finally, the 2022 *Code of Conduct for Military Personnel of the Armed Forces of Ukraine* calls upon service members to: "Be a disciplined soldier. Remember that violations of the law of war discredit the state, the army and the soldier. Instead of weakening the enemy's capacity to fight, such violations often strengthen it".[258] Discipline and initiative are also included among the military traditions listed in the 1999 *Code of Honor of an Officer of the Armed Forces of Ukraine*.[259]

In sum, all these doctrinal documents show that temperance understood as self-control or discipline is a key component of the professional behaviour expected of the militaries governed by said documents.

## 3 Concluding Remarks

This chapter has attempted to survey the meaning and different manifestations of the four cardinal virtues of justice, prudence, courage, and temperance as they relate to contemporary military doctrine across the world, considering the popularity that virtue ethics enjoys in Professional Military Ethics and Professional Military Education, which, nonetheless, has left the study of these cardinal virtues somewhat neglected in the literature. This gap should be addressed through analyses such as the one presented in this chapter, so that the additional normative standards that are needed to complement and

256 Ibid., pp. 1; 31.
257 Canadian Armed Forces, 'Trusted', pp. 38–39.
258 Armed Forces of Ukraine, 'Кодекс', p. 5.
259 'Code of honor'.

enhance the baseline legal instruction received by the military can be better understood and taught.

Before moving on to the Conclusions of this work, where military honour as refurbished with a modern notion of human dignity will be finally connected to the concept of military professionalism, it is important to keep in mind that all four cardinal virtues interact with, and mutually reinforce, each other.

Thus, in order to exercise courage, especially of the moral kind, it is a prerequisite to know what the right thing to do is in the first place, and that answer is provided by the virtue of justice. Similarly, in order to truly grasp the complexity and applicability of the abstract principles of justice to concrete situations, the virtue of prudence or common sense is also key. Temperance, as stated above, is also an enabling virtue that provides the necessary self-control for all the other virtues to arise and flourish. Accordingly, the military professional will ideally strike the right balance between them and skilfully navigate the extremes that define their contours in order to live up to the standards of military honour and human dignity.

This way, the main puzzle inspiring this investigation, namely the question about the need for additional normative standards beyond mere legal instruction to ensure decent behaviour on the battlefield, can be answered in a more robust way by including not only the echoes of chivalry known as military honour and human dignity, but also the transcendent four cardinal virtues as the vehicle whereby a practical codification of these additional normative standards can be found in the experience of many militaries around the world.

# Conclusions

## 1 Warrior or Soldier?

"If you are in a war, you are a warrior".[1] This statement by Grossman and Christensen sounds logical enough, in the same way enthymemes like "if you practice law, you are a lawyer" or "if you practice medicine, you are a medical doctor" make enough sense. But could it actually enclose a *non sequitur*? Beyond the statement's obvious omission regarding all those involved in war who are not warriors since in principle they do not take part in the hostilities, e.g. civilians and medical and religious personnel, it is worth probing the premise of this ostensibly logical assertion: can only *warriors* wage war? And if so, should warriors be the ultimate recipients of all the normative arguments that have thus far been unfolded in this inquiry?

The notion of *warrior* is widely used in both theory and practice to refer to those who, indeed, practice war. Michael Ignatieff's *The Warrior's Honor*,[2] Christopher Coker's *The Warrior Ethos*,[3] and Shannon French's *The Code of the Warrior*[4] are but a few examples of the currency of the concept in the literature. A recent publication praises Civil Affairs officers in the U.S. military as veritable "warrior diplomats" in the sense that they are not only expected to be prudent and judicious, but also display some attributes of the warrior who is by definition committed to operational excellence and is willing to take risks and sacrifice everything.[5] Grossman and Christensen similarly betray a rather laudatory use of the concept by focusing more on the service provided by warriors, namely protection, than the means to attain it, that is, killing.[6]

The expression remains popular also among some militaries across the world, including most notably the U.S. Army – which enshrines a *Warrior*

1 Dave Grossman and Loren W. Christensen, *On Combat. The Psychology and Physiology of Deadly Conflict in War and Peace*. 4th ed. (New York: Open Road Media, 2022), p. xviii.

2 Michael Ignatieff, *The Warrior's Honor. Ethnic War and the Modern Conscience* (New York: Holt Paperbacks, 1997).

3 Christopher Coker, *The Warrior Ethos. Military Culture and the War on Terror* (New York: Routledge, 2007).

4 Shannon E. French, *The Code of the Warrior. Exploring Warrior Values Past and Present*. 2nd ed. (Lanham: Rowman and Littlefield Publishers, 2017).

5 Arnel P. David, Sean Acosta and Nicholas Krohley (eds.), *Warrior Diplomats. Civil Affairs Forces on the Front Lines* (Amherst: Cambria, 2023), p. 13.

6 Grossman and Christensen, *Combat*, p. 367.

 | DOI:10.1163/9789004754096_010

*Ethos* as part of the broader *Soldier's Creed*[7] – and the New Zealand Army – which interestingly enough titled its ethical doctrinal publication *The Way of the New Zealand Warrior* in recognition of its hybrid heritage combining both the Māori warrior and the British soldier.[8]

On the other hand, practitioners are admittedly not always comfortable with this characterization,[9] and in fact some armed institutions have started to question the concept of *warrior* to describe their trade. For instance, after accusations of discrimination and harassment that led to some collective soul-searching in order to keep in touch with society,[10] some question the utility of the term for the modern Canadian Armed Forces ('CAF'). Although it is part of the CAF's foundational doctrine, Kent Gregory posits that, due to a lack of definition of the concept, a "male fighting culture" has suffused the institution leading to some dark passages in its recent history, in particular the infamous case of war crimes committed in 1993 by the Canadian Airborne Regiment in Somalia, after which that unit was disbanded.[11]

A similar crisis has taken place almost three decades later amidst the Australian Defence Forces ('ADF') after the publication of the *Brereton Report* on war crimes committed by special forces in Afghanistan, cited many times throughout this inquiry. Therein, the report decries the existence of a "warrior culture" that led to the excesses recounted in the report, in circumstances that "Special Forces operators should pride themselves on being model professional soldiers, not on being 'warrior heroes'".[12]

7 The *Warrior Ethos* is formulated as follows: "*I will always place the mission first. I will never accept defeat. I will never quit. I will never leave a fallen comrade*". See U.S. Army, 'ADRP-1: The Army Profession', https://irp.fas.org/doddir/army/adrp1.pdf, 25 May 2023, p. B-3. The notion of a "warrior ethos" was notably mentioned a few times during Pete Hegseth's confirmation hearing at the U.S. Senate in January of 2025. See Katherine Gypson, 'Trump Cabinet choice faces tough first day of questions on Capitol Hill', 15 January 2025; reaffirmed at 'Secretary Hegseth's Message to the Force', https://www.defense.gov/News/Releases/Release/Article/4040940/secretary-hegseths-message-to-the-force/, 28 January 2025.

8 New Zealand Army, 'The Way of the New Zealand Warrior', https://www.nzdf.mil.nz/assets/Uploads/DocumentLibrary/Way-of-the-New-Zealand-Warrior-2020.pdf, 23 May 2023, p. 13.

9 'Stop Calling Us Warriors', https://angrystaffofficer.com/2016/12/14/stop-calling-us-warriors/, 28 December 2023.

10 Paxton Mayer, 'What's in a Soldier? How to Rebrand the Canadian Armed Forces', *Policy Perspective – Canadian Global Affairs Institute* (2020), pp. 1–16.

11 Kent Gregory, 'Is the Term "Warrior" Suitable for the Canadian Armed Forces?', *Canadian Military Journal*, 22:4 (2022), pp. 55–56.

12 Inspector-General of the Australian Defence Force, *Afghanistan Inquiry Report* (Canberra: Commonwealth of Australia, 2020), p. 33.

However, there are some who believe that the concept of *warrior* can still be salvaged as it is not necessarily evil. Thus, Gregory recommends a "recalibration" of the warrior culture for the CAF, in the sense that "this new warrior culture must be anchored in professionalism".[13] Similarly, Andrew Hastie, a former Australian SAS officer, contends that a warrior culture is an important part of an elite unit, and it is worth promoting such a culture as long as it is infused with the right values, such as those stemming from the Just War Tradition ('JWT').[14]

Is it possible to successfully combine the warrior culture with professionalism? Is the dichotomy between 'warriors' and 'professionals' a false one?[15] And if so, is it more suitable to speak of *professional warriors* or of *professional soldiers*? I began this investigation by inquiring into all those conditions that make of war a permanent possibility in human affairs, namely the Circumstances of War ('CoW'), so that we may take war seriously and, by implication, take those who go to war seriously. But who are they? Who is the agent better positioned to manage the outcome of said circumstances in a restrained, rational, professional manner, the warrior or the soldier? Or perhaps a third, neo-Platonic category such as the 'guardian' as protector and upholder of the common good?[16] Who is better suited to carry on and implement the rejuvenated *ethos* incorporating humanitarian standards bearing on virtuous respect for human rights and human dignity as a matter of military honour that has been the main focus of this study?

First, it is crucial to dispel an important objection against the characterization of the entirety of the military as professionals. Fotion and Elfstrom argue that what defines a professional is not the mere fact of being remunerated for services rendered (as opposed to amateurs): "The narrower sense of professionals with which we are concerned includes receiving pay, possessing skill gained by training and includes even training that has a strong intellectual

13 Gregory, '"Warrior"', p. 57.

14 Andrew Hastie, 'SAS must put honour before glory', https://www.adso.org.au/andrew-hastie-sas-must-put-honour-before-glory/, 14 December 2022.

15 Mike Nelson, 'What Pete Hegseth Doesn't Understand About Soldiers', https://www.theatlantic.com/magazine/archive/2025/08/warrior-myth-lethality-pete-hegseth/683247/, 09 July 2025.

16 Pauline Shanks Kaurin, 'Warrior, Citizen Solider or Guardian: Thoughts After a Kerfuffle', https://shankskaurin.wordpress.com/2016/12/20/warrior-citizen-solider-or-guardian-thoughts-after-a-kerfuffle/, 28 December 2023; Pauline Shanks Kaurin, 'Necessity, Convenience, and Point of View. Military Necessity in Just War', in Eric Patterson and Marc LiVecche (eds.), Military Necessity and Just War Statecraft. The Principle of National Security Stewardship (New York: Routledge, 2024), pp. 77–87.

component to it".[17] By this standard, they conclude, draftees and volunteers do not qualify as professionals, even though they might still be expected to conduct themselves "in a professional manner".[18]

Now, as we examined in this investigation, the following traits usually identify professionals: (1) they are licensed by society and/or the state to provide a service; (2) they belong to a group with common rules of behaviour; (3) they possess specialized knowledge or expertise not found elsewhere in their communities; (4) they are autonomous in their work; and (5) they publicly pledge to assist those in need of their expertise.[19] More specifically, in the case of the military professional Samuel Huntington also points out the following defining traits: (i) Expertise or specialized knowledge and skill in a relevant field; (ii) Responsibility to society; and (iii) Corporateness, or a sense of organic unity.[20]

It is interesting to observe that none of these descriptions highlight the financial aspect of practicing a profession, even though the dictionary includes receiving financial return as a defining trait thereof.[21] Remuneration may be implied in concepts such as autonomy (i.e. the freedom to charge a fee for services rendered) or responsibility to society (i.e. the right to be remunerated counterweighing this liability). Yet, it is not explicitly listed as a defining feature of what it means to be a professional.[22]

In the case of warfighting, at least since Roman times soldiers have been paid in exchange for fighting wars.[23] In actuality, the word 'soldier' comes from the Latin *solidus*, namely the gold coin used to compensate legionaries.[24] Yet, the fact that a person engaged in hostilities is compensated for their service is also not something that belongs exclusively to the professional soldier. Other types of fighters or warriors are also remunerated for their services. In fact, the concept of "mercenary" is completely contingent on this condition.[25]

---

17 N. Fotion and Gerard Elfstrom, *Military Ethics. Guidelines for Peace and War* (New York: Routledge, 2021), p. 47.

18 Ibid.

19 Daryl Koehn, *The Ground of Professional Ethics* (New York: Routledge, 1994), p. 56.

20 Samuel Huntington, *The Soldier and the State* (Cambridge: Harvard University Press, 2000), pp. 8–10.

21 'professional', https://www.merriam-webster.com/dictionary/professional, 11 September 2023.

22 Daryl Koehn, *The Ground of Professional Ethics* (New York: Routledge, 1994), p. 19. See also Paul Camenisch, 'Business Ethics: On Getting to the Heart of the Matter', *Business and Professional Ethics Journal*, 1:1 (1981), pp. 59–69.

23 John Hackett, *The Profession of Arms* (London: Sidgwick & Jackson, 1983), p. 21.

24 'soldier (n.)', https://www.etymonline.com/word/soldier, 11 September 2023.

25 According to the 1989 International Convention against the Recruitment, Use, Financing and Training of Mercenaries, a mercenary is someone who, among other requirements,

However, the idea of fighting motivated mainly for private gain has always been looked down upon in the JWT. As Christine de Pizan declared in the Middle Ages: "it is dangerous in time of war for an army to be more driven by greed for pillage than by the intention to preserve the rightness of their cause or the honor of chivalry or to gain praise. Such men as these could better be called thieves or robbers than men-at-arms or knights".[26] Centuries later, even an archetypal realist such as Machiavelli would declare himself famously against using mercenaries or *condottieri* for national defence.[27] This widespread reluctancy could provide an element to negatively define what constitutes a military professional, namely, something other than the pursuit of (large) financial gain. This anti-materialism arguably can be traced back to the virtue of largesse or generosity of resources that characterized the medieval knight,[28] as the men and women in uniform of today decide to put their "talent"[29] or intellectual and physical resources in the service of an armed institution, thus foregoing more profitable opportunities in the private sector.

But, if not the mercenary's paycheque or the warrior's glory, what then makes a professional soldier or "professional man-at-arms"?[30] How can we positively define their trade? Writing after the revolution in military affairs that the Second World War brought about, Morris Janowitz postulated:

> The history of the modern military establishment can be described as a struggle between heroic leaders, who embody traditionalism and glory, and military 'managers,' who are concerned with the *scientific and rational* conduct of war. This distinction is fundamental. The *military manager* reflects the *scientific and pragmatic dimensions* of war-making; he is the *professional* with effective links to civilian society. The heroic leader is a

---

"Is motivated to take part in the hostilities essentially by the desire for private gain and, in fact, is promised, by or on behalf of a party to the conflict, material compensation substantially in excess of that promised or paid to combatants of similar rank and functions in the armed forces of that party" (art. 1.1.b).

26 Christine de Pizan, *The Book of Deeds of Arms and of Chivalry* (Pennsylvania: The Pennsylvania State University Press, 2003), p. 41. See also David Whetham, *Just Wars and Moral Victories. Surprise, Deception, and the Normative Framework of European War in the Later Middle Ages* (Leiden: Brill, 2009), p. 148.

27 Niccolò Machiavelli, *The Prince* (New York: Oxford University Press, 2005), pp. 87 *et seq.*

28 Richard W. Kaeuper, *Chivalry and Violence in Medieval Europe* (New York: Oxford University Press, 1999), p. 194.

29 British Army, 'Values and Standards of the British Army', https://www.army.mod.uk/media/5219/20180910-values_standards_2018_final.pdf, 24 May 2023, p. 26.

30 Hackett, *Profession*, p. 7.

> perpetuation of the warrior type, the mounted officer who embodies the martial spirit and the theme of personal valor.[31] (emphasis added)

The scientific, rational, restrained use of force, thus, becomes a defining feature of the professional in charge of managing the outcome of the CoW. As John Hackett puts it: "The function of the profession of arms is the *ordered* application of force in the resolution of a social problem" (emphasis added).[32] As pointed out in Chapter 1, the idea of *management* is tied to rationality and legitimacy, in the sense that force must be wielded only in a way that permits an effective return to a situation of non-violence.[33] Only such a *professional* management of force can make a return to peace more likely,[34] which is ultimately the goal of the JWT. As the *Ethos of the Chilean Army* remarks:

> [t]he exclusive trust in the use of arms, and in the use of rational and prudent violence that the social contract has placed in the Armed Forces, demands of the military professional certain aptitudes and competencies that make them, based on a committed adherence to professional military ethics, someone suitable to serve the nation and the Institution.[35]

## 2 Professionalism as a Virtue?

Professionalism is the quality or condition of being a professional, just as heroism is the quality or condition of being a hero or scepticism is the quality or condition of being a sceptic. In and of themselves, said qualities or conditions have no value independent of the value we assign to the main concept they derive from. If being a hero is a good thing, then *a fortiori* so will be heroism. If being a sceptic is a bad thing, so is scepticism. But some occasions call for a

31 Morris Janowitz, *The Professional Soldier* (New York: Free Press, 2017), p. 21.

32 Hackett, *Profession*, p. 9.

33 Juan Moliner, 'La educación y formación en ética militar', in Centro Conjunto de Desarollo de Conceptos, *Cuestiones sobre ética militar* (Madrid: Ministerio de Defensa, 2022), p. 24; Juan Moliner, *La ética militar como como marco de reflexión sobre la guerra y la profesión militar* (Madrid: Ministerio de Defensa, 2022), p. 29. See also Immanuel Kant, *Toward Perpetual Peace and Other Writings on Politics, Peace, and History* (New Haven: Yale University Press, 2006), p. 70.

34 Moliner, 'Educación', p. 29; Moliner, *Ética*, p. 34.

35 Free translation from Spanish. See Chilean Army, *Manual: Ethos del Ejército de Chile. MOLD – 02005* (Santiago: Ejército de Chile, Comando de Educación y Doctrina, 2018), pp. 3–5.

healthy amount of scepticism, for example, when engaging in critical thinking. Further, sometimes trying to play the hero might put more lives at risk if done imprudently. Then the tables will turn as we plead 'Don't be a hero!'

Professionalism, as the quality or condition of being a professional, is also axiologically neutral in this sense. We may highly value what a healthcare professional or a legal professional does to serve society, and therefore their professionalism will be deemed as a positive quality. But we may also regret that a professional mercenary or hitman is so skilled and effective that they can be said to inflict suffering and destruction on others with relentless professionalism. In this sense, professionalism resembles what some legal theorists believe about the concept of the 'rule of law'. For example, Joseph Raz postulates that the rule of law is one of the virtues that a legal system may (or may not) possess to a greater or lesser extent, without necessarily being committed to substantive values but only to the goal of restricting arbitrary power. The basic assumption is that the law must be capable of guiding the behaviour of its subjects, and arbitrariness is incompatible with such an expectation.[36] Thus, the rule of law is not a moral virtue, but a teleological virtue of the legal system that acts as a technique of social organisation,[37] just as a sharp knife is a tool that can be used for either good or evil. "Therefore, the rule of law is the specific excellence of the law".[38] Analogously, professionalism would amount to the specific excellence of any given profession, however laudable or despicable. This includes the military profession, and this is exactly the main concern of the field known as Professional Military Ethics ('PMEt') that has provided some of the theoretical foundations for this inquiry.

Indeed, in the volume dedicated to *Military Virtues* that has been referenced in this work as one of the latest contributions to the PMEt literature, professionalism is included among the list of virtues belonging to the profession of arms. In this sense, Daniel Lagacé-Roy and Carl Jacob call *Ethos* those professional guiding values, or professional military excellence.[39] "Professionalism" is, to these authors, a stage that is attained in the path from membership to the final idea of *Ethos*, across the following progression: (1) Member of the Profession of Arms – (2) Professionalization – (3) Professionalism –

36 Joseph Raz, *The Authority of Law: Essays on Law and Morality* (New York: Oxford University Press, 1979), pp. 210–218.

37 Hans Kelsen, *General Theory of Law and State* (Cambridge: Harvard University Press, 1949), p. 5.

38 Raz, *Authority*, pp. 219–225.

39 Daniel Lagacé-Roy and Carl Jacob, 'Professionalism. Overview: Professional Military Excellence Through Practice', in Michael Skerker, David Whetham and Don Carrick (eds.), *Military Virtues* (Havant: Howgate, 2019), p. 337.

(4) Professional – Professional Military Excellence (*Ethos*).[40] Professionalism is defined therein as the state of affairs whereby military professionals "display competence in their domain of expertise by the work they perform and the activities they complete".[41] Yet, this does not necessarily set apart the military professional, or any other professional who is good at their trade for that matter, such as the skilled professional assassin or criminal.

In order to dissipate this ambiguity, John Thomas clarifies the relationship between military professionalism and virtue ethics:

> [b]eing a military professional means not only mastering all the virtues examined in detail in the previous chapters,[42] but it also means having other qualities which fall outside the philosopher's strict definition of a virtue, for example technical skill, and physical and medical fitness. Crucially, professionalism also implies being accountable for one's actions (…). It means being personally accountable to one's comrades in arms, as well as being accountable under the law and, by extension, to society as a whole. This accountability is one key factor which distinguishes professionalism (…) from the often unaccountable actions of mercenaries, paramilitary forces and criminals masquerading as military.[43]

Professionalism, then, like a knife or the rule of law, is in principle a neutral tool, one that may be used for good or evil. And just as some legal theorists promote a substantive view of the rule of law (one that fosters values such as democracy, freedom, human rights and human dignity),[44] Thomas presents a robust account of professionalism requiring not only technical skill or expertise, but also commitment to virtue ethics as well as accountability to society under the law. He adds that professionalism "is about sustaining all the military virtues over the long haul"[45] and that "professionalism, like morale, is a fragile flower which has to be nurtured and actively encouraged".[46]

---

40 Ibid., p. 340.

41 Ibid., p. 341.

42 Of *Military Virtues*, namely justice, obedience, loyalty, courage, wisdom, honesty, integrity, perseverance, temperance, patience, humility, compassion, discipline, and professionalism.

43 John Thomas, 'Case Study: Professionalism in the Military', in Michael Skerker, David Whetham and Don Carrick (eds.), *Military Virtues* (Havant: Howgate, 2019), p. 348.

44 Margaret Jane Radin, 'Reconsidering the Rule of Law', *Boston University Law Review*, 69:4 (1989), pp. 783–791.

45 Thomas, 'Professionalism', p. 350.

46 Ibid., p. 359.

## 3 Military Honour as a Reward for Professionalism: a Scutcheon for the Wars of the 21st Century

This robust account of professionalism locates the excellence of the military profession in the continued cultivation and flourishment of all the military virtues. Thus conceived, professionalism is not a virtue in and of itself, but the epitome of all military virtues, much like according to Aristotle the virtue of magnanimity, greatness of soul or pride is "a sort of crown of the virtues".[47] We may say that the military person who displays professionalism is the magnanimous or proud man or woman of arms. In a similar way, human dignity is not the same as human rights, but as a legal status comprising a set of guarantees it can be conceived of as an abbreviation or "ellipsis" of said rights.[48]

Now, if professionalism is the epitome of the military profession's excellence, honour is the reward for professionalism. Indeed, we saw in Chapter 2 that military honour, rather than being a virtue itself, can be conceptualized as a reward for virtuous behaviour.[49] And although this way of thinking about honour can be problematic if prestige or a medal is all the supposedly virtuous soldier is really after, the fact remains that the reputational aspect to be found in any given "honour world"[50] can still provide a powerful additional motivation for agents to do the right thing and expect fair recognition for it.[51] This is a key consideration if what we are interested in finding are additional normative standards beyond the baseline legal instruction for soldiers to protect both civilians from unjustified harm and soldiers themselves from moral injury, since it is in one of those honour worlds that these additional standards may be found and (informally) enforced beyond mere legal regulations.

But no medal or distinction can provide what honour bestows upon the soldier as a marker of their professionalism. In her influential monography on the topic, Shannon French contends that the code of the warrior, which is a code

47 Aristotle, *The Nicomachean Ethics* (New York: Oxford University Press, 2005), IV.3, p. 69.

48 Jeremy Waldron, 'Is Dignity the Foundation of Human Rights?', *NYU Public Law and Legal Theory Research Paper Series*, 12–73 (2013), p. 25.

49 Peter Olsthoorn, *Military Ethics and Virtues* (New York: Routledge, 2011), p. 40. See also Céline Spector, 'A Montesquieu Dictionary. Honor', http://dictionnaire-montesquieu.ens-lyon.fr/en/article/1376474900/en/, 16 March 2022.

50 Kwame A. Appiah, *The Honor Code: How Moral Revolutions Happen* (New York: W.W. Norton & Company, 2010), p. 87; Leo Braudy, *From Chivalry to Terrorism* (New York: Vintage Books, 2005), pp. 87–88.

51 Olsthoorn, *Military*, pp. 15–16.

of honour,[52] is "a kind of moral and psychological armor that protects the warrior from becoming a monster in his or her own eyes".[53] Thus, the additional normative standards that go beyond simple legal instruction become a safeguard not only against committing unjustified harm to civilians, but also against the perils of moral injury to combatants themselves. This protective armour is, thus, a moral shield, a true scutcheon that is more than just an empty word or a simulacrum of morality,[54] but a meaningful interpretive concept.

As we saw in Chapter 2, Ronald Dworkin characterized an interpretive concept as one eliciting an 'interpretive attitude' among those who embrace it, an attitude which comprises two elements: (i) the assumption that the practice has value, namely that it serves some interest or purpose or enforces some principle, that there is a point to it; and (ii) that the practice is sensitive to its point or purpose and it must be interpreted and even modified as needed to fulfil that purpose, lest it becomes mechanical or mere ceremony. Only then the practice, and the interpretive concept underlying it, can be said to have true *meaning*.[55]

It has been the contention of this inquiry that military honour is one such interpretive concept and that, therefore, it has a meaning, that it is not just an empty formula ceremoniously inscribed in the motto of military academies as a mechanical simulacrum of military ethics devoid of any substance. On the contrary, the interpretive concept of military honour as the reward for professionalism in the 21st century has evolved in such a way that its chivalrous lineage has been infused with modern humanitarian contents.

Now, at the end of Chapter 2 I proposed a definition of military honour based on the analysis of different scholarly works bearing on this concept. In light of the ideas developed in the rest of this book, that definition can be adjusted to accommodate the four cardinal virtues of justice, prudence, courage, and temperance as follows:

> Military honour is a normative standard, in the form of a principle, value or ideal, that is applicable to a particular honour world comprising all those professionals of arms belonging to state armed forces and rooted in the chivalric tradition. The content of this normative standard includes

---

52 Shannon E. French, *The Code of the Warrior. Exploring Warrior Values Past and Present.* 2nd ed. (Lanham: Rowman and Littlefield Publishers, 2017), p. 4.

53 Ibid., p. 12.

54 Alasdair MacIntyre, *After Virtue*, 3rd ed. (Notre Dame: University of Notre Dame Press, 2007), pp. 1–2.

55 Ronald Dworkin, *Law's Empire* (Oxford: Hart Publishing, 1998), pp. 47–49.

> the cardinal virtues of justice, prudence, courage, and temperance. Professionalism amounts to the actualization of these and all the other military virtues, the epitome of the excellence of the profession of arms. As a result of observing such content, military honour can be construed as a reward for professionalism, while at the same time instilling a special sense of self-worth in the honourable individual and demanding a particular type of positive recognition respect by society.

These four cardinal virtues mutually reinforce each other, since in order to exercise courage, especially moral courage, we need to know what justice demands of us. Further, prudence or common sense tells us how when and how to better apply the standards of justice to concrete situations. And temperance is an enabling virtue providing the required self-control to continuously practice all the other virtues.

Furthermore, in the particular case of justice, respect for the dignity[56] of every human being, whether friend or foe, is at the heart of this cardinal virtue. The essentially contested concept of human dignity has been unpacked in Chapter 3 to show how many different competing conceptions thereof are used in contemporary normative discourse. By choosing the rank conception, in Chapter 4 I have attempted to show how the interpretive concept of military honour, as chivalry in modern guise, can be refurbished with a modern humanitarian content.

Indeed, if the essence or point of the interpretive practice of chivalry (or honour in its medieval guise) is the restriction of violence against both combatants and non-combatants, this humanitarian *desideratum* finds philosophical and normative articulation in the rank conception of dignity, in the form of a new *Jus Armorum* as the code of behaviour of the contemporary *miles protector* or guardian. By applying his or her moral capacity for scintillating between the understanding of the abstract concept of human dignity and recognizing its individual manifestations in each human face they encounter, the modern day *miles protector* may reignite that ember of chivalry that we call honour, which has never stopped burning throughout history. This keeps tradition alive, not by worshiping the ashes, but by preserving the fire, in Mahler's famous formula.

---

56 Edward Barrett, 'Justice. Overview: Just (and Unjust) Warriors: Nature and Causes', in Michael Skerker, David Whetham and Don Carrick (eds.), *Military Virtues* (Havant: Howgate, 2019), pp. 34–35; Lawrence Kohlberg, *The Philosophy of Moral Development. Moral Stages and the Idea of Justice* (San Francisco: Harper and Row, 1981), pp. 17–19; 409–412.

This new *Jus Armorum* finds formal articulation as International Humanitarian Law ('IHL') with its core chivalric standards such as distinction, the prohibition of perfidy, and humanity. Through IHL, a normative body where the legal archetype of dignity is at the heart of its many provisions,[57] the interpretive concept of military honour finds a new normative articulation to guide the conduct of the professional soldier of the 21st century as a steward of human dignity, for "If the chivalry of earlier times cannot be resurrected, it would be a positive development if the military could be encouraged to take a certain pride in the professionalism shown when behaving in accordance with humanitarian law".[58]

•••

We began this investigation by referencing the court-martial of U.S. Army Captain Roger Maynulet for his alleged mercy killing of a wounded Iraqi citizen. As part of his defence, Maynulet argued that when he received IHL/LOAC training he remembered a slide that read "Humanity – unnecessary suffering", which he took as a justification for shooting a wounded man. Yet, that slide reportedly was part of a longer presentation that also included another slide with the indication: "Soldiers collect and care for the wounded, whether friend or foe".[59] But even if this training and the fact that the ROEs he operated under were admittedly clear enough, perhaps further ethical discussions between Maynulet and his comrades might have dispelled the erroneous notion that mercy killings are something military professionals are allowed to do. A continuous, open dialogue among military professionals is key to their development and to the adequate practice of their craft.

Indeed, achieving the desired level of professionalism or excellence in the practice of the full panoply of the military virtues is not something that always comes naturally. It is, in fact, something that must be striven for every day with hard work and perseverance, such that these virtues may become true habits of the military professional. For this, Professional Military Education ('PME') is key, especially considering the importance of virtue ethics in that field. To this end, developing a culture among the military that values open debate and

57 International Criminal Tribunal for the Former Yugoslavia, Trial Chamber, *Prosecutor v. Anto Furundzija*, Judgment, 10 December 1998, Case No. IT-95-17/1-T, par. 183.

58 Louise Doswald-Beck and Sylvain Vité, 'International Humanitarian Law and Human Rights Law', *International Review of the Red Cross*, 293 (1993), pp. 118–119.

59 United States Court of Appeals for the Armed Forces, *United States v. Rogelio M. Maynulet, Captain, U.S. Army*, Crim. App. No. 20050412, Decided 3 March 2010, p. 8.

promotes routine, healthy discussions about ethical issues is of the utmost importance to achieve the excellence of each virtue. Given the importance of soft-role morality in this particular profession, it is key that said discussions are held openly and transparently vis-à-vis the society that tasks and funds these professionals of arms.

By critically inquiring about the meaning of household expressions such as military honour and human dignity, this book is intended to add complexity to this much needed conversation between the military and civil society. Thus, the additional normative standards beyond mere legal instruction that are needed to ensure appropriate behaviour by soldiers and avoid unjustified harm to civilians and moral injury to combatants themselves have found theoretical formulation in the echoes of chivalry known as military honour and human dignity, as well as practical articulation in the form of the cardinal virtues codified in contemporary military doctrine, as this investigation has attempted to show.

Once these additional normative standards have been ascertained and unpacked, the next logical step is finding the best way to convey them to their addressees. Aside from novel pedagogical tools harnessing the potential of technology and distance-learning, I have remarked the importance of traditional PME methods, including the enactment, study and application of doctrinal codes and manuals incorporating the main standards of PMEt in all its varied schools of thought, most notably virtue ethics but also some deontological and consequentialist contents. Only a consistent and effective PME process of socialization will endow the professional soldier with the armour or scutcheon that they need to face the main ethical dilemmas of the modern battlefield.

In this sense, we have seen how the cardinal virtues of justice, prudence, courage, and temperance have been codified in one way or the other in different doctrinal manuals issued by armed forces all around the world. These doctrinal publications bear out the modern humanitarian contents that have rejuvenated or reinvigorated the erstwhile code of chivalry and military honour with the mandate to respect human rights and human dignity as a matter of professionalism in the conduction of war.

After reflecting on the contents of the code governing the conduct of the particular type of professional tasked by society to wage war, we come now full circle by returning to the conditions making said professional services necessary, namely the Circumstances of War ('CoW').

As stated in Chapter 1, should statecraft fail in successfully navigating the interest thesis, the interplay between the latter and the mortality and the technology theses turns the outcome of war into a permanent possibility that societies must be ready to face when the time comes. The smartest, most responsible, and most ethical way to prepare for such a contingency, given that this possibility is itself permanent, is to permanently task a group of people to manage the situation should violence break out, i.e. military professionals. At the heart of the notion of management lie the concepts of rationality and legitimacy, such that a return to a situation of absence of violence or peace is possible.[60]

With their unique expertise in the efficient and proportionate use of force, and equipped with the normative aegis provided by Professional Military Ethics and its humanitarian message of rejuvenated chivalry, the professional soldiers of today are expected to fight our Just Wars for us by displaying full respect for human dignity, that they may leave the field of battle with their heads held high and their military honour untarnished.

60 Moliner, 'Educación', p. 24; Moliner, *Ética*, p. 29.

# References

## Doctrinal Works


Aalto, Janne, 'Challenges in combining ethical education for conscripts and professional military', Don Carrick, James Connelly and David Whetham (eds.), *Making the Military Moral. Contemporary Challenges and Responses in Military Ethics Education* (New York: Routledge, 2018), pp. 107–125.

Alexy, Robert, *Teoría de los Derechos Fundamentales* (Madrid: Centro de Estudios Constitucionales, 1993).

Allenby, Brad and Frame, Tom, 'Moral Injury', in Center on the Future of War, Arizona State University, *Moral Injury: Towards an International Perspective* (Tempe: Arizona State University, 2017), pp. 5–9.

Allison, Graham, *Destined for War. Can America and China Escape Thucydides's Trap?* (New York: Houghton Mifflin Harcourt, 2017).

Alston, Philip and Goodman, Ryan, *International Human Rights* (Oxford: Oxford University Press, 2013).

Antrobus, Sophy and West, Hannah, '"This Is All Very Academic": Critical Thinking in Professional Military Education', *RUSI Journal*, 167:3 (2022), pp. 78–86.

Appiah, Kwame A., *The Honor Code: How Moral Revolutions Happen* (New York: W.W. Norton & Company, 2010).

Applbaum, Arthur, *Ethics for Adversaries: The Morality of Roles in Public and Professional Life* (Princeton: Princeton University Press, 1999).

Aquinas, *Political Writings* (R.W. Dyson ed.) (Cambridge: Cambridge University Press, 2004).

Arendt, Hannah, *Between Past and Future* (New York: Penguin Classics, 1993).

Arendt, Hannah, *Eichmann in Jerusalem. A Report on the Banality of Evil* (London: Penguin, 2006).

Arendt, Hannah, *The Human Condition*, 2nd ed. (Chicago: University of Chicago Press, 1998).

Arendt, Hannah, *The Origins of Totalitarianism*, 2nd ed. (Cleveland: Meridian Books, 1962).

Aristotle, *The Nicomachean Ethics* (New York: Oxford University Press, 2005).

Arkin, Ronald, *Governing Lethal Behavior in Autonomous Robots* (Boca Raton: CRC Press, 2009).

Arman, Jemma, Henckaerts, Jean-Marie, Hiemstra, Heleen and Krotiuk, Kvitoslava, 'The Updated ICRC Commentary on the Third Geneva Convention', in Michael N. Schmitt and Christopher J. Koschnitzky (eds.), *Prisoners of War in Contemporary Conflict* (Oxford: Oxford University Press, 2023), pp. 343–374.

Aronovitch, Hilliard, 'Good Soldiers, A Traditional Approach', *Journal of Applied Philosophy*, 18:1 (2001), pp. 13–23.

Ashkin, Kelly, 'Treatment of Sexual Violence in Armed Conflicts: A Historical Perspective and the Way Forward', in Anne-Marie Brouwer et al (eds), *Sexual Violence as an International Crime: Interdisciplinary Approaches* (Cambridge: Intersentia, 2013), pp. 19–56.

Atienza, Manuel, *Sobre la dignidad humana* (Madrid: Trotta, 2022).

Atria, Fernando, *On Law and Legal Reasoning* (London: Bloomsbury Publishing, 2002).

Augustine, *City of God* (London: Penguin, 2003).

Axinn, Sidney, *A Moral Military*, 2nd ed. (Philadelphia: Temple University Press, 2009).

Aznar, Federico, '¿Qué es el honor militar?', in Centro Conjunto de Desarollo de Conceptos, *Cuestiones sobre ética militar* (Madrid: Ministerio de Defensa, 2022), pp. 49–73.

Bangerter, Olivier, 'Reasons why armed groups choose to respect international humanitarian law or not', *International Review of the Red Cross*, 93:882 (2011), pp. 353–384.

Barnes, David M., 'Case Study 2: Unit Temperance and the Haditha Case', in Michael Skerker, David Whetham and Don Carrick (eds.), *Military Virtues* (Havant: Howgate, 2019), pp. 231–239.

Barrett, Edward, 'Justice. Overview: Just (and Unjust) Warriors: Nature and Causes', in Michael Skerker, David Whetham and Don Carrick (eds.), *Military Virtues* (Havant: Howgate, 2019), pp. 31–40.

Barrett, Edward, 'Moral Injury: A Typology', *Journal of Military Ethics*, 22:3–4 (2023), pp. 158–167.

Bazeley, Pat, *Qualitative Data Analysis* (London: SAGE, 2013).

Beitz, Charles, 'Human Dignity in the Theory of Human Rights: Nothing But a Phrase?', *Philosophy and Public Affairs*, 41:3 (2013), pp. 259–290.

Bell, Andrew and Terry, Fionna, 'Combatant rank and socialization to norms of restraint: examining the Australian and Philippines armies', *International Interactions*, 47:5 (2021), pp. 825–854.

Bell, Andrew, 'Combatant socialization and norms of restraint: Examining officer training at the US Military Academy and Army ROTC', *Journal of Peace Research*, 59:2 (2022), pp. 180–196.

Bellamy, Alex, *Just Wars. From Cicero to Iraq* (Malden: Polity Press, 2012).

Bellamy, Alex, *Massacres and Morality: Mass Atrocities in the Age of Civilian Immunity* (Oxford: Oxford University Press, 2012).

Benbaji, Yitzhak, 'A Defense of the Traditional War Convention', *Ethics*, 118 (2008), pp. 464–495.

Benbaji, Yitzhak, 'The Moral Power of Soldiers to Undertake the Duty of Obedience, *Ethics*, 122 (2011), pp. 1–32.

Benbaji, Yitzhak, 'The Responsibility of Soldiers and the Ethics of Killing in War', *The Philosophical Quarterly*, 57:229 (2007), pp. 558–572.

Benbaji, Yitzhak, 'The War Convention and the Moral Division of Labour', *The Philosophical Quarterly*, 59:237 (2009), pp. 593–617.

Benbaji, Yitzhak, and Statman, Daniel, *War by Agreement. A Contractarian Ethics of War* (New York: Oxford University Press, 2019).

Bennett, Andrew and Elman, Colin, 'Case Study Methods in the International Relations Subfield', *Comparative Political Studies*, 40 (2007), pp. 170–195.

Benvenisti, Eyal, 'Human dignity in combat: The duty to spare enemy civilians', *Israel Law Review*, 39:2 (2006), pp. 81–109.

Benvenisti, Eyal and Cohen, Amichai, 'War is Governance: Explaining the Logic of the Laws of War From a Principal-Agent Perspective', *Michigan Law Review*, 112:8 (2014), pp. 1363–1415.

Berger, Peter, 'On the Obsolescence of the Concept of Honor', *European Journal of Sociology*, 11:2 (1970), pp. 339–347.

Berger, Thomas, 'Norms, Identity, and National Security in Germany and Japan', in Peter J. Katzenstein (ed.), *The Culture of National Security: Norms and Identity in World Politics* (New York: Columbia University Press, 1996), pp. 317–356.

Berman, Nathaniel, 'Privileging Combat? Contemporary Conflict and the Legal Construction of War', *Columbia Journal of Transnational Law*, 43:1 (2004), pp. 1–72.

Blackburn, Simon, *The Oxford Dictionary of Philosophy* (Oxford: Oxford University Press, 2005).

Blum, Gabriella, 'The Dispensable Lives of Soldiers', *Journal of Legal Analysis*, 2:1 (2010), pp. 69–124.

Blum, Gabriella, 'The Shadow of Success: How International Criminal Law Has Come to Shape the Battlefield', *International Law Studies*, 100:133 (2023), pp. 133–185.

Bobbio, Norberto, *El problema del positivismo jurídico* (Mexico D.F.: Fontamara, 1991).

Boddens Hosang, J.F.R., *Rules of Engagement and the International Law of Military Operations* (Oxford: Oxford University Press, 2020).

Boulette, Michael, 'Two concepts of role-morality – In search of a normative language of legal ethics', *AIO* 5:2 (2010), pp. 20–32.

Bourke, Joanna, *What it means to be human* (Berkeley: Counterpoint, 2011).

Boyle, Michael, 'The Cost and Consequences of Drone Warfare', *International Affairs*, 89:1 (2013), pp. 1–29.

Bradley, Peter and MacIntyre, Allister, 'Solving the military moral bystander problem with ethics instruction', in Don Carrick, James Connelly and David Whetham (eds.), *Making the Military Moral. Contemporary Challenges and Responses in Military Ethics Education* (New York: Routledge, 2018), pp. 30–51.

Brady, Henry E. and Collier, David, *Rethinking Social Inquiry: Diverse Tools, Shared Standards* (Lanham, MD: Rowman & Littlefield, 2004).

Braudy, Leo, *From Chivalry to Terrorism* (New York: Vintage Books, 2005).

Braun, Christian Nikolaus, *Limited Force and the Fight for the Just War Tradition* (Washington, DC: Georgetown University Press, 2023).

Bregman, Rutger, *Humankind. A Hopeful History* (London: Bloomsbury Publishing, 2021).

Brooks, Timothy, *Vermeer's Hat. The Seventeenth Century and the Dawn of the Global World* (London: Profile Books, 2009).

Brownlie, Ian, *International Law and the Use of Force by States* (Oxford: Clarendon Press, 1963).

Brownsword, Roger, 'Human dignity from a legal perspective' in Marcus Düwell, Jens Braarvig, Roger Brownsword, and Dietmar Mieth (eds.), *The Cambridge Handbook of Human Dignity* (Cambridge: Cambridge University Press, 2014), pp. 1–22.

Brunstetter, Daniel R. and O'Driscoll, Cian (eds.), *Just War Thinkers* (New York: Routledge, 2018).

Brunstetter, Daniel R., *Just and Unjust Uses of Limited Force. A Moral Argument with Contemporary Illustrations* (New York: Oxford University Press, 2021).

Bugnion, François, 'Just wars, wars of aggression and international humanitarian law', *International Review of the Red Cross*, 847:84 (2002), pp. 523–546.

Burke, Edmund, *Reflections on the Revolution in France* (New Haven: Yale University Press, 2003).

Camenisch, Paul, 'Business Ethics: On Getting to the Heart of the Matter', *Business and Professional Ethics Journal*, 1:1 (1981), pp. 59–69.

Camenisch, Paul, 'On the Matter of Good Moral Character', *The Linacre Quarterly*, 45:3 (1978), pp. 273–283.

Cañas de Pablos, Alberto, '"Worth More Than Life Itself": Military Honour and the Birth of Its Courts in Spain (1810–1870)', *Journal of Military Ethics*, 21:3–4 (2022), pp. 304–319.

Cançado Trindade, Antônio, 'Prefacio', in Pedro Calafate and Ramón Emilio Mandado Gutiérrez (eds.), *Escuela Ibérica de la Paz* (Santander: Ediciones Universidad Cantabria, 2014), pp. 43–109.

Carrick, Don, 'Integrity: Overview', in Michael Skerker, David Whetham and Don Carrick (eds.), *Military Virtues* (Havant: Howgate, 2019), pp. 171–176.

Carroll, Lewis, *Alice's Adventures in Wonderland & Through the Looking Glass* (London: MacMillam, 2016).

Cea, Sergio and Coronado, Ricardo, *Derecho Militar. Parte General* (Santiago: Legal Publishing, 2011).

Cerdá, David, *Ética para Valientes. El honor en nuestros días* (Madrid: Rialp, 2022).

Cervantes, Miguel de, *El Ingenioso Hidalgo Don Quijote De La Mancha* (Barcelona: Editorial Planeta, 2022).

Chilean Army, *Manual: Ethos del Ejército de Chile. MOLD – 02005* (Santiago: Ejército de Chile, Comando de Educación y Doctrina, 2018).

Clapham, Andrew, *War* (Oxford: Oxford University Press, 2021).

Clarke, Ben, Rouffaer, Christian and Sénéchaud, François, 'Beyond the Call of Duty: why shouldn't video game players face the same dilemmas as real soldiers?', *International Review of the Red Cross*, 94:886 (2013), pp. 711–737.

Clastres, Pierre, *Archeology of Violence* (Los Angeles: Semiotext(e), 2010).

Clausewitz, Carl von, *On War* (New York: Oxford University Press, 2008).

Coates, Anthony, *The Ethics of War* (Manchester: Manchester University Press, 1997).

Cochran, Patricia, *Common Sense and Legal Judgment. Community Knowledge, Political Power, and Rhetorical Practice* (Montreal: McGill-Queen's University Press, 2017).

Cohen, G.A., *If You're Egalitarian, How Come You're So Rich?* (Cambridge: Harvard University Press, 2001).

Coker, Christopher, *Barbarous Philosophers. Reflections on the Nature of War from Heraclitus to Heisenberg* (London: Hurst & Company, 2010).

Coker, Christopher, *Rebooting Clausewitz. 'On War' in the Twenty-First Century* (London: Hurst and Company, 2017).

Coker, Christopher, *The Warrior Ethos. Military Culture and the War on Terror* (New York: Routledge, 2007).

Connelly, James, 'On making the military moral', in Don Carrick, James Connelly and David Whetham (eds.), *Making the Military Moral. Contemporary Challenges and Responses in Military Ethics Education* (New York: Routledge, 2018), pp. 1–13.

Connolly, William E., *The Terms of Political Discourse*. 3rd ed. (Princeton: Princeton University Press, 1993).

Conrad, Joseph, *Heart of Darkness and Other Tales* (New York: Oxford University Press, 2008).

Conrad, Richard, 'The Holy Trinity as Source of Human Dignity according to St Thomas Aquinas', in John Loughlin (ed.), *Human Dignity in the Judaeo-Christian Tradition. Catholic, Orthodox, Anglican and Protestant Perspectives* (London: Bloomsbury, 2021), pp. 79–97.

Cook, James, 'Honesty. Overview', in Michael Skerker, David Whetham and Don Carrick (eds.), *Military Virtues* (Havant: Howgate, 2019), pp. 149–157.

Cook, Martin L. and Hamann, Phillip A., 'The Road to Basra: A Case Study in Military Ethics', *The Annual of the Society of Christian Ethics*, 14 (1994), pp. 207–228.

Cooper, Scott, 'Case Study 2: Moral Courage', in Michael Skerker, David Whetham and Don Carrick (eds.), *Military Virtues* (Havant: Howgate, 2019), pp. 118–126.

Copenhaver, Brian, 'Dignity, Vile Bodies, and Nakedness', in Remy Debes (ed.), *Dignity. A History* (New York: Oxford University Press, 2017), pp. 127–174.

Corn, G., Blank, L., Jenks, C. and Talbot Jensen, E., 'Belligerent Targeting and the Invalidity of a Least Harmful Means Rule', *International Law Studies*, 89 (2013), pp. 536–626.

Corn, G., Hansen, V., Jackson, R., Jenks, C., Talbot Jensen, E. and Schoettler, J., *The Law of Armed Conflict: An Operational Approach* (New York: Wolters Klumer, 2012).

Currier, Joseph M., Holland, Jason M., Drescher, Kent and Foy, David, 'Initial Psychometric Evaluation of the Moral Injury Questionnaire – Military Version', *Clinical Psychology and Psychotherapy*, 22 (2015), pp. 54–63.

Dallaire, Roméo, *Shake Hands With the Devil. The Failure of Humanity in Rwanda* (New York: Carroll & Graf, 2005).

Dan-Cohen, Meir, 'A Concept of Dignity', *Israel Law Review*, 44:9 (2011), pp. 9–23.

Dan-Cohen, Meir, 'Introduction: Dignity and its (Dis)content' in Jeremy Waldron, *Dignity, Rank and Rights. The Berkeley Tanner Lectures* (2009) (New York: Oxford University Press, 2012), pp. 3–10.

Darwall, Stephen, 'Two Kinds of Respect', *Ethics*, 88:1 (1977), pp. 36–49.

David, Arnel P., Acosta, Sean and Krohley, Nicholas (eds.), *Warrior Diplomats. Civil Affairs Forces on the Front Lines* (Amherst: Cambria, 2023).

Davis, Ian and van der Lijn, Jaïr, 'Global developments in armed conflicts, peace processes and peace operations', in Stockholm International Peace Research Institute, *SIPRI Yearbook 2020* (Oxford: Oxford University Press, 2020), Ch. 2.

Day, John, '"So God Created Humanity in His Own Image" (Genesis 1.27). What Does the bible Mean and What Have People Thought it Meant?', in John Loughlin (ed.), *Human Dignity in the Judaeo-Christian Tradition. Catholic, Orthodox, Anglican and Protestant Perspectives* (London: Bloomsbury, 2021), pp. 15–35.

De Beauvoir, Simone, *The Second Sex* (London: Vintage, 1956).

Deakin, Stephen, 'Education in an Ethos at the Royal Military Academy Sandhurst', in Paul Robinson, Nigel De Lee and Don Carrick (eds.), *Ethics Education in the Military* (New York: Routledge, 2016), pp. 15–30.

Deakin, Stephen, 'Temperance. Overview: The Virtue of Temperance', in Michael Skerker, David Whetham and Don Carrick (eds.), *Military Virtues* (Havant: Howgate, 2019), pp. 215–223.

Debes, Remy (ed.), *Dignity. A History* (New York: Oxford University Press, 2017).

dellaMirandola, Giovanni Pico, *Oration on the Dignity of Man* (Chicago: Henry Regnery Company, 1956).

Desjardins, Colonel Ivon, 'Canada's Defence Ethics Programme and Ethics Training', in Paul Robinson, Nigel De Lee and Don Carrick (eds.), *Ethics Education in the Military* (New York: Routledge, 2016), pp. 67–78.

Dickerhoff, Heinrich, '"We Must Also Reach the Soul"', *Ethics and Armed Forces*, 2 (2021), pp. 60–61.

Dimock, Wai Chee, 'High and Low', in Jeremy Waldron, *Dignity, Rank and Rights. The Berkeley Tanner Lectures* (2009) (New York: Oxford University Press, 2012), pp. 119–129.

Dinstein, Yoram, 'Law of Armed Conflict Manuals', *Yearbook of International Humanitarian Law*, 23 (2020), pp. 3–19.

Dinstein, Yoram, 'Legal Advisers in the Field During Armed Conflict', *International Law Studies*, 97 (2021), pp. 917–936.

Dinstein, Yoram, *The Conduct of Hostilities under the Law of International Armed Conflict*, 2nd ed. (Cambridge: Cambridge University Press, 2010).

Dinstein, Yoram, *War, Aggression and Self-Defence*. 5th ed. (Cambridge: Cambridge University Press, 2012).

Doswald-Beck, Louise, and Vité, Sylvain, 'International Humanitarian Law and Human Rights Law', *International Review of the Red Cross*, 293 (1993), pp. 94–119.

Dunlap, Charles, 'Lawfare Today: A Perspective', *Yale Journal or International Affairs*, 3 (2008), pp. 146–154.

Dunlap, Charles, 'Lawfare: A decisive Element of 21st Century Conflicts?', *Joint Forces Quarterly*, 54:3 (2009), pp. 34–39.

Durkheim, Émile, *Professional Ethics and Civic Morals* (New York: Routledge, 2019).

Düwell, Marcus, 'Human dignity: Concepts, discussions, philosophical perspectives', in Marcus Düwell, Jens Braarvig, Roger Brownsword, and Dietmar Mieth (eds.), *The Cambridge Handbook of Human Dignity* (Cambridge: Cambridge University Press, 2014), pp. 24–49.

Düwell, Marcus, Braarvig, Jens, Brownsword, Roger and Mieth, Dietmar (eds.), *The Cambridge Handbook of Human Dignity* (Cambridge: Cambridge University Press, 2014).

Dworkin, Ronald, *Is Democracy Possible Here?* (Princeton: Princeton University Press, 2006).

Dworkin, Ronald, *Justice for Hedgehogs* (Cambridge: Belknap Press, 2011).

Dworkin, Ronald, *Law's Empire* (Oxford: Hart Publishing, 1998).

Dworkin, Ronald, *Life's Dominion* (New York: Alfred A. Knopf, 1993).

Dworkin, Ronald, *Taking Rights Seriously* (Cambridge: Harvard University Press, 1977).

Eastwood, James, *Ethics as a Weapon of War. Militarism and Morality in Israel* (Cambridge: Cambridge University Press, 2020).

Eisenhower, Dwight D., *Crusade in Europe. A Personal Account of World War II* (New York: Vintage, 2021).

Emerson, Robert, Fretz, Rachel and Shaw, Linda, *Writing Ethnographic Fieldnotes*, 2nd ed. (Chicago: University of Chicago Press, 2011).

Ewen, Shane, *Fighting Fires. Creating the British Fire Service, 1800–1978* (New York: Palgrave Macmillan, 2010).

Ferguson, Niall, *Colossus. The rise and fall of the American empire* (New York: Penguin Books, 2004).

Fikfak, Veronica and Izvorova, Lora, 'Language and Persuasion: Human Dignity at the European Court of Human Rights', *iCourts Working Paper Series*, 287 (2022), pp. 4–29.

Finnis, John, Boyle, Joseph, and Grisez, Germain, *Nuclear Deterrence, Morality and Realism* (Oxford: Clarendon Press, 1987).

Firth, John, *Studies in Linguistic Analysis* (Oxford: Basil Blackwell, 1962).

Fisher, Andrew, *Metaethics. An Introduction* (New York: Routledge, 2014).

Fisher, David, 'Why morality matters to the military', in Don Carrick, James Connelly and David Whetham (eds.), *Making the Military Moral. Contemporary Challenges and Responses in Military Ethics Education* (New York: Routledge, 2018), pp. 14–24.

Fotion, N. and Elfstrom, Gerard, *Military Ethics. Guidelines for Peace and War* (New York: Routledge, 2021).

Foucault, Michel, *Society Must Be Defended* (London: Penguin Books, 2003).

Frantzen, Allen J., *Bloody Good. Chivalry, Sacrifice, and the Great War* (Chicago: University of Chicago Press, 2004).

French, Shannon E., 'An American military ethicist's perspective', in Charles Reed and David Ryall (eds.), *The Price of Peace. Just War in the Twenty-First Century* (Cambridge: Cambridge University Press, 2007), pp. 295–303.

French, Shannon E., *The Code of the Warrior. Exploring Warrior Values Past and Present* (Lanham: Rowman and Littlefield Publishers, 2005).

French, Shannon E., *The Code of the Warrior. Exploring Warrior Values Past and Present.* 2nd ed. (Lanham: Rowman and Littlefield Publishers, 2017).

Frowe, Helen, *Defensive Killing* (Oxford: Oxford University Press, 2014).

Frulli, Micaela, 'The Promise of International Criminal Justice: Achievements and Failures in Protecting Human Dignity', in Andrea Gattini, Rosana Garciandia and Philippa Webb, *Human Dignity and International Law* (Leiden: Brill-Nijhoff, 2021), pp. 52–70.

Fuller, Lon, *The Morality of Law.* 2nd ed. (New Haven: Yale University Press, 1969).

Gallie, W.B., 'Essentially Contested Concepts', *Proceedings of the Aristotelian Society*, 56 (1955–1956), pp. 167–198.

Gattini, Andrea, 'Setting the Scene: 100 Years of Human Dignity', in Andrea Gattini, Rosana Garciandia and Philippa Webb, *Human Dignity and International Law* (Leiden: Brill-Nijhoff, 2021), pp. 1–8.

George, Alexander L. and Bennett, Andrew, *Case Studies and Theory Development in the Social Sciences* (Cambridge: MIT Press, 2004).

Germano, Kate and Smith, David, 'Case Study 2: Gender Equity as Fairness in the Military Institution', in Michael Skerker, David Whetham and Don Carrick (eds.), *Military Virtues* (Havant: Howgate, 2019), pp. 51–61.

Gerring, John, 'What Makes a Concept Good? A Criterial Framework for Understanding Concept Formation in the Social Sciences', *Polity*, 31:3 (1999), pp. 357–393.

Gilabert, Pablo, *Human Dignity and Human Rights* (New York: Oxford University Press, 2018).

Giladi, Rotem, 'The Enactment of Irony: Reflections on the Origins of the Martens Clause', *The European Journal of International Law*, 25(3) (2014), pp. 847–869.

Gilbert, Paul, 'Civilian Immunity in the "New Wars"', in Igor Primoratz (ed.), *Civilian Immunity in War* (Oxford, Oxford University Press, 2007), pp. 201–216.

Gilbert, Paul, 'Compassion: Definitions and controversies', in Paul Gilbert (ed.), *Compassion. Concepts, Research and Applications* (New York: Routledge, 2017), pp. 2–15.

Gill, Terry, 'Chivalry: A Principle of the Law of Armed Conflict?', in Mariëlle Matthee, Brigit Toebes, and Marcel Brus (eds.), *Armed Conflict and International Law: In Search of the Human Face* (The Hague: Asser Press, 2013), pp. 33–51.

Gilligan, Carol, *In a Different Voice* (Cambridge: Harvard University Press, 2003).

Gillner, Matthias, 'Ethical Education in the German Armed Forces: Embraced Values and Moral Judgment', *Ethics and Armed Forces*, 2 (2019), pp. 22–29.

Golding, William, *Lord of the Flies* (Pomodoro Books, 2023).

Goodman, Ryan, 'The Power to Kill or Capture Enemy Combatants: A Rejoinder to Michael N. Schmitt', *The European Journal of International Law*, 24(3) (2013), pp. 865–866.

Goodman, Ryan, 'The Power to Kill or Capture Enemy Combatants', *The European Journal of International Law*, 24(3) (2013), pp. 841–842.

Grayling, A.C., *Wittgenstein. A Very Short Introduction* (New York: Oxford University Press, 2001).

Greenwood, Christopher, 'Historical Development and Legal Basis', in Dieter Fleck (ed.), *The Handbook of International Humanitarian Law*, 2nd ed. (Oxford: Oxford University Press, 2010), pp. 1–44.

Gregory, Gordon, 'The Trial of Peter von Hagenbach', in Kevin Heller and Gerry Simpson (eds.), *The Hidden Histories of War Crimes Trials* (Oxford: Oxford University Press, 2013), pp. 13–49.

Gregory, Kent, 'Is the Term "Warrior" Suitable for the Canadian Armed Forces?', *Canadian Military Journal*, 22:4 (2022), pp. 52–57.

Griffin, James, *On Human Rights* (Oxford: Oxford University Press, 2013).

Grimm, Dieter, 'Dignity in a Legal Context and as an Absolute Right', in Christopher McCrudden (ed.), *Understanding Human Dignity* (Oxford: Oxford University Press, 2015), pp. 381–391.

Grimsrud, Ted, *The Good War That Wasn't – and Why It Matters* (Eugene: Cascade Books, 2014).

Grossman, Dave and Christensen, Loren W., *On Combat. The Psychology and Physiology of Deadly Conflict in War and Peace*. 4th ed. (New York: Open Road Media, 2022).

Grossman, Dave, *On Killing. The Psychological Cost of Learning to Kill in War and Society* (New York: Back Bay Books, 1996).

Grotius, Hugo, *The Right of War and Peace* (Indianapolis: Liberty Fund, 2005).

Habermas, Jürgen, 'The concept of human dignity and the realistic utopia of human rights', *Metaphilosophy*, 41:4 (2010), pp. 465–480.

Habermas, Jürgen, *Between Facts and Norms. Contributions of a Discourse Theory of Law and Democracy* (Cambridge: MIT Press, 1996).

Habermas, Jürgen, *The Inclusion of the Other. Studies in Political Theory* (Cambridge: MIT Press, 1998).

Habermas, Jürgen, *Theory and Practice* (Boston: Beacon Press, 1974).

Hackett, John, *The Profession of Arms* (London: Sidgwick & Jackson, 1983).

Hampson, Françoise J., 'The relationship between international humanitarian law and international human rights law', in Scott Sheera and Sir Nigel Rodley, (eds.), *Routledge Handbook of International Human Rights Law* (New York: Routledge, 2014), pp. 185–213.

Harari, Yuval Noah, *Nexus* (New York: Random House, 2024).

Hart, H.L.A., 'Positivism and the Separation of Law and Morals', *Harvard Law Review*, 71:613 (1958).

Hart, H.L.A., *The Concept of Law*, 3rd ed. (Oxford: Oxford University Press, 2012).

Hart, Henry and Sacks, Albert, *The Legal Process. Basic Problems in the Making and Application of Law* (New York: Westbury, 1994).

Hartnett, Liane and O'Driscoll, Cian, 'Sad and laughable and Strange: At War with Just War', *Global Society*, 35:1 (2021), pp. 27–44.

Hathaway, Oona and Shapiro, Scott, *The Internationalists. How a Radical Plan to Outlaw War Remade the World* (New York: Simon & Schuster, 2017).

Hauser, Tzvi, 'The Spirit of the IDF', *Azure*, 5757 (1997), pp. 47–72.

Headquarters Army Training Command, *Indian Army Doctrine* (Shimla: Headquarters Army Training Command, 2004).

Hegel, G.W.F., *Elements of the Philosophy of Right* (Cambridge: Cambridge University Press, 2003).

Heidegger, Martin, *Being and Time* (Cornwall: Blackwell, 2005).

Heidegger, Martin, *Filosofía, ciencia y técnica* (Santiago: Editorial Universitaria, 2004).

Heller, Kevin Jon, 'The Concept of the "Human" in the Critique of Autonomous Weapons', *Harvard National Security Journal*, 14 (2023), pp. 1–73.

Hemingway, Ernest (ed.), *Men at War* (New York: Berkeley Publishing, 1958).

Henckaerts, Jean-Marie, and Doswald-Beck, Louise, *Customary International Humanitarian Law. Vol. I: Rules* (New York: Cambridge University Press-ICRC, 2009).

Henderson, Ian and Reece, Kate, 'Proportionality under International Humanitarian Law: The "Reasonable Military Commander" Standard and Reverberating Effects', *Vanderbilt Journal of Transnational Law*, 51:835 (2018), pp. 835–855.

Hennette-Vauchez, Stéphanie, 'A human *dignitas*? Remnants of the ancient legal concept in contemporary dignity jurisprudence', *I-CON*, 9:1 (2011), pp. 32–57.

Henschke, Adam, 'Rethinking the Nature of States and Political Violence', *Ethics and International Affairs*, 35:1 (2021), pp. 145–158.

Herzog, Don, 'Aristocratic Dignity?', in Jeremy Waldron, *Dignity, Rank and Rights. The Berkeley Tanner Lectures* (2009) (New York: Oxford University Press, 2012), pp. 99–118.

Heuser, Beatrice, *War. A Genealogy of Western Ideas and Practices* (New York: Oxford University Press, 2022).

Hewitt, H.J., *The Black Prince's Expeditions of 1355–1357* (Manchester: Manchester University Press, 1958).

Hobbes, Thomas, *Leviathan* (Oxford: Oxford University Press, 1998).

Hobbes, Thomas, *Man and Citizen* (Indianapolis: Hackett, 1991).

Högl, Eva, 'Civil courage in the military – not a contradiction in terms!', *Ethics and Armed Forces*, 2 (2021), pp. 46–48.

Høiback, Harald, *Understanding Military Doctrine* (New York: Routledge, 2017).

Hollenbach, David, 'Human dignity in Catholic thought', in Marcus Düwell, Jens Braarvig, Roger Brownsword, and Dietmar Mieth (eds.), *The Cambridge Handbook of Human Dignity* (Cambridge: Cambridge University Press, 2014), pp. 250–259.

Hörnle, Tatjana and Kremnitzer, Mordechai, 'Human Dignity as a Protected Interest in Criminal Law', *Israel Law Review*, 44 (2011), pp. 143–167.

Howard, Michael, *The causes of wars* (London: Counterpoint, 1983).

Howard, Michael, *War and the Liberal Conscience* (London: Hurst, 2008).

Hude, Henri, 'Reshaping the Ethical Training of Future French Commissioned Officers', in Paul Robinson, Nigel De Lee and Don Carrick (eds.), *Ethics Education in the Military* (New York: Routledge, 2016), pp. 109–118.

Huizinga, Johan, *Homo Ludens* (London: Routledge and Kegan Paul, 1980).

Huizinga, Johan, *The Autumn of the Middle Ages* (Chicago: The University of Chicago Press, 1996).

Hume, David, *A Treatise of Human Nature*, Vol. 1 (New York: Oxford University Press, 2007).

Hume, David, *An Enquiry Concerning the Principles of Morals* (Indianapolis: Hackett, 1983).

Hunt, William, 'Civic Chivalry and the English Civil War', in Anthony Grafton and Ann Blair (eds.), *The Transmission of Culture in Early Modern Europe* (Philadelphia: University of Pennsylvania Press, 1990), pp. 204–237.

Huntington, Samuel, *The Soldier and the State* (Cambridge: Harvard University Press, 2000).

ICRC, *International Humanitarian Law and the Challenges of Contemporary Armed Conflicts* (Geneva: ICRC, 2019).

ICRC, *The Roots of Behaviour in War* (Geneva: ICRC, 2004).

ICRC, *The Roots of Restraint in War* (Geneva: ICRC, 2018).

Ignatieff, Michael, *The Warrior's Honor. Ethnic War and the Modern Conscience* (New York: Holt Paperbacks, 1997).

Inspector-General of the Australian Defence Force, *Afghanistan Inquiry Report* (Canberra: Commonwealth of Australia, 2020).

International Institute of Humanitarian Law, *Sanremo Handbook on Rules of Engagement* (Sanremo: IIHL, 2009).

International Law Commission, *73rd Session. A/CN.4/L.967. Texts of the draft conclusions and Annex adopted by the Drafting Committee on second reading* (Geneva: ILC, 2022).

Isaac, Jeffrey C., 'A New Guarantee on Earth: Hannah Arendt on Human Dignity and the Politics of Human Rights', *The American Political Science Review*, 90:1 (1996), pp. 61–73.

Ishiguro, Kazuo, *The Remains of the Day* (London: Faber & Faber, 1989).

Jakobs, Günther, *Sociedad, norma y persona en una teoría de un Derecho penal funcional* (Bogotá: Universidad Externado de Colombia, 1996).

Janowitz, Morris, *The Professional Soldier* (New York: Free Press, 2017).

Jinks, Derek, 'Protecting Prisoners of War in Contemporary Conflicts', in Michael N. Schmitt and Christopher J. Koschnitzky (eds.), *Prisoners of War in Contemporary Conflict* (Oxford: Oxford University Press, 2023), pp. 159–180.

Jo, Hyeron, Alley, Joshua K., Park, Yohan, and Jordan, Soren, 'Signaling restraint: international engagement and rebel groups' commitment to international law', *International Interactions*, 47:5 (2021), pp. 928–954.

Johansen, Sigrid Redse, *The Military Commander's Necessity. The Law of Armed Conflict and Its Limits* (Cambridge: Cambridge University Press, 2021).

Johnson, James Turner, 'Historical Tradition and Moral Judgment: The Case of Just War Tradition', *The Journal of Religion*, 64:3 (1984), pp. 299–317.

Johnson, James Turner, *Just War Tradition and the Restraint of War. A Moral and Historical Inquiry* (Princeton: Princeton University Press, 1984).

Jones, Craig, *The War Lawyers. The United States, Israel, and Juridical Warfare* (Oxford: Oxford University Press, 2020).

Jorgensen, Marianne and Phillips, Louise, *Discourse Analysis as Theory and Method* (London: SAGE, 2002).

Jünger, Ernst, *Storm of Steel* (London: Penguin, 2004).

Junger, Sebastian, *War* (New York: Twelve, 2011).

Kaeuper, Richard W., *Chivalry and Violence in Medieval Europe* (New York: Oxford University Press, 1999).

Kagan, Donald, *On the Origins of War and the Preservation of Peace* (New York: Doubleday, 1995).

Kahn, Paul, 'The Paradox of Riskless Warfare', *Philosophy and Public Policy Quarterly*, 22:3 (2002), pp. 2–8.

Kalshoven, Frits and Zegveld, Liesbeth, *Constraints on the Waging of War. An introduction to International Humanitarian Law*. 3rd ed. (Geneva: ICRC, 2001).

Kant, Immanuel, *Critique of Judgment* (Indianapolis: Hackett, 1987).

Kant, Immanuel, *Critique of Pure Reason* (New York: Cambridge University Press, 1998).

Kant, Immanuel, *Groundwork of the Metaphysics of Morals* (Cambridge: Cambridge University Press, 2012).

Kant, Immanuel, *The Metaphysics of Morals* (Cambridge: Cambridge University Press, 1996).

Kant, Immanuel, *Toward Perpetual Peace and Other Writings on Politics, Peace, and History* (New Haven: Yale University Press, 2006).

Kasher, Asa, 'Combatant's Life and Human Dignity', *Israel Yearbook on Human Rights*, 24 (2014), pp. 219–246.

Kasher, Asa, 'Teaching and Training Military Ethics: An Israeli Experience', in Paul Robinson, Nigel De Lee and Don Carrick (eds.), *Ethics Education in the Military* (New York: Routledge, 2016), pp. 133–146.

Katzenstein, Peter J., 'Introduction: Alternative Perspectives on National Security', in Peter J. Katzenstein (ed.), *The Culture of National Security: Norms and Identity in World Politics* (New York: Columbia University Press, 1996), pp. 1–32.

Kaurin, Pauline Shanks, 'Courage. Overview', in Michael Skerker, David Whetham and Don Carrick (eds.), *Military Virtues* (Havant: Howgate, 2019), pp.102–110.

Kaurin, Pauline Shanks, 'Necessity, Convenience, and Point of View. Military Necessity in Just War', in Eric Patterson and Marc LiVecche (eds.), *Military Necessity and Just War Statecraft. The Principle of National Security Stewardship* (New York: Routledge, 2024), pp. 77–87.

Keegan, John, *A History of Warfare* (New York: Vintage Books, 1993).

Keegan, John, *The Face of Battle* (London: Pimlico, 2004).

Kelsay, John, 'Just War Thinking as a Social Practice', *Ethics and International Affairs*, 27:1 (2013), pp. 67–86.

Kelsen, Hans, *General Theory of Law and State* (Cambridge: Harvard University Press, 1949).

Kelsen, Hans, *Pure Theory of Law*, 2nd ed. (Clark: The Lawbook Exchange, 2005).

Kennedy, David, *Of War and Law* (Princeton: Princeton University Press, 2006).

Kent, Bonnie, 'In the Image of God. Human Dignity After the Fall', in Remy Debes (ed.), *Dignity. A History* (New York: Oxford University Press, 2017), pp. 73–98.

Kinsella, Helen M., *The Image before the Weapon. A Critical History of the Distinction between Combatant and Civilian* (Ithaca: Cornell University Press, 2011).

Kittrie, Orde, *Lawfare. Law as a Weapon of War* (New York: Oxford University Press, 2016).

Klabbers, Jan, *International Law*, 3rd ed. (Cambridge: Cambridge University Press, 2020).

Klabbers, Jan, *Virtue in Global Governance* (Cambridge: Cambridge University Press, 2022).

Kleinman, Steven M., 'Case Study 2: Operationalizing Wisdom: aggressive Restraint in the global War on Terror', in Michael Skerker, David Whetham and Don Carrick (eds.), *Military Virtues* (Havant: Howgate, 2019), pp. 141–148.

Koch, Bernhard, '"God, How I hate the 20th Century". On Chivalry as a Myth and as an Ethical Virtue', *Ethics and Armed Forces*, 2 (2021), pp. 30–37.

Koch, Bernhard, 'Chivalry between History, Tradition and Obsolescence: Overcoming One-Dimensionality in the Ethics of War. An Introduction to this Volume', in Bernhard Koch (ed.), *Chivalrous Combatants? The Meaning of Military Virtue Past and Present* (Baden-Baden: Nomos, 2019), pp. 7–28.

Koehn, Daryl, *The Ground of Professional Ethics* (New York: Routledge, 1994).

Kohlberg, Lawrence, *The Philosophy of Moral Development. Moral Stages and the Idea of Justice* (San Francisco: Harper and Row, 1981).

Koltermann, Jens O., 'Citizen in Uniform: Democratic Germany and the Changing "Bundeswehr"', *Parameters*, 42:2 (2012), pp. 108–126.

Kramer, Eric-Hans and Molendijk, Tine, 'Introduction', in Eric-Hans Kramer and Tine Molendijk (eds.), *Violence in Extreme Conditions. Ethical Challenges in Military Practice* (Cham: Springer, 2023), pp. 1–16.

Lagacé-Roy, Daniel and Jacob, Carl, 'Professionalism. Overview: Professional Military Excellence Through Practice', in Michael Skerker, David Whetham and Don Carrick (eds.), *Military Virtues* (Havant: Howgate, 2019), pp. 337–347.

Latinovic, Vladimir, 'Christ as *Imago Dei* – A Missed Opportunity of Ante-Nicene Christian Theology', in John Loughlin (ed.), *Human Dignity in the Judaeo-Christian Tradition. Catholic, Orthodox, Anglican and Protestant Perspectives* (London: Bloomsbury, 2021), pp. 57–78.

Le Moli, Ginevra, *Human Dignity in International Law* (Cambridge: Cambridge University Press, 2021).

Levi, Primo, *The Drowned and the Saved* (London: Abacus, 2013).

Lin, Patrick, Mehlman, Maxwell J. and Abney, Keith, *Enhanced Warfighters: Risk, Ethics, and Policy* (San Luis Obispo: California Polytechnic States University, 2013).

Liivoja, Rain, 'Chivalry Without a Horse: Military Honour and the Modern Law of Armed Conflict', *ENDC Proceedings*, Vol. 15 (2012), pp. 75–100.

Liivoja, Rain, 'Law and Honor: Normative Pluralism in the Regulation of Military Conduct', in Jan Klabbers and Touko Piiparinen (eds.), *Normative Pluralism and International Law: Exploring Global Governance* (Cambridge: Cambridge University Press, 2013), pp. 143–165.

Lindisfarne, Nancy and Neale, Jonathan, *Why Men? A Human History of Violence and Inequality* (London: Hurst & Co., 2023).

Lobo, Francisco, 'A conception of human dignity. The normative case against female genital mutilation', *Journal of Human Dignity and Wellbeing*, 7 (2019), pp. 80–98.

Lobo, Francisco, 'Abolishing atomic warfare? Nuclear power and natural-international law in the twenty-first century', *Transnational Legal Theory* (2019), pp. 1–27.

Lobo, Francisco, 'Aborto y Diversas Concepciones de Dignidad Humana', *Libertades Públicas, Colección Breviarios*, 8 (2017), pp. 1–19.

Lobo, Francisco, 'Kant's Conception of Human Dignity and the Importance of Singularity within Commonality', *International Journal of Law and Political Sciences*, 13:2 (2019), pp. 214–219.

Lobo, Francisco, 'The "capture or kill" debate revisited: Putting the "human" back in "human enhancement of soldiers"', *The Military Law and the Law of War Review*, 58:1 (2020), pp. 85–120.

Lobo, Francisco, 'The quest for the Ukrainian "Araucana". The case for the humanization of the Orc', *Revista Electrónica Iberoamericana*, 18:2 (2024), pp. 241–263.

Lobo, Francisco, 'Training and war games', https://www.euroisme.eu/index.php/en/events/past-conferences/berlin-2020, 9 October 2023.

Lobo, Francisco, *Teoría y Práctica de la Intervención Humanitaria en la Tradición de la Guerra Justa* (Mexico D.F.: Tirant lo Blanch, 2016).

Locke, John, *Second Treatise of Government* (Indianapolis: Hackett, 1980).

Lott, Micah, 'The Knowledge of Human Dignity', in Roger Teichmann (ed.), *The Oxford Handbook of Elizabeth Anscombe* (New York: Oxford University Press, 2022), pp. 292–307.

Loughlin, John, 'Human Dignity and Human Wretchedness from Iranaeus to Pico della Mirandola', in John Loughlin (ed.), *Human Dignity in the Judaeo-Christian Tradition. Catholic, Orthodox, Anglican and Protestant Perspectives* (London: Bloomsbury, 2021), pp. 99–119.

Loughlin, John, 'Introduction', in John Loughlin (ed.), *Human Dignity in the Judaeo-Christian Tradition. Catholic, Orthodox, Anglican and Protestant Perspectives* (London: Bloomsbury, 2021), pp. 1–14.

Luban, David, 'A Theory of Crimes Against Humanity', *Yale Journal of International Law*, 29 (2004), pp. 85–167.

Luban, David, 'Military Lawyers and the Two Cultures Problem', *Georgetown Public Law and Legal Theory Research Paper*, No. 12–057 (2012), pp. 1–55.

Luban, David, 'What is Military Necessity? A Defense of the Marginal Interpretation', in Eric Patterson and Marc LiVecche (eds.), *Military Necessity and Just War Statecraft. The Principle of National Security Stewardship* (New York: Routledge, 2024), pp. 41–54.

Luban, David, *Legal Ethics and Human Dignity* (Cambridge: Cambridge University Press, 2009).

Lucas, George R., *Law, Ethics and Emerging Military Technologies. Confronting Disruptive Innovation* (Oxon: Routledge, 2023).

Maalouf, Amin, *The Crusades through Arab Eyes* (London: Saqi Books, 2012).

Machiavelli, Niccolò, *The Prince* (New York: Oxford University Press, 2005).

MacIntyre, Alasdair, 'Military Ethics: A Discipline in Crisis', in George Lucas (ed.), *Routledge Handbook of Military Ethics* (New York: Routledge, 2015), pp. 3–14.

MacIntyre, Alasdair, *After Virtue*, 3rd ed. (Notre Dame: University of Notre Dame Press, 2007).

Madden, Mike, 'Of Wolves and Sheep: A Purposive Analysis of Perfidy Prohibitions in International Humanitarian Law', *Journal of Conflict and Security Law*, 17:3 (2012), pp. 439–463.

Madziwa, Edward, 'Advancing honour and dignity in death for victims of armed conflicts: Exploring the challenges and opportunities of AI and machine learning in humanitarian forensic action under IHL', *International Review of the Red Cross*, 106: 926 (2024), pp. 760–794.

Maier-Katkin, Birgit and Maier-Katkin, Daniel, 'At the Heart of Darkness: Crimes against Humanity and the Banality of Evil', *Human Rights Quarterly*, 26:3 (2004), pp. 584–604.

Mainländer, Philipp, *Filosofía de la redención* (Santiago: FCE, 2011).

Mangas, LCDR Rachel JAGC, USN and Festa, MAJ Matthew USAR (eds.), *Operational Law Handbook*, 16th ed. (Charlottesville: JAGC Legal Centre and School, 2016).

Marconi, Rachele, 'Between Outdated Morality and Evolutive Interpretation: The Concept of "Honour" under Article 27(2) of the Fourth Geneva Convention', *MPIL Research Paper Series*, No 2021–22.

Margalit, Avishai, *The Decent Society* (Cambridge: Harvard University Press, 1996).

Martin, Daniel and Heineberg, Yotam, 'Positive leadership, power and compassion, in Paul Gilbert (ed.), *Compassion. Concepts, Research and Applications* (New York: Routledge, 2017), pp. 221–236.

Mason, Jennifer, *Qualitative Researching*, 3rd ed. (London: SAGE, 2018).

May, Larry, *After War Ends. A Philosophical Perspective* (Cambridge: Cambridge University Press, 2012).

May, Larry, *War Crimes and Just War* (Cambridge: Cambridge University Press, 2007).

Mayer, Jane, *The Dark Side* (New York: Doubleday, 2008).

Mayer, Paxton, 'What's in a Soldier? How to Rebrand the Canadian Armed Forces', *Policy Perspective – Canadian Global Affairs Institute* (2020), pp. 1–16.

McCormack, Philip, 'Case Study 1: Levels of Loyalty: Country, Service, Mission, Troops', in Michael Skerker, David Whetham and Don Carrick (eds.), *Military Virtues* (Havant: Howgate, 2019), pp. 87–93.

McCormack, Philip, 'Compassion: Overview', in Michael Skerker, David Whetham and Don Carrick (eds.), *Military Virtues* (Havant: Howgate, 2019), pp. 287–295.

McCormack, Philip, 'Virtues or Values?', in Michael Skerker, David Whetham and Don Carrick (eds.), *Military Virtues* (Havant: Howgate, 2019), pp. 15–30.

McCormack, Wayne, *Understanding the Law of Terrorism* (Danvers: Lexis Nexis, 2007).

McCormick, Matt, 'Is it wrong to play violent video games?', *Ethics and Information Technology*, 3:4 (2001), pp. 277–287.

McCrudden, Christopher (ed.), *Understanding Human Dignity* (Oxford: Oxford University Press, 2015).

McCrudden, Christopher, 'Human Dignity and Judicial Interpretation of Human Rights', *The European Journal of International Law*, 19:4 (2008), pp. 655–724.

McDonald, Jack, *Enemies Known and Unknown* (Oxford: Oxford university Press, 2017).

McDonald, Jack, *What is War For?* (Bristol: Bristol University Press, 2023).

McDougal, Myers and Laswell, Harold, 'The identification and appraisal of diverse systems of public order', *The American Journal of International Law*, 53 (1959), pp. 1–29.

McMahan, Jeff, 'Just War Theory and the Russia-Ukraine War', *Studia Philosophica Estonica*, 17 (2024), pp. 54–67.

McMahan, Jeff, 'The Ethics of Killing in War', *Ethics*, 114 (2004), pp. 693–733.

McMahan, Jeff, 'The Morality of War and the Law of War', in David Rodin and Henry Shue (eds.), *Just and Unjust Warriors. The Moral and Legal Status of Soldiers* (New York: Oxford University Press, 2008), pp. 19–43.

McMahan, Jeff, *Killing in War* (New York: Oxford University Press, 2009).

McMaster, H.R., 'Preserving Soldiers' Moral Character in Counter-insurgency Operations', in Don Carrick, James Connelly and Paul Robinson (eds.), *Ethics Education for Irregular Warfare* (Cornwall: Ashgate, 2009), pp. 15–26.

McNeill, William, *Keeping together in time* (Cambridge: Harvard University Press, 1995).

McQuinn, Brian, Terry, Fiona, Kaplan, Oliver and Gutiérrez-Sanin, Francisco, 'Introduction: promoting restraint in war', *International Interactions*, 47:5 (2021), pp. 795–824.

Meagher, Robert Emmet, *Killing from the Inside Out. Moral Injury and Just War* (Eugene: Cascade Books, 2014).

Meireis, Torsten, 'Chivalry and Law-sustaining Force', in Bernhard Koch (ed.), *Chivalrous Combatants? The Meaning of Military Virtue Past and Present* (Baden-Baden: Nomos, 2019), pp. 121–138.

Melgaard, Nicholas and Whetham, David, 'Jus ad vim. War, peace and the ethical status of the in-between', in Seumas Miller, Mitt Regan and Patrick F. Walsh (eds.), *National Security Intelligence and Ethics* (London: Routledge, 2021), pp. 186–198.

Melnychuk, Svitlana, Zagorui, Ivan, Zagorui, Liudmyla, Kravchenko, Ihor and Kuderska, Nadiia, 'Freedom and Human Dignity as Fundamental Constittuional Values: The Challenge of Modernity', *Lex humana*, 15:3 (2023), pp. 424–437.

Melzer, Nils, *Interpretive Guidance on the Notion of Direct Participation in Hostilities Under International Humanitarian Law* (Geneva: ICRC, 2009).

Merkl, Alexander, 'The Meaning of Military Virtues for Peace – a Moral Theological Approach', in Bernhard Koch (ed.), *Chivalrous Combatants? The Meaning of Military Virtue Past and Present* (Baden-Baden: Nomos, 2019), pp. 107–120.

Meron, Theodor, 'Shakespeare's Henry the Fifth and the Law of War', *The American Journal of International Law*, 86 (1992), pp. 1–45.

Meron, Theodor, *Bloody Constraint: War and Chivalry in Shakespeare* (New York: Oxford University Press, 1998).

Meron, Theodor, *Standing Up for Justice* (New York: Oxford University Press, 2021).

Meyer, Michael, 'Kant's concept of dignity and modern political thought', *History of European Ideas*, 8:3 (1987), pp. 319–332.

Milbank, John, 'The Dignity of the Ancients and the Dignity of the Moderns', in John Loughlin (ed.), *Human Dignity in the Judaeo-Christian Tradition. Catholic, Orthodox, Anglican and Protestant Perspectives* (London: Bloomsbury, 2021), pp. 173–192.

Milburn, Andrew, *When the Tempest Gathers* (Bransley: Pen & Sword, 2020).

Miller, Dale E., 'Rule utilitarianism', in Ben Eggleston and Dale E. Miller (eds.), *The Cambridge Companion to Utilitarianism* (Cambridge: Cambridge University Press, 2014), pp. 146–165.

Miller, William Ian, *The Mystery of Courage* (Cambridge: Harvard University Press, 2000).

Ministry of Defence of Ukraine, *Кодекс поведінки учасників бойових дій* (Kyiv: Ministry of Defence of Ukraine, 1998).

Molendijk, Tine, 'War Is Back in Post-Heroic Europe: Change and Continuity in the Relationship Between the Armed Forces and Society', *Armed Forces and Society*, 00 (2024), pp. 1–25.

Molendijk, Tine, *Moral Injury and Soldiers in Conflict* (Oxon: Routledge, 2021).

Moliner, Juan, 'La educación y formación en ética militar', in Centro Conjunto de Desarollo de Conceptos, *Cuestiones sobre ética militar* (Madrid: Ministerio de Defensa, 2022), pp. 21–48.

Moliner, Juan, *La ética militar como como marco de reflexión sobre la guerra y la profesión militar* (Madrid: Ministerio de Defensa, 2022).

Montaigne, Michel de, *The Complete Essays* (London: Penguin Books, 2003).

Mouffe, Chantal, *The Return of the Political* (Brooklyn: Verso, 2005).
Moyn, Samuel, 'The Secret History of Constitutional Dignity', in Christopher McCrudden (ed.), *Understanding Human Dignity* (Oxford: Oxford University Press, 2015), pp. 95–111.
Moyn, Samuel, *Humane* (New York: Farrar, Straus and Giroux, 2021).
Nabulsi, Karma, *Traditions of War* (New York: Oxford University Press, 2007).
Narvaez, Darcia, 'Evolution, child raising, and compassionate morality', in Paul Gilbert (ed.), *Compassion. Concepts, Research and Applications* (New York: Routledge, 2017), pp. 173–186.
Nash, Claudio, *La concepción de derechos fundamentales en Latinoamérica* (Mexico D.F.: Fontamara, 2010).
Neitzel, Sönke, 'Tribal Cultures and *Innere Führung* – A Contradiction?', *Ethics and Armed Forces*, 2 (2021), pp. 4–11.
Neuhäuser, Christian and Stoekcer, Ralf, 'Human dignity as universal nobility', in Marcus Düwell, Jens Braarvig, Roger Brownsword, and Dietmar Mieth (eds.), *The Cambridge Handbook of Human Dignity* (Cambridge: Cambridge University Press, 2014), pp. 298–309.
Norton, John, 'Prolegomenon to the jurisprudence of Myers McDougal and Harold Lasswell', *Virginia Law Review*, 54 (1968), pp. 662–688.
Nussbaum, Martha, *Poetic Justice. The Literary Imagination and Public Life* (Boston: Beacon Press, 1995).
O'Brien, Tim, *The Things They Carried* (London: 4th Estate, 2015).
O'Brien, William, *The Conduct of Just and Limited War* (New York: Praeger Publishers, 1981).
O'Driscoll, Cian, 'Christine de Pizan', in Daniel R. Brunstetter and Cian O'Driscoll (eds.), *Just War Thinkers* (New York: Routledge, 2018), pp. 64–76.
O'Driscoll, Cian, *Victory. The Triumph and Tragedy of Just War* (New York: Oxford University Press, 2020).
Oeter, Stefan, 'The (Non-)Importance of Chivalry in International Humanitarian Law', in Bernhard Koch (ed.), *Chivalrous Combatants? The Meaning of Military Virtue Past and Present* (Baden-Baden: Nomos, 2019), pp. 45–68.
Ohlin, Jens David, 'The Duty to Capture', *Minnesota Law Review*, 97 (2013), pp. 1268–1342.
Olsthoorn, Peter, 'Educating for Restraint', in Eric-Hans Kramer and Tine Molendijk (eds.), *Violence in Extreme Conditions. Ethical Challenges in Military Practice* (Cham: Springer, 2023), pp. 119–130.
Olsthoorn, Peter, 'Introduction. Military Virtues and Moral Relativism', in Michael Skerker, David Whetham and Don Carrick (eds.), *Military Virtues* (Havant: Howgate, 2019), pp. 1–14.
Olsthoorn, Peter, 'Military Virtues for Today', *Ethics and Armed Forces*, 2 (2021), pp. 24–29.

Olsthoorn, Peter, 'Risks, Robots, and the Honorableness of the military Profession', in Bernhard Koch (ed.), *Chivalrous Combatants? The Meaning of Military Virtue Past and Present* (Baden-Baden: Nomos, 2019), pp. 161–178.

Olsthoorn, Peter, 'The Ethics Curriculum at the Netherlands Defence Academy, and Some Problems with its Theoretical Underpinnings', in Paul Robinson, Nigel De Lee and Don Carrick (eds.), *Ethics Education in the Military* (New York: Routledge, 2016), pp. 119–130.

Olsthoorn, Peter, *Military Ethics and Virtues* (New York: Routledge, 2011).

Ortega y Gasset, José, *Meditaciones del Quijote y otros ensayos* (Madrid: Alianza, 2014).

Ortega y Gasset, José, *Obras Completas.* Vol. IV. 6th ed. (Madrid: Revista de Occidente, 1966).

Osswald, Silvia, Frey, Dieter and Streicher, Bernhard, 'Moral Courage', in E. Kals and J. Maes (eds.), *Justice and Conflicts* (Berlin: Springer-Verlag, 2012), pp. 391–405.

Ota, Fumio, 'Ethics Training for the Samurai Warrior', in Paul Robinson, Nigel De Lee and Don Carrick (eds.), *Ethics Education in the Military* (New York: Routledge, 2016), pp. 147–158.

Pacheco Gómez, Alejandro, 'The incorporation of lex artis in the Law', *Mexican Bioethics Review ICSa*, 3:6 (2022), pp. 21–25.

Pamuk, Zeynep, 'Artificial Intelligence and the Problem of Judgment', *Ethics and International Affairs*, 37:2 (2023), pp. 232–243.

Parker, Philip, *The Atlas of Atlases* (London: Ivy Press, 2022).

Parks, Hays, 'Part IX of the ICRC "Direct Participation in Hostilities" Study: No Mandate, No Expertise, and Legally Incorrect', *International Law and Politics*, 42 (2010), pp. 769–830.

Patrikarakos, David, *War in 140 Characters. How Social Media Is Reshaping Conflict in the Twenty-First Century* (New York: Basic Books, 2017).

Patterson, Eric, 'Returning Military Necessity to the *Jus in Bello*', in Eric Patterson and Marc LiVecche (eds.), *Military Necessity and Just War Statecraft. The Principle of National Security Stewardship* (New York: Routledge, 2024), pp. 1–13.

Peperkamp, Lonneke and Braun, Christian Nikolaus, 'Contemporary Just War Thinking and Military Education', in Eric-Hans Kramer and Tine Molendijk (eds.), *Violence in Extreme Conditions. Ethical Challenges in Military Practice* (Cham: Springer, 2023), pp. 101–117.

Pepper, Stephen, 'The Lawyer's Amoral Ethical Role: A Defense, A Problem, and Some Possibilities', *Law and Social Inquiry*, 11:4 (1986), pp. 613–634.

Pérez Rosales, Vicente, *Recuerdos del Pasado. 1814–1860*. 3rd ed. (Santiago: Imprenta Gutenberg, 1886).

Perrow, Charles, *Normal Accidents. Living with High-Risk Technologies* (Princeton: Princeton University Press, 1999).

Persson, Ingmar and Savulescu, Julian, *Unfit for the Future: The Need for Moral Enhancement* (Oxford: Oxford University Press, 2012).

Pickering, Guillermo, *Profesión soldado. Apuntes de un general del Ejército de Chile* (Santiago: LOM Ediciones, 2022).

Pinker, Steven, *The Better Angels of Our Nature. Why Violence Has Declined* (New York: Penguin, 2012).

Pizan, Christine de, *The Book of Deeds of Arms and of Chivalry* (Pennsylvania: The Pennsylvania State University Press, 2003).

Plato, *The Republic* (Luton: Andrews UK Limited, 2012).

Plokhy, Serhii, *The Russo-Ukrainian War* (London: Allen Lane, 2023).

Poggi, Francesca, 'Defeasibility, Law, and Argumentation: A Critical View from an Interpretative Standpoint', *Argumentation*, 35 (2021), pp. 409–434.

Prescott, Jody, *Empirical Assessment in IHL Education and Training* (London: Anthem Press, 2021).

Prieto Rudolphy, Marcela, *The Morality of the Laws of War: War, Law, and Murder* (Oxford: Oxford University Press, 2023).

Puscas, Ioana Maria, 'Military Human Enhancement', in William H. Boothby (ed.), *New Technologies and the Law in War and Peace* (Cambridge: Cambridge University Press, 2018), pp. 182–229.

Qerimi, Qerim, 'Dignity in *transition*: the constitutional and operational potential and limits of human dignity seen from the lens of post-conflict societies', *The International Journal of Human Rights*, No. 8 (2021), pp. 1211–1232.

Quinn, Josephine, *How the World Made the West. A 4,000 Year History* (New York: Random House, 2024).

Radin, Margaret Jane, 'Reconsidering the Rule of Law', *Boston University Law Review*, 69:4 (1989), pp. 781–819.

Ramsey, Paul, *The Just War. Force and Political Responsibility* (New York: Charles Scribner's Sons, 1968).

Rau, Zbigniew, '"Free with the free, equal with the equal". Knightly freedom-lovingness against Moscow despotism is a common heritage of the First Polish-Lithuanian Commonwealth in the political culture of Poland and Ukraine', in in Dmytro Kuleba (ed.), *Війна і нові горизонти* (Kyiv: Knygolove, 2024), pp. 193–230.

Rawls, John, 'Two Concepts of Rules', *The Philosophical Review*, 64:1 (1955), pp. 3–32.

Rawls, John, *A Theory of Justice* (Cambridge: Harvard University Press, 2005).

Raz, Joseph, *The Authority of Law: Essays on Law and Morality* (New York: Oxford University Press, 1979).

Reichberg, Gregory, Syse, Henrik and Begby, Endre (eds.), *The Ethics of War. Classic and Contemporary Readings* (Oxford: Blackwell, 2006).

Renic, Neil C., *Asymmetric Killing. Risk Avoidance, Just War, and the Warrior Ethos* (Oxford: Oxford University Press, 2020).

Reynolds, Susan, *Before Eminent Domain. Toward a History of Expropriation of Land for the Common Good* (Chapel Hill: University of North Carolina Press, 2010).

Ritchie, Jane, 'The Applications of Qualitative Methods to Social Research', in Jane Ritchie and Jane Lewis, *Qualitative Research Practice* (London: SAGE, 2003), pp. 24–46.

Roberts, Adam, 'The Principle of Equal Application of the Laws of War', in David Rodin and Henry Shue (eds.), *Just and Unjust Warriors. The Moral and Legal Status of Soldiers* (New York: Oxford University Press, 2008), pp. 226–254.

Roberts, Peter, *The Western Way of War* (Havant: Howgate, 2024).

Robinson, Paul, 'Discipline. Overview', in Michael Skerker, David Whetham and Don Carrick (eds.), *Military Virtues* (Havant: Howgate, 2019), pp. 311–318.

Robinson, Paul, 'Integrity and Selective Conscientious Objection', *Journal of Military Ethics*, 8:1 (2009), pp. 34–47.

Robinson, Paul, 'Introduction: Ethics education for Irregular Warfare', in Don Carrick, James Connelly and Paul Robinson (eds.), *Ethics Education for Irregular Warfare* (Cornwall: Ashgate, 2009), pp. 1–14.

Robinson, Paul, 'Introduction: Ethics Education in the Military', in Paul Robinson, Nigel De Lee and Don Carrick (eds.), *Ethics Education in the Military* (New York: Routledge, 2016), pp. 1–14.

Robinson, Paul, *Military Honour and the Conduct of War. From Ancient Greece to Iraq* (New York: Routledge, 2006).

Rodin, David and Shue, Henry (eds.), *Just and Unjust Warriors. The Moral and Legal Status of Soldiers* (New York: Oxford University Press, 2008).

Rodin, David, 'Justice between Wars', *Ethics and International Affairs*, 35:3 (2021), pp. 435–442.

Rodin, David, 'The Moral Inequality of Soldiers: Why *jus in bello* Asymmetry is Half Right', in David Rodin and Henry Shue (eds.), *Just and Unjust Warriors. The Moral and Legal Status of Soldiers* (New York: Oxford University Press, 2008), pp. 44–68.

Rodin, David, *War and Self-Defense* (Oxford: Oxford University Press, 2002).

Rodriguez, Philippe-André, 'Human dignity as an essentially contested concept', *Cambridge Review of International Affairs*, 28:4 (2015), pp. 743–756.

Roff, Heather M., 'Jeff McMahan (1954–present)', in Daniel R. Brunstetter and Cian O'Driscoll (eds.), *Just War Thinkers* (New York: Routledge, 2018), pp. 238–249.

Rohan, Sally, 'An organic professional military ethic and the educational challenge', in Don Carrick, James Connelly and David Whetham (eds.), *Making the Military Moral. Contemporary Challenges and Responses in Military Ethics Education* (New York: Routledge, 2018), pp. 71–91.

Rosen, Michael, 'Dignity Past and Present', in Jeremy Waldron, *Dignity, Rank and Rights. The Berkeley Tanner Lectures* (2009) (New York: Oxford University Press, 2012), pp. 79–98.

Rosen, Michael, *Dignity. It's History and Meaning* (Cambridge: Harvard University Press, 2012).

Rosenthal, Joel H., 'Foreword', in Daniel R. Brunstetter and Cian O'Driscoll (eds.), *Just War Thinkers* (New York: Routledge, 2018), pp. xiv–xv.

Rossman, Gretchen, and Rallis, Sharon, *An Introduction to Qualitative Research*, 4th ed. (London: SAGE, 2017).

Roth, Hans Ingvar, 'P.C. Chang and Charles Malik: The Two Philosophers of the Universal Declaration of Human Rights', *Human Rights Quarterly*, 45:4 (2023), pp. 545–567.

Rousseau, Jean-Jacques, *Discourse on the Origins of Inequality* (*Second Discourse*) (Hanover: University Press of New England, 1992).

Rousseau, Jean-Jacques, *The Social Contract* (Oxford: Oxford University Press, 1999).

Royal, Benoit, 'Case Study 1: The Necessity of Self Control and the Perils of Anger', in Michael Skerker, David Whetham and Don Carrick (eds.), *Military Virtues* (Havant: Howgate, 2019), pp. 319–325.

Rubel, Rick, 'Wisdom. Overview', in Michael Skerker, David Whetham and Don Carrick (eds.), *Military Virtues* (Havant: Howgate, 2019), pp. 127–132.

Russell, Bertrand, *Human Society in Ethics and Politics* (London: Routledge, 1992).

Saborido, Jorge and Borrelli, Marcelo, 'Por la "dignidad Militar": la revista Cabildo y el levantamiento carapintada en la Semana Santa de 1987', *La Trama de la Comunicación*, 18 (2014), pp. 293–311.

Salomon, Richard, '2023 DoD Manual Revision – What's Chivalry Got to Do with It?', https://lieber.westpoint.edu/whats-chivalry-got-to-do-with-it/, 26 August 2024.

Sandel, Michael, *Justice. What's the Right Thing to Do?* (New York: Farrar, Straus and Giroux, 2010).

Sangiovanni, Andrea, *Humanity without Dignity* (Cambridge: Harvard University Press, 2017).

Sassòli, Marco, Bouvier, Antoine, and Quintin, Ann, *How does law protect in war?* 3rd ed. Vol. I (Geneva: ICRC, 2011).

Sattler, John and Skerker, Michael, 'Case study 1: Compassion toward Enemies', in Michael Skerker, David Whetham and Don Carrick (eds.), *Military Virtues* (Havant: Howgate, 2019), pp. 298–300.

Scanlon, Tim M., *What We Owe to Each Other* (Cambridge: Harvard University Press, 2000).

Schachter, Oscar, 'Human Dignity as a Normative Concept', *American Journal of International Law*, 77 (1983), pp. 848–854.

Schauer, Frederick, *Playing by the Rules: A Philosophical Examination of Rule-Based Decision -Making in Law and Life* (Oxford: Oxford University Press, 1993).

Scheler, Max, *El Puesto del Hombre en el Cosmos* (Buenos Aires: Losada, 1938).

Schelling, Thomas, *Arms and Influence* (New Haven: Yale University Press, 1966).

Schmitt, Carl, *The Concept of the Political* (Chicago: The University of Chicago Press, 2007).

Schmitt, Michael, 'Military Necessity and Humanity in International Humanitarian Law: Preserving a Delicate Balance', *Virginia Journal of International Law*, 50:4 (2010).

Schmitt, Michael, 'Wound, Capture, or Kill: A Reply to Ryan Goodman's "The Power to Kill or Capture Enemy Combatants"', *The European Journal of International Law*, 24(3) (2013), p. 856.

Schörnig, Niklas, 'Chivalry and Sniping – Simply Incompatible?', in Bernhard Koch (ed.), *Chivalrous Combatants? The Meaning of Military Virtue Past and Present* (Baden-Baden: Nomos, 2019), pp. 179–198.

Schwartz, Jonathan Peter, *Arendt's Judgment: Freedom, Responsibility, Citizenship* (Philadelphia: University of Pennsylvania Press, 2016).

Schwarzbauer, Matthias, 'Make *Innere Führung* Attractive Again! A Personal Essay', *Ethics and Armed Forces*, 2 (2019), pp. 49–54.

Schweitzer, Albert, *The Philosophy of Civilization* (New York: Prometheus Books, 1987).

Scott, James C., *Seeing Like a State* (New Haven: Yale University Press, 2020).

Scott, Wilbur J., Modesto De Angelis, Karin and Segal, David R., *Military Sociology. A Guided Introduction* (New York: Routledge, 2023).

Searle, John, *The construction of social reality* (New York: The Free Press, 1995).

Sensen, Oliver, 'Kant's Conception of Human Dignity', *Kant-Studien*, 100 (2009), pp. 309–331.

Shay, Jonathan, *Achilles in Vietnam. Combat Trauma and the undoing of Character* (New York: Scribner, 2003).

Sherman, Nancy, *Stoic Warriors. The Ancient Philosophy Behind the Military Mind* (New York: Oxford University Press, 2005).

Sherman, Nancy, *Stoic Wisdom. Ancient Lessons for Modern Resilience* (New York: Oxford University Press, 2021).

Shue, Henry, 'Torture', *Philosophy and Public Affairs*, 7:2 (1978), pp. 124–143.

Simons, Anna, 'The Military and Society: A Refresher', *2024 Index of U.S. Military Strength* (2024), pp. 63–71.

Skerker, Michael, 'Preface', in Michael Skerker, David Whetham and Don Carrick (eds.), *Military Virtues* (Havant: Howgate, 2019), pp. xxv–xxvi.

Skerker, Michael, *The Moral Status of Combatants. A New Theory of Just War* (New York: Routledge, 2020).

Skerker, Michael, Whetham, David and Carrick, Don (eds.), *Military Virtues* (Havant: Howgate, 2019).

Sledge, Eugene B., *With the Old Breed. At Peleliu and Okinawa* (New York: Presidio Press, 2007).

Smart, J.J.C., 'Extreme and Restricted Utilitarianism', *The Philosophical Quarterly*, 6:25 (1956), pp. 344–354.

Snow, Nancy E., 'Teaching Virtues in the Military, *Journal of Military Ethics*, 22:3–4 (2023), pp. 185–199.

Spaulding, Norman W., 'Is Human Judgment Necessary? Artificial Intelligence, Algorithmic Governance, and the Law', in Markus D. Dubber et al (eds.), *The Oxford Handbook of Ethics of AI* (New York: Oxford University Press, 2020), pp. 375–402.

Spikins, Penny, 'Prehistoric origins. The compassion of far distant strangers', in Paul Gilbert (ed.), *Compassion. Concepts, Research and Applications* (New York: Routledge, 2017), pp. 16–30.

Stanar, Dragan, 'The right to die with dignity: Soldiers in post-modern warfare', *Yearbook of Human Rights Protection: The Right to Human Dignity*, 3 (2020), pp. 519–531.

Starčević, Srđan, 'Military Command and the Right to Human Dignity', *Yearbook of Human Rights Protection. The Right to Human Dignity*, 3 (2020), pp. 133–144.

Steinhoff, Uwe, *The Ethics of War and the Force of Law. A Modern Just War Theory* (New York: Routledge, 2021).

Stoecker, Ralf, 'Three Crucial Turns on the Road to an Adequate Understanding of Human Dignity', in P. Kaufmann, H. Kuch, C. Neuhäuser, and E. Webster (eds.), *Humiliation, Degradation, Dehumanization. Human Dignity Violated* (New York: Springer, 2011), pp. 7–17.

Suzuki, Eisuke, 'The New Haven School of international law: An invitation to a policy-oriented jurisprudence', *Yale Studies of World Public Order*, 1 (1974), pp. 1–48.

Tadros, Victor, *To Do, To Die, To Reason Why. Individual Ethics in War* (Oxford: Oxford University Press, 2020).

Teitel, Ruti, *Humanity's Law* (New York: Oxford University Press, 2011).

Thaler, Mathias, *Naming Violence. A Critical Theory of Genocide, Torture, and Terrorism* (New York: Columbia University Press, 2018).

Theletsane, K.I., 'Form and Content of the Ethics Programme in the South African National Defence Force', *African Journal of Public Affairs*, 11:1 (2019), pp. 75–92.

Thomas, John 'Case Study: Professionalism in the Military', in Michael Skerker, David Whetham and Don Carrick (eds.), *Military Virtues* (Havant: Howgate, 2019), pp. 348–364.

Thomas, John 'Ethical challenges for the modern military', in Don Carrick, James Connelly and David Whetham (eds.), *Making the Military Moral. Contemporary Challenges and Responses in Military Ethics Education* (New York: Routledge, 2018), pp. 92–106.

Thomas, Ward, 'Norms and Security: The Case of International Assassination', *International Security*, 25 (2000), pp. 105–133.

Thompson, Maj. J. David, 'Military Reasons for Civilian Harm Mitigation', *Liaison*, 13:2 (2021), pp. 54–59.

Tocqueville, Alexis de, *Democracy in America* (Indianapolis: Liberty Fund, 2010).

Traven, David, *Law and Sentiment in International Politics. Ethics, Emotions, and the Evolution of the Laws of War* (New York: Cambridge University Press, 2021).

Twain, Mark, *A Connecticut Yankee in King Arthur's Court* (New York: Barnes & Noble, 2005).

Tzu, Sun, *The Art of War* (Pax Librorum, 2009).

UK Parliament, 'Overseas Operations (Service Personnel and Veterans) Bill, https://bills.parliament.uk/bills/2727, 9 April 2021.

Urmson, J.O., 'The Interpretation of the Moral Philosophy of J.S. Mill', *The Philosophical Quarterly*, 3:10 (1953), pp. 33–39.

US Department of Defense, *Law of War Manual* (Washington D.C.: DoD, 2015).

Vale, Malcolm, 'Chivalry and the Conduct of Warfare – Illusion and Reality', in Bernhard Koch (ed.), *Chivalrous Combatants? The Meaning of Military Virtue Past and Present* (Baden-Baden: Nomos, 2019), pp. 29–43.

van der Wilt, H., 'War Crimes and the Requirement of a Nexus with an Armed Conflict', *Journal of International Criminal Justice*, 10:5 (2012), pp. 1113–1128.

van Schooten, Hanneke, 'War as an Institutional Fact: Semiotics and Institutional Legal Theory', *International Journal for the Semiotics of Law*, 22:3 (2009), pp. 307–320.

VanLandingham, Rachel, 'The Law of War is Not About "Chivalry"', https://www.justsecurity.org/24773/laws-war-chivalry/, 26 August 2024.

Varaki, Maria, 'The Quest for *Phronesis* in the Holy Land', in Jan Klabbers, Maria Varaki, and G.V. Vilaça, *Towards Responsible Global Governance* (Helsinki: Unigrafia, 2018), pp. 131–142.

Verbruggen, J.F., *The Art of Warfare in Western Europe During the Middle Ages* (Rochester: The Boydell Press, 1997).

Verdiesen, Ilse, *Agency Perception and Moral Values Related to Autonomous Weapons* (Leiden: Brill-Nijhoff, 2022).

Vitoria, Francisco de, *Political Writings* (Anthony Pagden and Jeremy Lawrance eds.) (Cambridge: Cambridge University Press, 2010).

Vitoria, Francisco de, *Relecciones sobre los Indios y el Derecho de Guerra*. 3rd ed. (Madrid: Espasa-Calpe, 1975).

Vlastos, Gregory, 'Justice and Equality', in Jeremy Waldron (ed.), *Theories of Rights* (New York: Oxford University Press, 1984), pp. 41–76.

Waldron, Jeremy, 'Against', in Tamar Meisels and Jeremy Waldron, *Debating Targeted Killing* (New York: Oxford University Press, 2020), pp. 146–257.

Waldron, Jeremy, 'Citizenship and Dignity', in Christopher McCrudden (ed.), *Understanding Human Dignity* (Oxford: Oxford University Press, 2015), pp. 327–343.

Waldron, Jeremy, 'Deep Morality and the Laws of War', in Seth Lazar and Helen Frowe (eds.), *The Oxford Handbook of Ethics of War* (Oxford: Oxford University Press, 2018), pp. 80–93.

Waldron, Jeremy, 'Dignity and Rank', *European Journal of Sociology*, 48:2 (2007), pp. 201–237.

Waldron, Jeremy, 'How Law Protects Dignity', *The Cambridge Law Journal*, 71:1 (2012), pp. 200–222.

Waldron, Jeremy, 'Is Dignity the Foundation of Human Rights?', *NYU Public Law and Legal Theory Research Paper Series*, 12–73 (2013), pp. 1–29.

Waldron, Jeremy, 'Is the Rule of Law and Essentially Contested Concept (in Florida)', *Law and Philosophy*, 21 (2002), pp. 137–164.

Waldron, Jeremy, *Dignity, Rank and Rights. The Berkeley Tanner Lectures (2009)* (New York: Oxford University Press, 2012).

Waldron, Jeremy, *One Another's Equals. The Basis of Human Equality* (Cambridge: Harvard University Press, 2017).

Waldron, Jeremy, *Torture, Terror and Trade-offs. Philosophy for the White House* (New York: Oxford University Press, 2010).

Wallach, Evan, 'Pray Fire First Gentlemen of France: Has 21st Century Chivalry Been Subsumed by Humanitarian Law?', *Harvard National Security Journal*, 3 (2012), pp. 431–469.

Walzer, Michael, 'Response to McMahan's paper', *Philosophia*, 34:43 (2006), pp. 43–45.

Walzer, Michael, *Arguing about War* (New Haven: Yale University Press, 2004).

Walzer, Michael, *Just and Unjust Wars. A Moral Argument with Historical Illustrations*. 4th ed. (New York: Basic Books, 2006).

Walzer, Michael, *Just and Unjust Wars. A Moral Argument with Historical Illustrations*. 5th ed. (New York: Basic Books, 2015).

Walzer, Michael, *Spheres of Justice* (New York: Basic Books, 1983).

Warner, Cristopher H. et. al., 'Effectiveness of Battlefield-Ethics Training During Combat Deployment: A Programme Assessment', *The Lancet*, 378: 9794 (2011), pp. 915–924.

Watts, Sean, 'The DOD Law of War Manual's Return to Principles', https://www.justsecurity.org/24270/dod-law-war-manuals-return-principles/, 26 August 2024.

Weber, Max, *The Vocation Lectures* (Indianapolis: Hacket, 2004).

Weil, Simone, 'The Iliad, or the Poem of Force', *Chicago Review*, 18:2 (1965), pp. 5–30.

Weil, Simone, *The Need for Roots* (New York: Routledge, 2002).

Wendel, Bradley, 'Legal Ethics as Political Moralism or the Morality of Politics', *Cornell Law Review*, 93:6 (2008), pp. 1413–1436.

Werle, Gerhard, *Principles of International Criminal Law*, 2ª ed. (The Hague: TMC Asser Press, 2009).

Wertheimer, Roger, 'The Moral Singularity of Military Professionalism', in Roger Wertheimer (ed.), *Empowering our Military Conscience. Transforming Just War Theory and Military Moral Education* (New York: Routledge, 2010).

Whetham, David, 'Case Study 2: Should Service Personnel Refuse to Fight in Unjust Wars?', in Michael Skerker, David Whetham and Don Carrick (eds.), *Military Virtues* (Havant: Howgate, 2019), pp. 75–80.

Whetham, David, 'Challenges to the professional military ethics education landscape', in Don Carrick, James Connelly and David Whetham (eds.), *Making the Military Moral. Contemporary Challenges and Responses in Military Ethics Education* (New York: Routledge, 2018), pp. 141–158.

Whetham, David, 'Ethics and the Special Forces', *In-Depth Briefing-CHACR*, 55 (2023), pp. 1–6.

Whetham, David, 'Special Operations Command: Leadership and Ethics Review', in Inspector-General of the Australian Defence Force, *Afghanistan Inquiry Report* (Canberra: Commonwealth of Australia, 2020), pp. 504–531.

Whetham, David, *Just Wars and Moral Victories. Surprise, Deception, and the Normative Framework of European War in the Later Middle Ages* (Leiden: Brill, 2009).

Whitman, James, 'Enforcing Civility and Respect: Three Societies', *The Yale Law Journal*, 109 (2000), pp. 1279–1378.

Wilson, Jeffrey, 'An Ethics Curriculum for an Evolving Army', in Paul Robinson, Nigel De Lee and Don Carrick (eds.), *Ethics Education in the Military* (New York: Routledge, 2016), pp. 31–42.

Witt, John Fabian, *Lincoln's Code* (New York: Free Press, 2012).

Wittgenstein, Ludwig, *Philosophical Investigations* (Croydon: Blackwell Publishing, 2009).

Wittrock, Jon, 'A human right to friendship? Dignity, autonomy, and social deprivation', *The International Journal of Human Rights*, 26:9 (2022), pp. 1590–1607.

Wolfendale, Jessica, 'What is the Point of Teaching Ethics in the Military?', in Paul Robinson, Nigel De Lee and Don Carrick (eds.), *Ethics Education in the Military* (New York: Routledge, 2016), pp. 161–174.

Wollstonecraft, Mary, *A Vindication of the Rights of Men* (London: J. Johnson, 1790).

Wright, Georg Von, *Norm and Action* (London: Routledge & Kegan Paul, 1963).

Zając, Maciek, 'AWS compliance with the ethical principle of proportionality: three possible solutions', *Ethics and Information Technology*, 25:13 (2023), pp. 1–13.

Zalaquett, José, 'Prólogo', in Francisco Lobo, *Teoría y Práctica de la Intervención Humanitaria en la Tradición de la Guerra Justa* (Mexico D.F.: Tirant lo Blanch, 2016), pp. 17–22.

Zilincik, Samuel, 'Why the "Fear, Honour and Interest" Trinity Harms Our Understanding of War', *The RUSI Journal*, (2021), pp. 2–9.

Zupan, Dan, 'A Presumption of the Moral Equality of Combatants', in David Rodin and Henry Shue (eds.), *Just and Unjust Warriors. The Moral and Legal Status of Soldiers* (New York: Oxford University Press, 2008), pp. 214–225.

## Electronic Sources

'Ancient History Source Book: Josephus (37–after 93 CE): The Roman Army in the First Century CE', https://sourcebooks.fordham.edu/ancient/josephus-warb.asp, 9 April 2021.

'Code of honor of an officer of the Armed Forces of Ukraine', https://sprotyvg7.com.ua/lesson/kodeks-chesti-oficera-zbrojnix-sil-ukraini, 16 October 2024.

'Convention (III) relative to the Treatment of Prisoners of War. Geneva, 12 August 1949. Commentary of 1960. Article 4 – Prisoners of War', https://ihl-databases.icrc.org/en/ihl-treaties/gciii-1949/article-4/commentary/1960?activeTab=undefined, 2 May 2023.

'Core Code of Ethics for Fire and Rescue Services – England', https://www.local.gov.uk/publications/core-code-ethics-fire-and-rescue-services-england, 3 October 2022.

'Crusader II Cruiser Tank', https://www.iwm.org.uk/collections/item/object/70000137, 16 October 2024.

'Factsheet', https://www.westpoint.edu/about/public-affairs/news/fact-sheets, 4 October 2023.

'Final Report to the Prosecutor by the Committee Established to Review the NATO Bombing Campaign Against the Federal Republic of Yugoslavia', http://www.icty.org/x/file/Press/nato061300.pdf, 8 April 2021.

'Firefighter Code of Ethics', https://www.usfa.fema.gov/downloads/pdf/code_of_ethics.pdf, 3 October 2022.

'Former NATO General: Western self-deterrence only prolongs Ukraine war', https://www.youtube.com/watch?v=QbwYBv_vARU&list=WL&index=6&t=157s, 26 September 2023.

'General Dwight D. Eisenhower's Order of the Day (1944)', https://www.archives.gov/milestone-documents/general-eisenhowers-order-of-the-day, 14 October 2024.

'George Santayana 1863–1952. Spanish-born philosopher and critic', https://www.oxfordreference.com/view/10.1093/acref/9780191843730.001.0001/q-oro-ed5-00009114, 5 April 2021.

'Instruction *Dignitas Personae* on Certain Bioethical Questions', https://www.vatican.va/roman_curia/congregations/cfaith/documents/rc_con_cfaith_doc_20081208_dignitas-personae_en.html, 6 September 2022.

'Joint Statement of the Russian Federation and the People's Republic of China on the International Relations Entering a New Era and the Global Sustainable Development', http://en.kremlin.ru/supplement/5770, 4 February 2022.

'Manifesto: Definitions of the concept of liberal profession at European level', https://www.eesc.europa.eu/en/documents/manifesto-definitions-concept-liberal-profes sion-european-level, 3 October 2022.

'Maynulet testifies in own defense, says killing wounded Iraqi "right thing to do"', https://www.stripes.com/news/maynulet-testifies-in-own-defense-says-killing -wounded-iraqi-right-thing-to-do-1.31154, 26 September 2023.

'Memorandum for the President', https://nsarchive2.gwu.edu/NSAEBB/NSAEBB127 /02.01.25.pdf, 6 November 2024.

'Merlin', https://www.royalnavy.mod.uk/equipment/aircraft/merlin, 16 October 2024.

'My trip to Europe is about America rallying the world's democracies', https://www .washingtonpost.com/opinions/2021/06/05/joe-biden-europe-trip-agenda/, 7 June 2021.

'Narendra Modi chides Vladimir Putin over Ukraine war', https://www.ft.com/content /d0ac0361-c101-4605-ba22-ee20f9f92233, 21 September 2022.

'New App Helps Military Service Members Consider Issues of Ethics In and Out of War', https://www.kcl.ac.uk/news/new-app-helps-military-service-members-consi der-issues-of-ethics-in-and-out-of-war, 21 December 2022.

'On the Disciplinary Statute of the Armed Forces of Ukraine', https://zakon.rada.gov .ua/laws/show/551-14#Text, 14 November 2024.

'professional', https://www.merriam-webster.com/dictionary/professional, 11 September 2023.

'Remarks by President Biden on the Terrorist Attacks in Israel", https://www.white house.gov/briefing-room/speeches-remarks/2023/10/10/remarks-by-president-bid en-on-the-terrorist-attacks-in-israel-2/, 11 October 2023.

'Samantha Power's democracy promotion plan', https://www.devex.com/news/devex -newswire-samantha-power-s-democracy-promotion-plan-103414?utm_campaign =wp_todays_worldview&utm_medium=email&utm_source=newsletter&wpisrc =nl_todayworld, 17 June 2022.

'SAS Rogue Heroes', https://www.bbc.co.uk/iplayer/episodes/p0d5z0xy/sas-rogue -heroes, 22 September 2023.

'Secretary Hegseth's Message to the Force', https://www.defense.gov/News/Releases /Release/Article/4040940/secretary-hegseths-message-to-the-force/, 28 January 2025.

'Servicemen of Ukraine trained with Paladin self-propelled howitzers', https://mil.in .ua/en/news/servicemen-of-ukraine-trained-with-paladin-self-propelled-howit zers/, 16 October 2024.

'soldier (n.)', https://www.etymonline.com/word/soldier, 11 September 2023.

'Statement by General Angus J. Campbell, AO, DSC Chief of the Defence Force Australia, 19 November 2020', https://afghanistaninquiry.defence.gov.au/sites/default/files/2020-11/CDF-Statement-19-Nov-20-Check-against-Delivery.pdf, 9 April 2021.

'Stop Calling Us Warriors', https://angrystaffofficer.com/2016/12/14/stop-calling-us-warriors/, 28 December 2023.

'The AI Arms Race is Changing Everything', https://time.com/6255952/ai-impact-chatgpt-microsoft-google/?utm_campaign=wp_todays_worldview&utm_medium=email&utm_source=newsletter&wpisrc=nl_todayworld, 26 July 2023.

'The Military Order of the Saint Grand Martyr and the Triumphant George has been established', https://www.prlib.ru/en/history/619789, 21 October 2024.

'Ukrainian soldiers showcased operations with M982 Excalibur shells', https://mil.in.ua/en/news/ukrainian-soldiers-showcased-operations-with-m982-excalibur-shells/, 16 October 2024.

'UN Secretary General describes war in Ukraine as "absurdity" in 21st century', https://www.theguardian.com/world/2022/apr/28/un-secretary-general-describes-war-in-ukraine-as-absurdity-in-21st-century, 28 April 2022.

'We share common values – Zelensky after talks with von der Leyen', https://interfax.com.ua/news/general/822505.html, 9 April 2022.

Armed Forces of Ukraine, 'Кодекс поведінки військовослужбовців Збройних Сил України', https://www.mil.gov.ua/content/pdf/Code_of_Conduct_for_Military_Personnel.pdf, 08 November 2024.

Australian Defence Forces, 'Military Ethics', https://theforge.defence.gov.au/sites/default/files/2021-12/ADF-P-0%20Military%20Ethics%20Ed%201_0.pdf, 10 December 2022.

Balzac, Honoré de, 'Colonel Chabert', https://www.gutenberg.org/files/1954/1954-h/1954-h.htm, 3 October 2022.

Bell, Andrew, 'Can IHL training influence military conduct in war?', https://blogs.icrc.org/law-and-policy/2024/05/07/can-ihl-training-influence-military-conduct-in-war/, 13 May 2024.

Borys, Christian, 'The story of Saint Javelin', https://www.nato.int/docu/review/articles/2024/02/22/the-story-of-saint-javelin/index.html, 16 October 2024.

Boulette, Michael, 'Two Concepts of Role-Morality', https://papers.ssrn.com/sol3/papers.cfm?abstract_id=1527253, 3 October 2022.

Bray, Bill, 'From Fat Leonard Ethics Alerts to Classical Ethics: The Stockdale Exemplar', https://www.usni.org/magazines/proceedings/2018/february/fat-leonard-ethics-alerts-classical-ethics-stockdale-exemplar, 22 September 2022.

British Army, 'Values and Standards of the British Army', https://www.army.mod.uk/media/5219/20180910-values_standards_2018_final.pdf, 24 May 2023.

Brooks, Rosa, 'Fighting words. Has the nature of "war" changed since the days of Clausewitz?', https://foreignpolicy.com/2014/02/04/fighting-words/, 04 February 2014.

Canadian Armed Forces, 'Duty with Honour: The Profession of Arms in Canada', https://www.canada.ca/en/department-national-defence/corporate/reports-publications/duty-with-honour-2009.html, 21 March 2023.

Canadian Armed Forces, 'Joint Doctrine Manual: Law of Armed Conflict at the Operational and Tactical Levels', https://www.fichl.org/fileadmin/_migrated/content_uploads/Canadian_LOAC_Manual_2001_English.pdf, 10 June 2022.

Canadian Armed Forces, 'Statement of Defence Ethics', https://www.canada.ca/en/department-national-defence/services/benefits-military/defence-ethics/about/statement.html, 9 April 2021.

Canadian Armed Forces, 'The Canadian Armed Forces Ethos – Trusted to Serve', https://www.canada.ca/en/department-national-defence/corporate/reports-publications/canadian-armed-forces-ethos-trusted-to-serve.html, 21 March 2023.

Chilean Army, 'Comunicado Oficial / Ataque incendiario al Monumento del General Baquedano', https://www.ejercito.cl/prensa/visor/comunicado-oficial-ataque-incendiario-al-monumento-del-general-baquedano, 6 April 2022.

Chilean Army, 'Military Values', https://www.ejercito.cl/our-commitment/military-values, 23 February 2022.

Code of Warriors of Light, 'Welcome to the LOAC learning platform', https://www.armedconflict.law/, 23 April 2025.

Comité d'éthique de la défense, 'Avis sur l'éthique dans la formation des militaires', https://www.defense.gouv.fr/sites/default/files/tronc_commun/20220413_Comit%C3%A9%20d%27%C3%A9thique%20de%20la%20d%C3%A9fense%20-%20Avis%20sur%20l%27%C3%A9thique%20dans%20la%20formation%20des%20militaires.pdf, 7 July 2023.

Corn, G., 'Contemplating the meaning of "responsibility" in responsible command', https://papers.ssrn.com/sol3/papers.cfm?abstract_id=2546594, 1 October 2020.

État-major de l'armée de Terre, 'Honneur, courage et dignité. Le comportement du soldat de l'armée de Terre', https://www.info-reglement.terre.defense.gouv.fr/images/multimedia/photo/illustrations/livre_orange-Comportement_du_soldat-web-VD.pdf, 7 July 2023.

Federal Ministry of Justice, 'Basic Law for the Federal Republic of Germany', https://www.gesetze-im-internet.de/englisch_gg/englisch_gg.html, 6 July 2023.

Felton, James, 'Researchers Improve ChatGPT By Getting It To Learn From Its Own Mistakes', https://www.iflscience.com/researchers-improve-chatgpt-by-getting-it-to-learn-from-its-own-mistakes-68299, 26 July 2023.

Ferguson, Michael P., 'The nature of war is not changing in Ukraine', https://thehill.com/opinion/national-security/3526558-the-nature-of-war-is-not-changing-in-ukraine/?fbclid=IwAR30UkkAy-DUdmhcrE90UjWXu1NzYxUbq0N07nr9YZkDjg7ZfY53Cp6myr4&fs=e&s=cl, 16 June 2022.

Geneva Call, 'Their Words', http://theirwords.org/, 1 March 2022.

Gibbons-Neff, Thomas, 'In Ukraine, Killings of Surrendering Russians Divide an American-Led Unit', https://www.nytimes.com/2024/07/06/world/europe/ukraine-russia-killings-us.html, 7 July 2024.

Goldberg, Jeffrey, 'Trump: "I Need the Kind of Generals that Hitler Had"', https://www.theatlantic.com/politics/archive/2024/10/trump-military-generals-hitler/680327/, accessed 24 October 2024.

Gray, John, 'The human era is ending', https://www.newstatesman.com/ideas/2023/08/the-end-of-the-human-era?, 13 August 2023.

Gypson, Katherine, 'Trump Cabinet choice faces tough first day of questions on Capitol Hill', 15 January 2025.

Halbertal, Moshe, 'The Goldstone Illusion', https://newrepublic.com/article/70956/the-goldstone-illusion, 7 April 2021.

Harari, Yuval Noah, 'Yuval Noah Harari argues that what's at stake in Ukraine is the direction of human history', https://www.economist.com/by-invitation/2022/02/09/yuval-noah-harari-argues-that-whats-at-stake-in-ukraine-is-the-direction-of-human-history?itm_source=parsely-api, 14 February 2022.

Harper, Jon, 'How Technology Could Create 'Super Soldiers'', http://www.nationaldefensemagazine.org/articles/2016/8/1/2016august-how-technology-could-create-super-soldiers, 01 August 2016.

Hastie, Andrew, 'SAS must put honour before glory', https://www.adso.org.au/andrew-hastie-sas-must-put-honour-before-glory/, 14 December 2022.

Henschke, Adam, ''Supersoldiers': Ethical concerns in human enhancement technologies', http://blogs.icrc.org/law-and-policy/2017/07/03/supersoldiers-ethical-concerns-human-enhancement-technologies-2/, 03 July 2017.

Heyns, Christof, 'Report of the Special Rapporteur on extrajudicial, summary or arbitrary executions', https://digitallibrary.un.org/record/755741?ln=en, 25 July 2023.

Hodge, Nathan, 'https://edition.cnn.com/2022/02/08/europe/putin-coarse-remarks-ukraine-intl/index.html', 22 September 2023.

Hugo, Victor, 'Détruire la misère', https://www2.assemblee-nationale.fr/decouvrir-l-assemblee/histoire/grands-discours-parlementaires/victor-hugo-9-juillet-1849, 27 June 2023.

Hugo, Victor, 'Speech to the Peace Congress at Paris', https://trove.nla.gov.au/newspaper/article/12914658, 27 June 2023.

Human Rights Committee, 'General Comment No 36 (2018) on article 6 of the International Covenant on Civil and Political Rights, on the right to life', https://tbinternet.ohchr.org/Treaties/CCPR/Shared%20Documents/1_Global/CCPR_C_GC_36_8785_E.pdf, 22 March 2022.

International Committee of the Red Cross, 'Convention (III) relative to the Treatment of Prisoners of War. Geneva, 12 August 1949. Commentary of 2020. Article 27 – Dissemination of the Convention', https://ihl-databases.icrc.org/en/ihl-treaties

/gciii-1949/article-127/commentary/2020?activeTab=undefined#_Toc42507340, 07 March 2023.

International Committee of the Red Cross, 'IHL Database. Customary IHL. Practice Relating to Rule 14. Proportionality in Attack', https://ihl-databases.icrc.org/customary-ihl/eng/docs/v2_rul_rule14, 13 July 2021.

International Committee of the Red Cross, 'IHL Database. Customary IHL. Sources', https://ihl-databases.icrc.org/en/customary-ihl/sources, 11 January 2023.

Israel Defense Forces, 'The Spirit of the IDF', https://www.idf.il/en/mini-sites/spirit-of-the-idf/, 6 July 2023.

Japanese National Defence Academy, 'The National Defence Academy Cadets' Pledge', https://www.mod.go.jp/nda/english/about/pledge.html', 23 February 2022.

Kant, Immanuel, 'What is Enlightenment?', http://www.columbia.edu/acis/ets/CCREAD/etscc/kant.html, 19 December 2022.

Kaurin, Pauline Shanks, 'Warrior, Citizen Solider or Guardian: Thoughts After a Kerfuffle', https://shankskaurin.wordpress.com/2016/12/20/warrior-citizen-solider-or-guardian-thoughts-after-a-kerfuffle/, 28 December 2023.

Khurshudyan, Isabelle, Ilyushina, Mary and Khudov, Kostiantyn, 'Russia and Ukraine are fighting the first full-scale drone war', https://www.washingtonpost.com/world/2022/12/02/drones-russia-ukraine-air-war/, 15 October 2024.

Knesset, 'Basic Law: Human Dignity and Liberty', https://m.knesset.gov.il/EN/activity/documents/BasicLawsPDF/BasicLawLiberty.pdf, 13 July 2023.

Lobo, Francisco, 'Chile and a global revolution for dignity', https://www.openglobalrights.org/chile-and-a-global-revolution-for-dignity/, 12 May 2021.

Lobo, Francisco, 'Defending the Rules-Based Order: The US at a Crossroads', https://rusi.org/explore-our-research/publications/commentary/defending-rules-based-order-us-crossroads, 26 September 2023.

Lobo, Francisco, 'From "Lawfare" to "Lawcraft": Law in the Service of Contemporary Statecraft and Foreign Policy', https://blogs.kcl.ac.uk/warcrimes/2021/08/12/from-lawfare-to-lawcraft-law-in-the-service-of-contemporary-statecraft-and-foreign-policy/, 12 August 2021.

Lobo, Francisco, 'Military Honor in the Twenty-First Century: Some Contemporary Challenges', https://www.e-ir.info/2021/05/25/military-honor-in-the-twenty-first-century-some-contemporary-challenges/, 25 May 2021.

Lobo, Francisco, 'Parody or deadly-serious commitment? Non-state armed groups upholding humanitarian standards in war', (https://www.kcl.ac.uk/parody-or-deadly-serious-commitment-non-state-armed-groups-upholding-humanitarian-standards-in-war), 08 June 2022.

Miller, Amanda, 'Space Force Uniform Prototype Has Diagonal Buttons, PT Uniforms Are Black and Gray', https://www.airandspaceforces.com/space-force-uniform-prototype-has-diagonal-buttons-pt-uniforms-are-black-and-gray/, 28 September 2023.

Ministry of Defence of the United Kingdom of Great Britain and Northern Ireland, 'The Joint Service Manual of the Law of Armed Conflict', https://assets.publishing.service.gov.uk/government/uploads/system/uploads/attachment_data/file/27874/JSP3832004Edition.pdf, 20 June 2022.

Ministry of Defence of Ukraine, 'Наказ 23.03.2017 No. 164', https://zakon.rada.gov.ua/laws/show/z0704-17#Text, 08 November 2024.

Molendijk, Tine, 'Just War Theory for Morale and Moral Injury: Beyond Individual Resilience', https://www.tandfonline.com/doi/full/10.1080/15027570.2024.2442802?src=, 17 January 2025.

Nelson, Mike, 'What Pete Hegseth Doesn't Understand About Soldiers', https://www.theatlantic.com/magazine/archive/2025/08/warrior-myth-lethality-pete-hegseth/683247/, 09 July 2025.

New Zealand Army, 'The Way of the New Zealand Warrior', https://www.nzdf.mil.nz/assets/Uploads/DocumentLibrary/Way-of-the-New-Zealand-Warrior-2020.pdf, 23 May 2023.

Ohlin, Jens David, 'War's Rustic Code of Honor', https://ssrn.com/abstract=4931591, 12 September 2024.

Orr, Scott W., 'Just War Theory Reloaded: The Ethics of SOF in Modern Conflict', https://apps.dtic.mil/sti/pdfs/AD1060027.pdf, 6 June 2023.

Pérez de Oliva, Fernán, 'Diálogo de la dignidad del hombre (1586)', http://www.cervantesvirtual.com/obra-visor/dialogo-de-la-dignidad-del-hombre--0/html/fedde6c2-82b1-11df-acc7-002185ce6064_2.html, 19 April 2021.

Philipps, Dave, 'To Stand Out, the Army Picks a New Uniform With a World War II Look', https://www.nytimes.com/2019/05/05/us/new-army-greens-uniform.html, 28 September 2023.

Prykhodko, Ihor et al., 'Army Values of the Ukrainian Soldier: Its Contents and Its Assessment by Combatants', https://doi.org/10.1080/15027570.2025.2468015, 12 May 2025.

Riaño, Peio, 'La Guerra por la estatua del general Baquedano incendia Chile', https://www.eldiario.es/internacional/guerra-estatuas-general-baquedano-simbolo-incendia-chile_1_7322077.html, 6 April 2022.

Ryan, Mick, 'Kursk and the Battle of Wills', https://mickryan.substack.com/p/kursk-and-the-battle-of-wills, 21 August 2024.

Schiller, Friedrich, 'On Grace and Dignity', https://archive.schillerinstitute.com/educ/aesthetics/Schiller_On_Grace_and_Dignity.pdf, 7 April 2021.

Schragger, Richard C., 'Cooler Heads. The difference between the president's lawyers and the military's', https://slate.com/news-and-politics/2006/09/what-administration-lawyers-could-learn-from-military-lawyers.html, 30 July 2021.

Schwarz, Elke and Renic, Neil, 'Beyond Law: Reaffirming the Centrality of Ethics in War', https://www.justsecurity.org/103464/beyond-law-reaffirming-the-centrality-of-ethics-in-war/, 8 October 2024.

SIPRI, 'Global developments in armed conflicts, peace processes and peace operations', https://www.sipri.org/yearbook/2021/02, 1 March 2022.

Snider, Don, Oh, Paul and Toner, Kevin, 'The Army's Professional Military Ethic in an Era of Persistent Conflict', https://catalog.hathitrust.org/Record/007099091, 7 April 2021.

South African National Defence Forces, 'Code of Conduct', https://www.resdal.org/Archivo/d0000124.htm#:~:text=I%20accept%20personal%20responsibility%20for,risk%20of%20my%20own%20life, 10 July 2023.

Spanish Army, 'Los Valores en el Ejército de Tierra', https://ame1.org.es/wp-content/uploads/2018/03/EME-Valores-del-Ejercito-de-Tierra-2018.pdf, 31 July 2023.

Spector, Céline, 'A Montesquieu Dictionary. Honor', http://dictionnaire-montesquieu.ens-lyon.fr/en/article/1376474900/en/, 16 March 2022.

U.S. Army, 'ADRP-1: The Army Profession', https://irp.fas.org/doddir/army/adrp1.pdf, 25 May 2023.

U.S. Army, 'The Army Values', https://www.army.mil/values/, 23 February 2022.

U.S. Department of Defense, 'Directive 2311.01. DoD Law of War Program', https://www.esd.whs.mil/Portals/54/Documents/DD/issuances/dodd/231101p.pdf?ver=2020-07-02-143157-007, 11 December 2023.

UN International Law Commission, 'Draft conclusions on identification of customary international law', https://legal.un.org/ilc/texts/instruments/english/draft_articles/1_13_2018.pdf, 11 January 2023.

Verkhovna Rada of Ukraine, 'Law of Ukraine on the Statute of the Internal Service of the Armed Forces of Ukraine', https://zakon.rada.gov.ua/laws/show/548-14#Text, 07 May 2025.

Vineyard, Chaplain (Lt. Col.) Jared L., 'Cardinal Virtues as Warrior Virtues', https://www.armyupress.army.mil/journals/military-review/online-exclusive/2025-ole/cardinal-virtues/, 09 June 2025.

Wolfendale, Jessica, 'Beyond Law: When States Use Ethics to Excuse War Crimes', https://www.justsecurity.org/104969/states-ethics-excuse-war-crimes/, 21 November 2024.

## Case Law and Judicial Opinions

Decision of the Second Senate of the Constitutional Court of Ukraine No. 3-r(II)/2023 dated March 22, 2023 in the case upon the constitutional complaint of Ihor Lazurenko regarding the conformity of the provisions of Articles 70.2.4 and 70.2.5 of the Law of Ukraine "On Enforcement Proceedings", Articles 50.2.3 and 50.2.4 of the Law of Ukraine "On General Compulsory State Pension Insurance" with the

Constitution (constitutionality) (regarding guaranteed pension, which is the main source of living, not lower than the subsistence minimum).

European Court of Human Rights, Ireland v. The United Kingdom (*Application no. 5310/71*), Judgment of 18 January 1978, Separate Opinion of Judge Fitzmaurice.

European Court of Human Rights, Pretty v. The United Kingdom (*Application no. 2346/02*), Fourth Section, Judgment of 29 April 2002.

European Court of Justice (First Chamber), Case C-36/02, Omega Spielhallen- und Automatenaufstellungs-GmbH v. Oberbürgermeisterin der Bundesstadt Bonn, Judgment, 14 October 2004.

German Federal Constitutional Court, 1 BvR 357/07, 15 February 2006.

High Court of Justice of Israel, HCJ 2056/04, *Beit Sourik Vill. Council v. Gov't of Israel*, 58(5) PD 817.

High Court of Justice of Israel, HCJ 769/02, *Pub. Comm. against Torture in Israel v. Gov't of Israel*, 62(1) PD 507 (2006) (Isr.), reprinted in 46 I.L.M. 375.

International Court of Justice (ICJ), *Application of the Convention on the Prevention and Punishment of the Crime of Genocide (Bosnia and Herzegovina v. Serbia and Montenegro), Judgment, I.C.J. Reports 2007*, p. 43.

International Court of Justice (ICJ), *Armed Activities on the Territory of the Congo (Democratic Republic of Congo v. Uganda), Judgement, I.C.J. Reports 2005*, p. 168.

International Court of Justice (ICJ), *Legal Consequences of the Construction of a Wall in the Occupied Palestinian Territory. Advisory Opinion, I.C.J. Reports 2004*, p. 136.

International Court of Justice (ICJ), *Legality of the Threat or Use of Nuclear Weapons, Advisory Opinion, I.C.J. Reports 1996*, p. 226.

International Court of Justice (ICJ), *Military and Paramilitary Activities in and against Nicaragua (Nicaragua v. United States), Merits, Judgment, I.C.J. Reports 1986*, p. 14.

Inter-American Court of Human Rights, Case of "In Vitro Fertilization" (Artavia Murillo et al) v. Costa Rica, Judgment of November 28, 2012 (*Merits*).

Inter-American Court of Human Rights, Case of "Masacre de Mapiripán" v. Colombia, Judgment of September 15, 2005.

Inter-American Court of Human Rights, Case of the "Street Children" (Villagran-Morales et al) v. Guatemala, Judgment of November 19, 1999 (*Merits*).

Inter-American Court of Human Rights, Vera Rojas et al v. Chile, Judgment of October 01, 2021 (*Merits*).

International Criminal Court, Pre-Trial Chamber I, *The Prosecutor v. Germain Katanga and Mathieu Ngudjolo Chui*, Decision on the confirmation of charges, 30 September 2008, ICC-01/04-01/07.

International Criminal Tribunal for the former Yugoslavia, Appeals Chamber, *Prosecutor v. Dusco Tadic*, Decision on the Defence Motion for Interlocutory Appeal on Jurisdiction, 2 October 1995, Case No. IT-94-1.

International Criminal Tribunal for the Former Yugoslavia, Trial Chamber, *Prosecutor v. Anto Furundzija*, Judgment, 10 December 1998, Case No. IT-95-17/1-T.
International Criminal Tribunal for the Former Yugoslavia, Trial Chamber, *Prosecutor v. Galić*, Judgment, 5 December 2003, Case No. IT-98-29-T.
Supreme Court of India, 'Francis Coralie Mullin v. Dehli', AIR 1981 SC 746.
Supreme Court of the Republic of Chile, Case CS No 921-09, 13 August 2009.
Supreme Court of the Republic of Chile, Case CS No 2182-98, 08 July 2010.
United States Court of Appeals for the Armed Forces, *United States v. Rogelio M. Maynulet, Captain, U.S. Army*, Crim. App. No. 20050412, Decided 3 March 2010.
United States Military Tribunal, *The Hostages Trial*, Case No. 7, Judgment, 19 February 1948.

# Index

www.ingramcontent.com/pod-product-compliance
Lightning Source LLC
LaVergne TN
LVHW102105300926
849161LV00001B/27
* 9 7 8 9 0 0 4 7 5 4 0 8 9 *